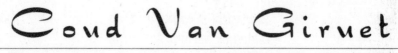

Coud Van Giruet

Elemental Gelade I / Mayumi Azuma

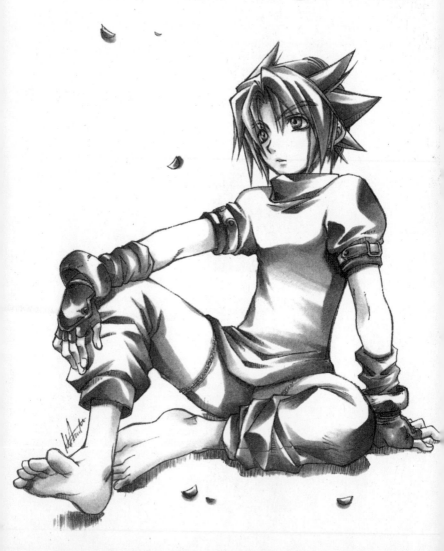

Elemental Gelade Vol. 1
Created by Mayumi Azuma

Translation - Alethea Nibley
English Adaptation - Jordan Capell
Copy Editor - Peter Ahlstrom
Retouch and Lettering - Jose Macasocol, Jr.
Production Artist - Fawn Lau
Graphic Designer - James Lee

Editor - Troy Lewter
Digital Imaging Manager - Chris Buford
Production Manager - Liz Brizzi
Managing Editor - Lindsey Johnston
VP of Production - Ron Klamert
Editor-in-Chief - Rob Tokar
Publisher - Mike Kiley
President and C.O.O. - John Parker
C.E.O. and Chief Creative Officer - Stuart Levy

A **TOKYOPOP** Manga

TOKYOPOP Inc.
5900 Wilshire Blvd. Suite 2000
Los Angeles, CA 90036

E-mail: info@TOKYOPOP.com
Come visit us online at www.TOKYOPOP.com

ISBN: 1-59816-598-4

First TOKYOPOP printing: July 2006
10 9 8 7 6 5 4
Printed in the USA

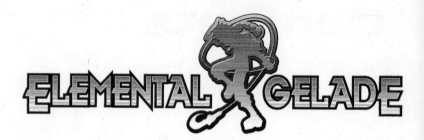

ELEMENTAL GELADE

Volume 1

by
Mayumi Azuma

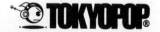

HAMBURG // LONDON // LOS ANGELES // TOKYO

Contents

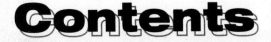

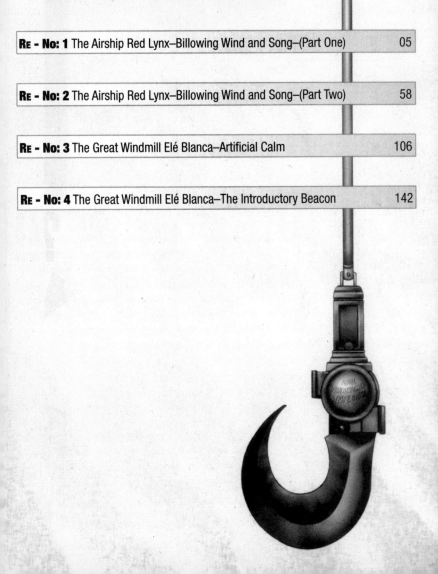

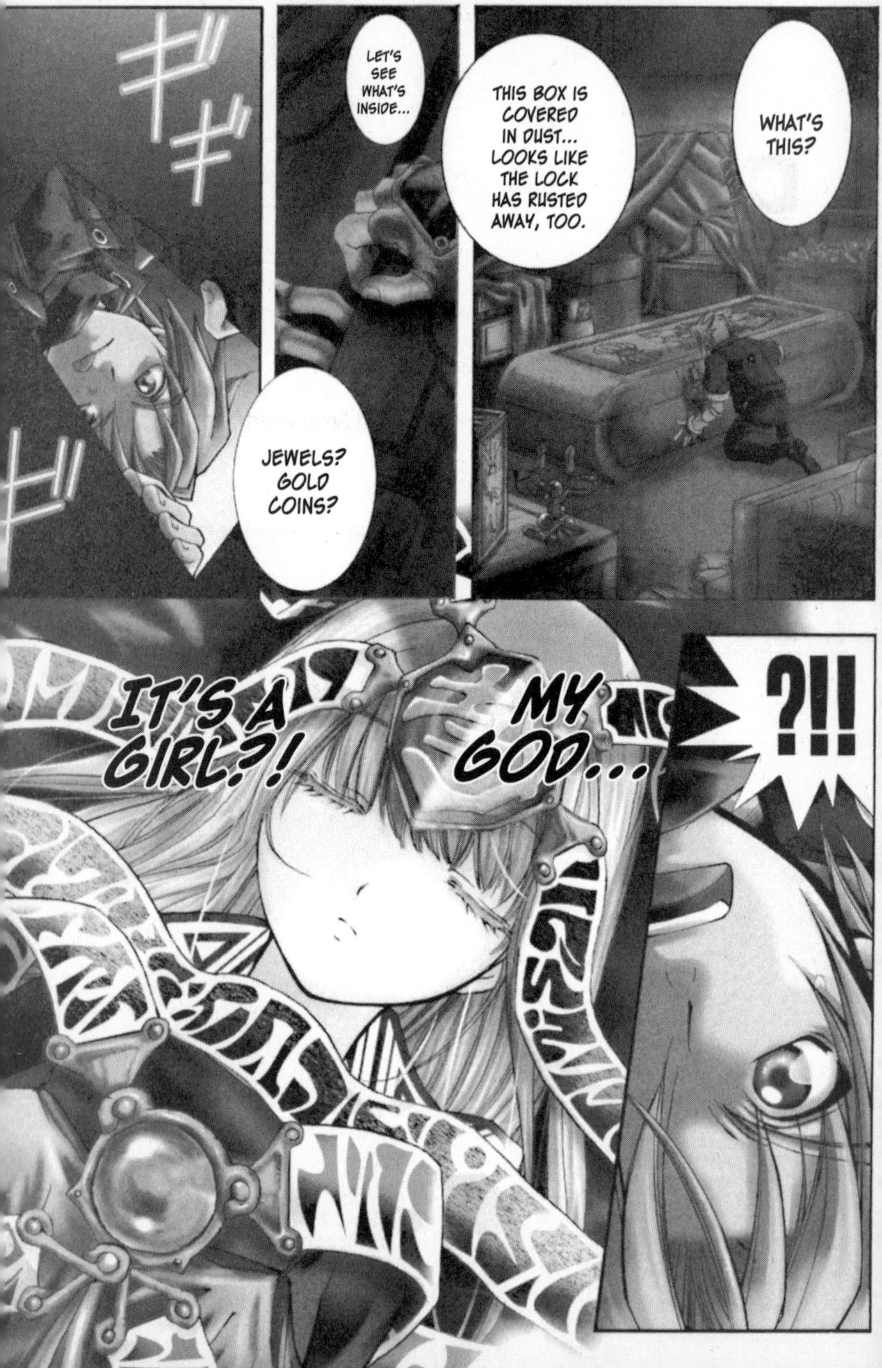
WHAT'S THIS?
THIS BOX IS COVERED IN DUST... LOOKS LIKE THE LOCK HAS RUSTED AWAY, TOO.
LET'S SEE WHAT'S INSIDE...
JEWELS? GOLD COINS?
ギギ
?!!
MY GOD...
IT'S A GIRL?!

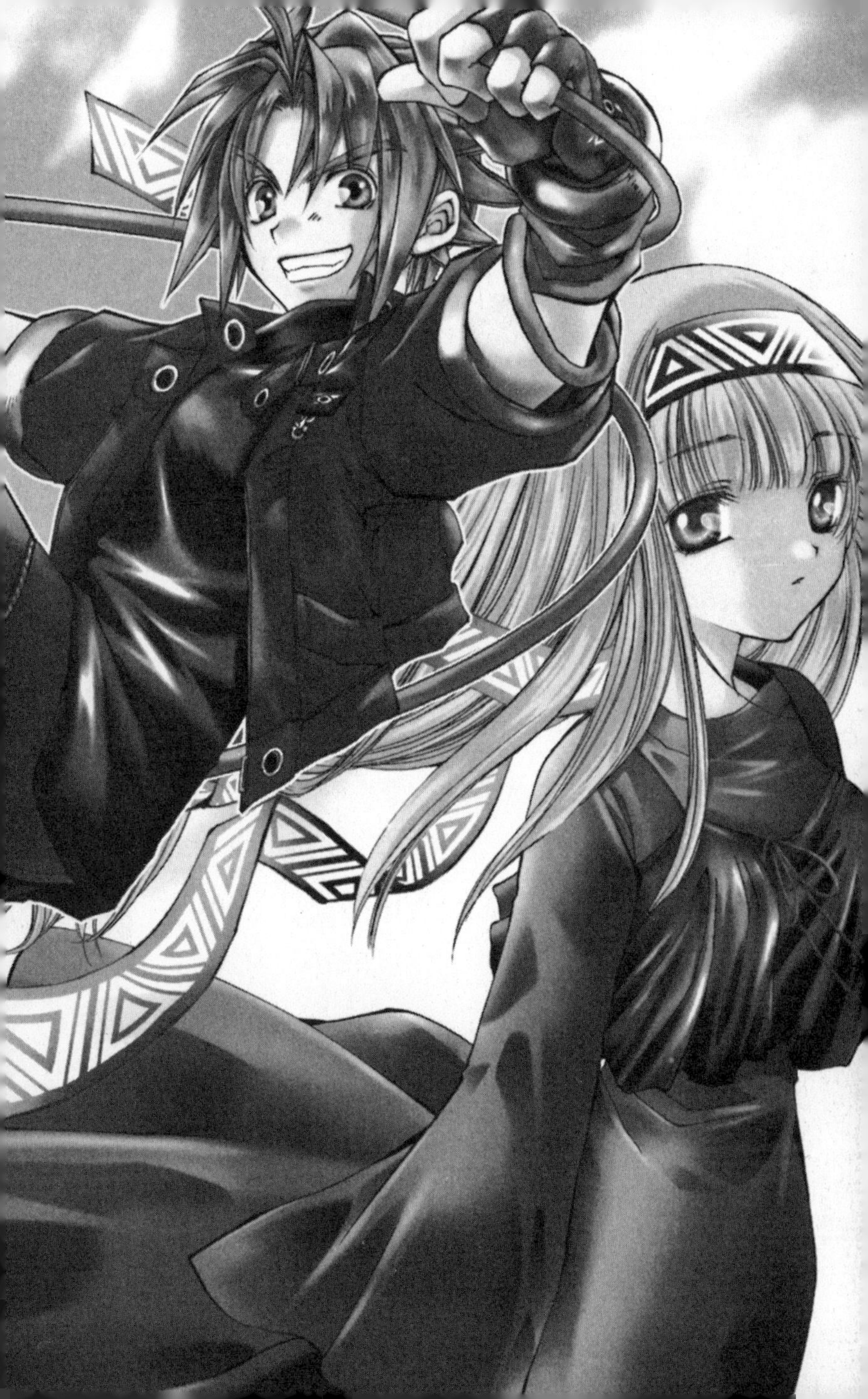

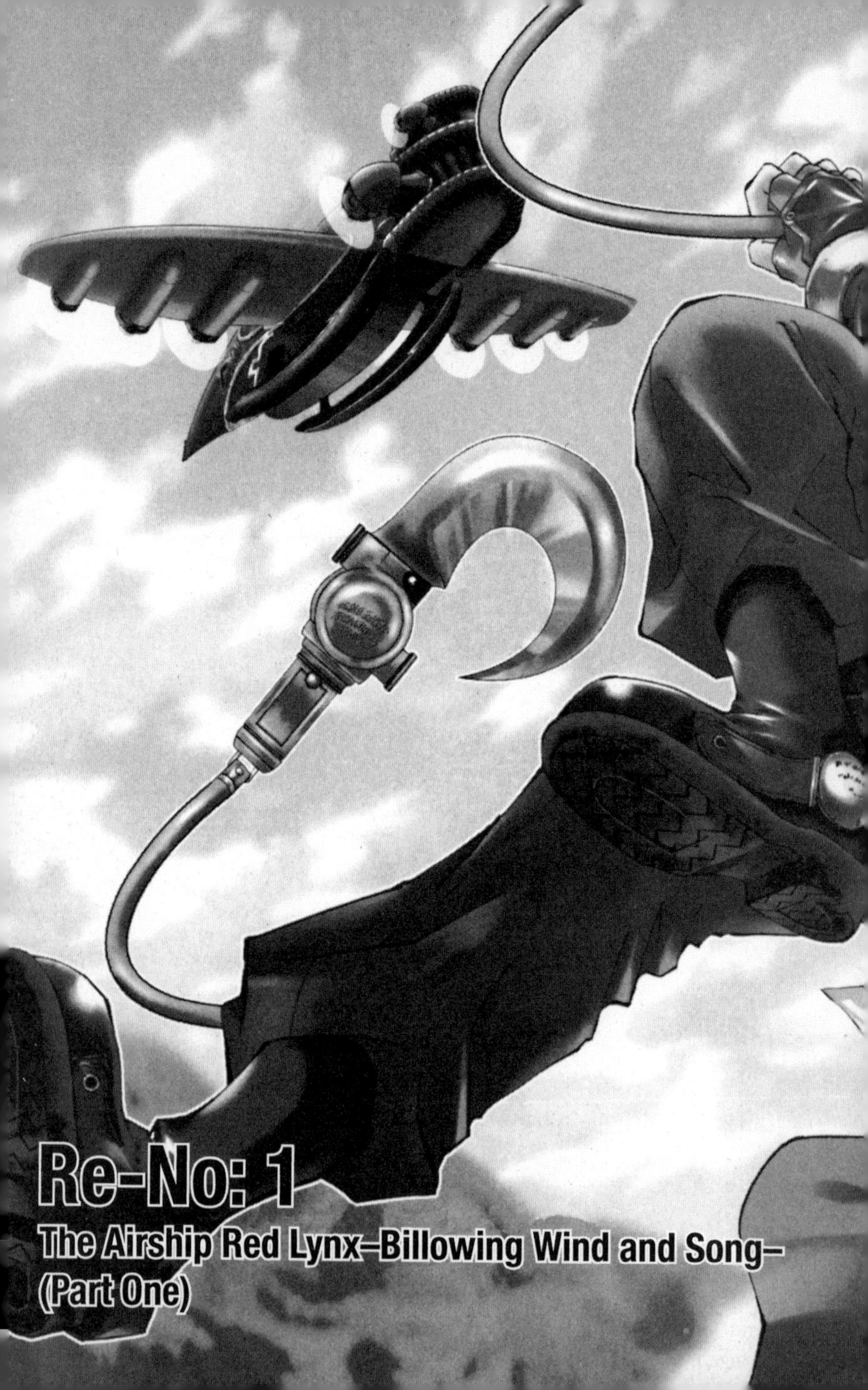
Re-No: 1
The Airship Red Lynx–Billowing Wind and Song–
(Part One)

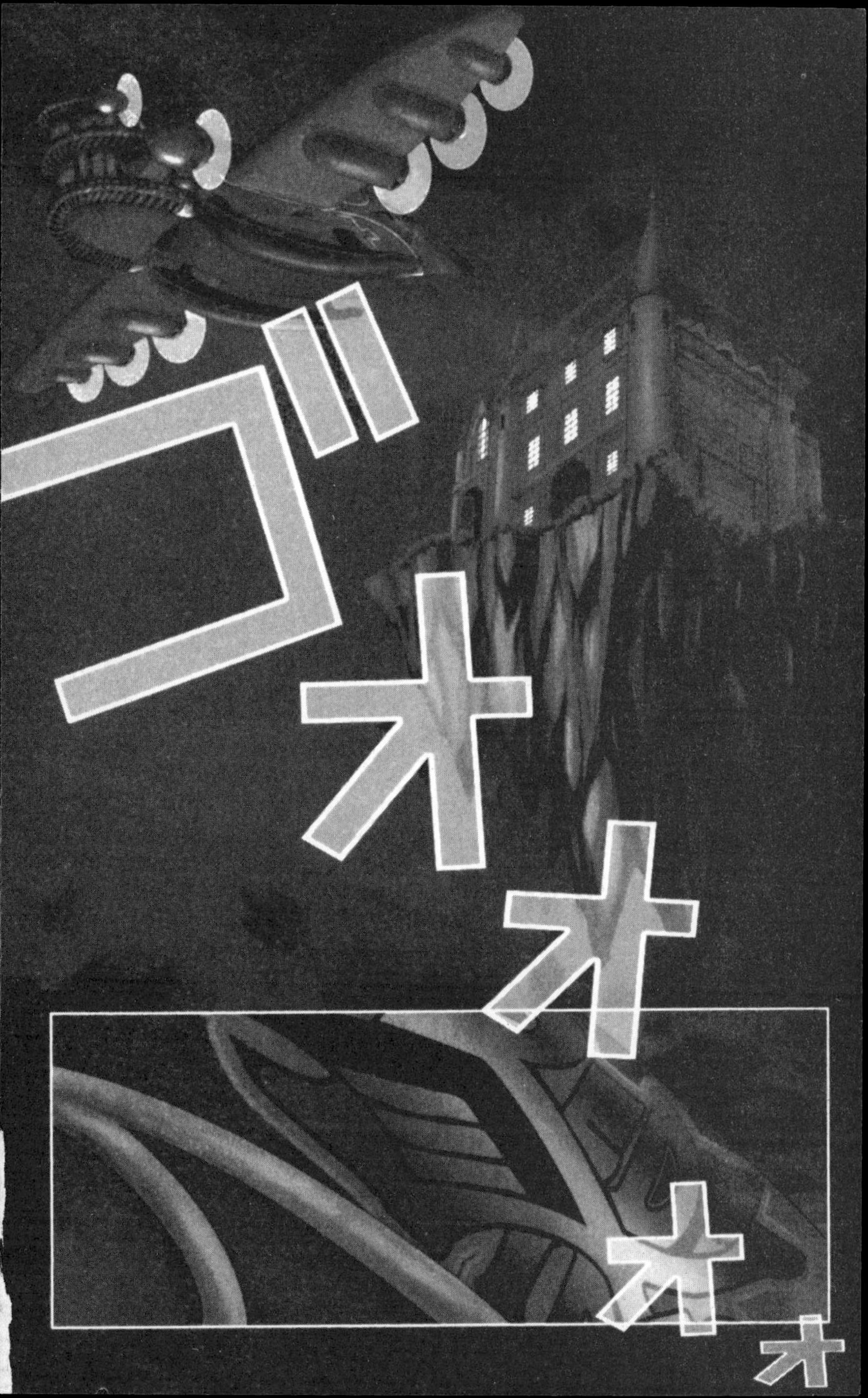
ゴオオオオ

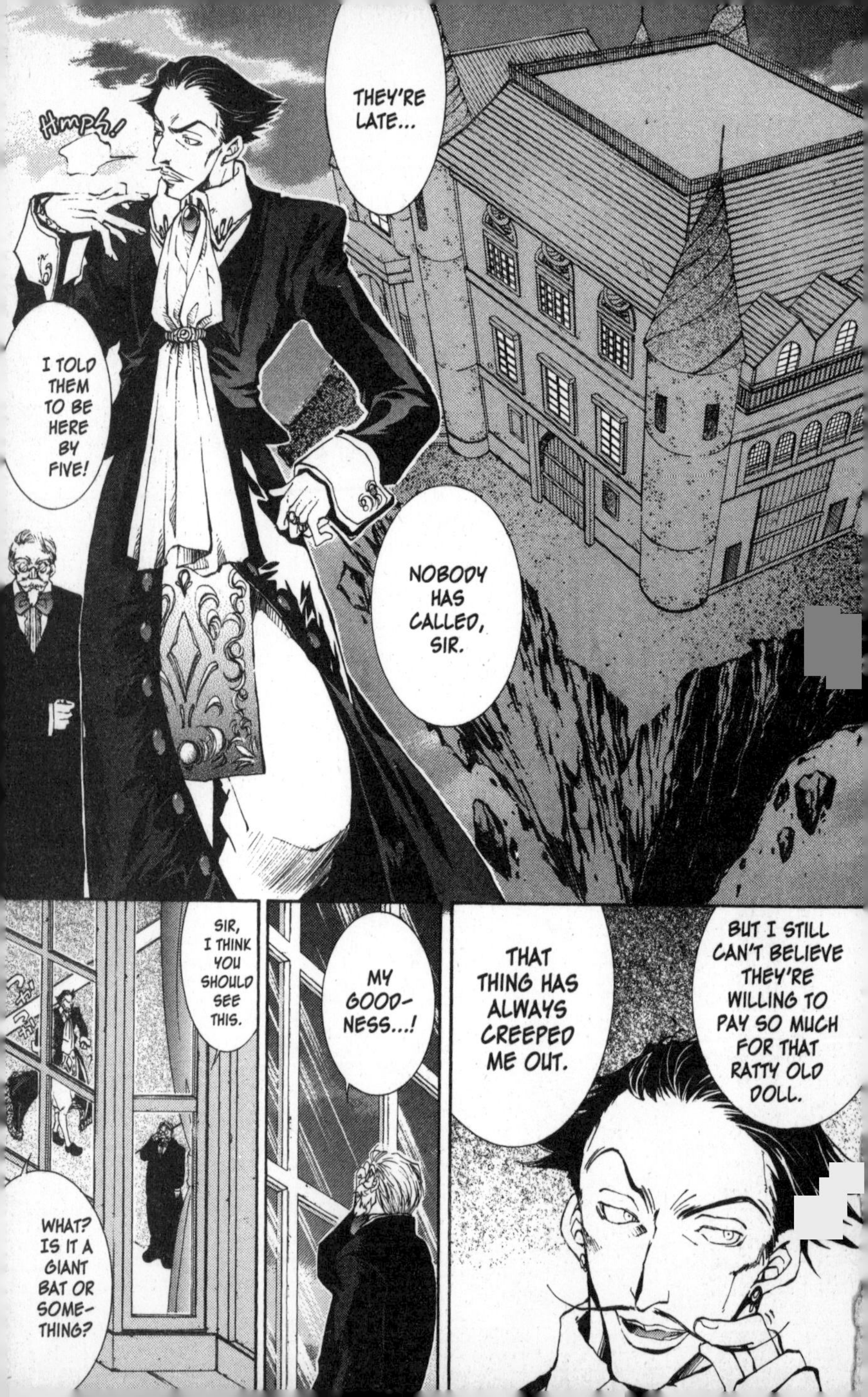
THEY'RE LATE...
Hmph!
I TOLD THEM TO BE HERE BY FIVE!
NOBODY HAS CALLED, SIR.
BUT I STILL CAN'T BELIEVE THEY'RE WILLING TO PAY SO MUCH FOR THAT RATTY OLD DOLL.
THAT THING HAS ALWAYS CREEPED ME OUT.
MY GOOD-NESS...!
SIR, I THINK YOU SHOULD SEE THIS.
WHAT? IS IT A GIANT BAT OR SOME-THING?

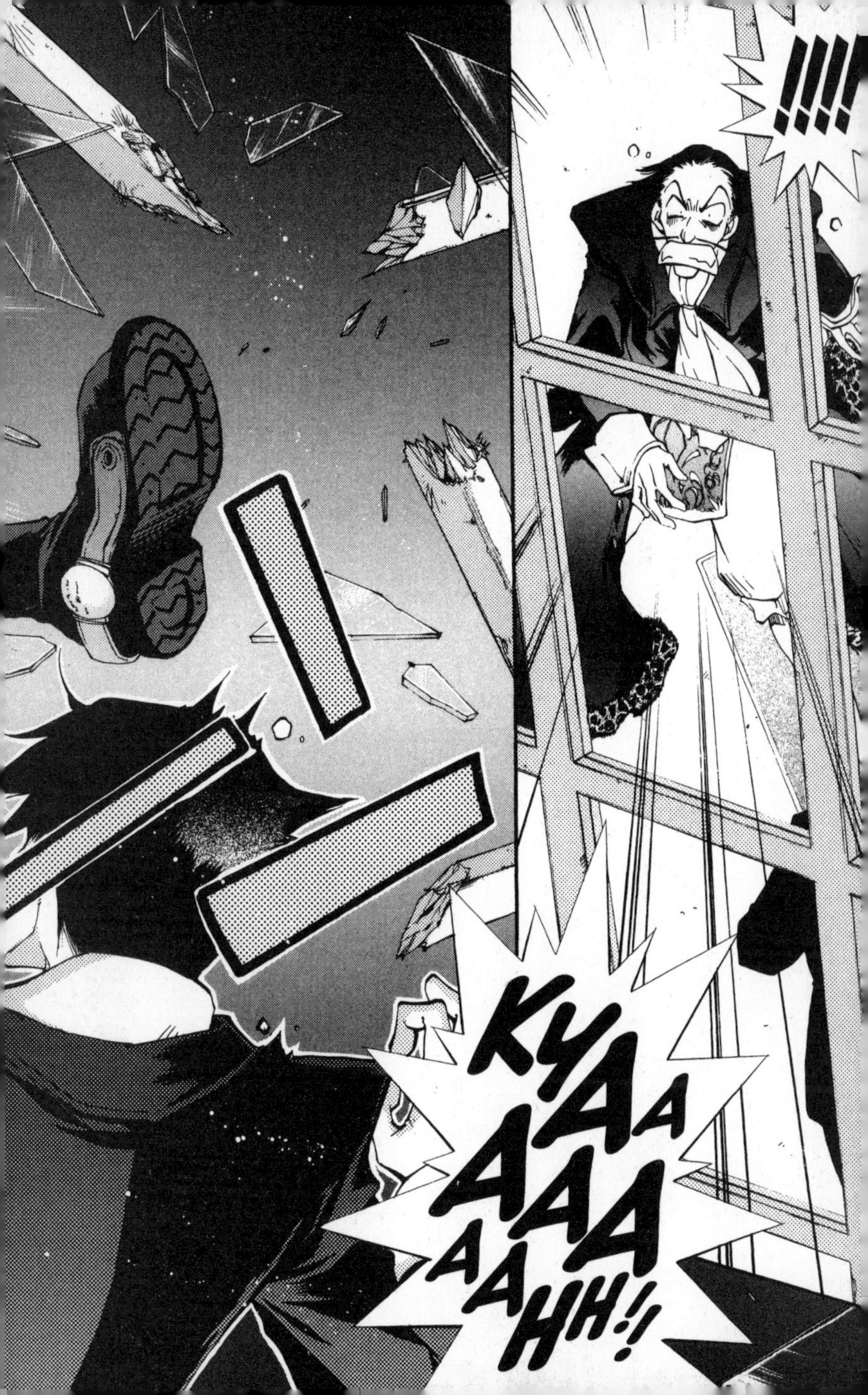
!!!!
KYAAAAAAAHH!!

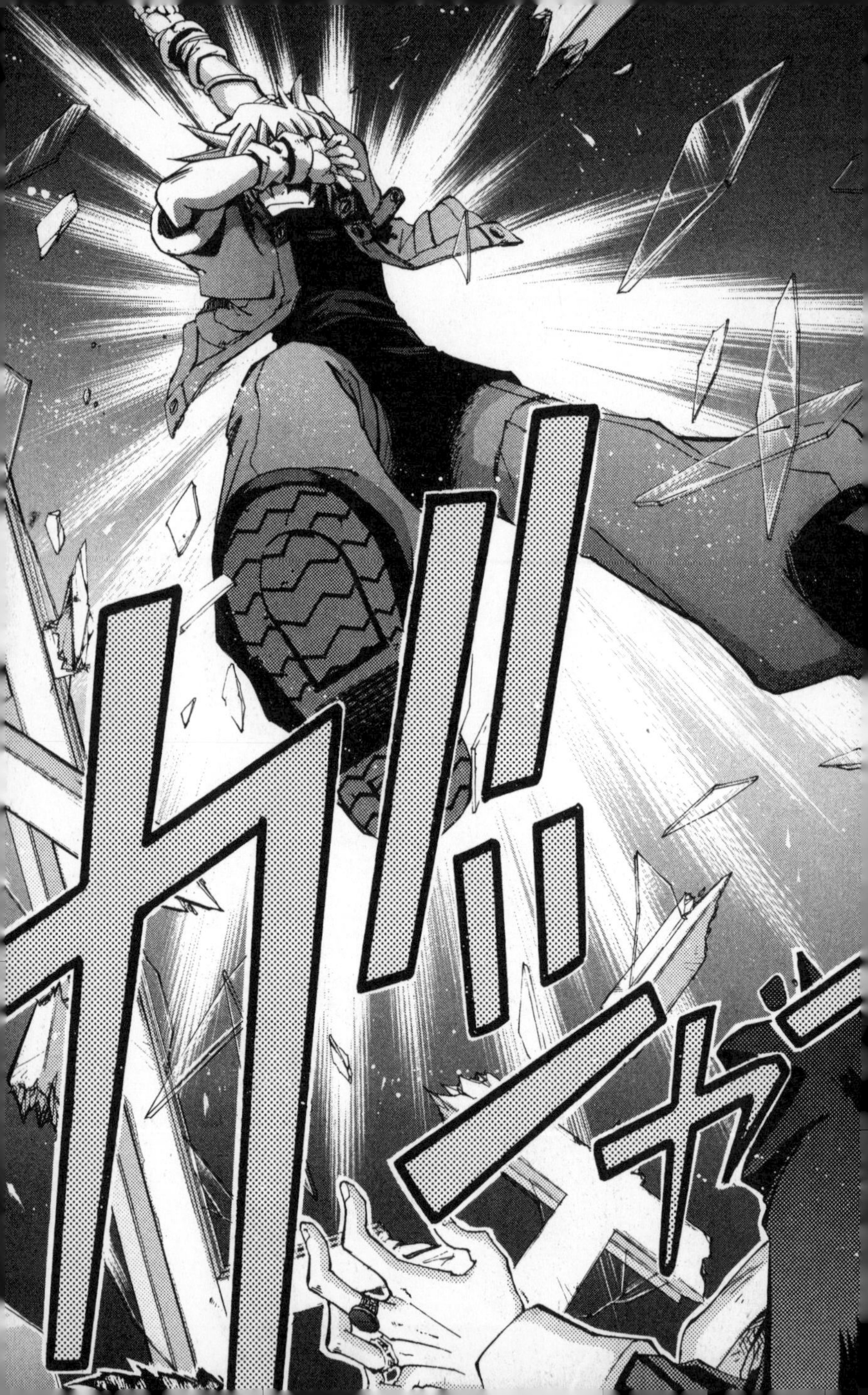

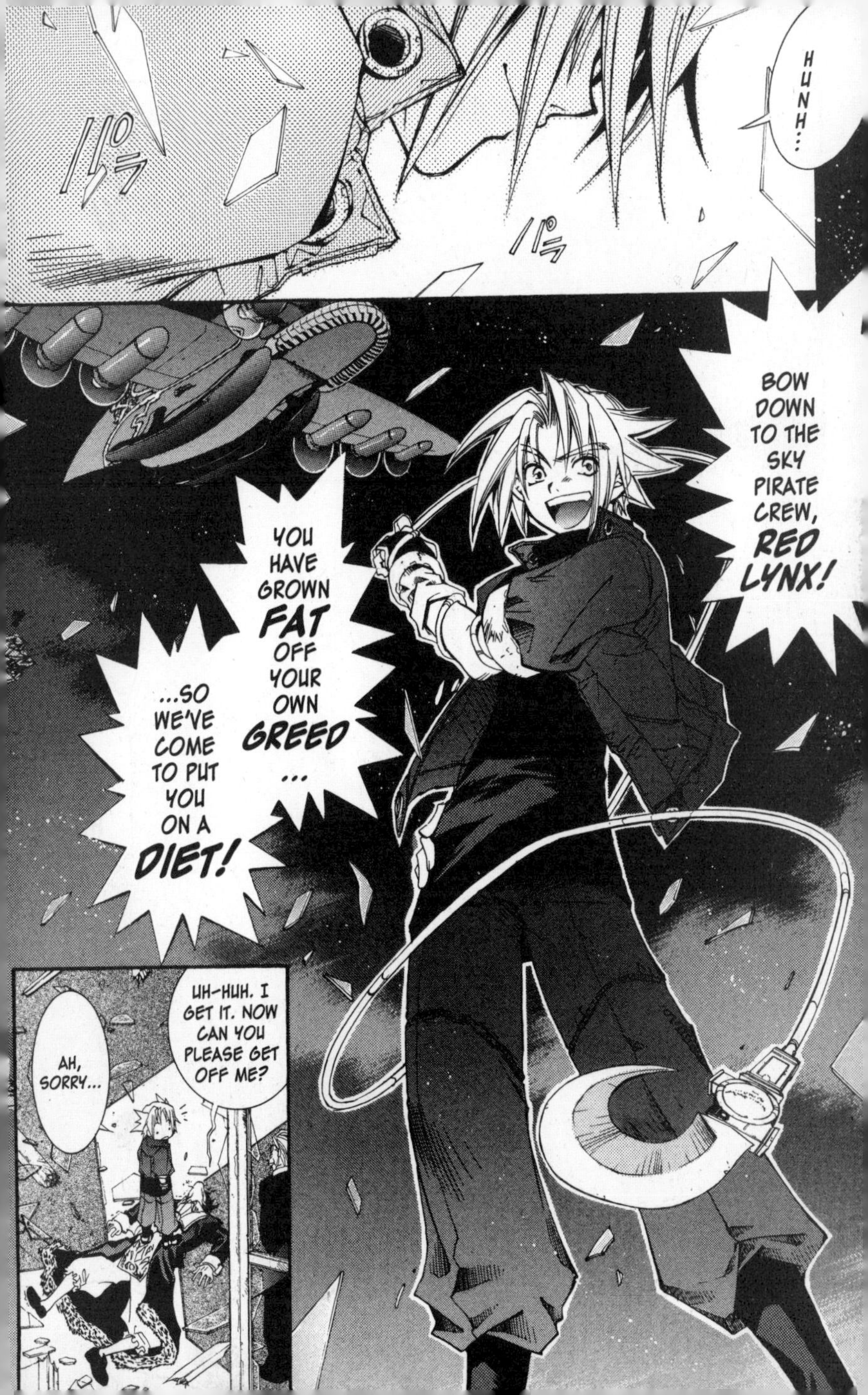
HUNH...
パラ
パラ
BOW DOWN TO THE SKY PIRATE CREW, RED LYNX!
YOU HAVE GROWN FAT OFF YOUR OWN GREED...
...SO WE'VE COME TO PUT YOU ON A DIET!
UH-HUH. I GET IT. NOW CAN YOU PLEASE GET OFF ME?
AH, SORRY...

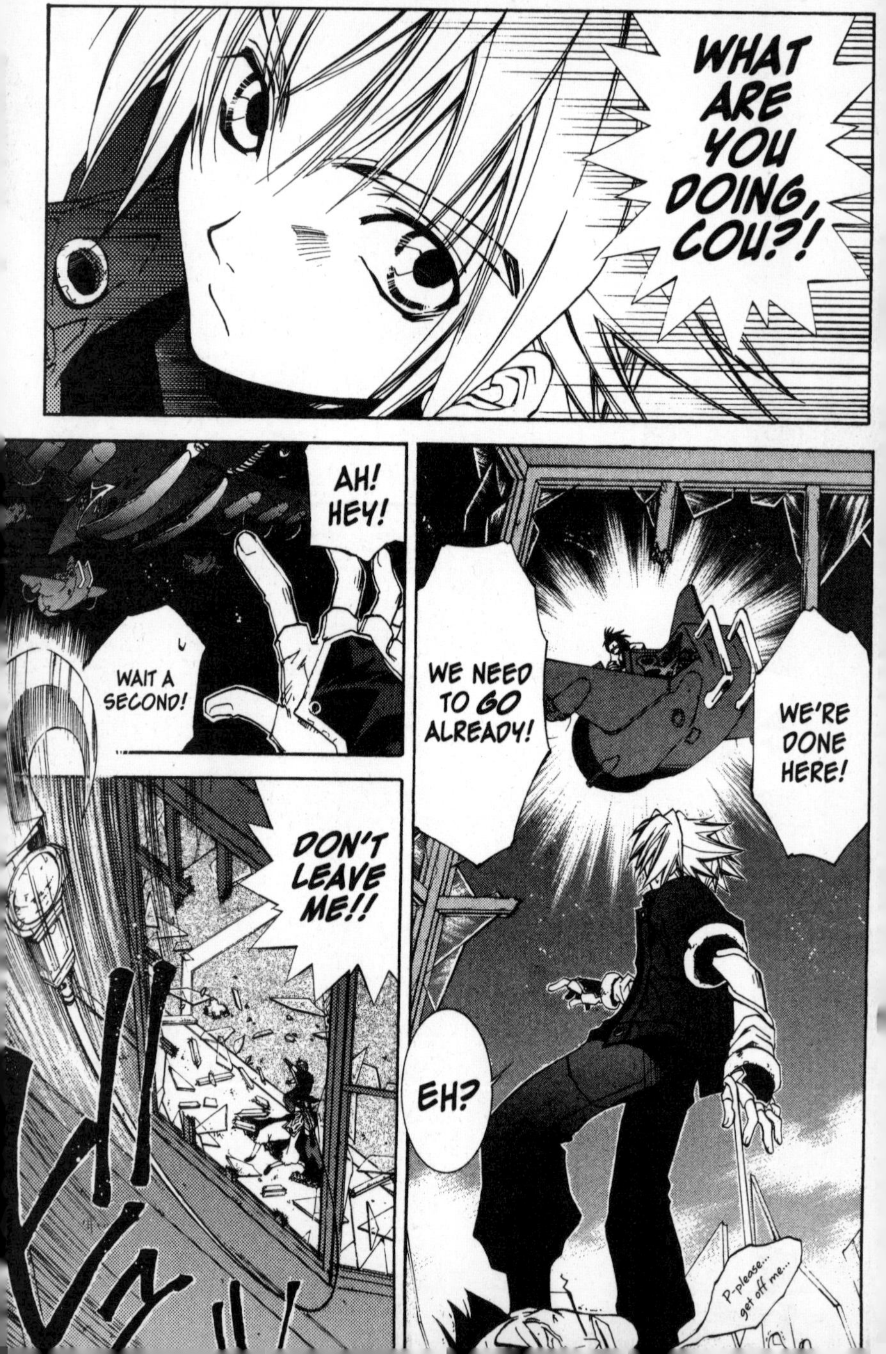
WHAT ARE YOU DOING, COU?!
WE'RE DONE HERE!
WE NEED TO GO ALREADY!
EH?
P-please... get off me...
AH! HEY!
WAIT A SECOND!
DON'T LEAVE ME!!

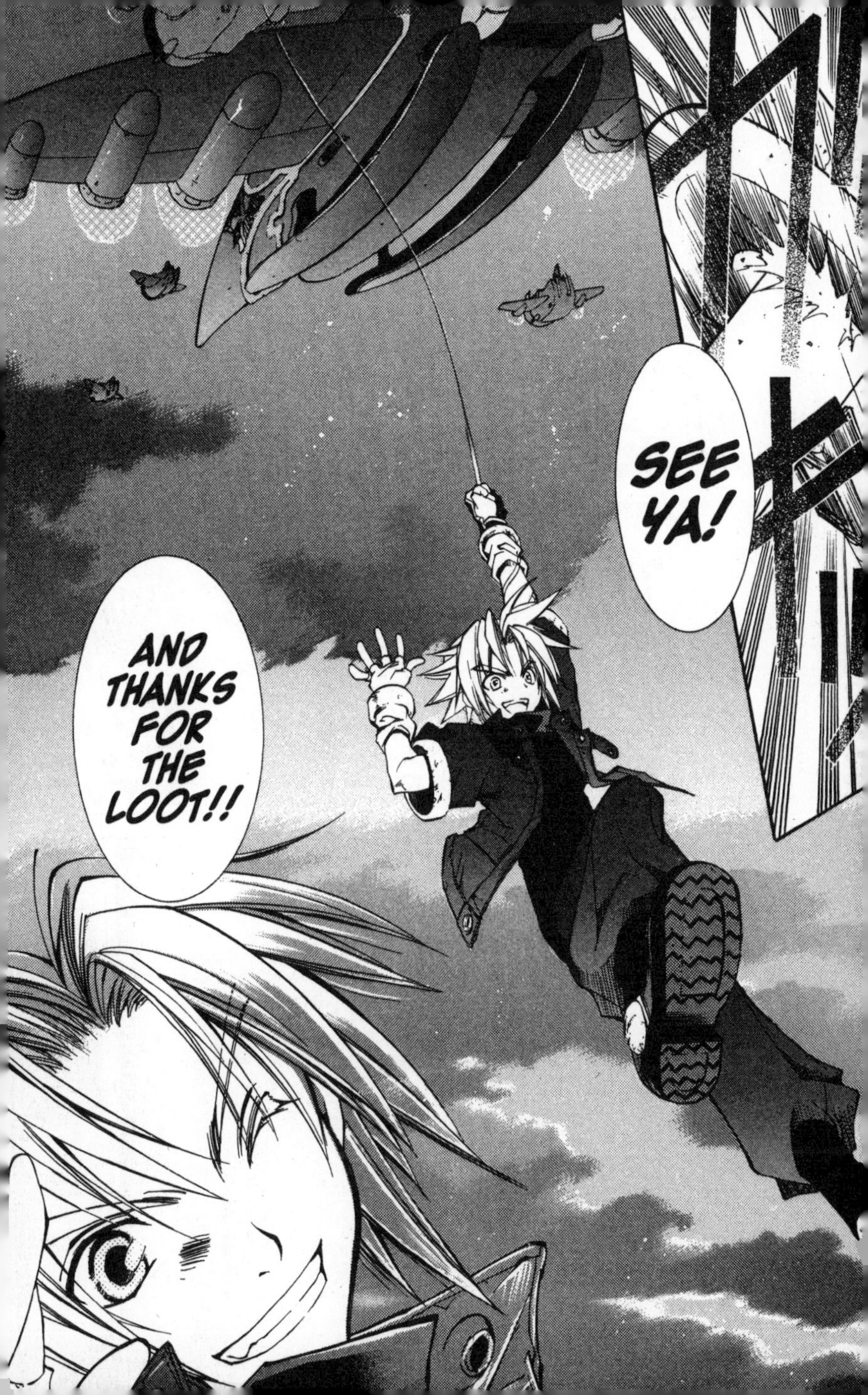
SEE YA!
AND THANKS FOR THE LOOT!!

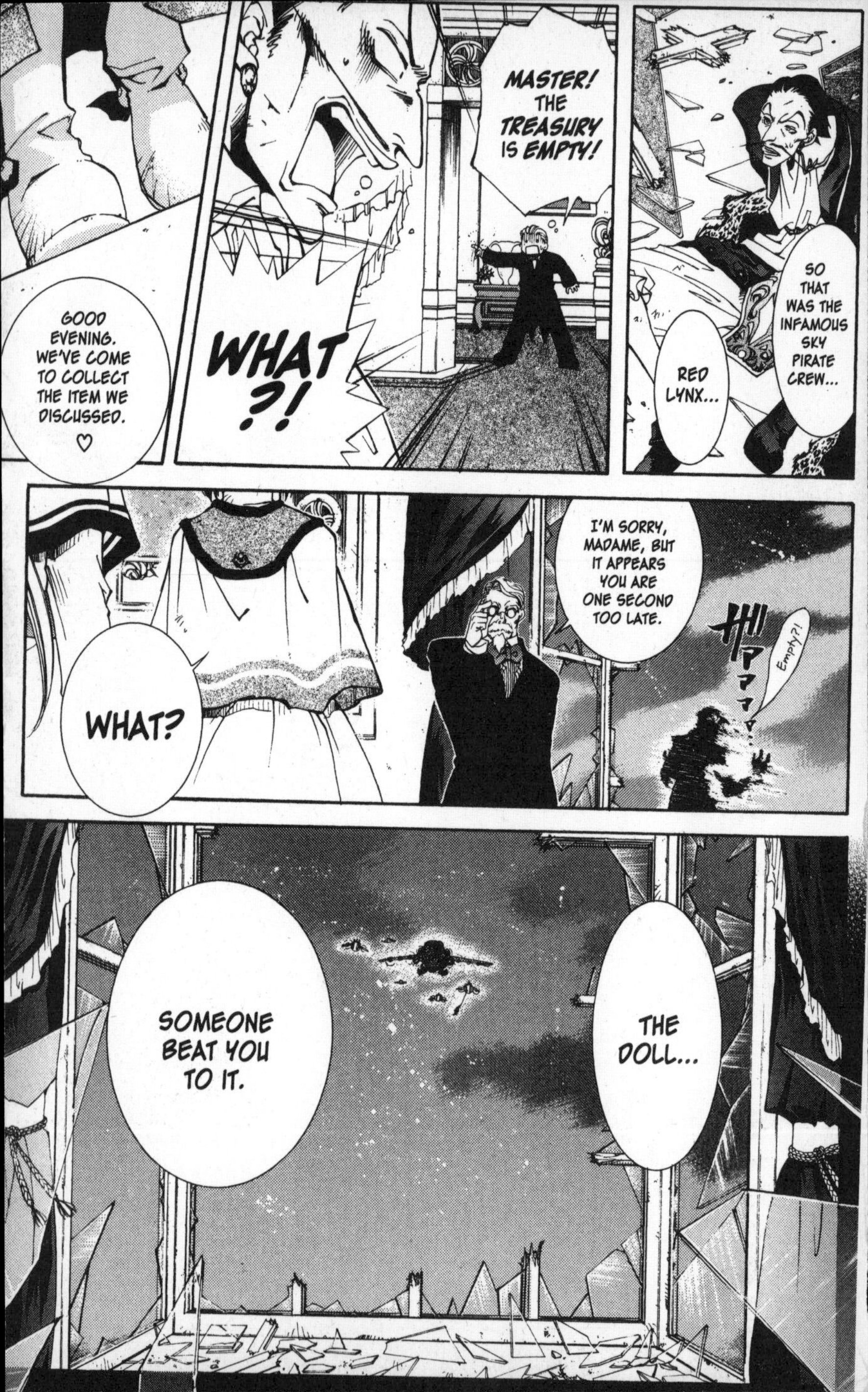
SO THAT WAS THE INFAMOUS SKY PIRATE CREW...
RED LYNX...
MASTER! THE TREASURY IS EMPTY!
WHAT ?!
GOOD EVENING. WE'VE COME TO COLLECT THE ITEM WE DISCUSSED. ♡
I'M SORRY, MADAME, BUT IT APPEARS YOU ARE ONE SECOND TOO LATE.
Empty?!
WHAT?
THE DOLL...
SOMEONE BEAT YOU TO IT.

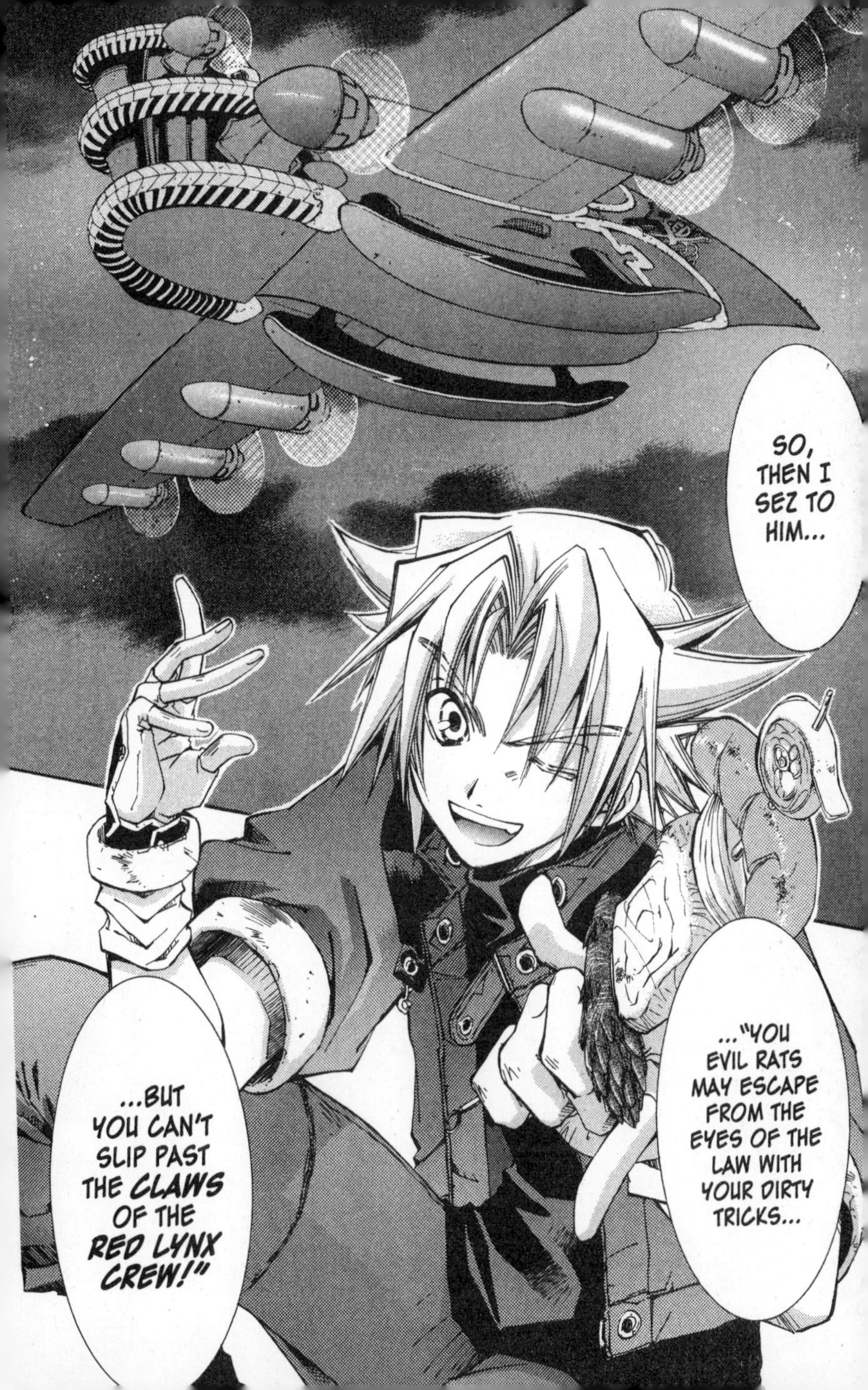
SO, THEN I SEZ TO HIM...
..."YOU EVIL RATS MAY ESCAPE FROM THE EYES OF THE LAW WITH YOUR DIRTY TRICKS...
...BUT YOU CAN'T SLIP PAST THE *CLAWS* OF THE *RED LYNX CREW!"*

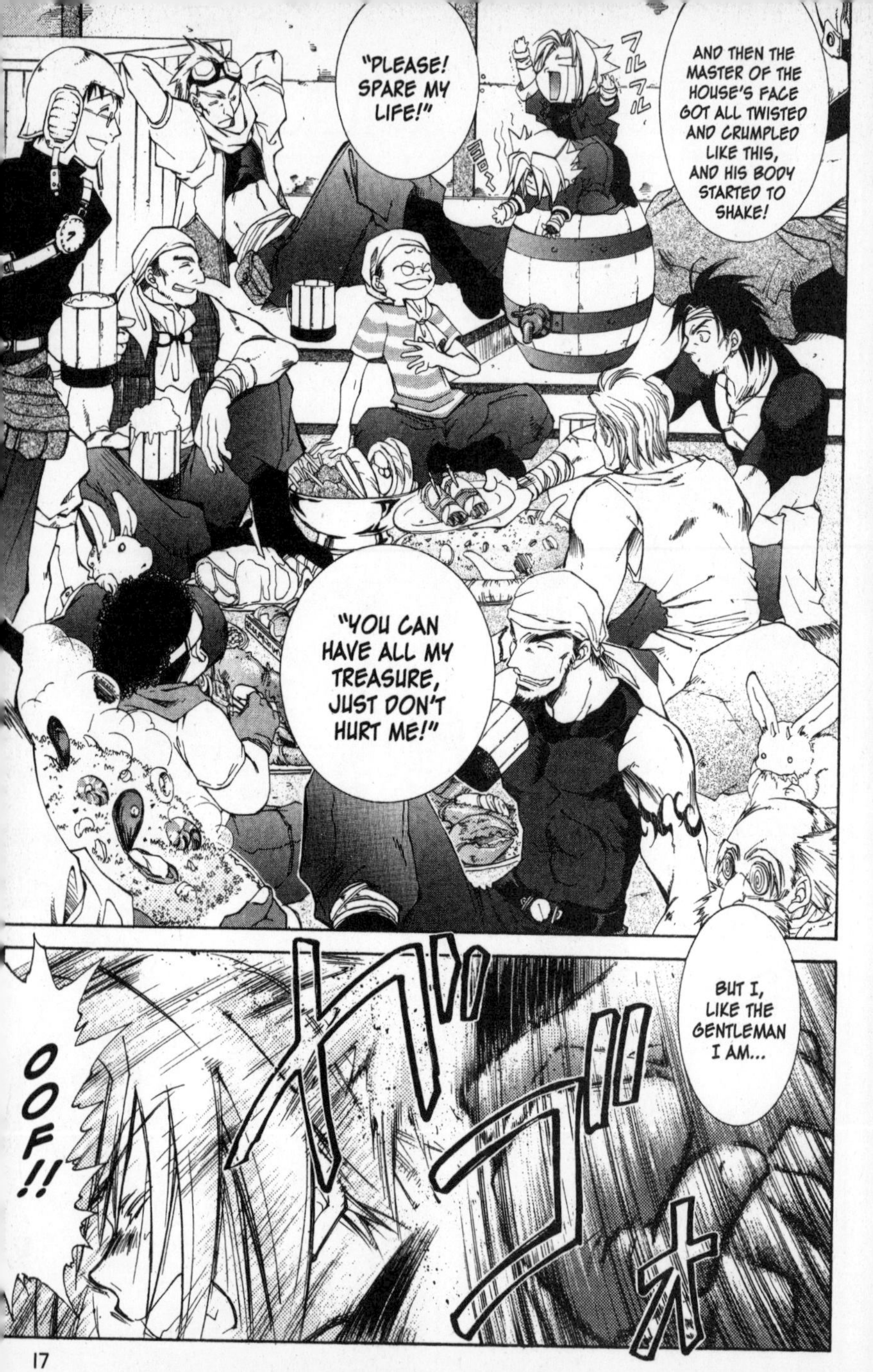
AND THEN THE MASTER OF THE HOUSE'S FACE GOT ALL TWISTED AND CRUMPLED LIKE THIS, AND HIS BODY STARTED TO SHAKE!
"PLEASE! SPARE MY LIFE!"
"YOU CAN HAVE ALL MY TREASURE, JUST DON'T HURT ME!"
BUT I, LIKE THE GENTLEMAN I AM...
OOF!!

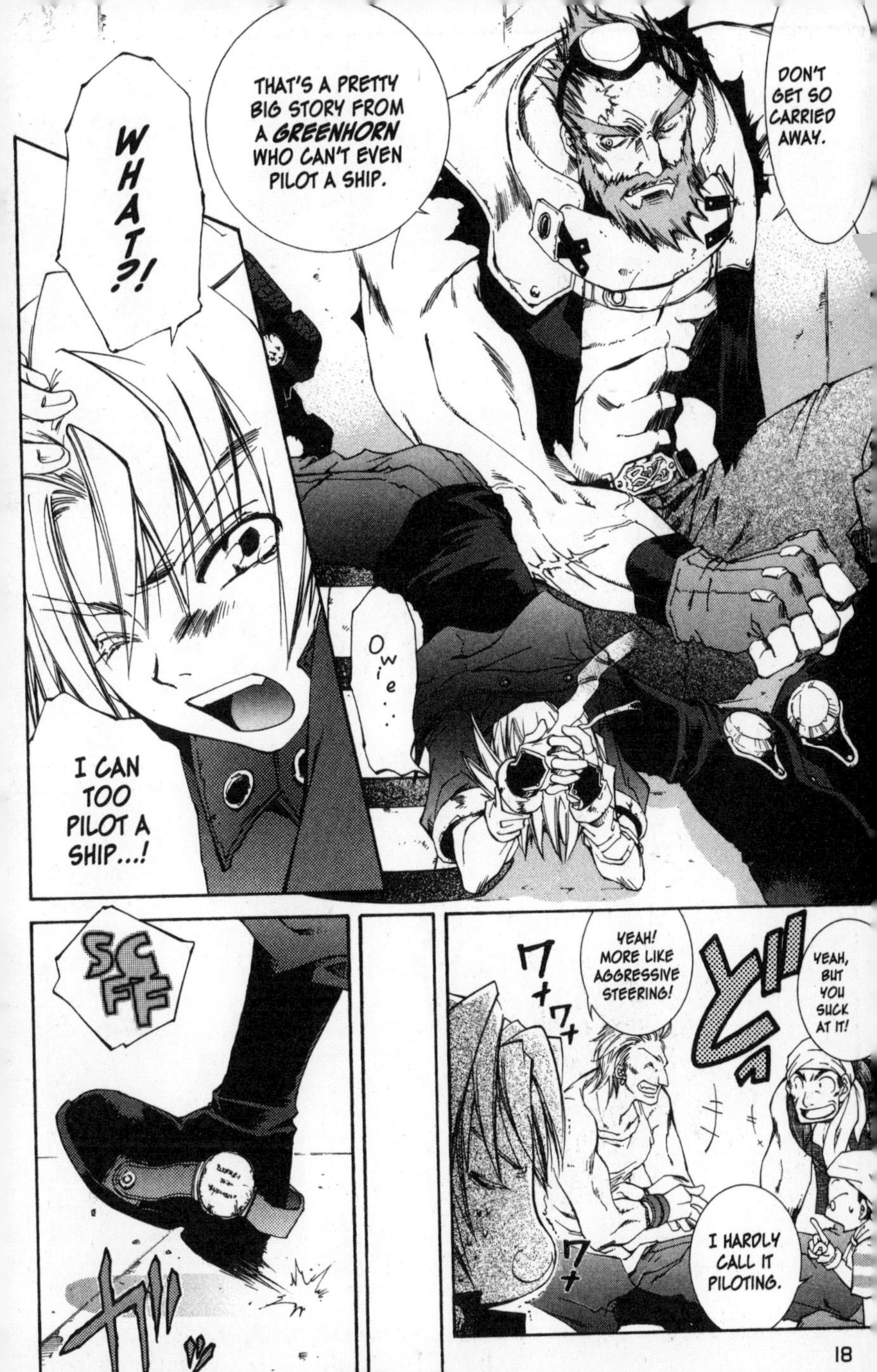
DON'T GET SO CARRIED AWAY.
THAT'S A PRETTY BIG STORY FROM A *GREENHORN* WHO CAN'T EVEN PILOT A SHIP.
WHAT?!
Owie...
I CAN TOO PILOT A SHIP...!
YEAH, BUT YOU SUCK AT IT!
YEAH! MORE LIKE AGGRESSIVE STEERING!
I HARDLY CALL IT PILOTING.
SCFF

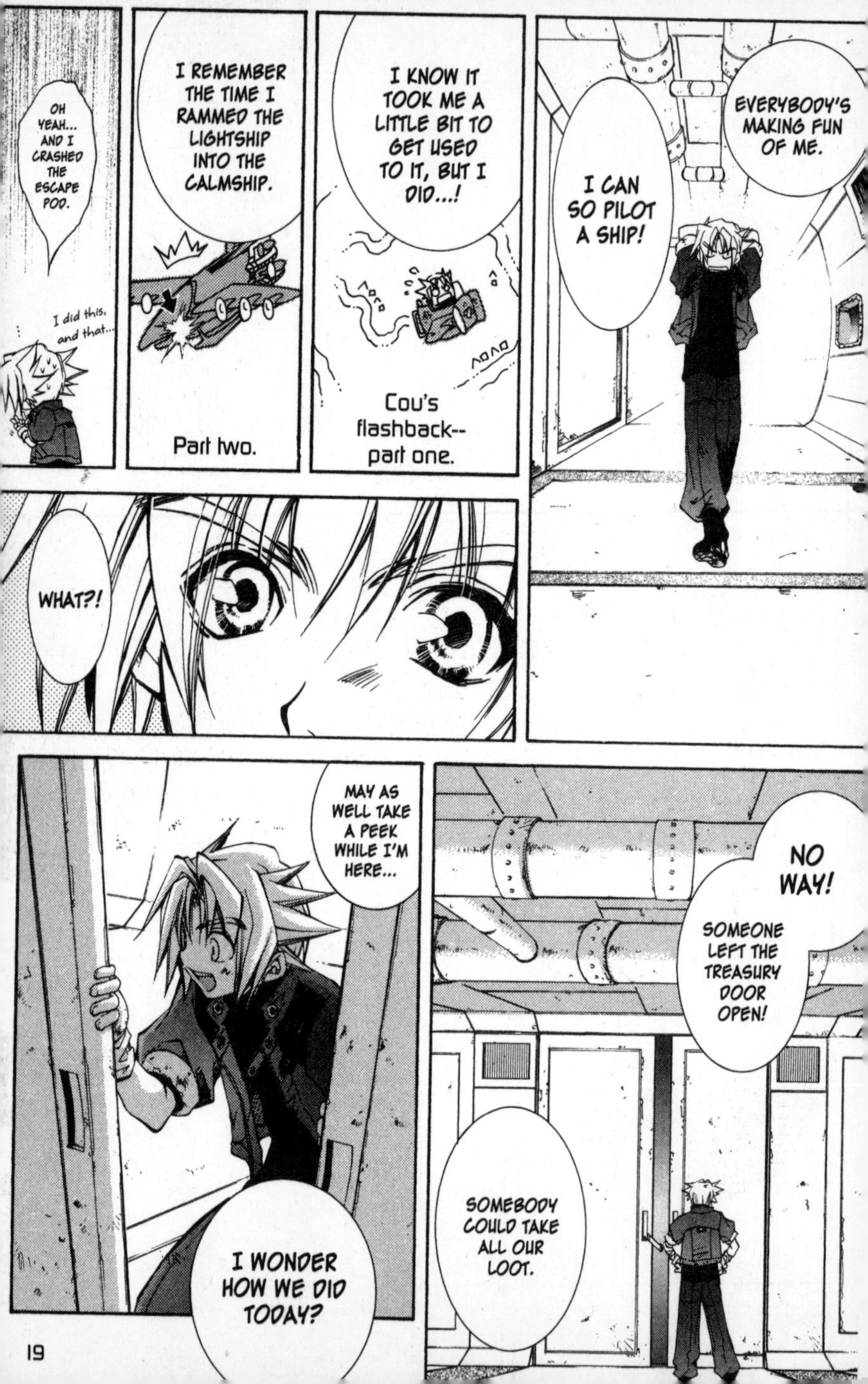

EVERYBODY'S MAKING FUN OF ME.
I CAN SO PILOT A SHIP!
I KNOW IT TOOK ME A LITTLE BIT TO GET USED TO IT, BUT I DID...!
Cou's flashback-- part one.
I REMEMBER THE TIME I RAMMED THE LIGHTSHIP INTO THE CALMSHIP.
Part two.
OH YEAH... AND I CRASHED THE ESCAPE POD.
I did this, and that...
WHAT?!
NO WAY!
SOMEONE LEFT THE TREASURY DOOR OPEN!
SOMEBODY COULD TAKE ALL OUR LOOT.
MAY AS WELL TAKE A PEEK WHILE I'M HERE...
I WONDER HOW WE DID TODAY?

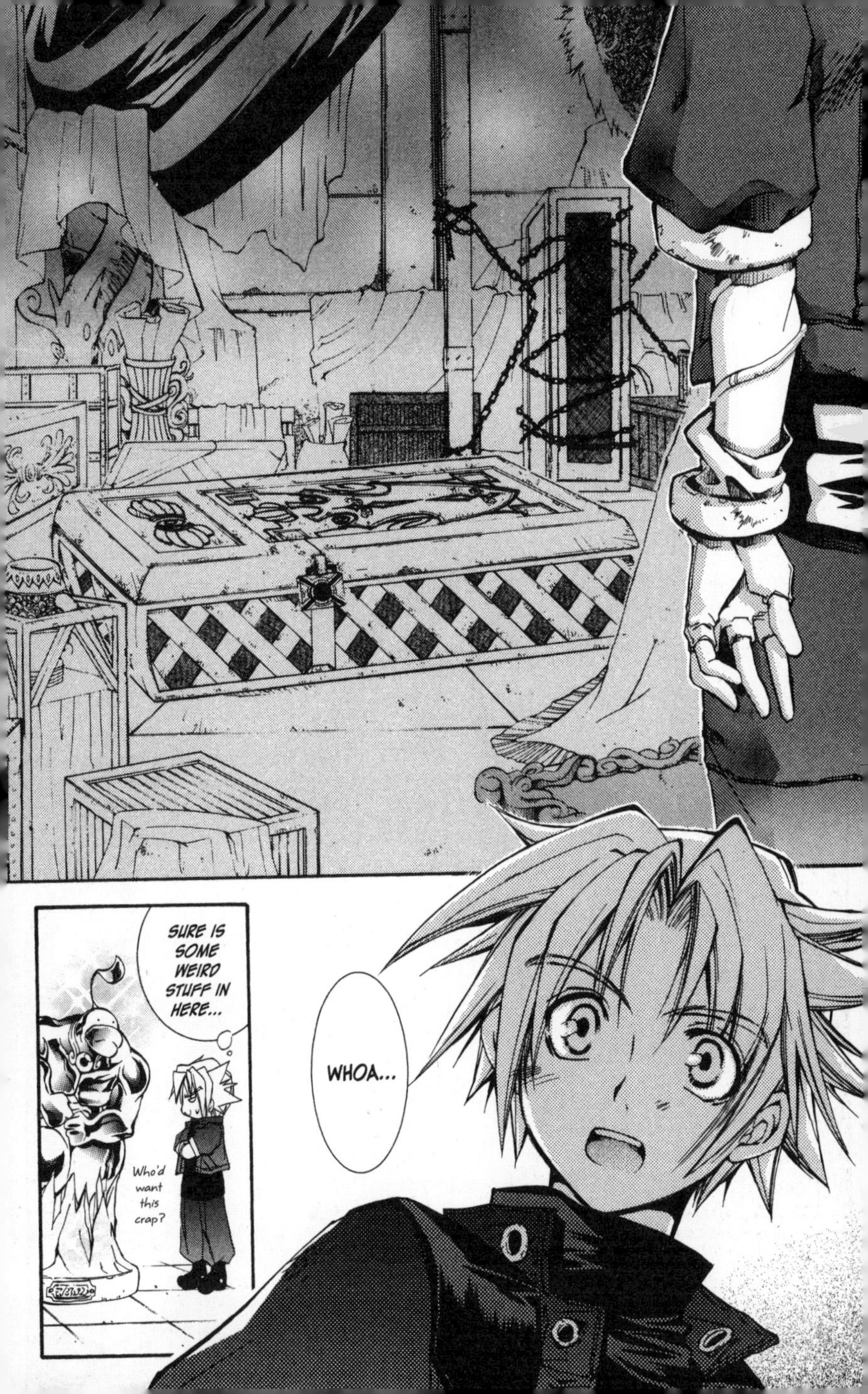
WHOA...
SURE IS SOME WEIRD STUFF IN HERE...
Who'd want this crap?

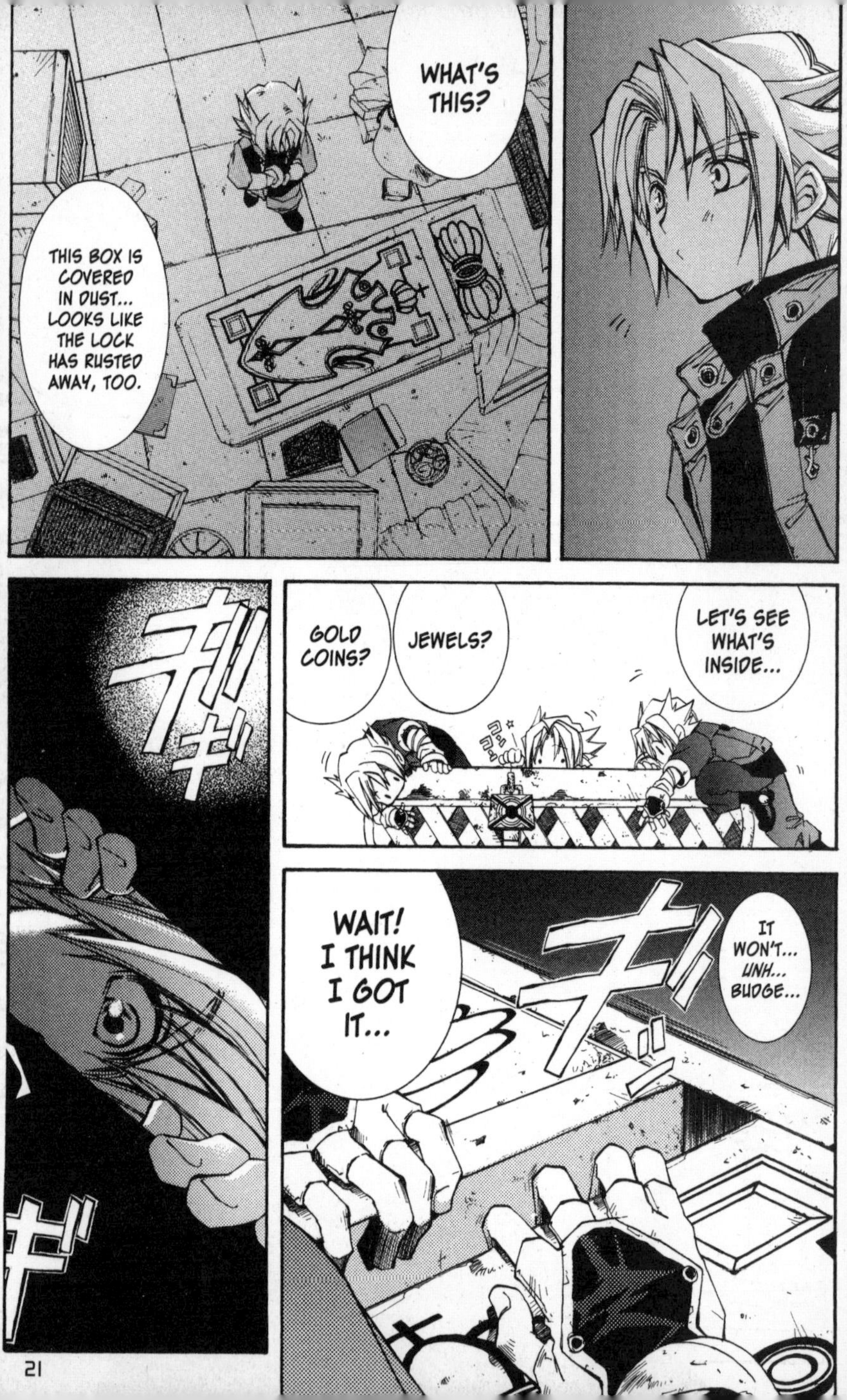
WHAT'S THIS?
THIS BOX IS COVERED IN DUST... LOOKS LIKE THE LOCK HAS RUSTED AWAY, TOO.
LET'S SEE WHAT'S INSIDE...
JEWELS?
GOLD COINS?
IT WON'T... UNH... BUDGE...
WAIT! I THINK I GOT IT...

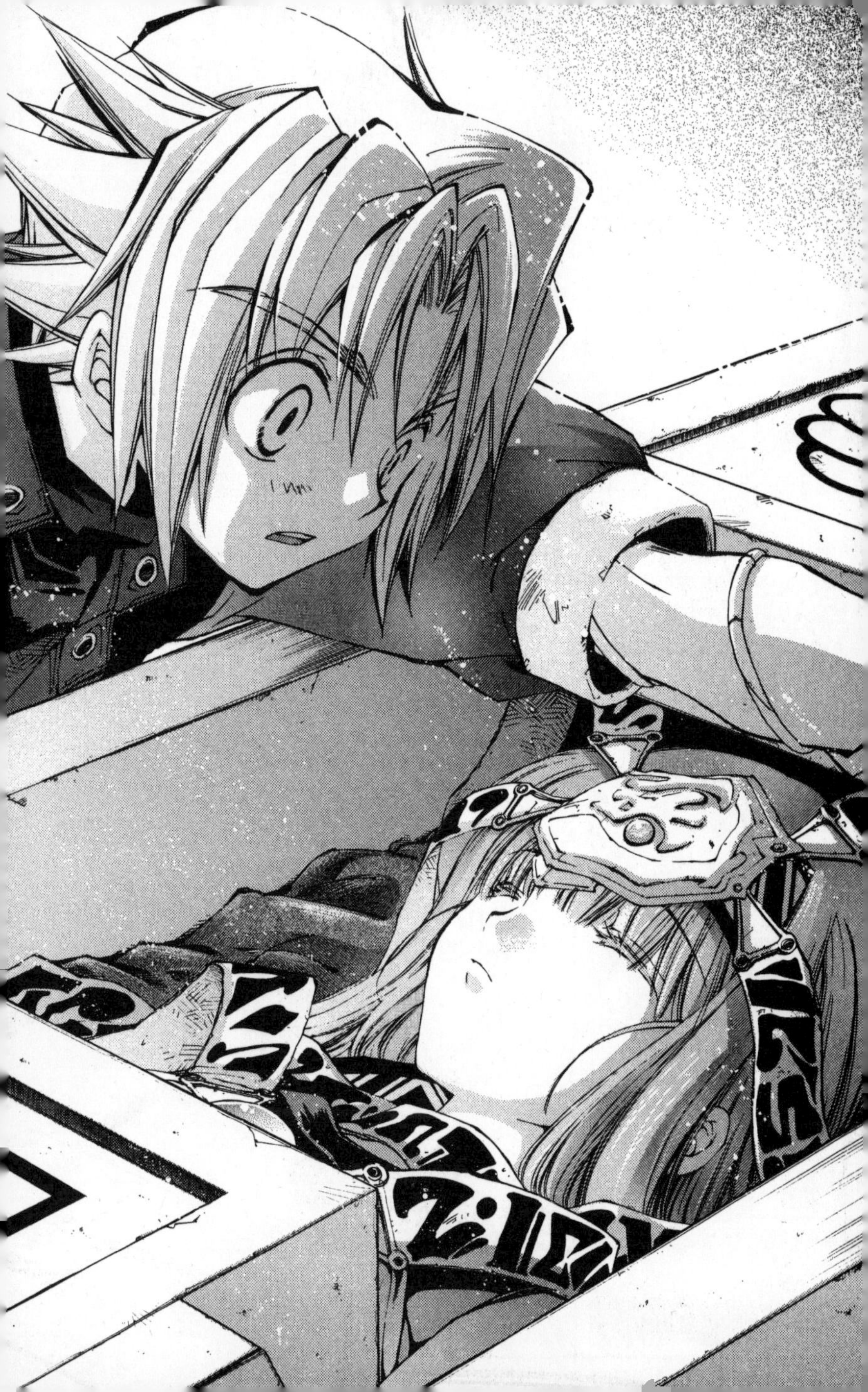

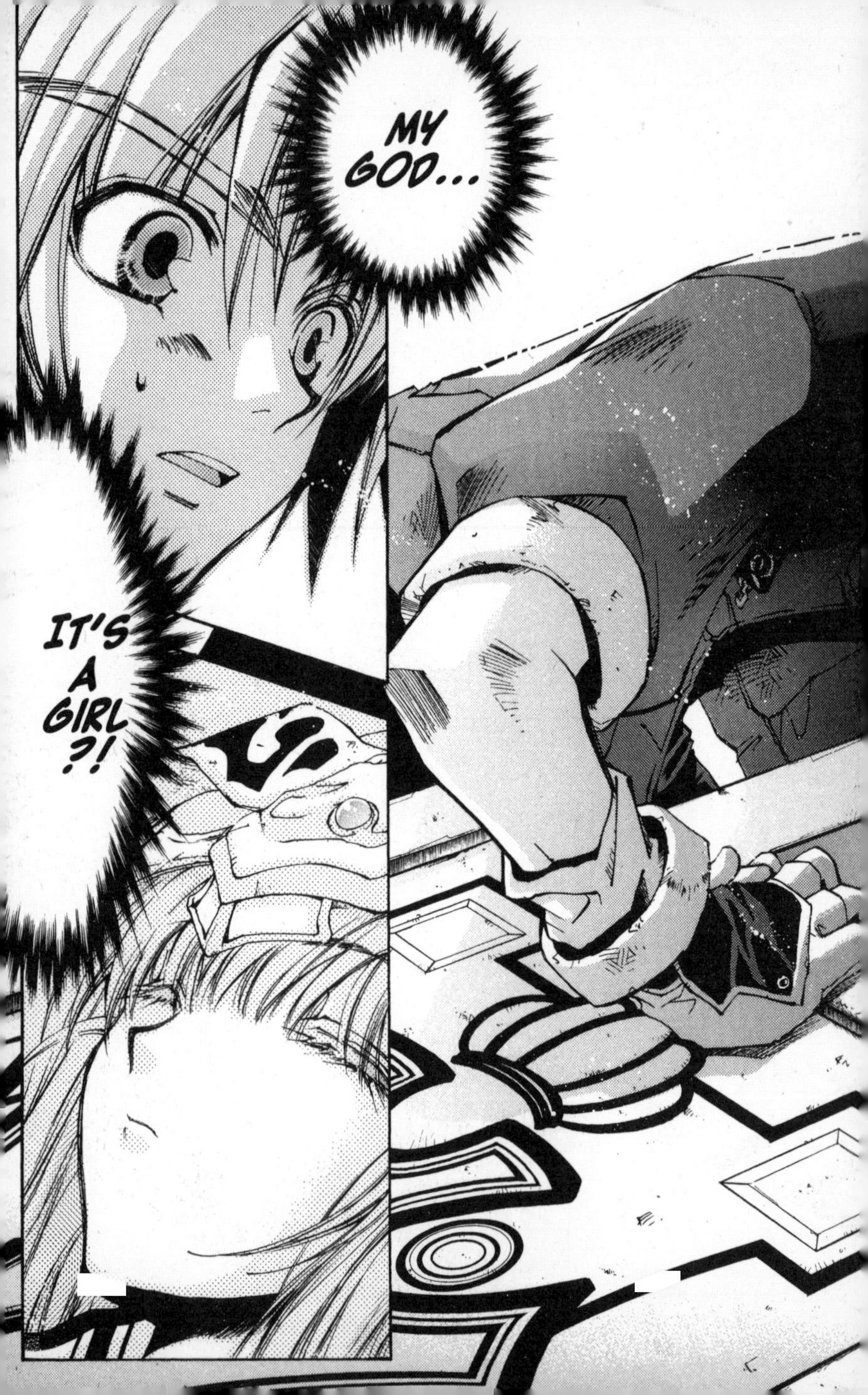
MY GOD...
IT'S A GIRL?!

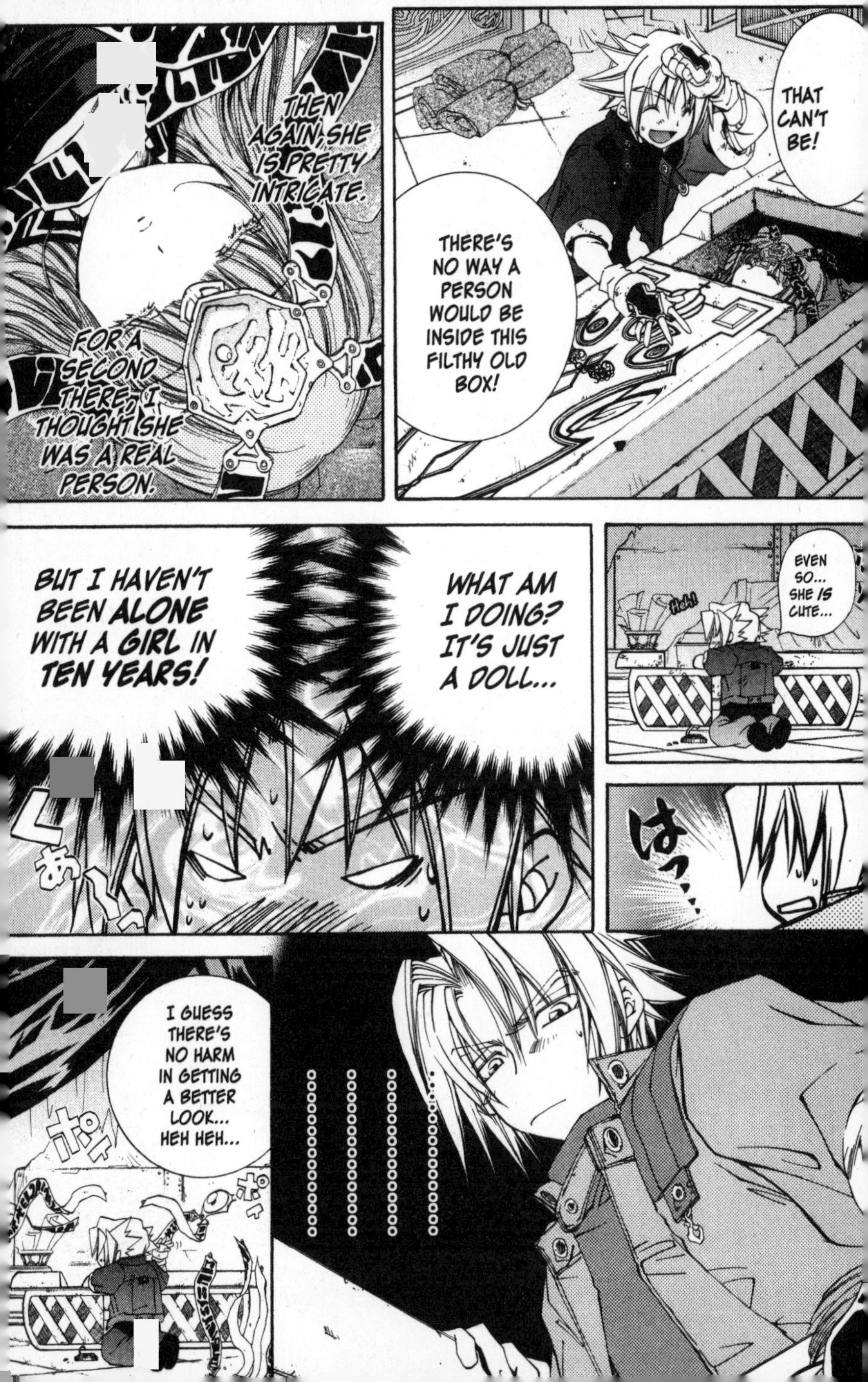
THAT CAN'T BE!
THERE'S NO WAY A PERSON WOULD BE INSIDE THIS FILTHY OLD BOX!
THEN AGAIN, SHE IS PRETTY INTRICATE.
FOR A SECOND THERE, I THOUGHT SHE WAS A REAL PERSON.
EVEN SO... SHE IS CUTE...
Heh!
はっ…
WHAT AM I DOING? IT'S JUST A DOLL...
BUT I HAVEN'T BEEN ALONE WITH A GIRL IN TEN YEARS!
I GUESS THERE'S NO HARM IN GETTING A BETTER LOOK... HEH HEH...
ポッ
ポッ

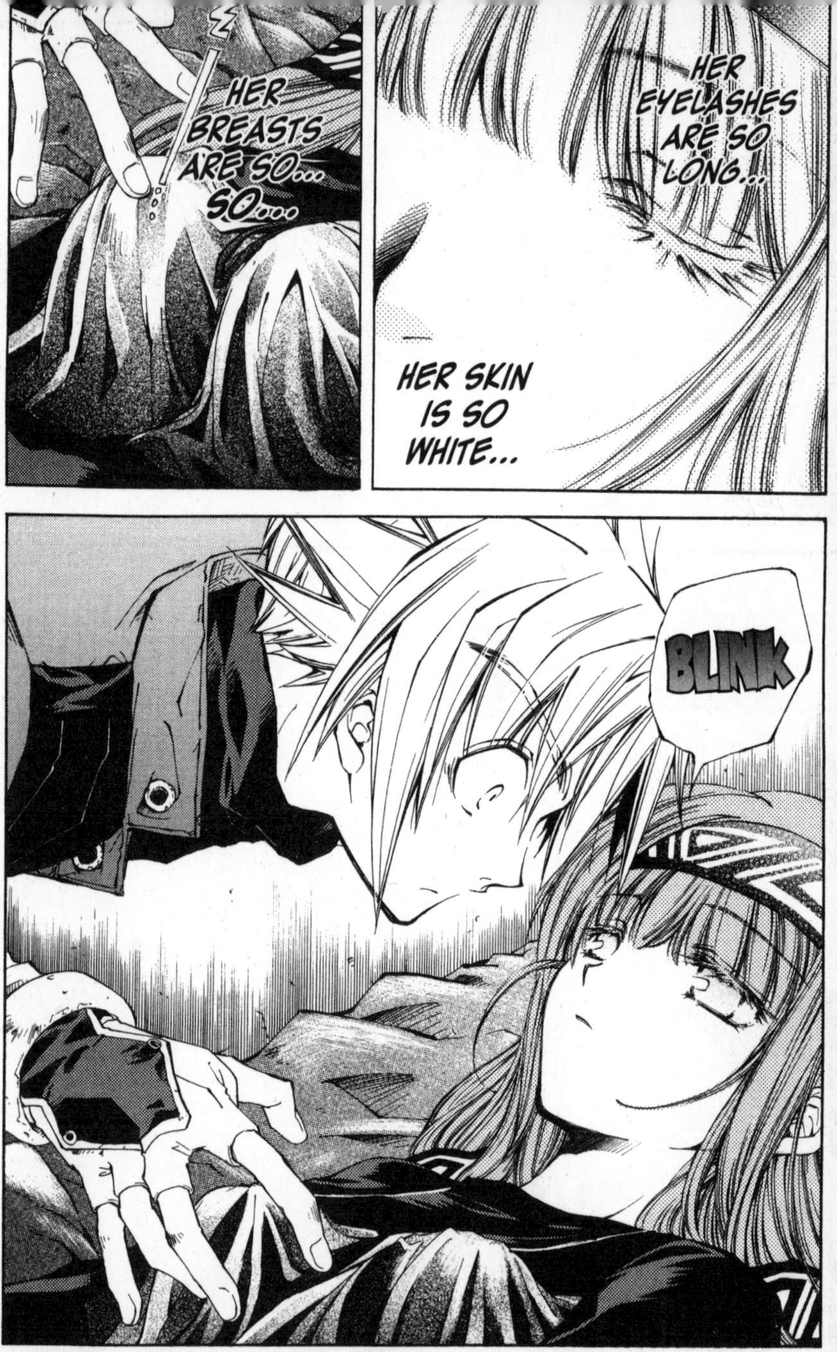
HER EYELASHES ARE SO LONG...
HER SKIN IS SO WHITE...
HER BREASTS ARE SO... SO...
BLINK

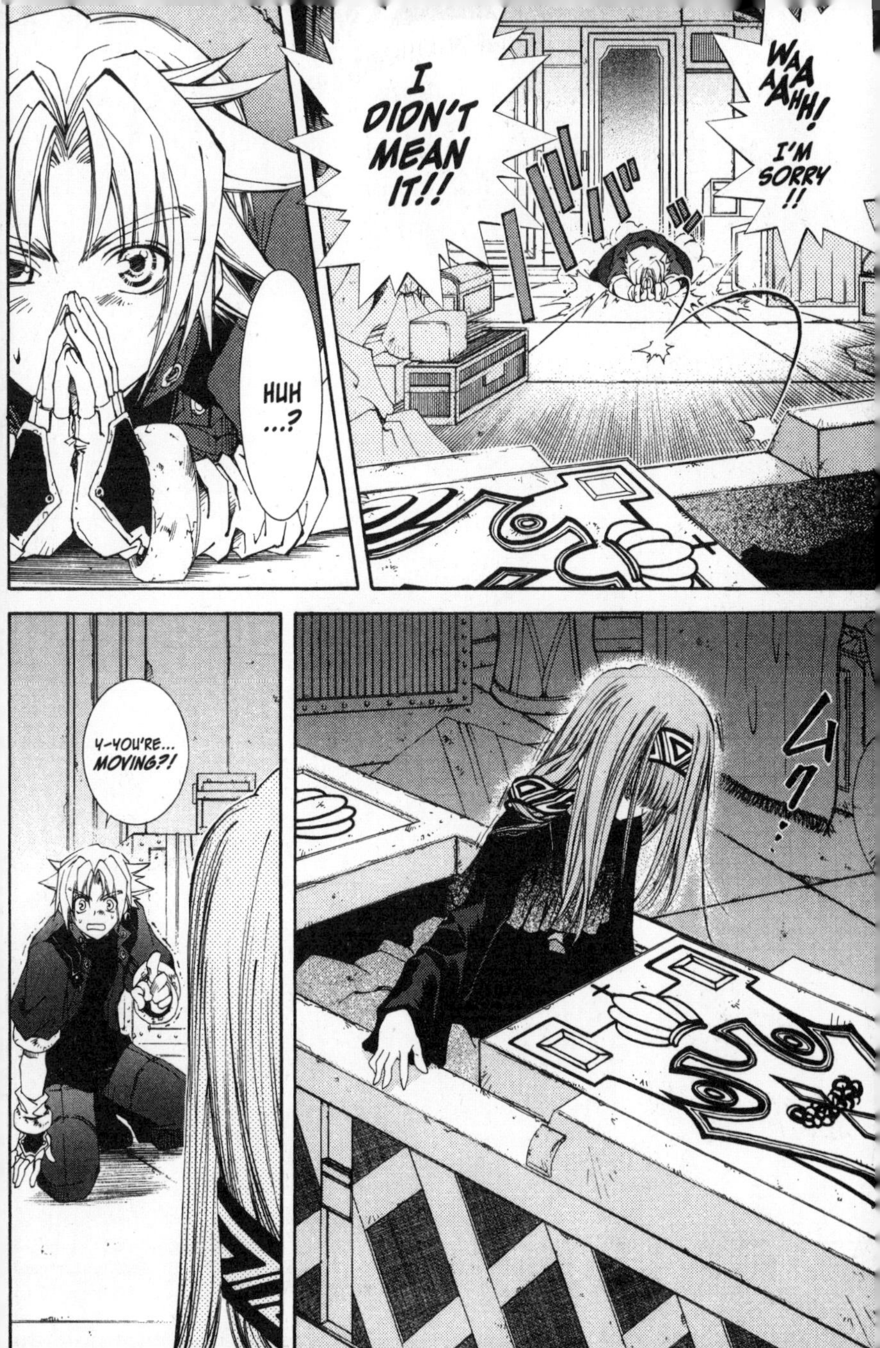
WAAAAHH!
I'M SORRY!!
I DIDN'T MEAN IT!!
HUH...?
Y-YOU'RE... MOVING?!

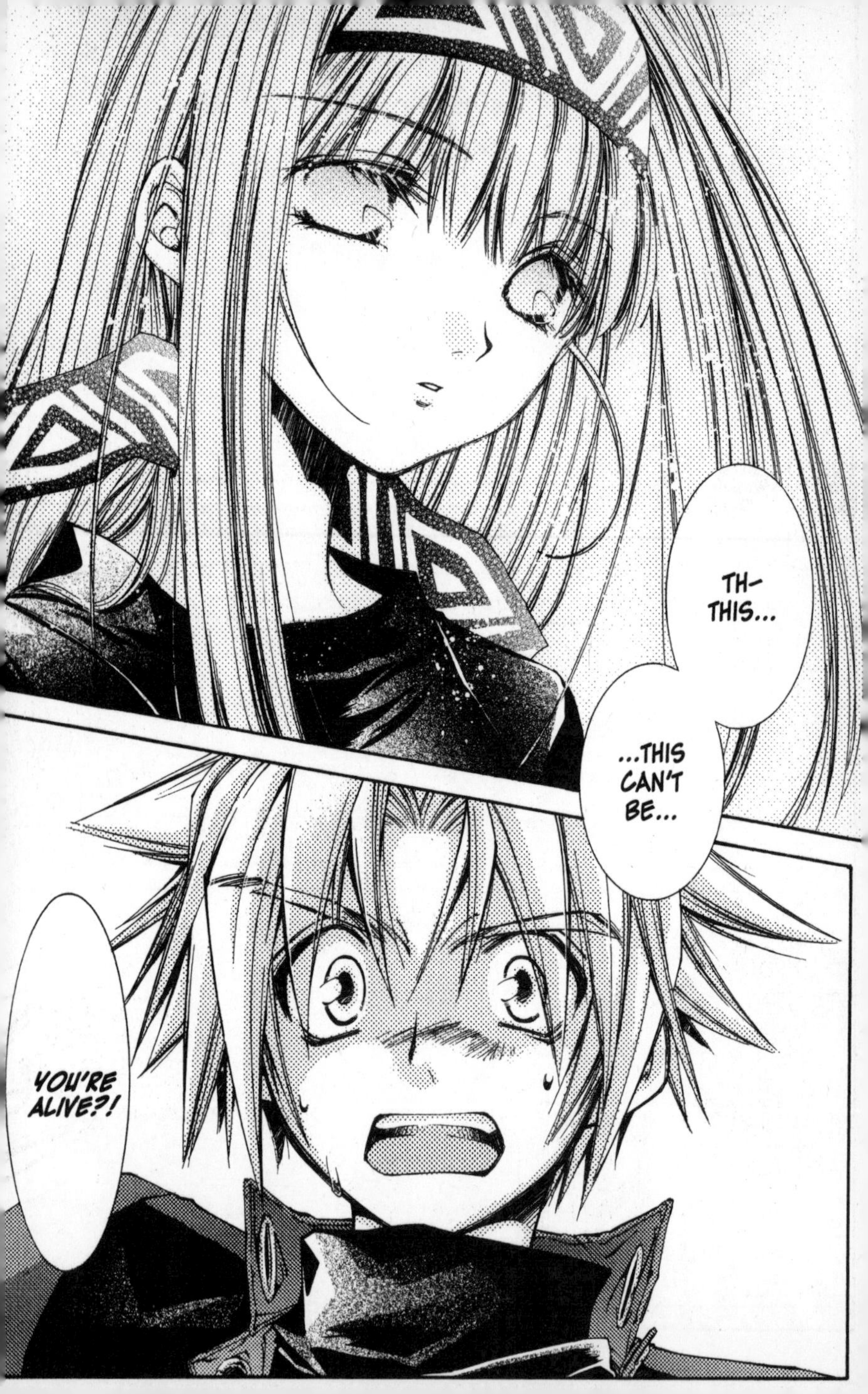
TH- THIS...
...THIS CAN'T BE...
YOU'RE ALIVE?!

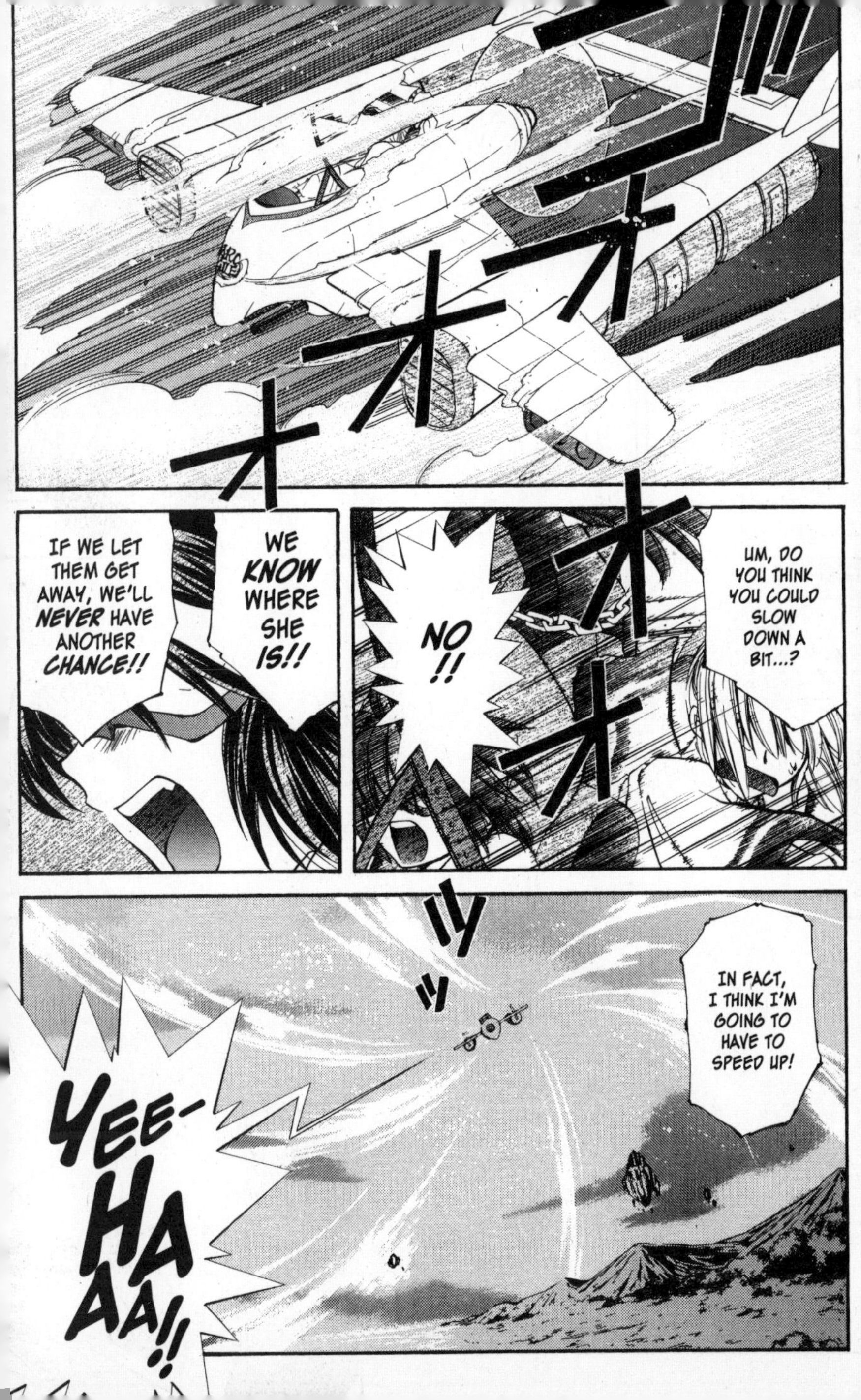
UM, DO YOU THINK YOU COULD SLOW DOWN A BIT...?
NO!!
WE KNOW WHERE SHE IS!!
IF WE LET THEM GET AWAY, WE'LL NEVER HAVE ANOTHER CHANCE!!
IN FACT, I THINK I'M GOING TO HAVE TO SPEED UP!
YEE-HAHAAA!!

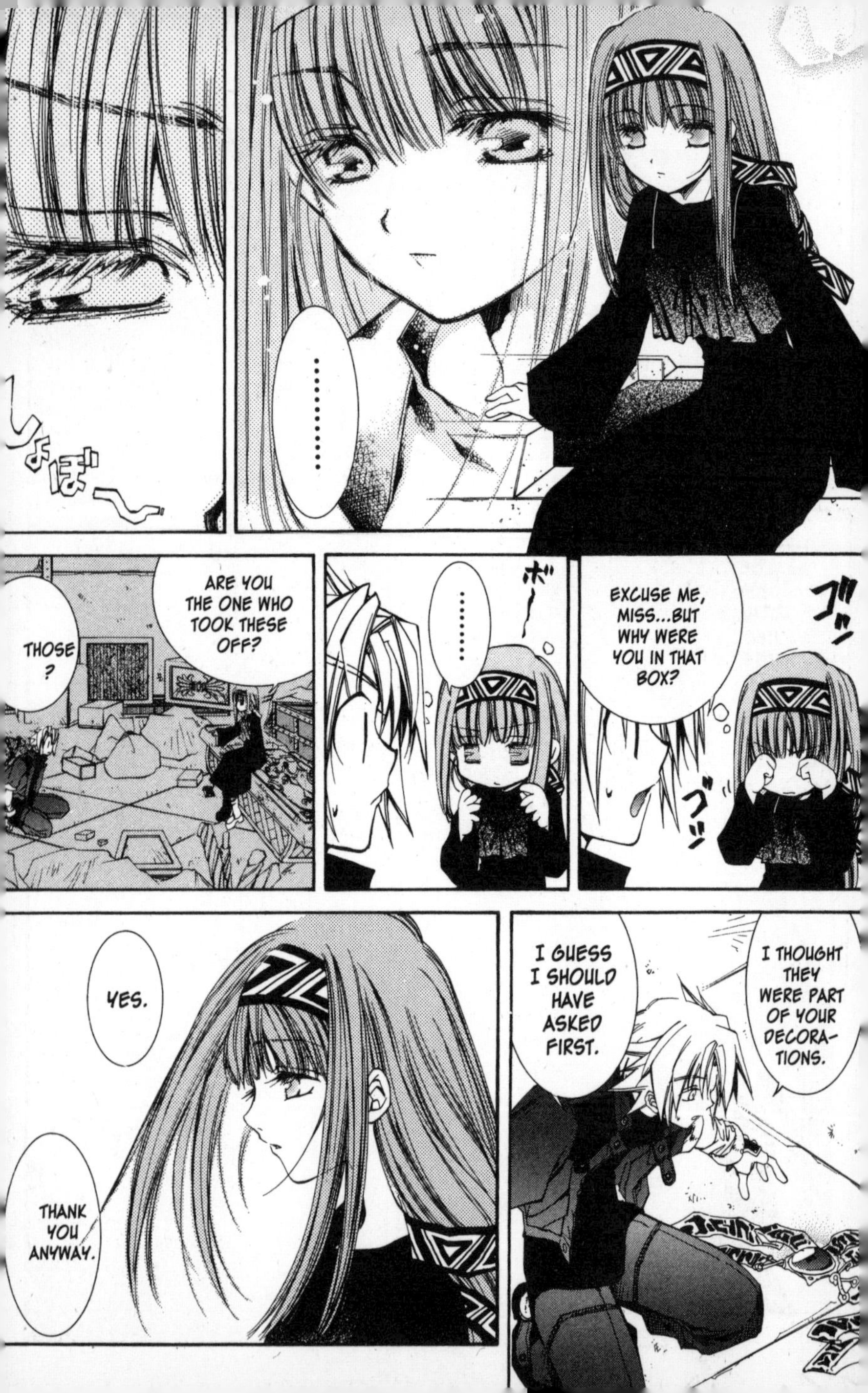
......
しょぼ〜
EXCUSE ME, MISS...BUT WHY WERE YOU IN THAT BOX?
ゴッ
ゴッ
......
ボー
ARE YOU THE ONE WHO TOOK THESE OFF?
THOSE?
I THOUGHT THEY WERE PART OF YOUR DECORATIONS.
I GUESS I SHOULD HAVE ASKED FIRST.
YES.
THANK YOU ANYWAY.

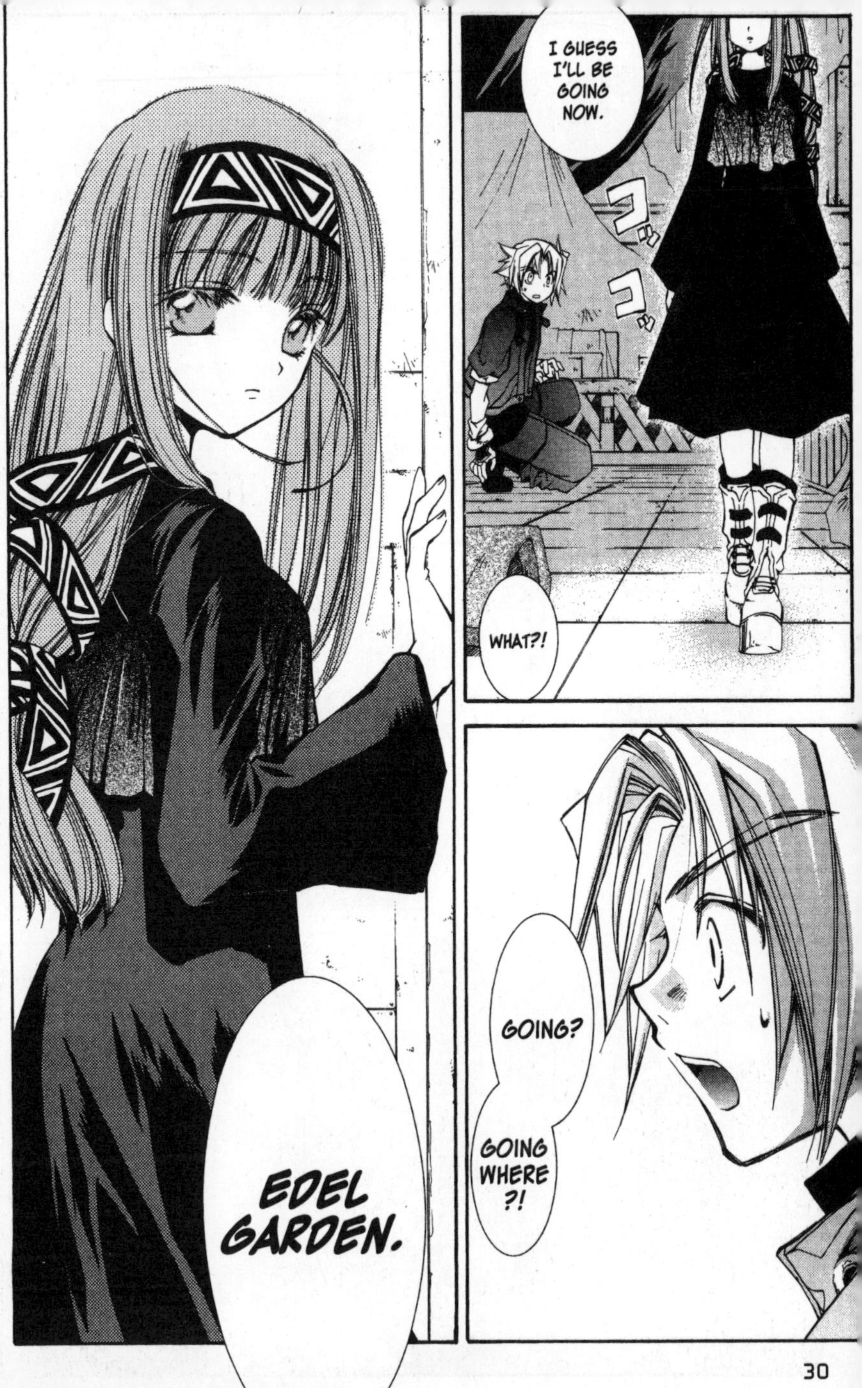
I GUESS I'LL BE GOING NOW.
WHAT?!
GOING?
GOING WHERE ?!
EDEL GARDEN.

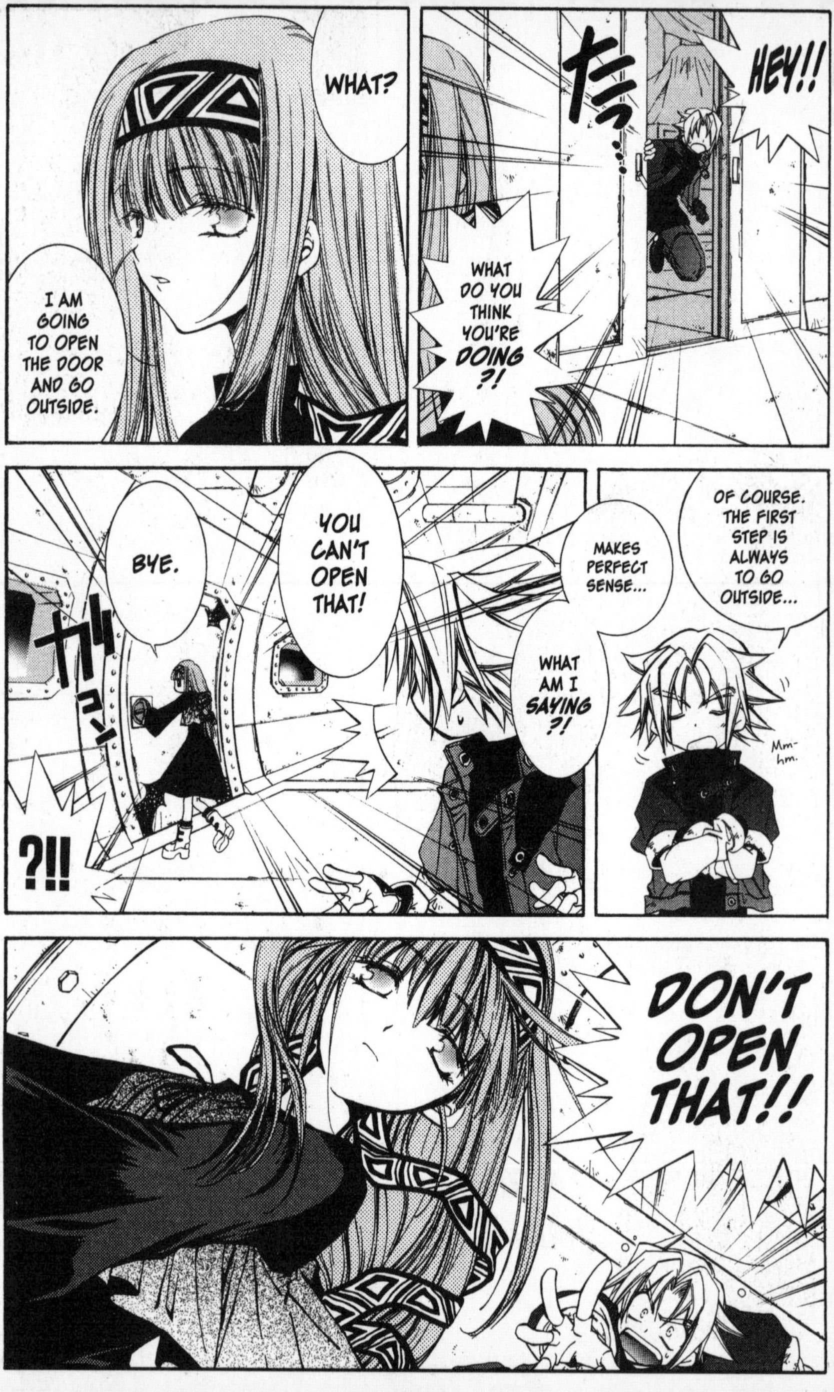
HEY!!
WHAT DO YOU THINK YOU'RE DOING?!
WHAT?
I AM GOING TO OPEN THE DOOR AND GO OUTSIDE.
OF COURSE. THE FIRST STEP IS ALWAYS TO GO OUTSIDE...
Mm-hm.
MAKES PERFECT SENSE...
WHAT AM I SAYING?!
YOU CAN'T OPEN THAT!
BYE.
?!!
DON'T OPEN THAT!!

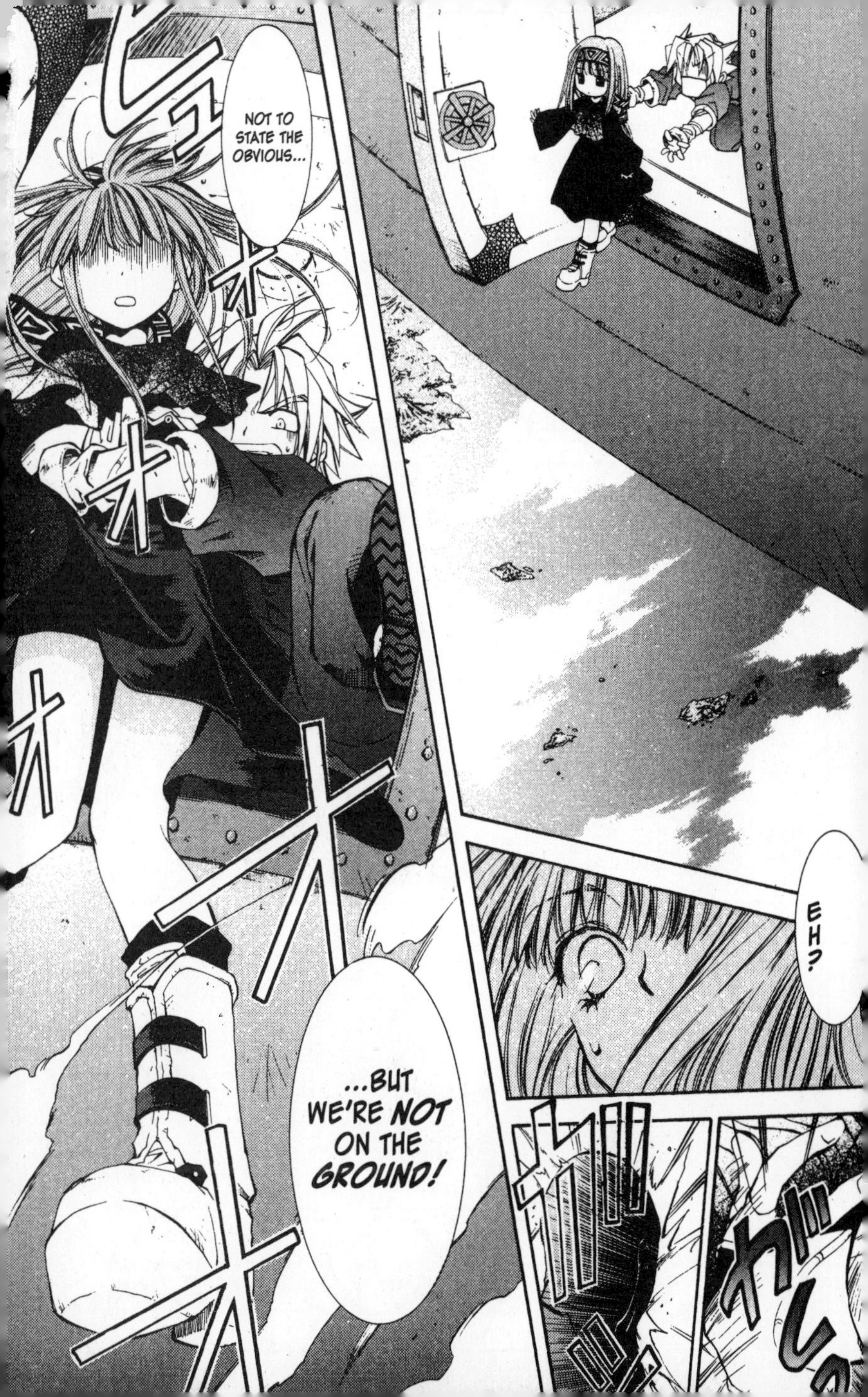
EH?
NOT TO STATE THE OBVIOUS...
...BUT WE'RE NOT ON THE GROUND!

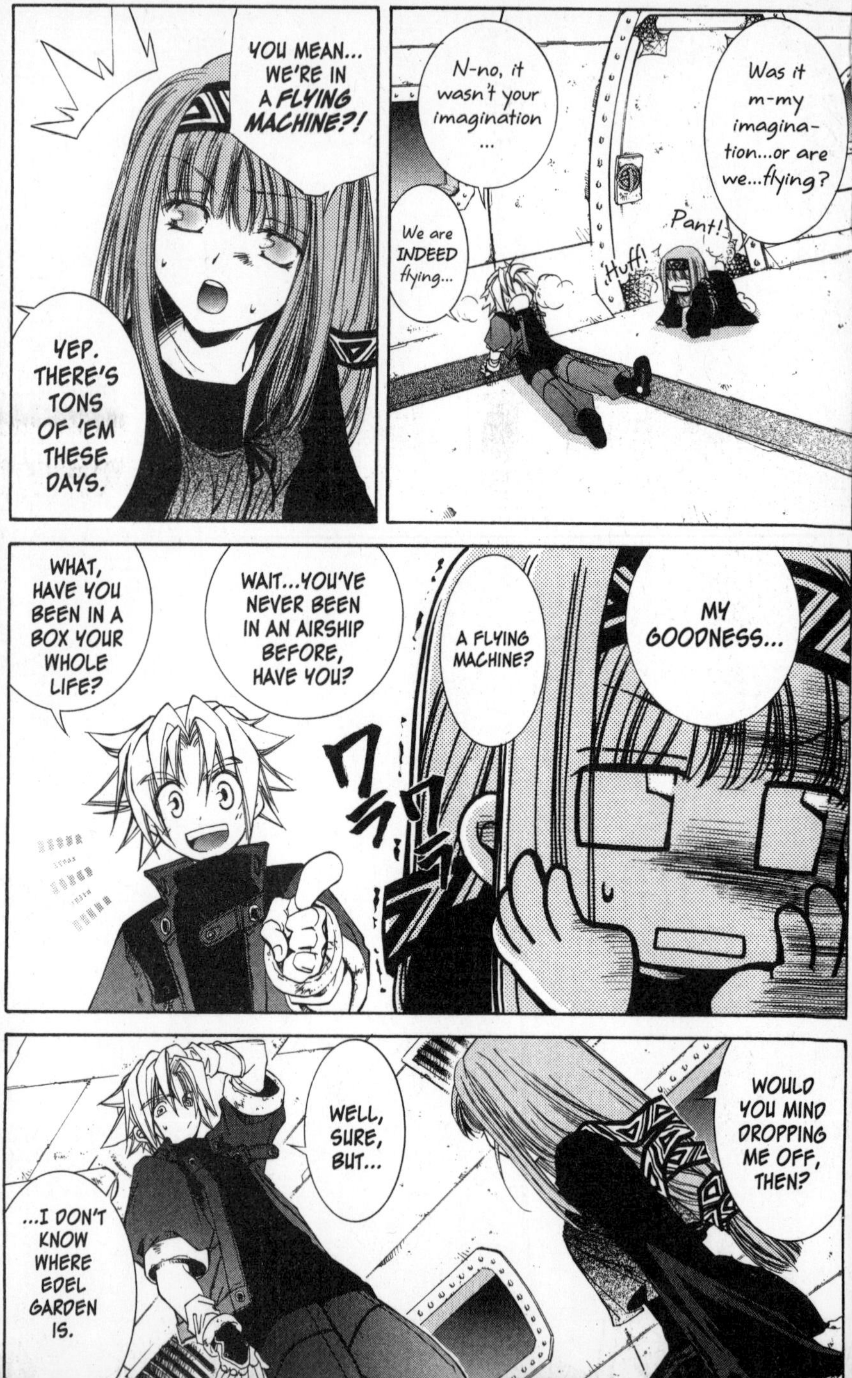
Was it m-my imagination...or are we...flying?
N-no, it wasn't your imagination...
Pant!
Huff!
We are INDEED flying...
YOU MEAN... WE'RE IN A *FLYING MACHINE?!*
YEP. THERE'S TONS OF 'EM THESE DAYS.
MY GOODNESS...
A FLYING MACHINE?
WAIT...YOU'VE NEVER BEEN IN AN AIRSHIP BEFORE, HAVE YOU?
WHAT, HAVE YOU BEEN IN A BOX YOUR WHOLE LIFE?
WOULD YOU MIND DROPPING ME OFF, THEN?
WELL, SURE, BUT...
...I DON'T KNOW WHERE EDEL GARDEN IS.

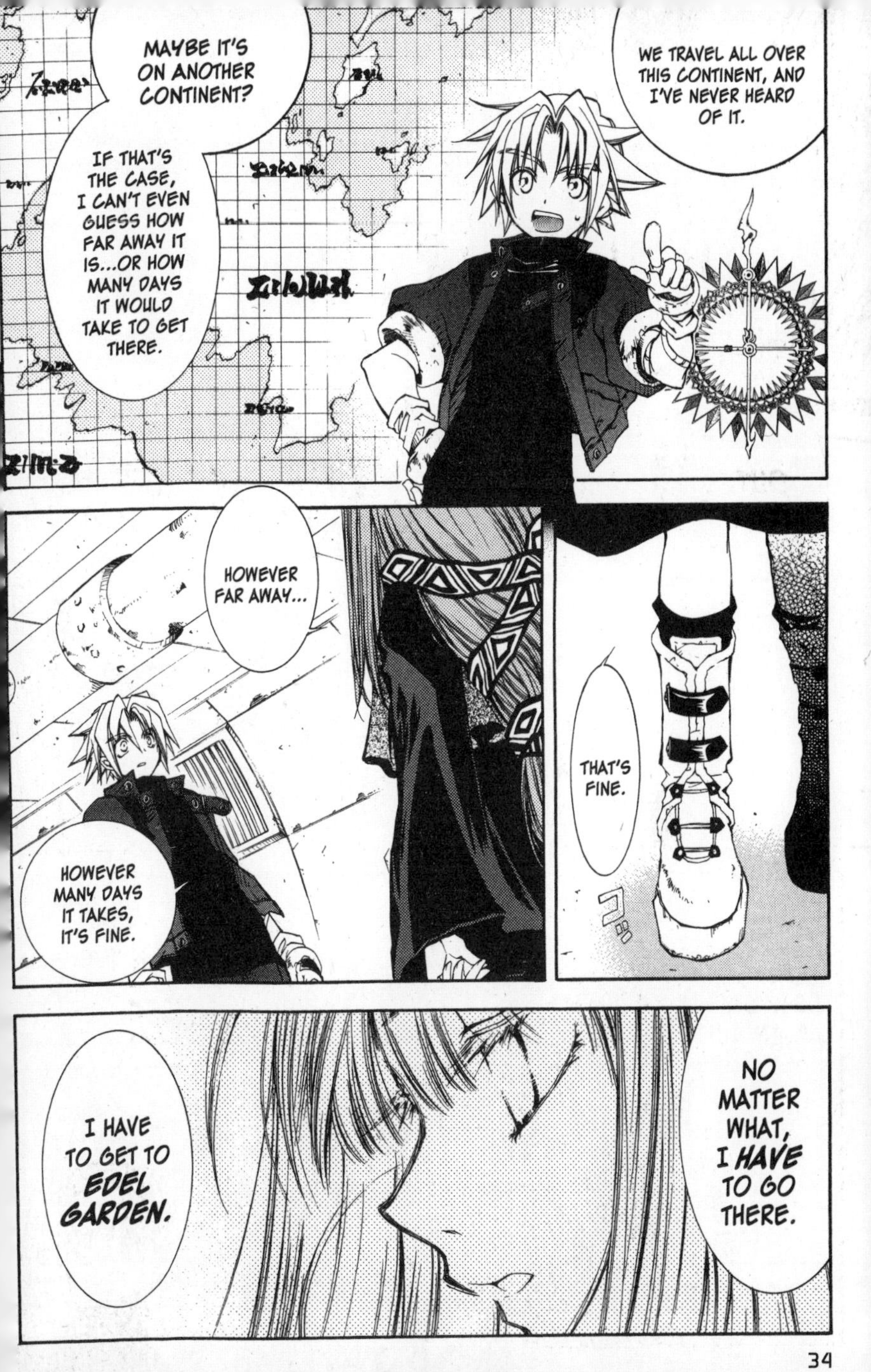
WE TRAVEL ALL OVER THIS CONTINENT, AND I'VE NEVER HEARD OF IT.
MAYBE IT'S ON ANOTHER CONTINENT?
IF THAT'S THE CASE, I CAN'T EVEN GUESS HOW FAR AWAY IT IS...OR HOW MANY DAYS IT WOULD TAKE TO GET THERE.
THAT'S FINE.
HOWEVER FAR AWAY...
HOWEVER MANY DAYS IT TAKES, IT'S FINE.
NO MATTER WHAT, I *HAVE* TO GO THERE.
I HAVE TO GET TO **EDEL GARDEN.**

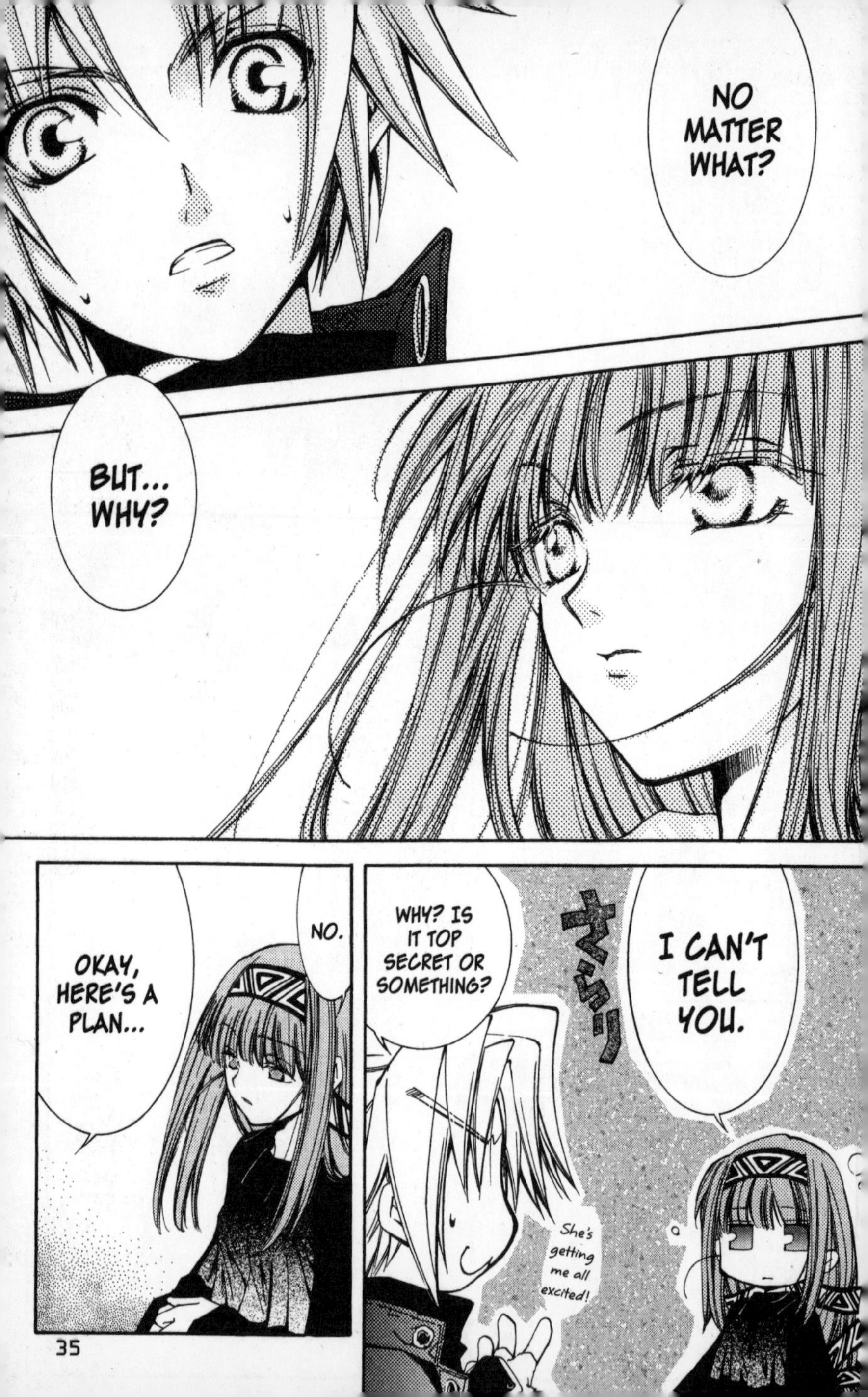
NO MATTER WHAT?
BUT... WHY?
I CAN'T TELL YOU.
WHY? IS IT TOP SECRET OR SOMETHING?
She's getting me all excited!
NO.
OKAY, HERE'S A PLAN...

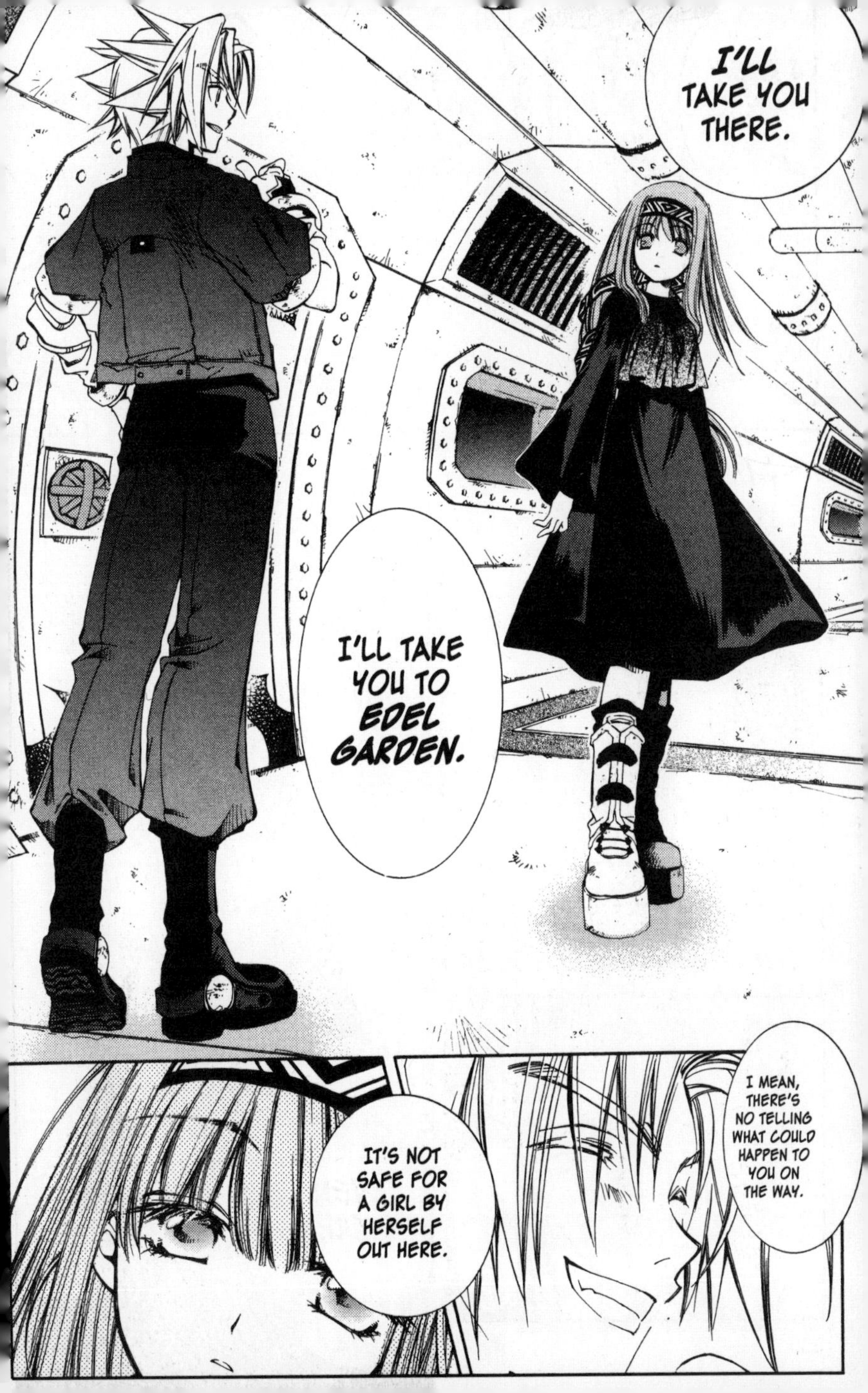
I'LL TAKE YOU THERE.
I'LL TAKE YOU TO EDEL GARDEN.
I MEAN, THERE'S NO TELLING WHAT COULD HAPPEN TO YOU ON THE WAY.
IT'S NOT SAFE FOR A GIRL BY HERSELF OUT HERE.

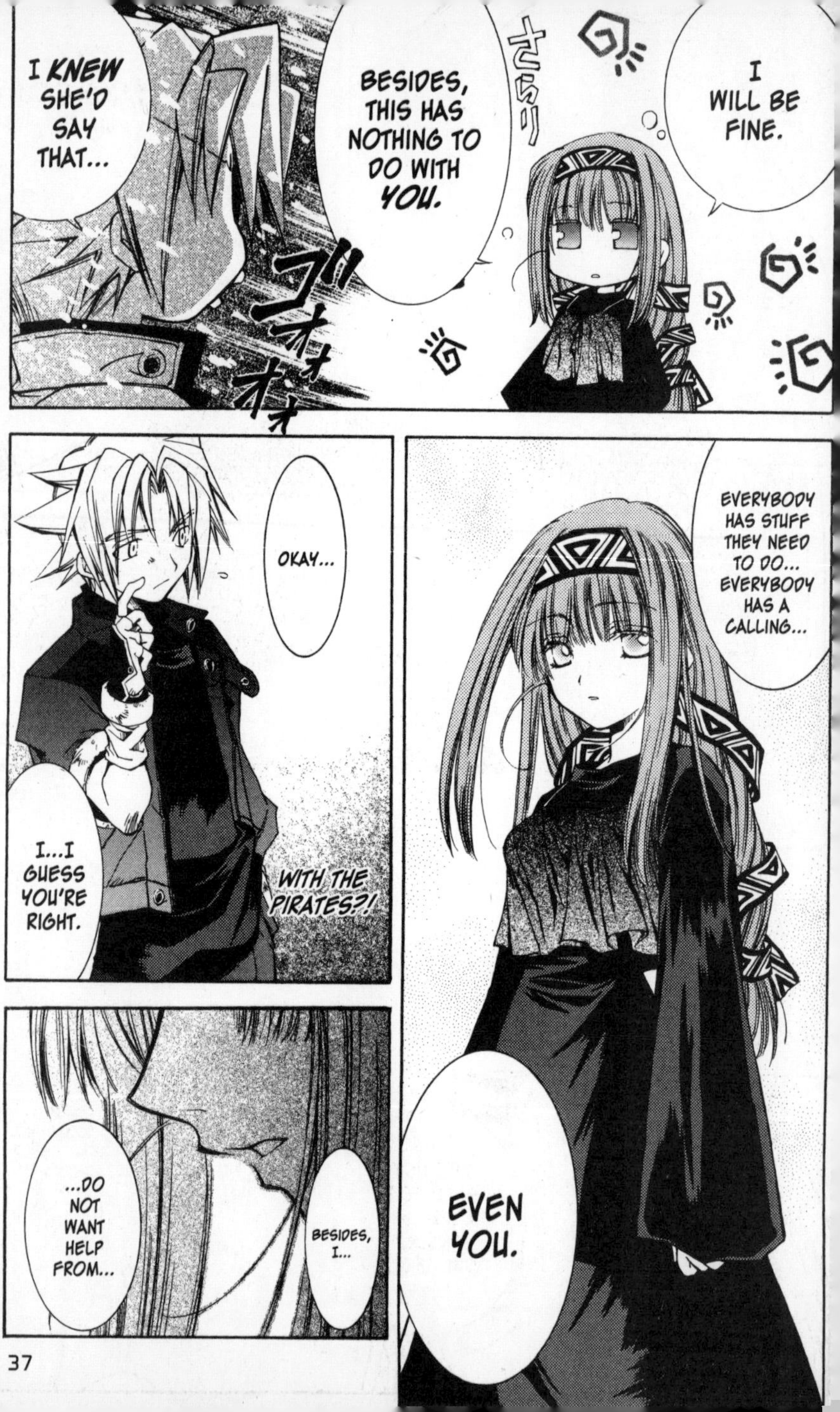
I WILL BE FINE.
さらり
BESIDES, THIS HAS NOTHING TO DO WITH *YOU*.
ゴオオオ
I *KNEW* SHE'D SAY THAT...
EVERYBODY HAS STUFF THEY NEED TO DO... EVERYBODY HAS A CALLING...
EVEN YOU.
OKAY...
WITH THE PIRATES?!
I...I GUESS YOU'RE RIGHT.
BESIDES, I...
...DO NOT WANT HELP FROM...

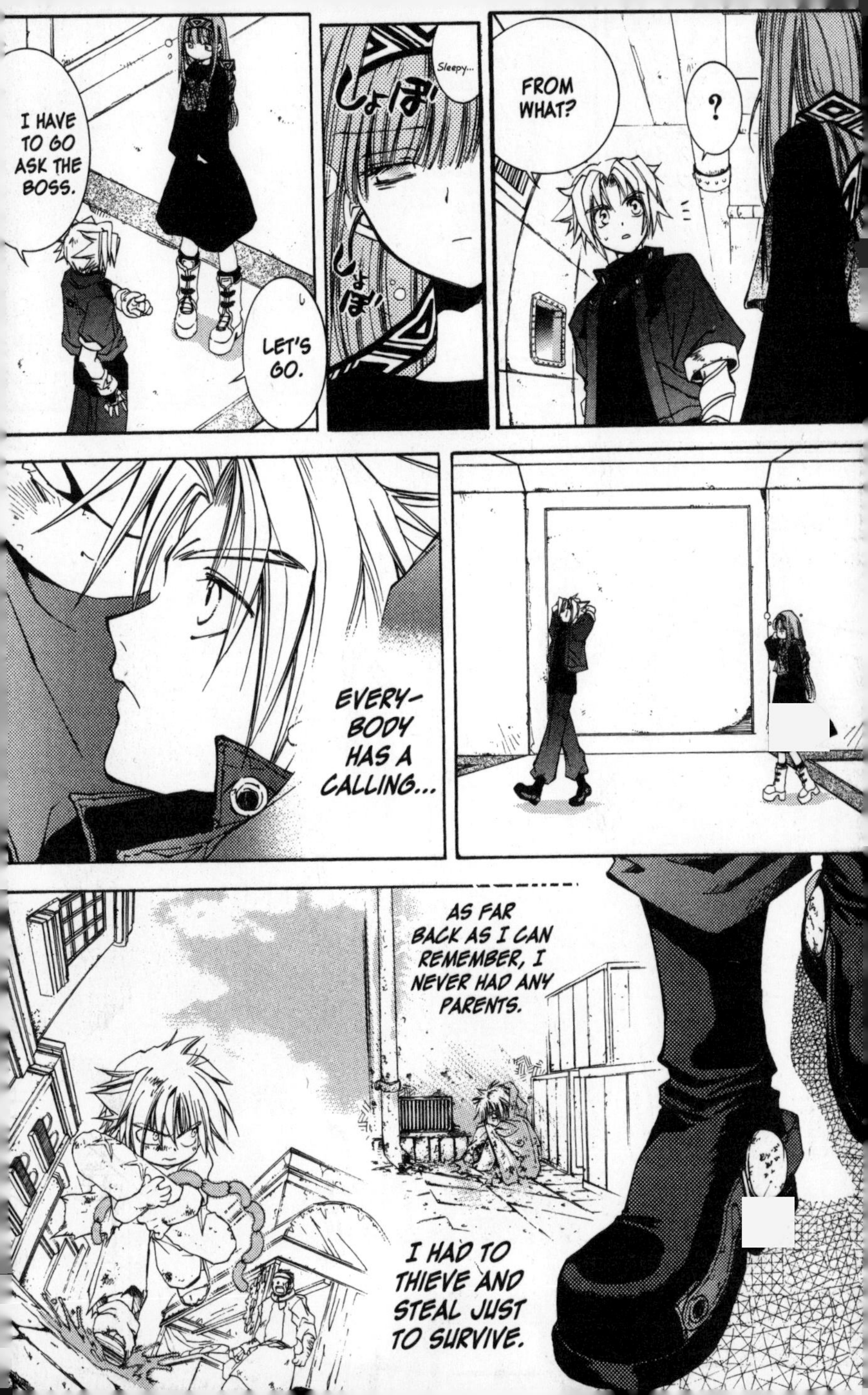
?
FROM WHAT?
Sleepy...
しょぼ
しょぼ
I HAVE TO GO ASK THE BOSS.
LET'S GO.
EVERY-BODY HAS A CALLING...
AS FAR BACK AS I CAN REMEMBER, I NEVER HAD ANY PARENTS.
I HAD TO THIEVE AND STEAL JUST TO SURVIVE.

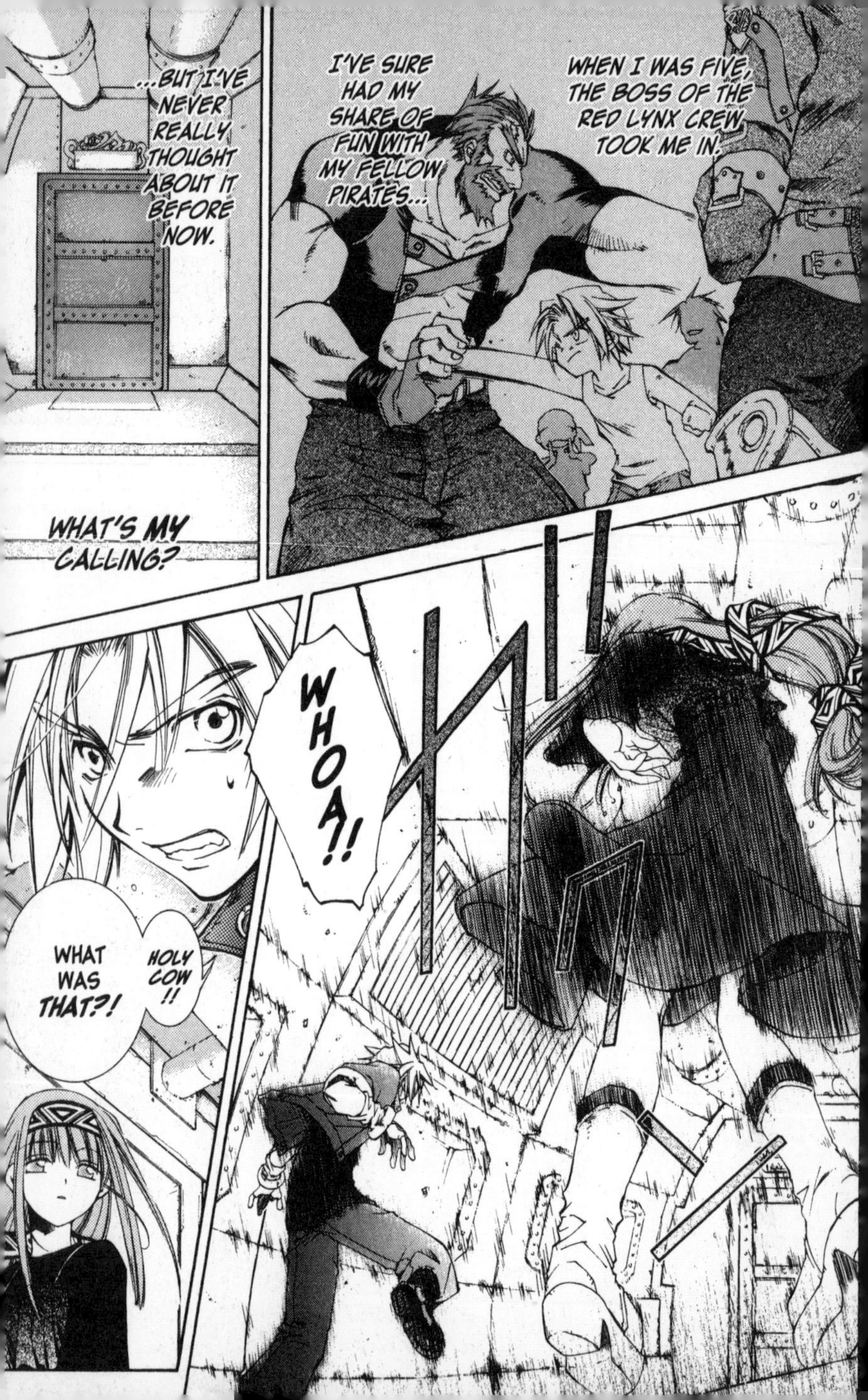
WHEN I WAS FIVE, THE BOSS OF THE RED LYNX CREW TOOK ME IN.
I'VE SURE HAD MY SHARE OF FUN WITH MY FELLOW PIRATES...
...BUT I'VE NEVER REALLY THOUGHT ABOUT IT BEFORE NOW.
WHAT'S MY CALLING?
WHOA!!
HOLY COW!!
WHAT WAS THAT?!

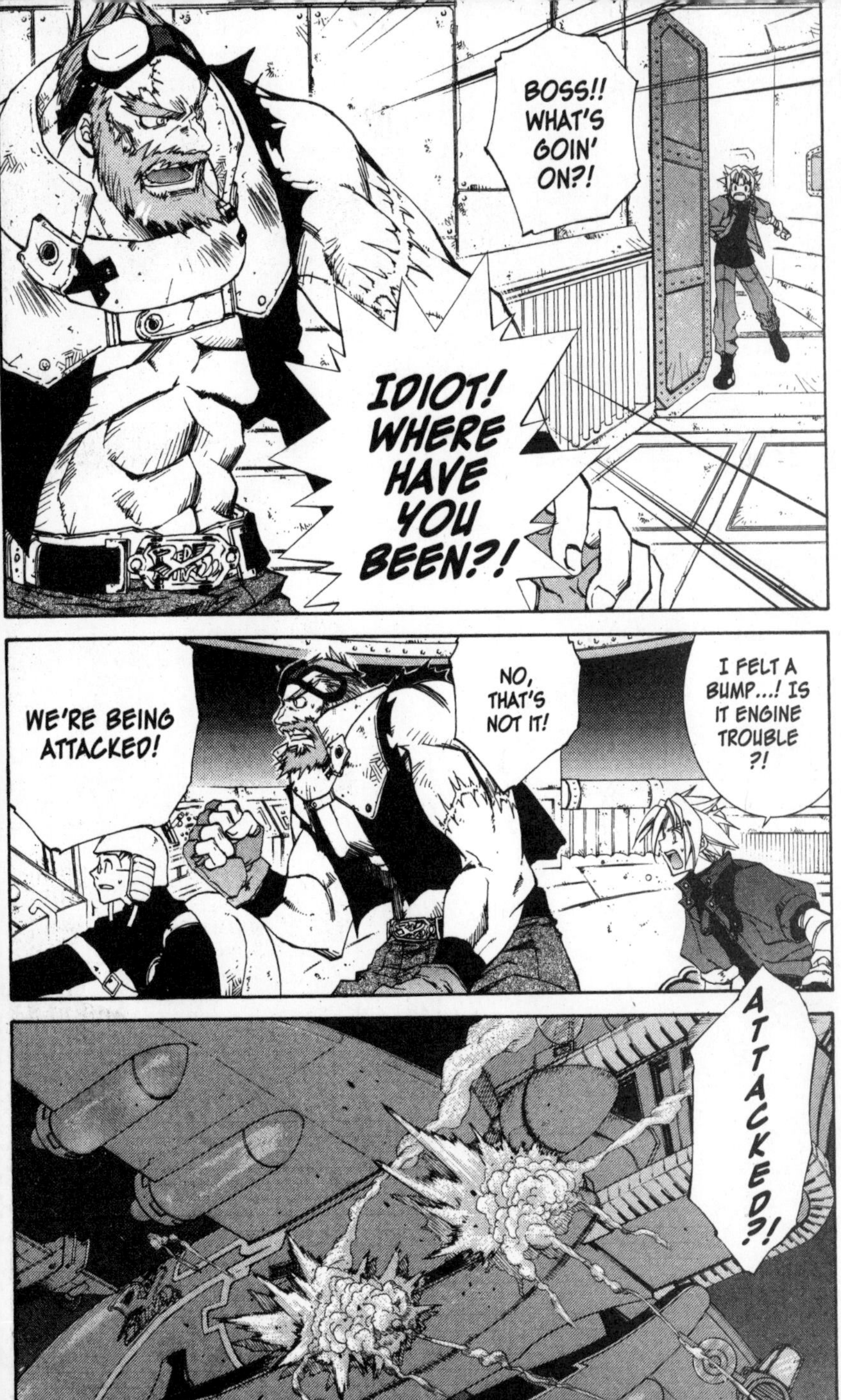
BOSS!! WHAT'S GOIN' ON?!
IDIOT! WHERE HAVE YOU BEEN?!
I FELT A BUMP...! IS IT ENGINE TROUBLE?!
NO, THAT'S NOT IT!
WE'RE BEING ATTACKED!
ATTACKED?!

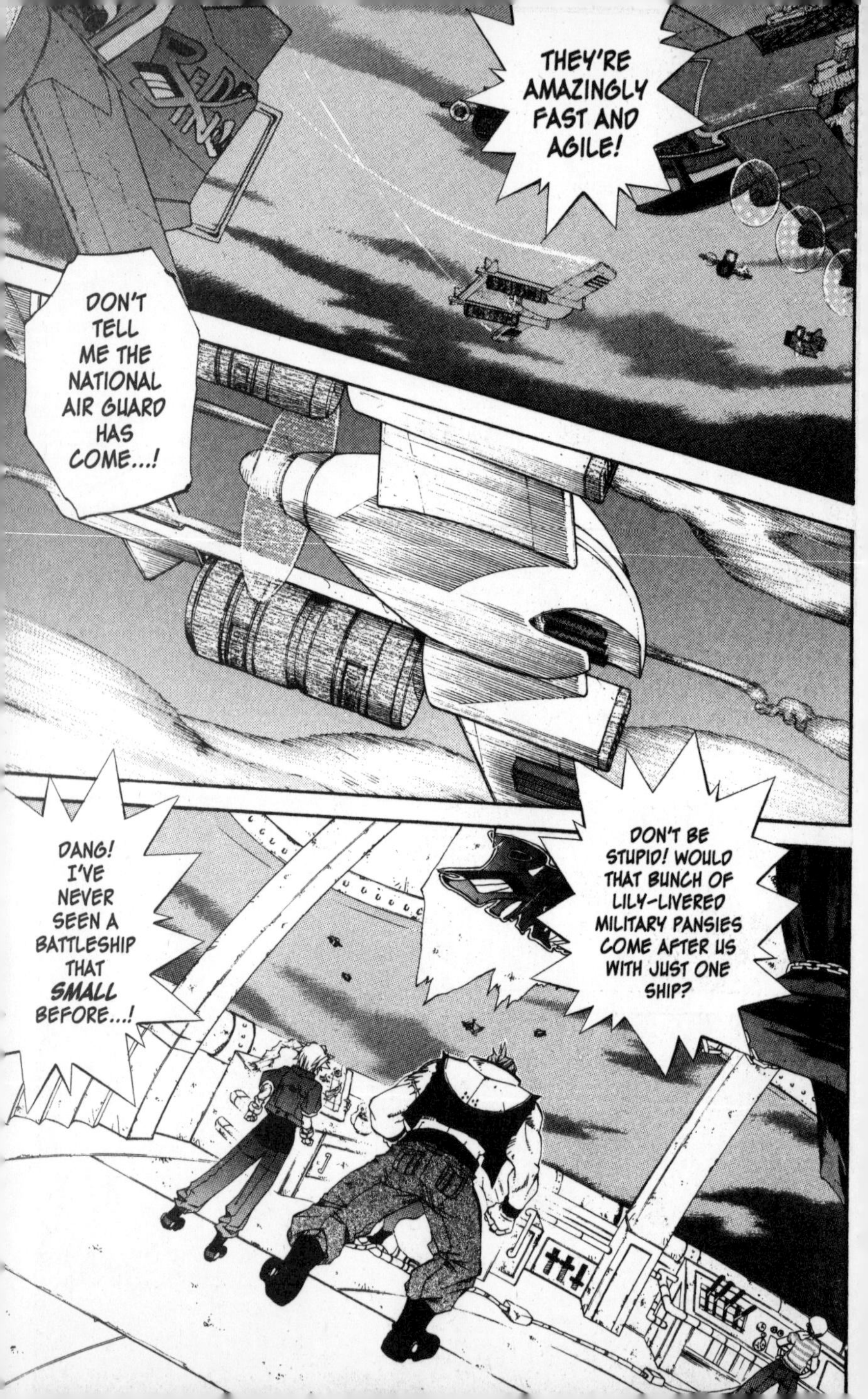
THEY'RE AMAZINGLY FAST AND AGILE!
DON'T TELL ME THE NATIONAL AIR GUARD HAS COME...!
DON'T BE STUPID! WOULD THAT BUNCH OF LILY-LIVERED MILITARY PANSIES COME AFTER US WITH JUST ONE SHIP?
DANG! I'VE NEVER SEEN A BATTLESHIP THAT SMALL BEFORE...!

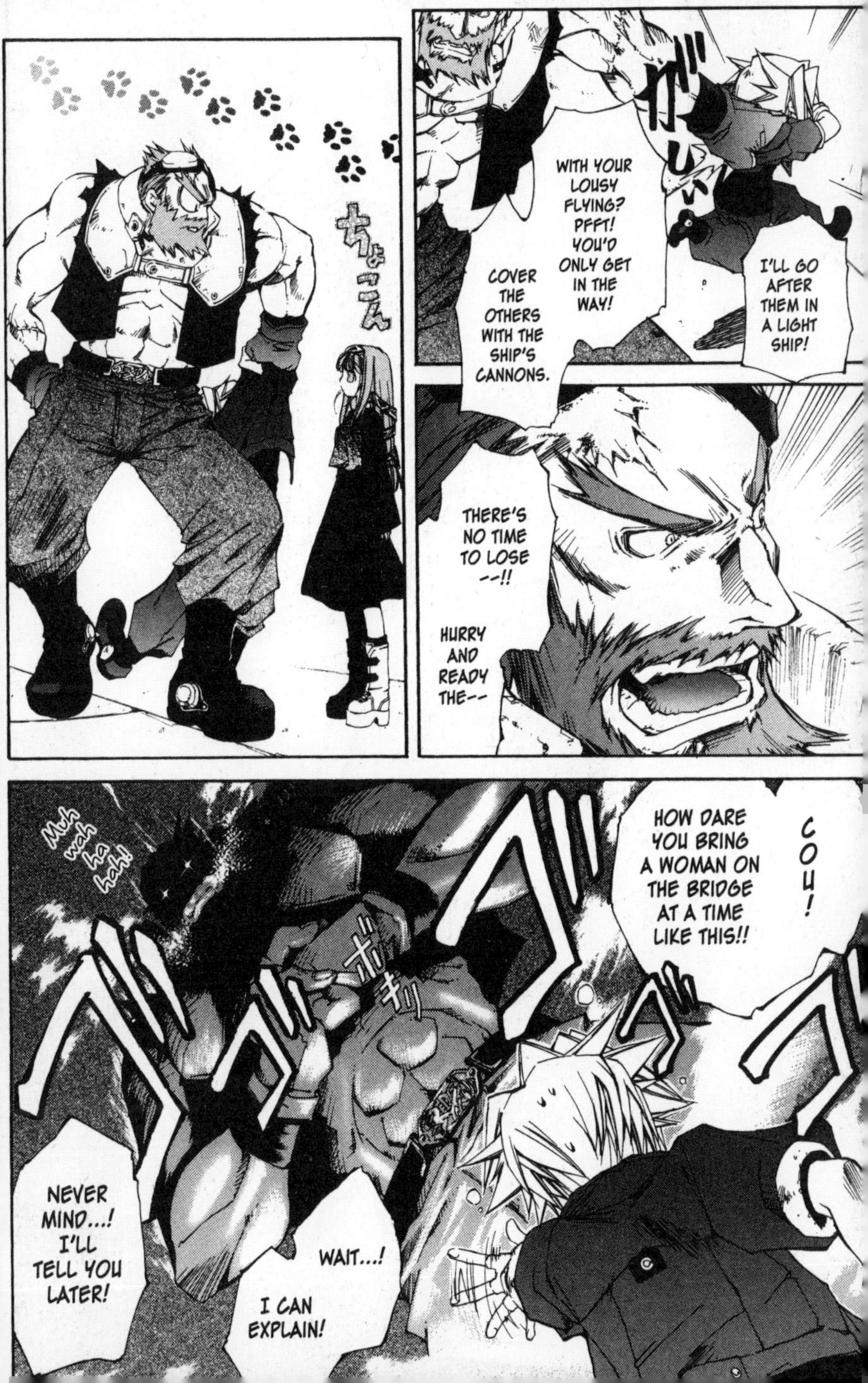
I'LL GO AFTER THEM IN A LIGHT SHIP!
WITH YOUR LOUSY FLYING? PFFT! YOU'D ONLY GET IN THE WAY!
COVER THE OTHERS WITH THE SHIP'S CANNONS.
THERE'S NO TIME TO LOSE --!!
HURRY AND READY THE--
ちょこん
COU!
HOW DARE YOU BRING A WOMAN ON THE BRIDGE AT A TIME LIKE THIS!!
Muh wah ha hah!
WAIT...!
I CAN EXPLAIN!
NEVER MIND...! I'LL TELL YOU LATER!

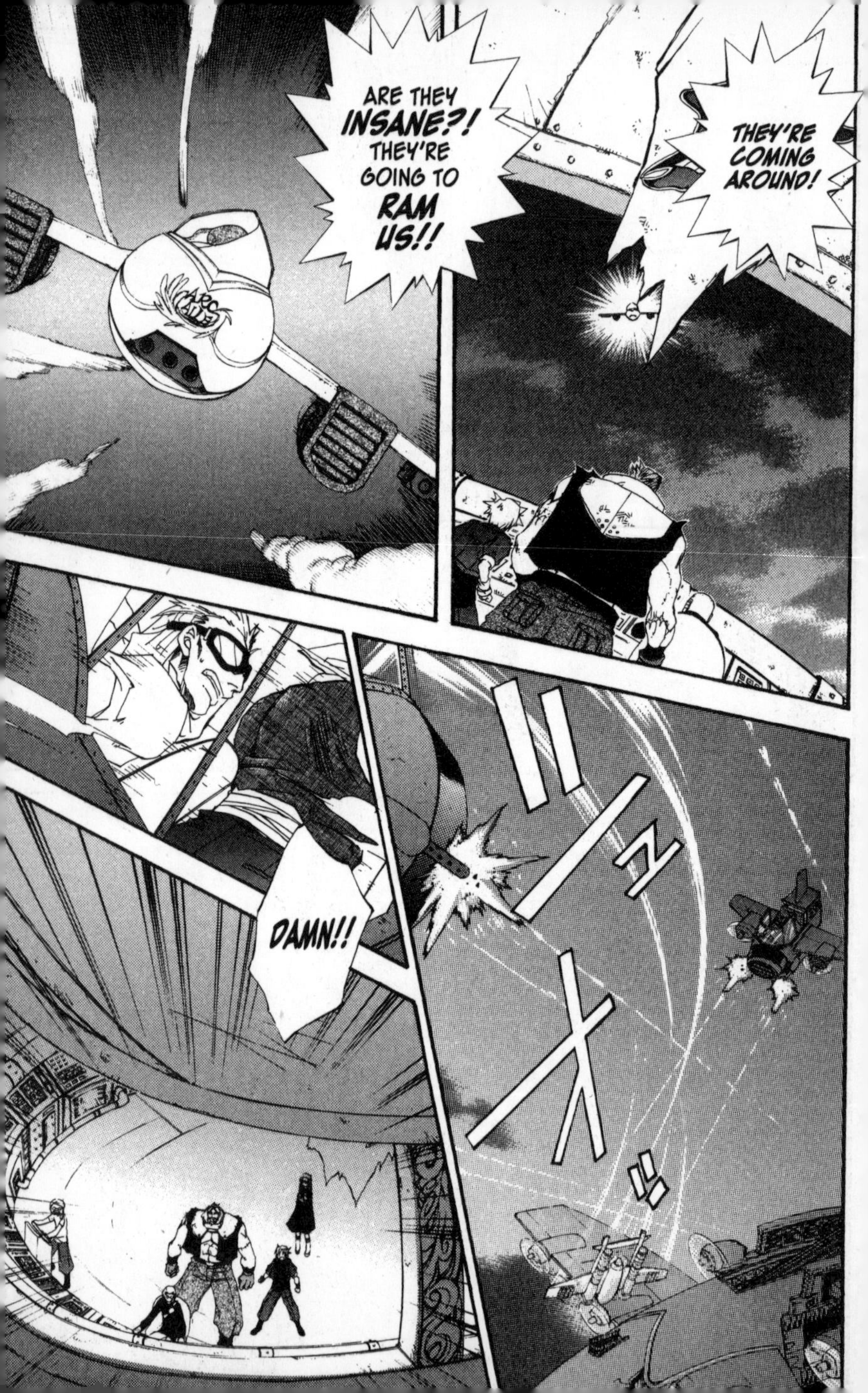
THEY'RE COMING AROUND!
ARE THEY INSANE?! THEY'RE GOING TO RAM US!!
DAMN!!

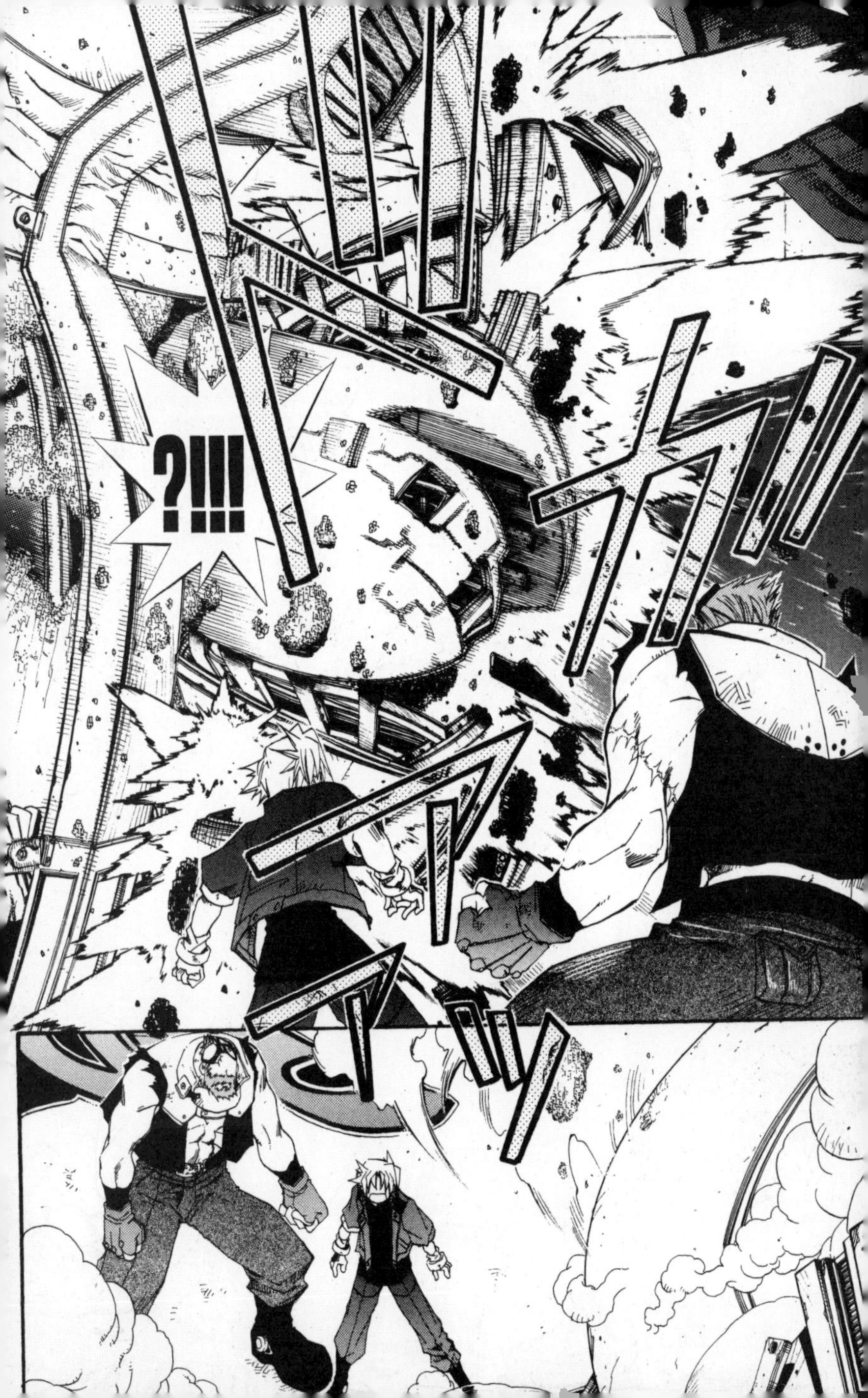
?!!!

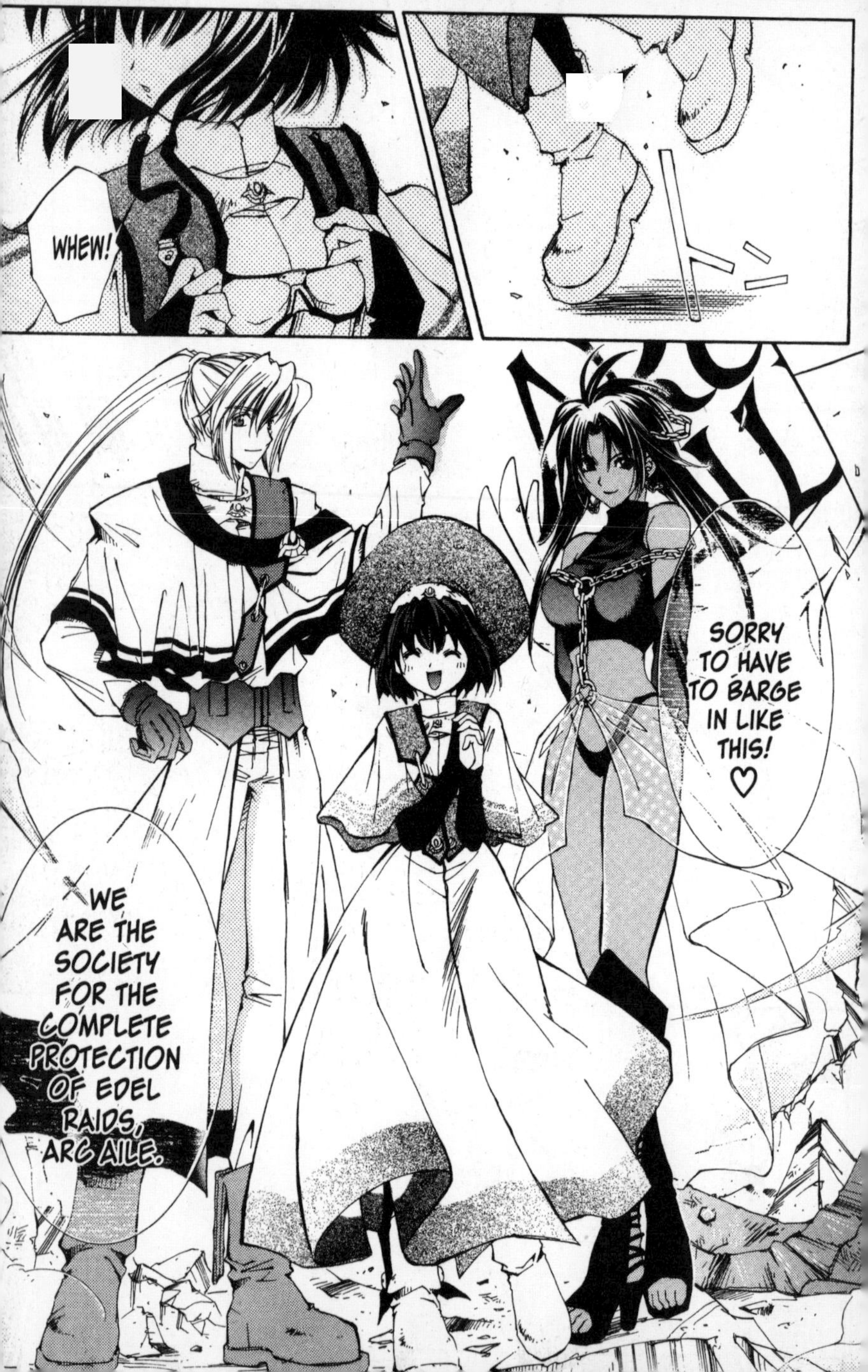
WHEW!
SORRY TO HAVE TO BARGE IN LIKE THIS! ♡
WE ARE THE SOCIETY FOR THE COMPLETE PROTECTION OF EDEL RAIDS, ARC AILE.

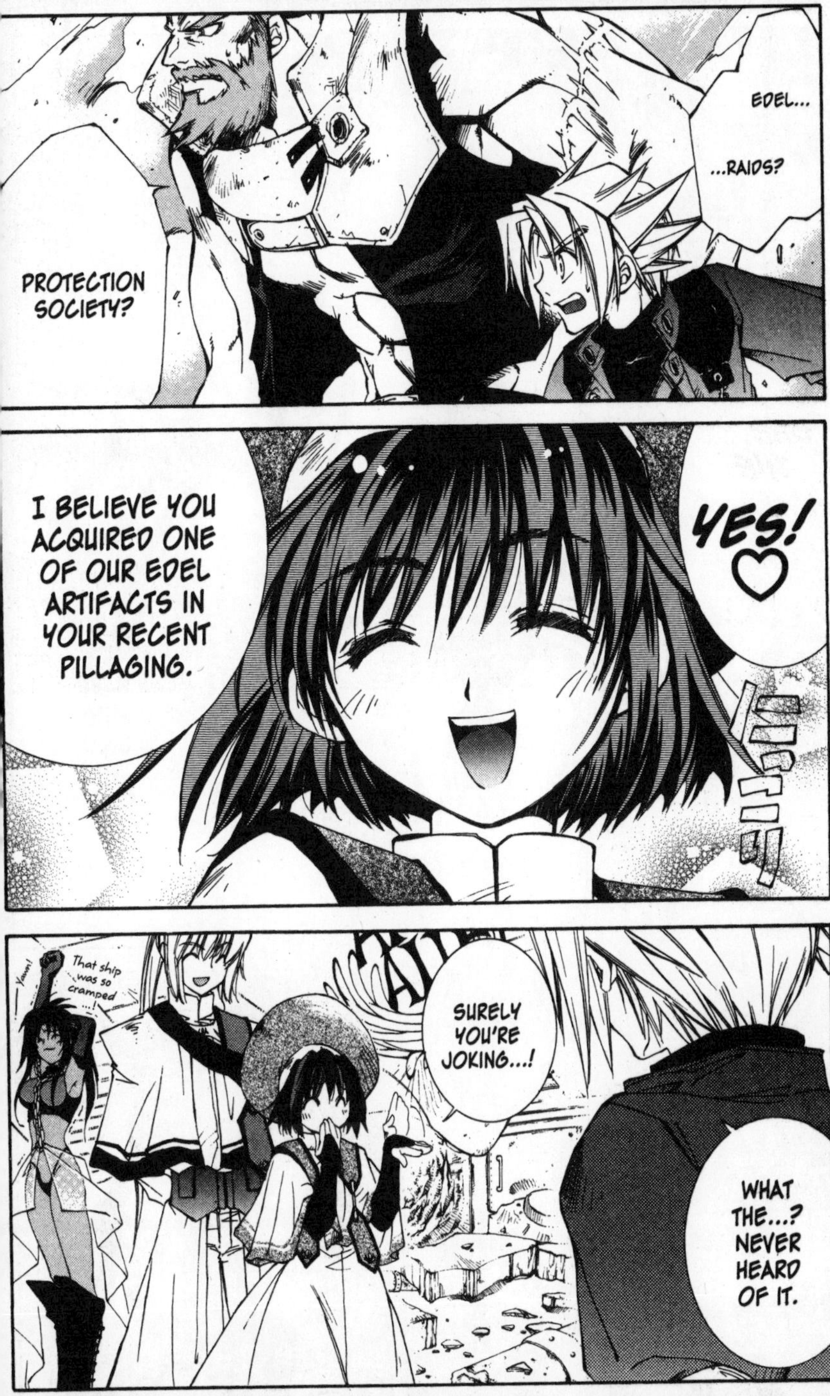
EDEL...
...RAIDS?
PROTECTION SOCIETY?
YES! ♡
I BELIEVE YOU ACQUIRED ONE OF OUR EDEL ARTIFACTS IN YOUR RECENT PILLAGING.
WHAT THE...? NEVER HEARD OF IT.
SURELY YOU'RE JOKING...!
That ship was so cramped...!
Yawn!

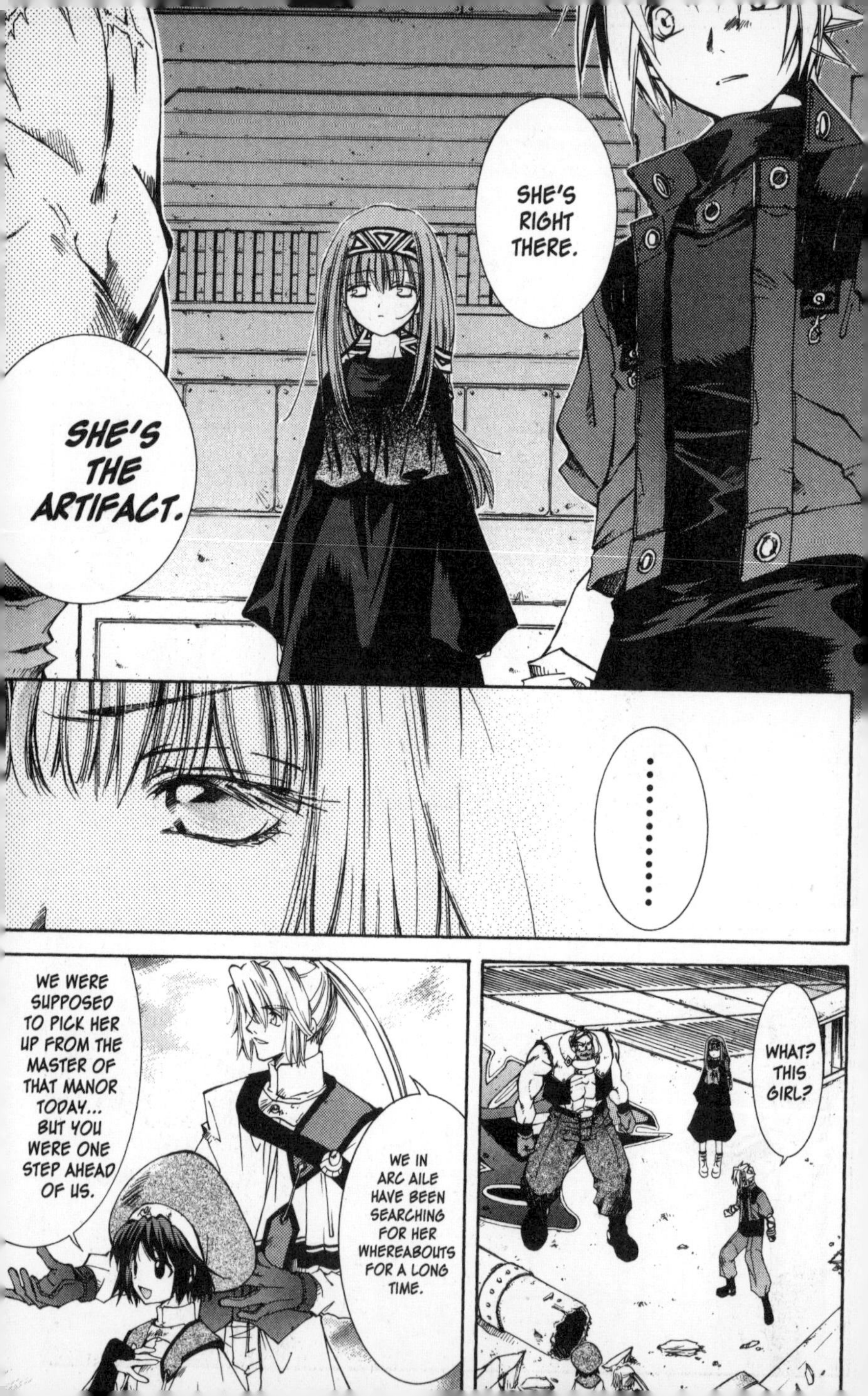
SHE'S RIGHT THERE.
SHE'S THE ARTIFACT.
....
WHAT? THIS GIRL?
WE IN ARC AILE HAVE BEEN SEARCHING FOR HER WHEREABOUTS FOR A LONG TIME.
WE WERE SUPPOSED TO PICK HER UP FROM THE MASTER OF THAT MANOR TODAY... BUT YOU WERE ONE STEP AHEAD OF US.

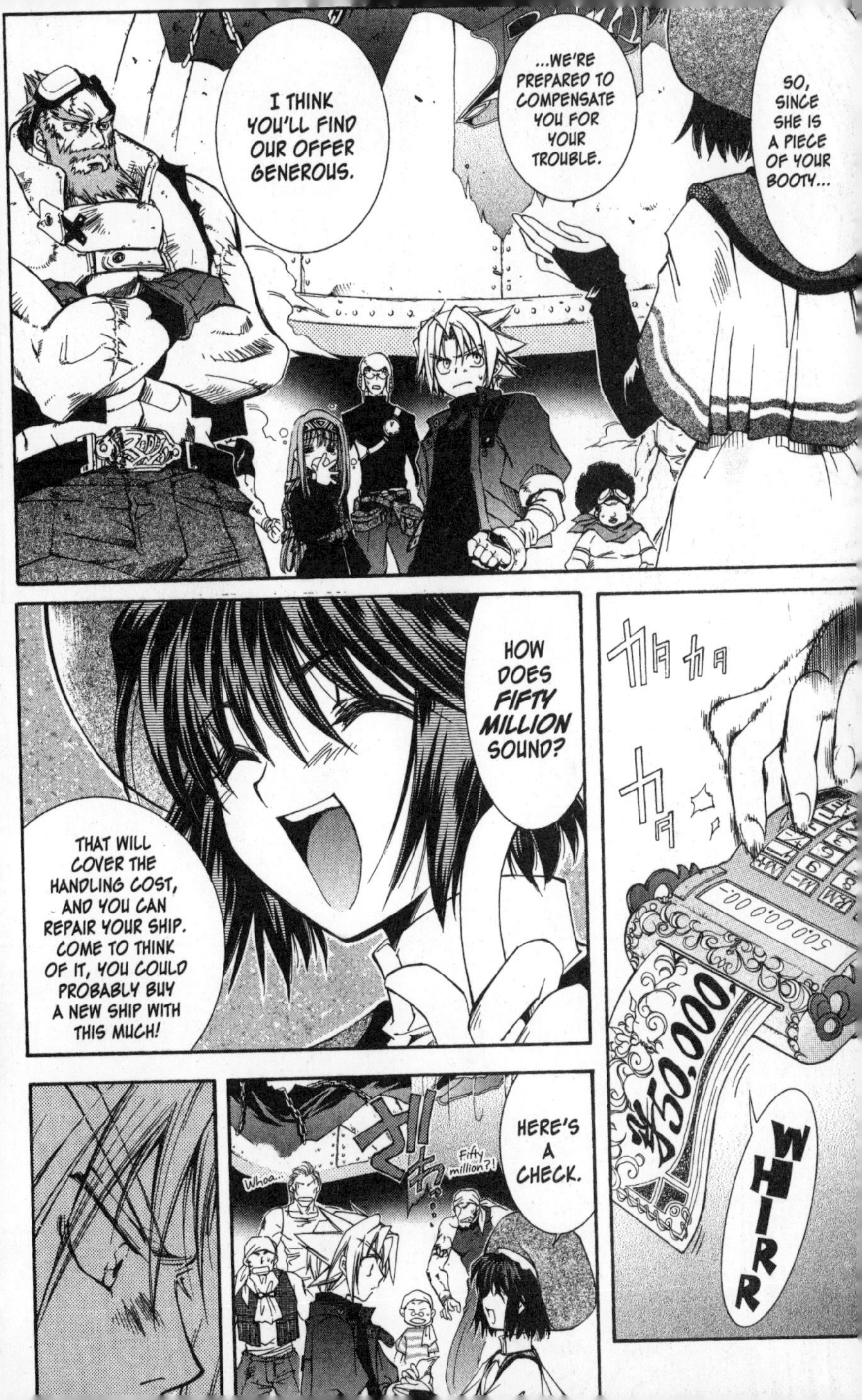
SO, SINCE SHE IS A PIECE OF YOUR BOOTY...
...WE'RE PREPARED TO COMPENSATE YOU FOR YOUR TROUBLE.
I THINK YOU'LL FIND OUR OFFER GENEROUS.
HOW DOES *FIFTY MILLION* SOUND?
THAT WILL COVER THE HANDLING COST, AND YOU CAN REPAIR YOUR SHIP. COME TO THINK OF IT, YOU COULD PROBABLY BUY A NEW SHIP WITH THIS MUCH!
カタカタ
カタ
50,000,000.-
¥50,000,
WHIRR
HERE'S A CHECK.
Fifty million?!
Whoa...

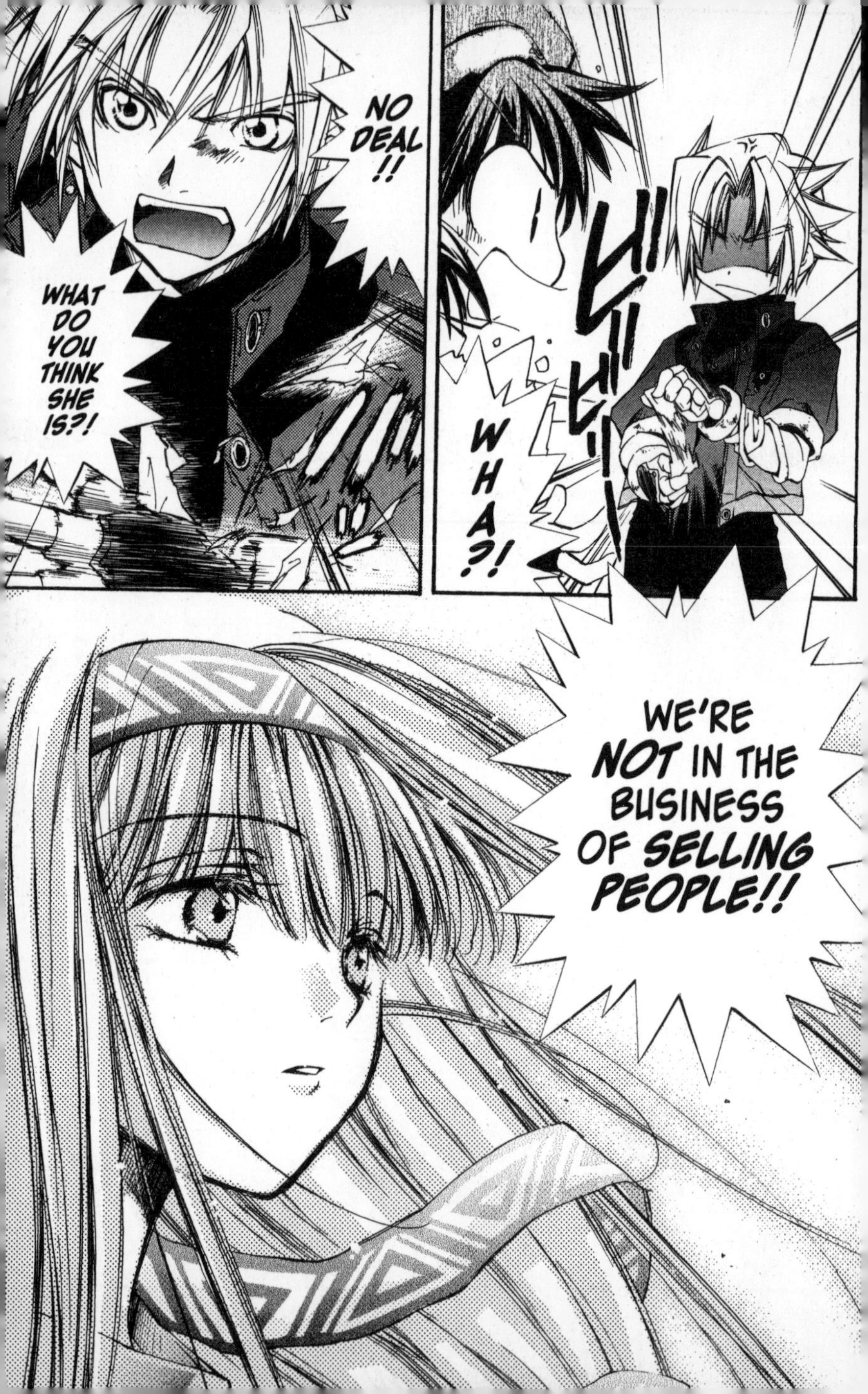
WHA?!
NO DEAL!!
WHAT DO YOU THINK SHE IS?!
WE'RE NOT IN THE BUSINESS OF SELLING PEOPLE!!

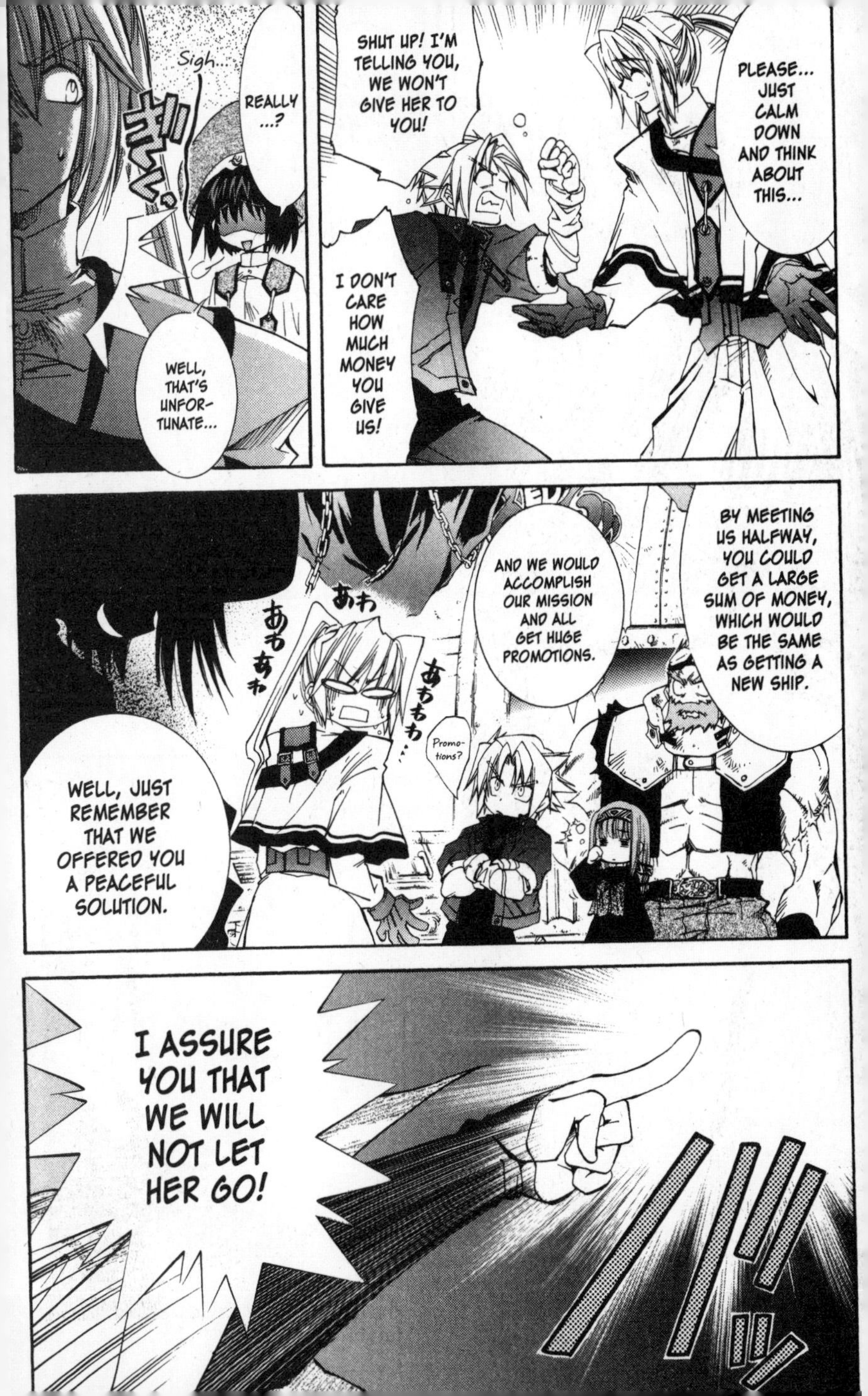
PLEASE... JUST CALM DOWN AND THINK ABOUT THIS...
SHUT UP! I'M TELLING YOU, WE WON'T GIVE HER TO YOU!
I DON'T CARE HOW MUCH MONEY YOU GIVE US!
REALLY ...?
Sigh...
WELL, THAT'S UNFOR-TUNATE...
BY MEETING US HALFWAY, YOU COULD GET A LARGE SUM OF MONEY, WHICH WOULD BE THE SAME AS GETTING A NEW SHIP.
AND WE WOULD ACCOMPLISH OUR MISSION AND ALL GET HUGE PROMOTIONS.
あわ
あわあわ
あわわわ...
Promo-tions?
WELL, JUST REMEMBER THAT WE OFFERED YOU A PEACEFUL SOLUTION.
I ASSURE YOU THAT WE WILL NOT LET HER GO!

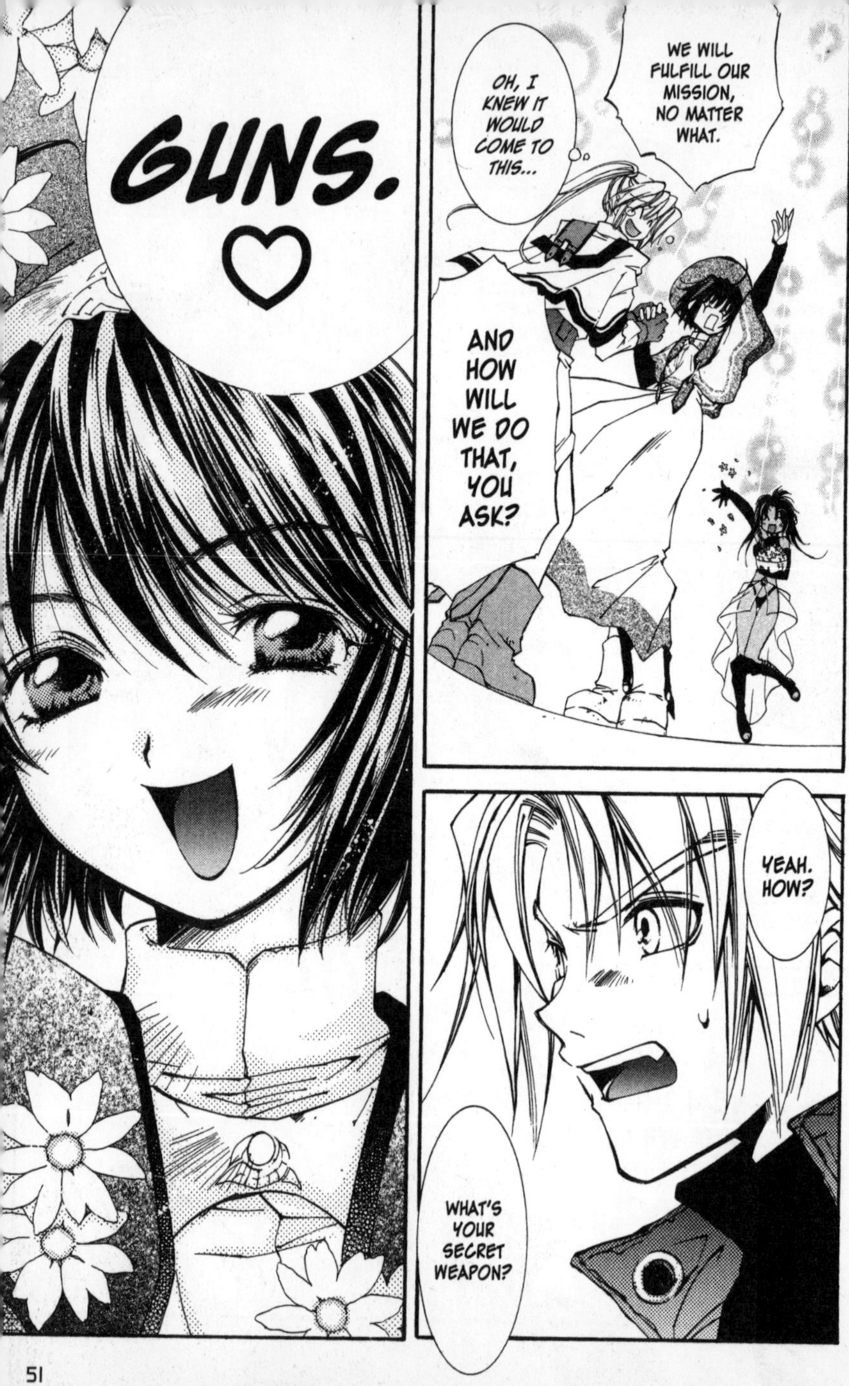
WE WILL FULFILL OUR MISSION, NO MATTER WHAT.
OH, I KNEW IT WOULD COME TO THIS...
AND HOW WILL WE DO THAT, YOU ASK?
YEAH. HOW?
WHAT'S YOUR SECRET WEAPON?
GUNS. ♡

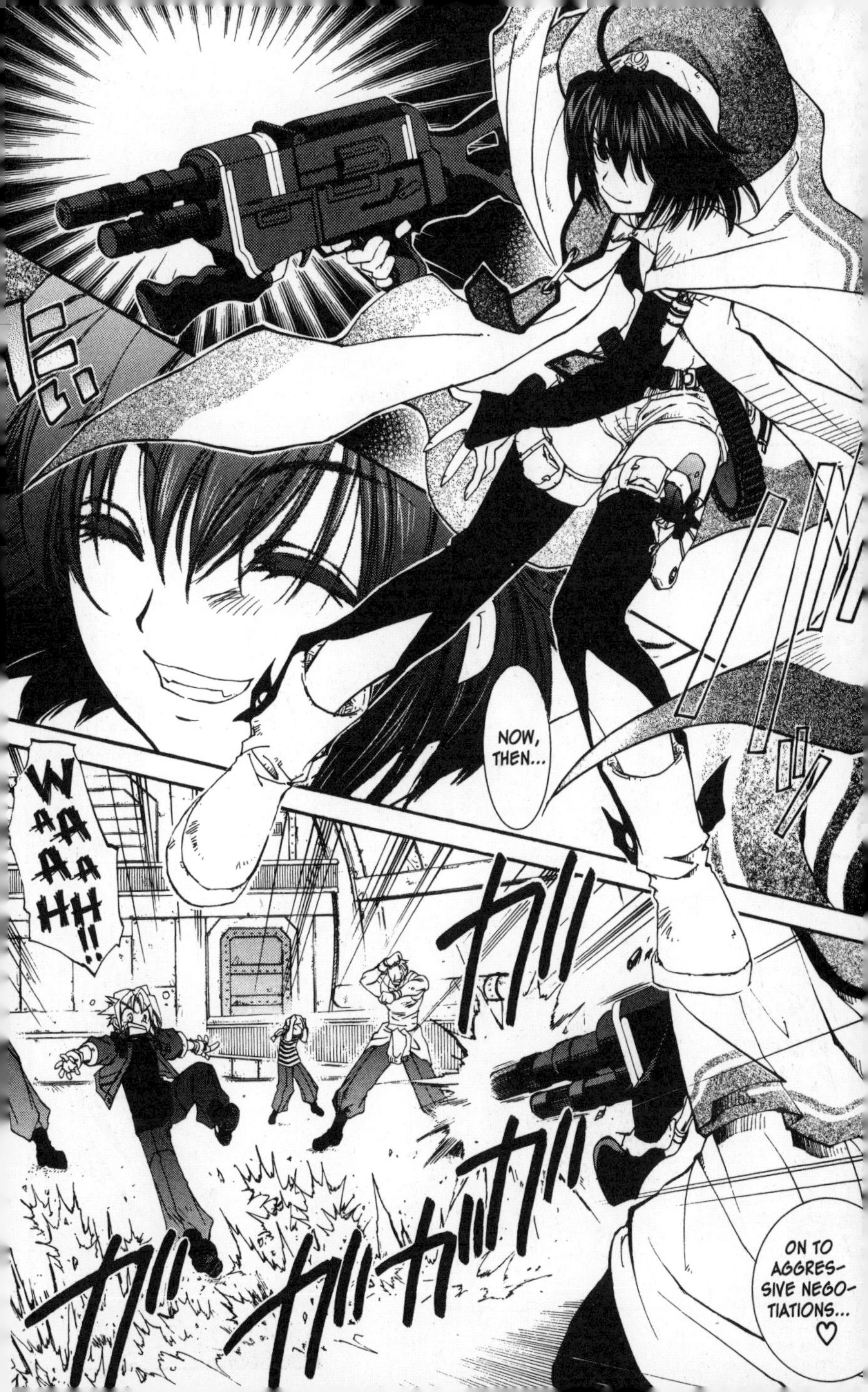
NOW, THEN...
ON TO AGGRES-SIVE NEGO-TIATIONS... ♡
WAAAAAHH!!

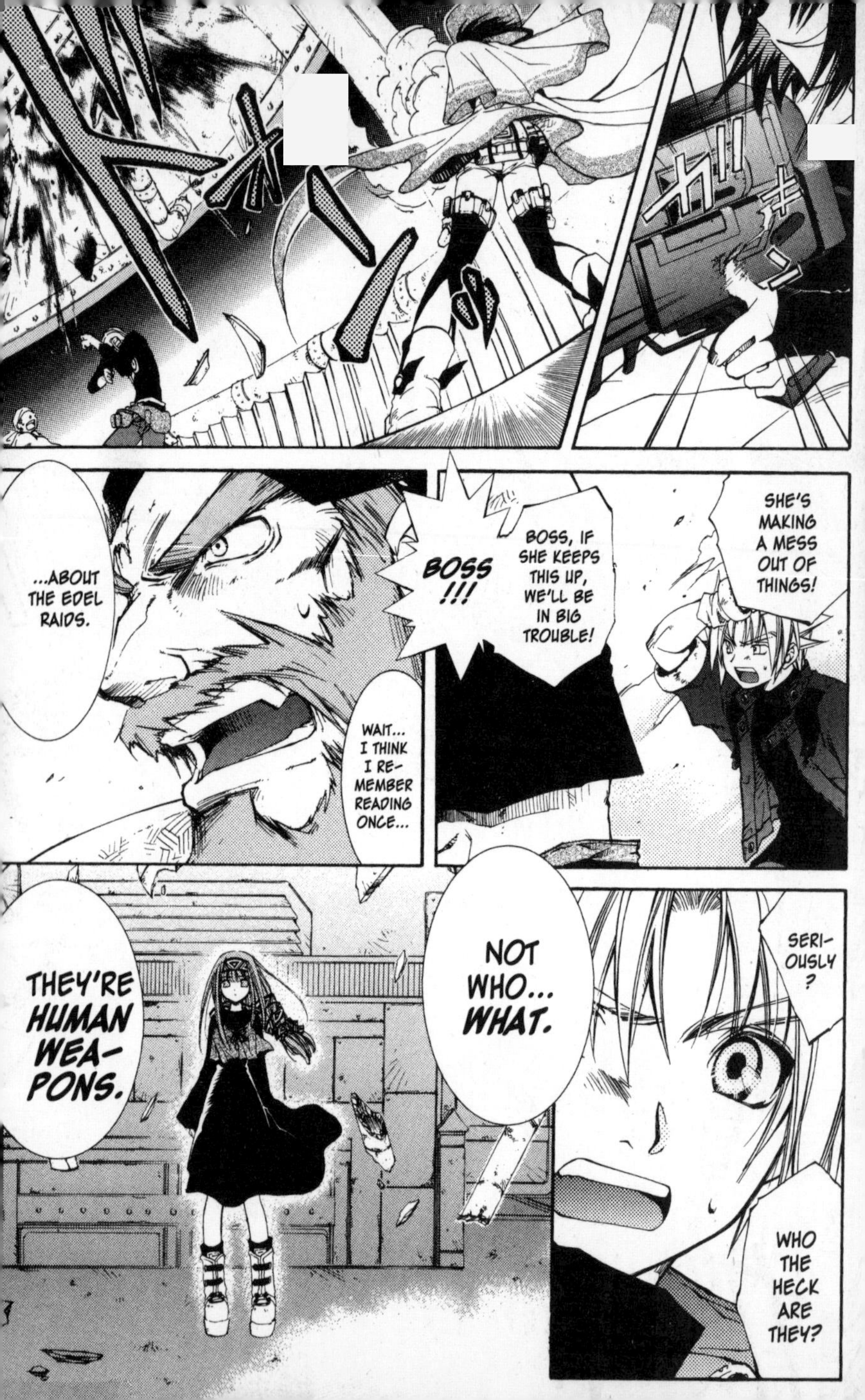

SHE'S MAKING A MESS OUT OF THINGS!
BOSS, IF SHE KEEPS THIS UP, WE'LL BE IN BIG TROUBLE!
BOSS!!!
WAIT... I THINK I RE-MEMBER READING ONCE...
...ABOUT THE EDEL RAIDS.
SERI-OUSLY?
WHO THE HECK ARE THEY?
NOT WHO... WHAT.
THEY'RE HUMAN WEA-PONS.

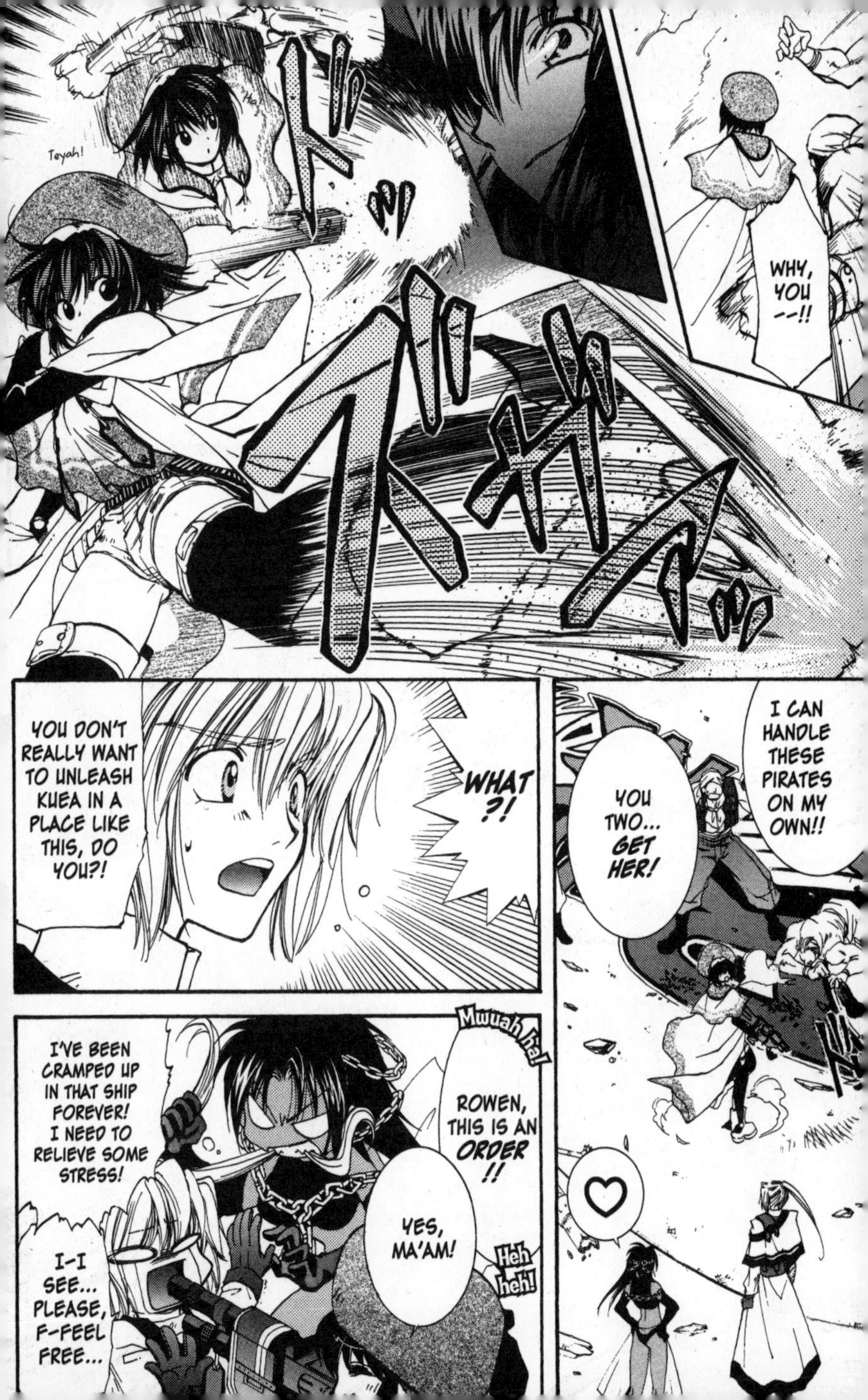
WHY, YOU --!!
Teyah!
I CAN HANDLE THESE PIRATES ON MY OWN!!
YOU TWO... GET HER!
WHAT?!
YOU DON'T REALLY WANT TO UNLEASH KUEA IN A PLACE LIKE THIS, DO YOU?!
Mwuah ha!
ROWEN, THIS IS AN ORDER!!
I'VE BEEN CRAMPED UP IN THAT SHIP FOREVER! I NEED TO RELIEVE SOME STRESS!
Heh heh!
YES, MA'AM!
I-I SEE... PLEASE, F-FEEL FREE...

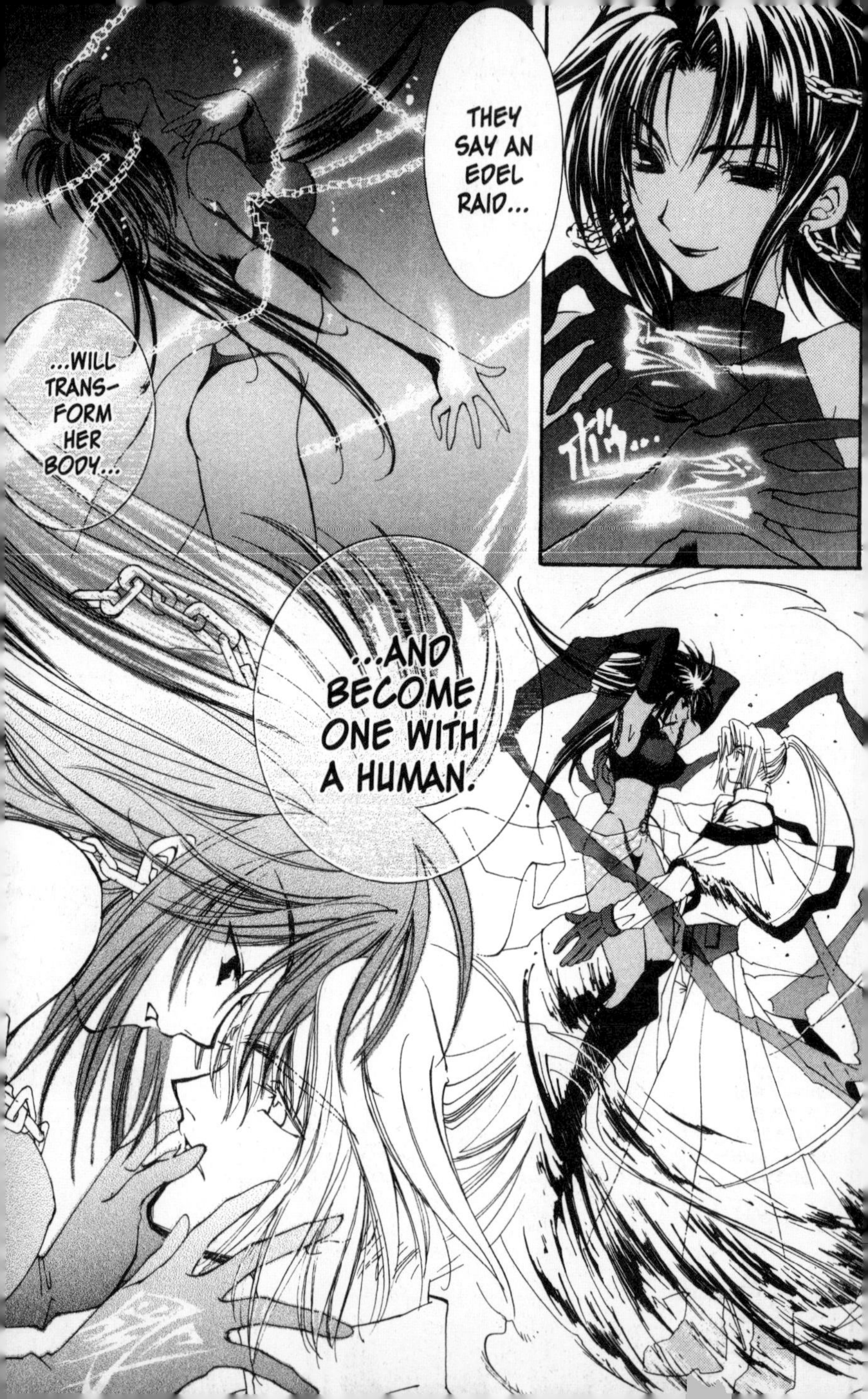
THEY SAY AN EDEL RAID...
...WILL TRANS-FORM HER BODY...
...AND BECOME ONE WITH A HUMAN.

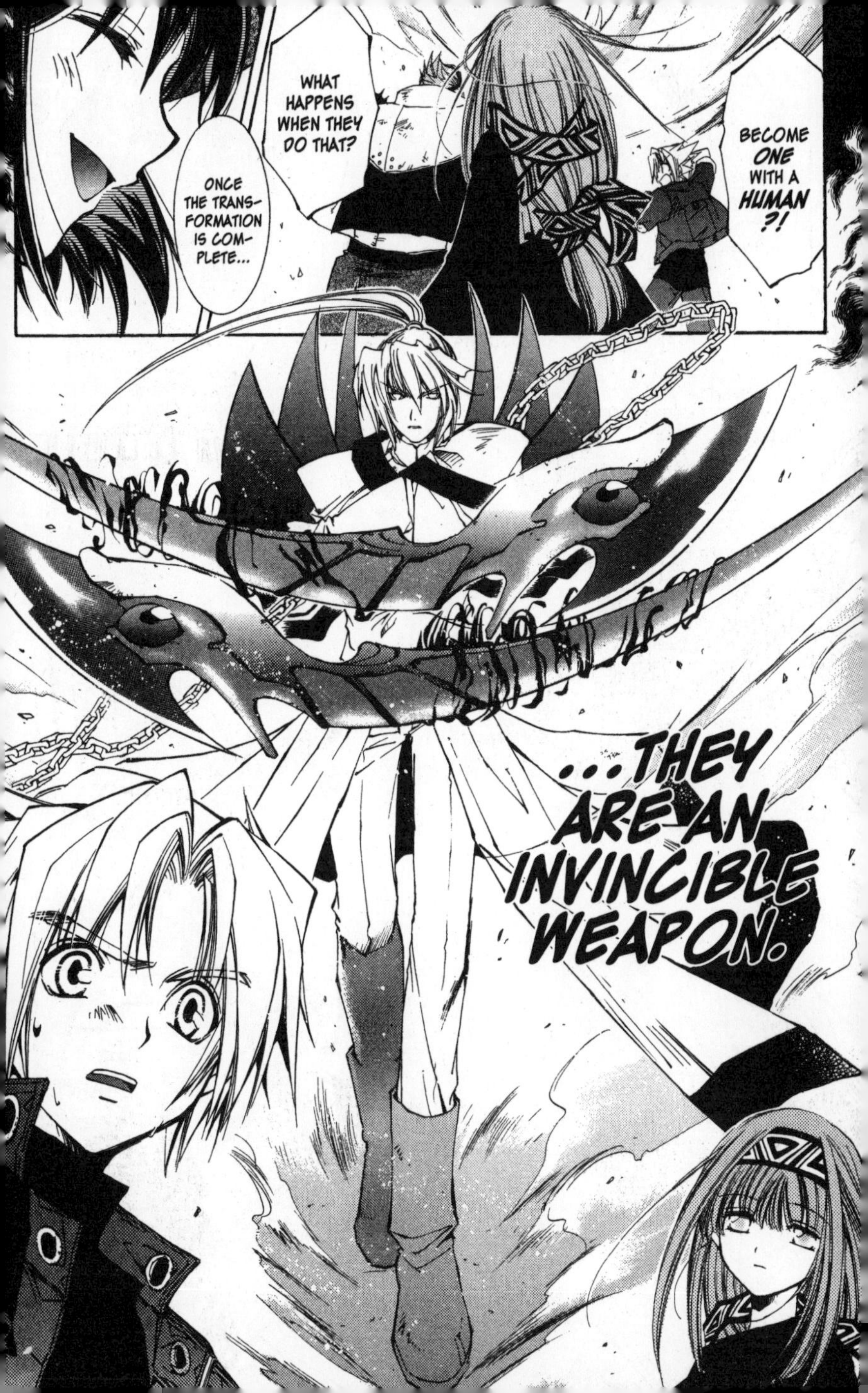
BECOME ONE WITH A HUMAN?!
WHAT HAPPENS WHEN THEY DO THAT?
ONCE THE TRANS-FORMATION IS COM-PLETE...
...THEY ARE AN INVINCIBLE WEAPON.

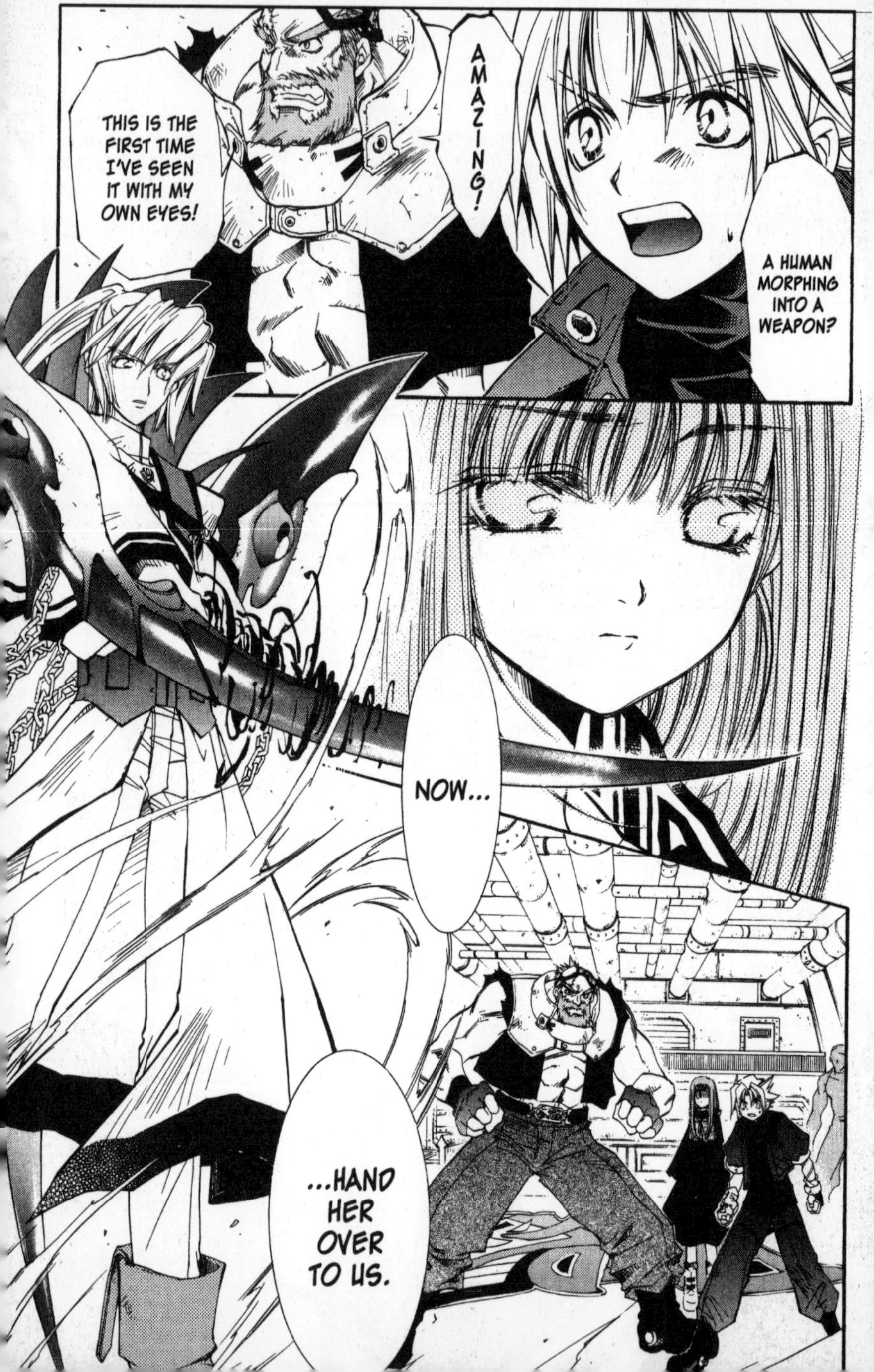
AMAZING!
A HUMAN MORPHING INTO A WEAPON?
THIS IS THE FIRST TIME I'VE SEEN IT WITH MY OWN EYES!
NOW...
...HAND HER OVER TO US.

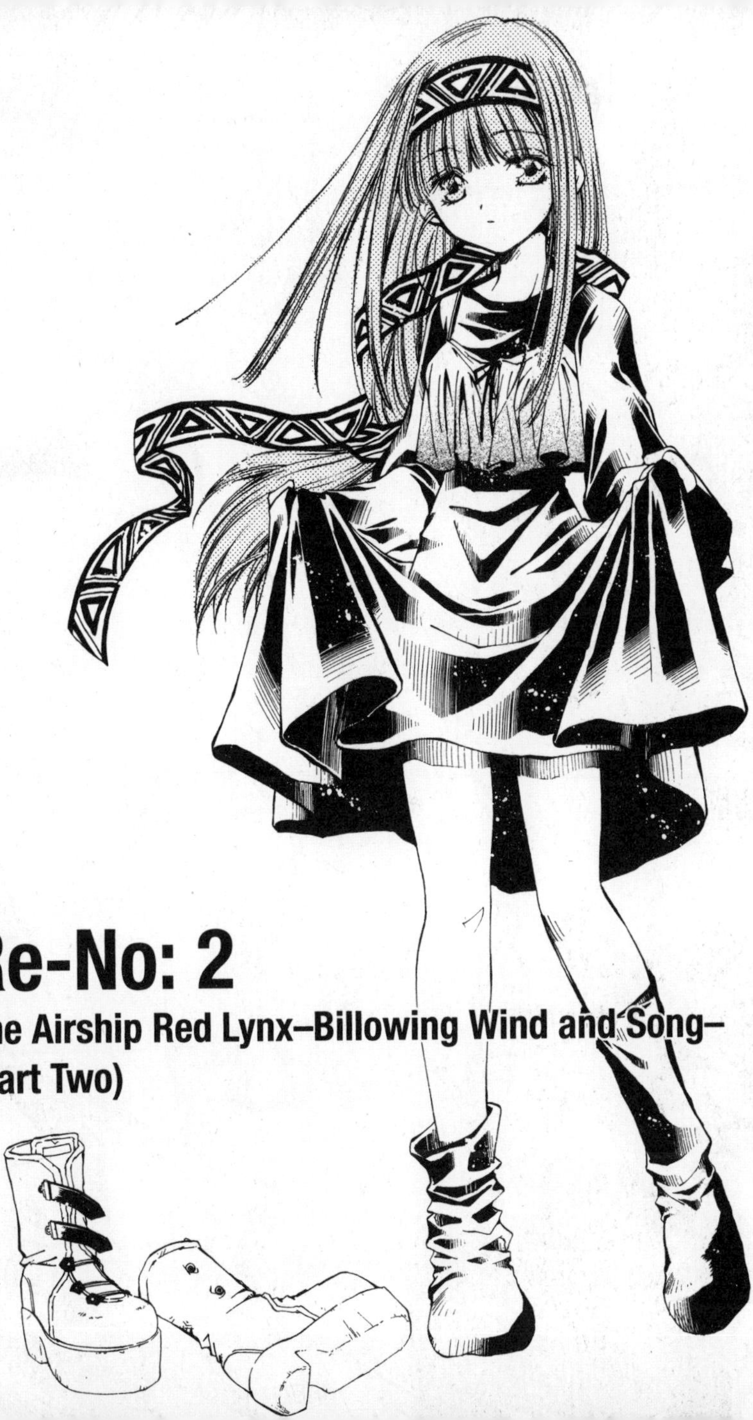

Re-No: 2
The Airship Red Lynx–Billowing Wind and Song–
(Part Two)

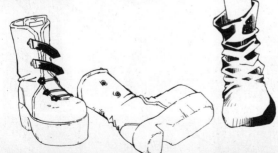

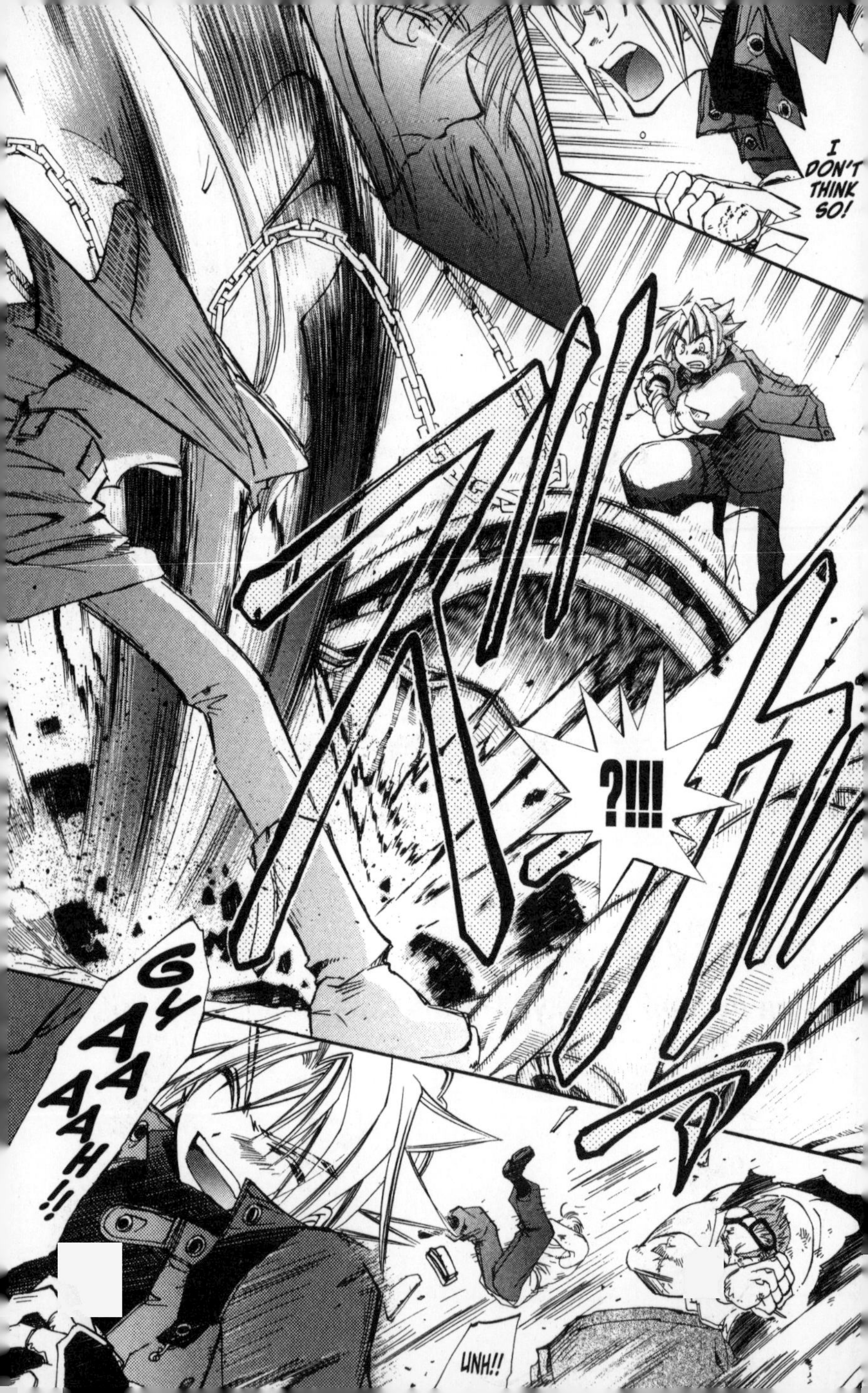
I DON'T THINK SO!
?!!!
GYAAAAAH!!
UNH!!

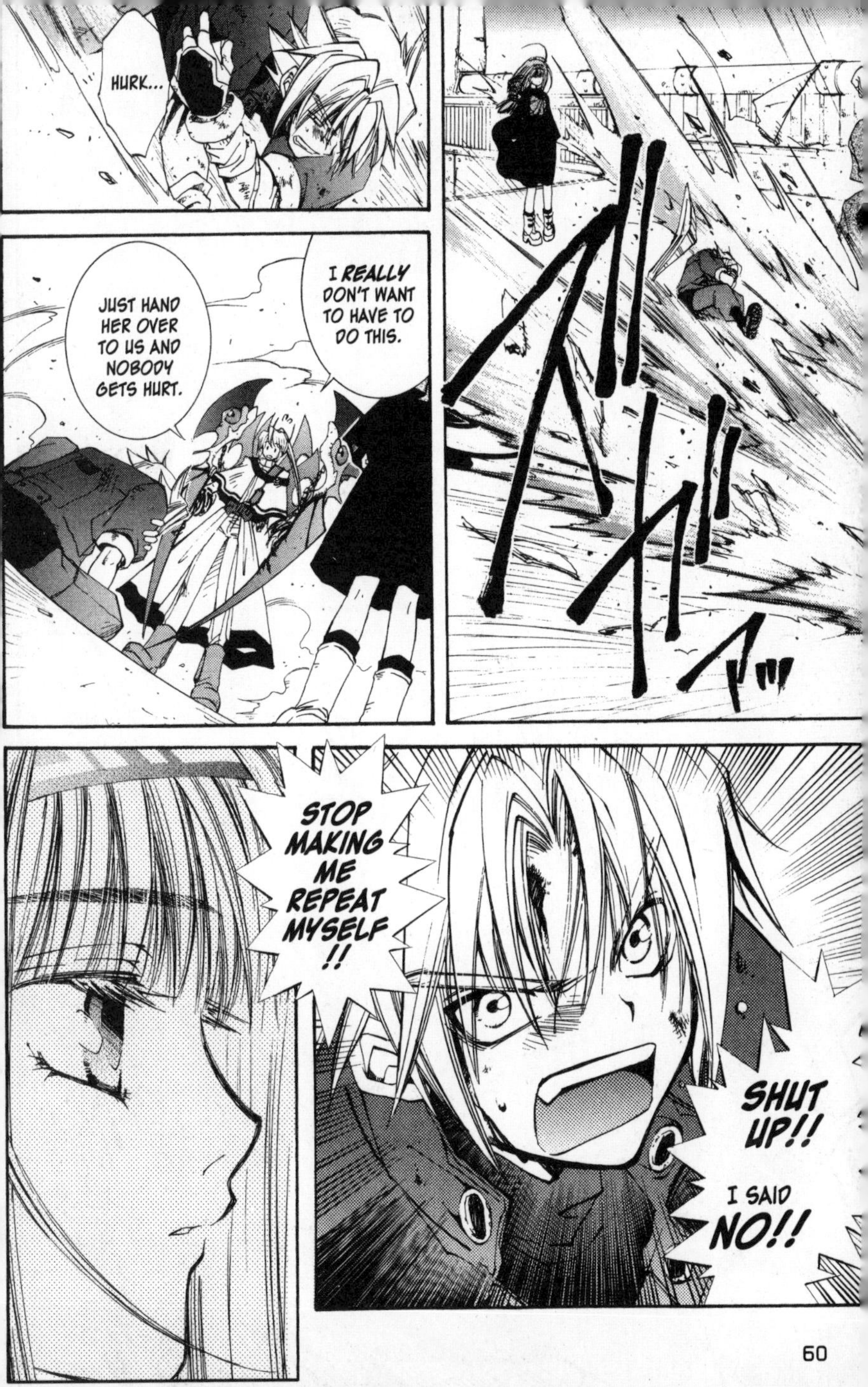
HURK...
I REALLY DON'T WANT TO HAVE TO DO THIS.
JUST HAND HER OVER TO US AND NOBODY GETS HURT.
SHUT UP!!
I SAID NO!!
STOP MAKING ME REPEAT MYSELF!!

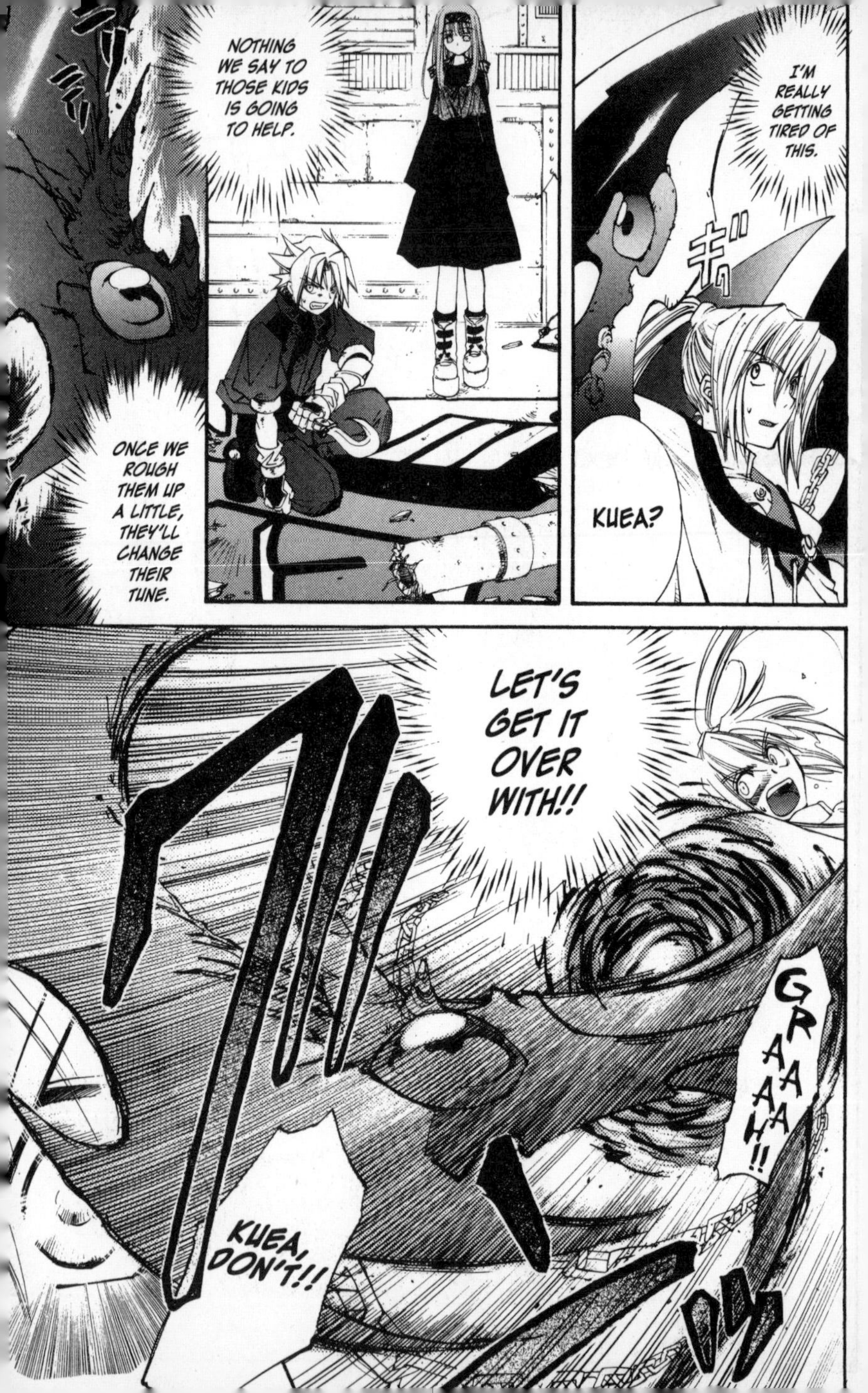
I'M REALLY GETTING TIRED OF THIS.
KUEA?
NOTHING WE SAY TO THOSE KIDS IS GOING TO HELP.
ONCE WE ROUGH THEM UP A LITTLE, THEY'LL CHANGE THEIR TUNE.
LET'S GET IT OVER WITH!!
GRAAAAH!!
KUEA, DON'T!!

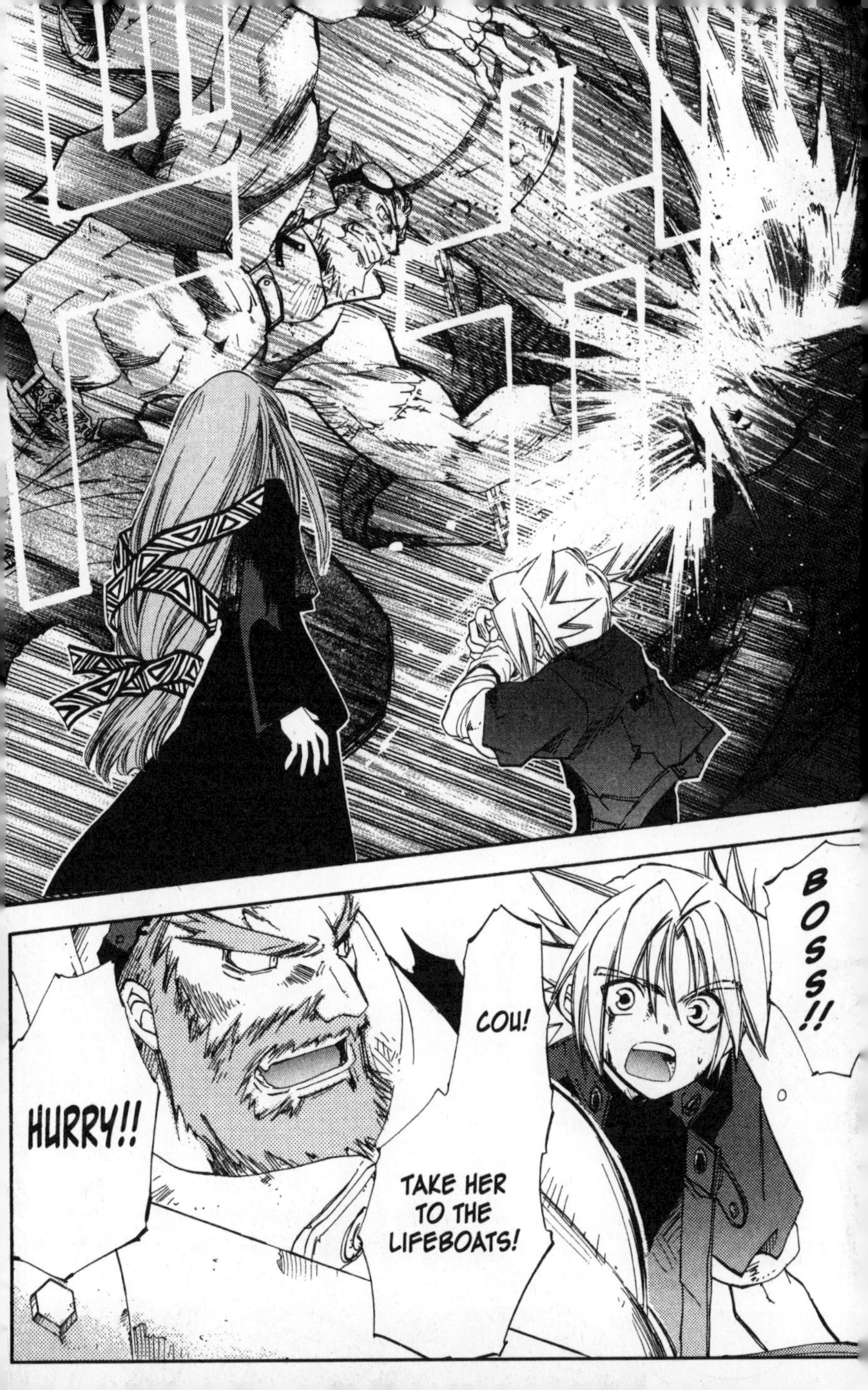
BOSS!!
COU!
TAKE HER TO THE LIFEBOATS!
HURRY!!

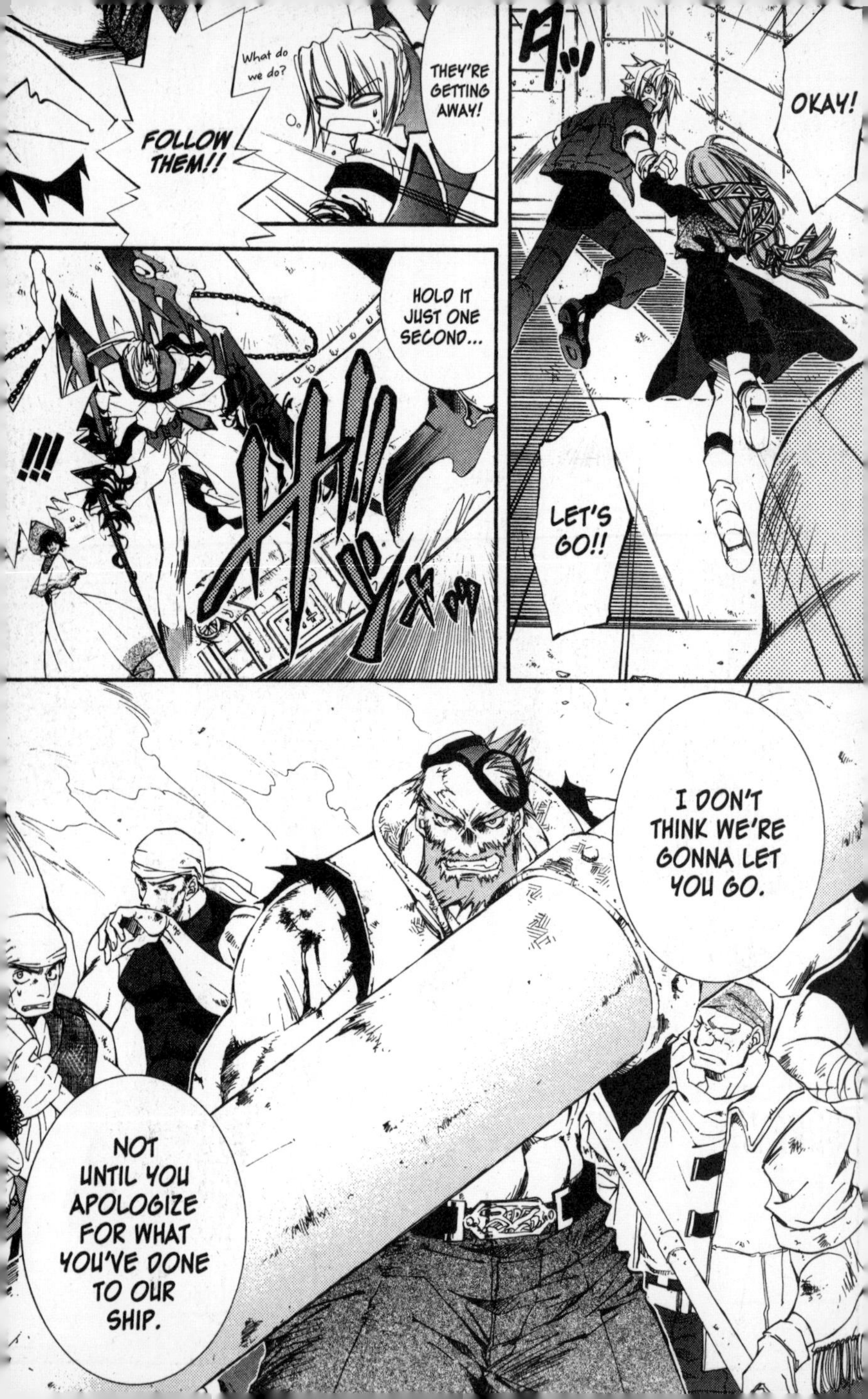
OKAY!
LET'S GO!!
THEY'RE GETTING AWAY!
What do we do?
FOLLOW THEM!!
HOLD IT JUST ONE SECOND...
!!!
I DON'T THINK WE'RE GONNA LET YOU GO.
NOT UNTIL YOU APOLOGIZE FOR WHAT YOU'VE DONE TO OUR SHIP.

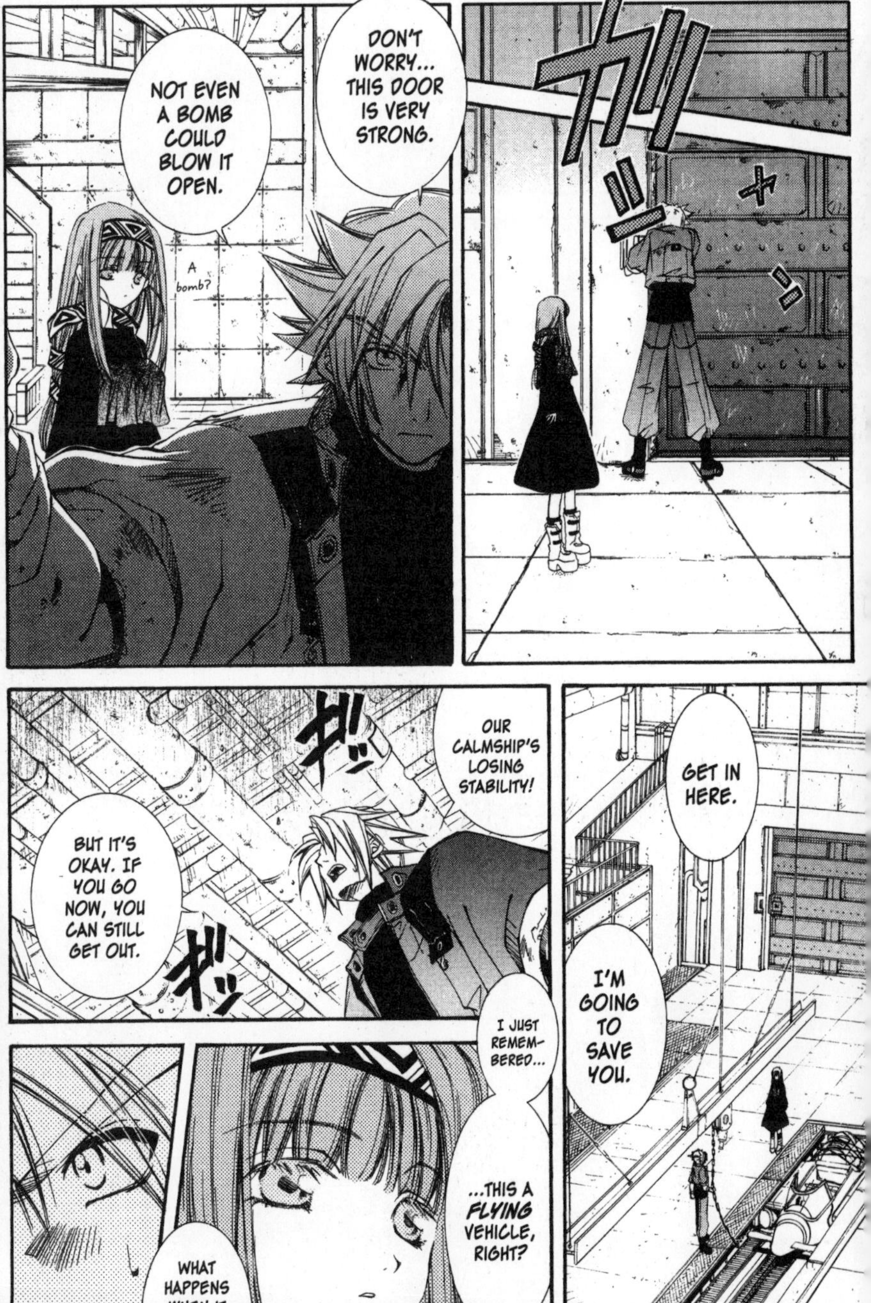
DON'T WORRY... THIS DOOR IS VERY STRONG.
NOT EVEN A BOMB COULD BLOW IT OPEN.
A bomb?
GET IN HERE.
I'M GOING TO SAVE YOU.
OUR CALMSHIP'S LOSING STABILITY!
BUT IT'S OKAY. IF YOU GO NOW, YOU CAN STILL GET OUT.
I JUST REMEMBERED...
...THIS A *FLYING* VEHICLE, RIGHT?
WHAT HAPPENS WHEN IT CAN'T FLY?

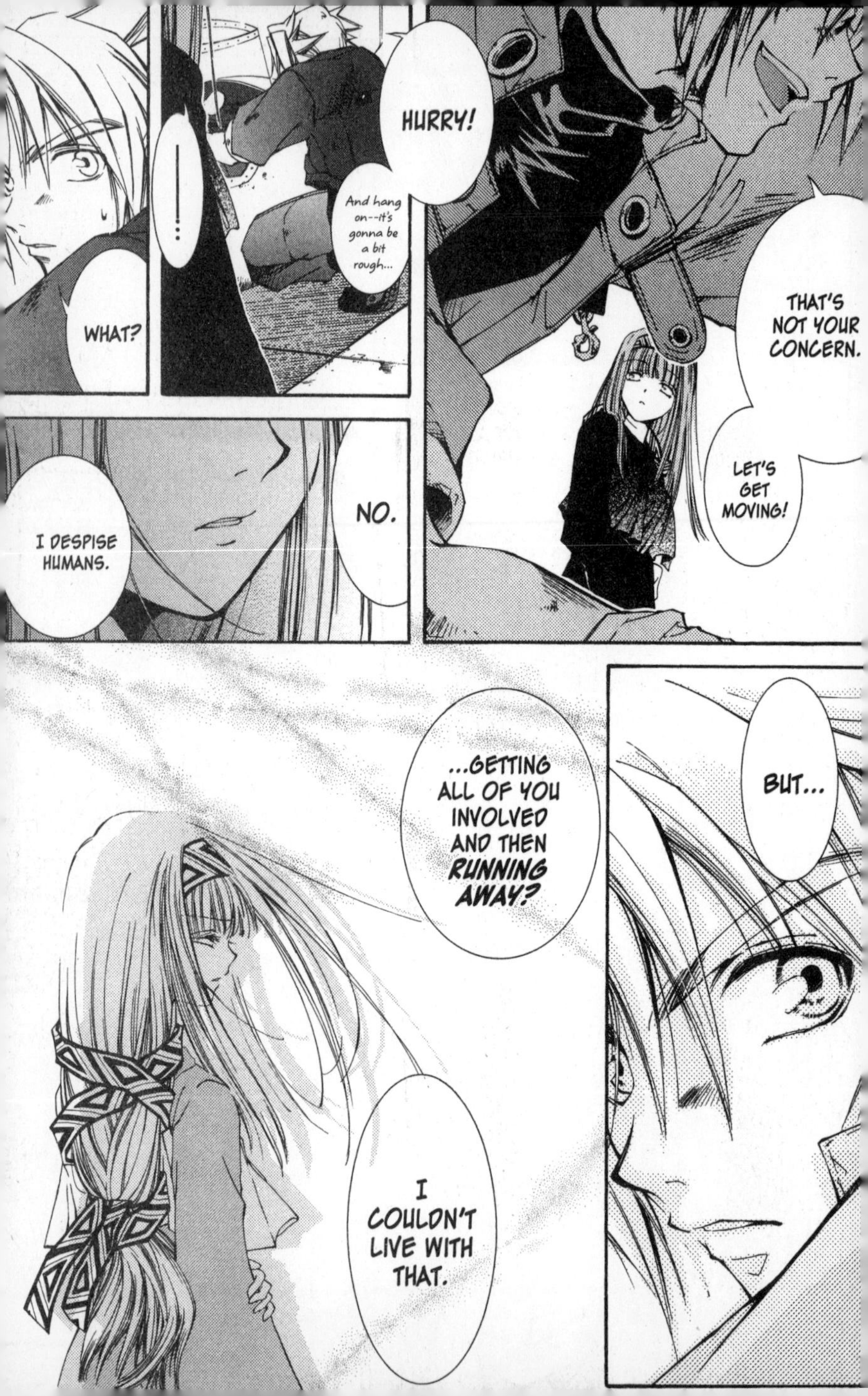
HURRY!
And hang on--it's gonna be a bit rough...
...!
WHAT?
THAT'S NOT YOUR CONCERN.
LET'S GET MOVING!
NO.
I DESPISE HUMANS.
BUT...
...GETTING ALL OF YOU INVOLVED AND THEN RUNNING AWAY?
I COULDN'T LIVE WITH THAT.

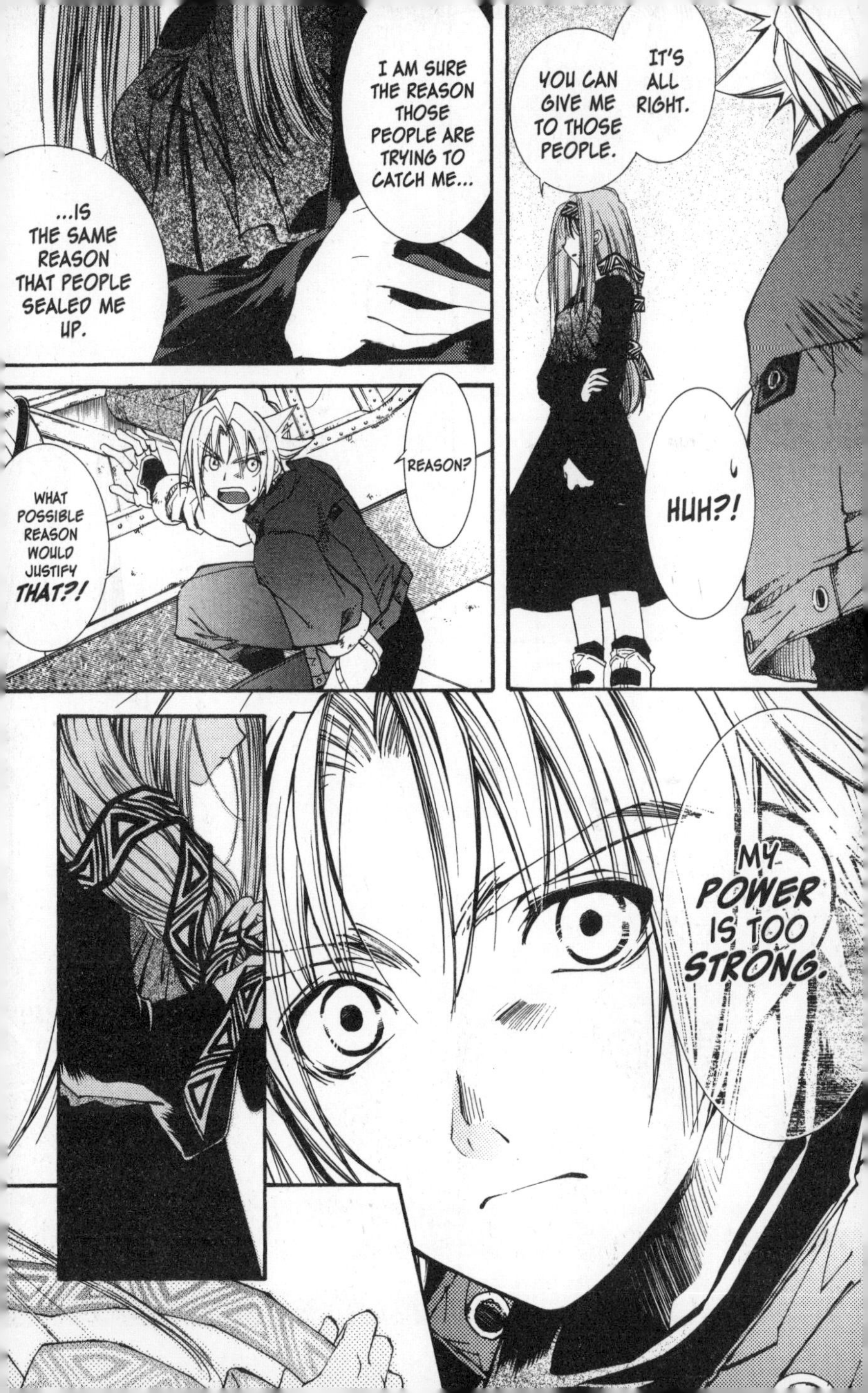
IT'S ALL RIGHT.
YOU CAN GIVE ME TO THOSE PEOPLE.
HUH?!
I AM SURE THE REASON THOSE PEOPLE ARE TRYING TO CATCH ME...
...IS THE SAME REASON THAT PEOPLE SEALED ME UP.
REASON?
WHAT POSSIBLE REASON WOULD JUSTIFY *THAT?!*
MY *POWER* IS TOO *STRONG.*

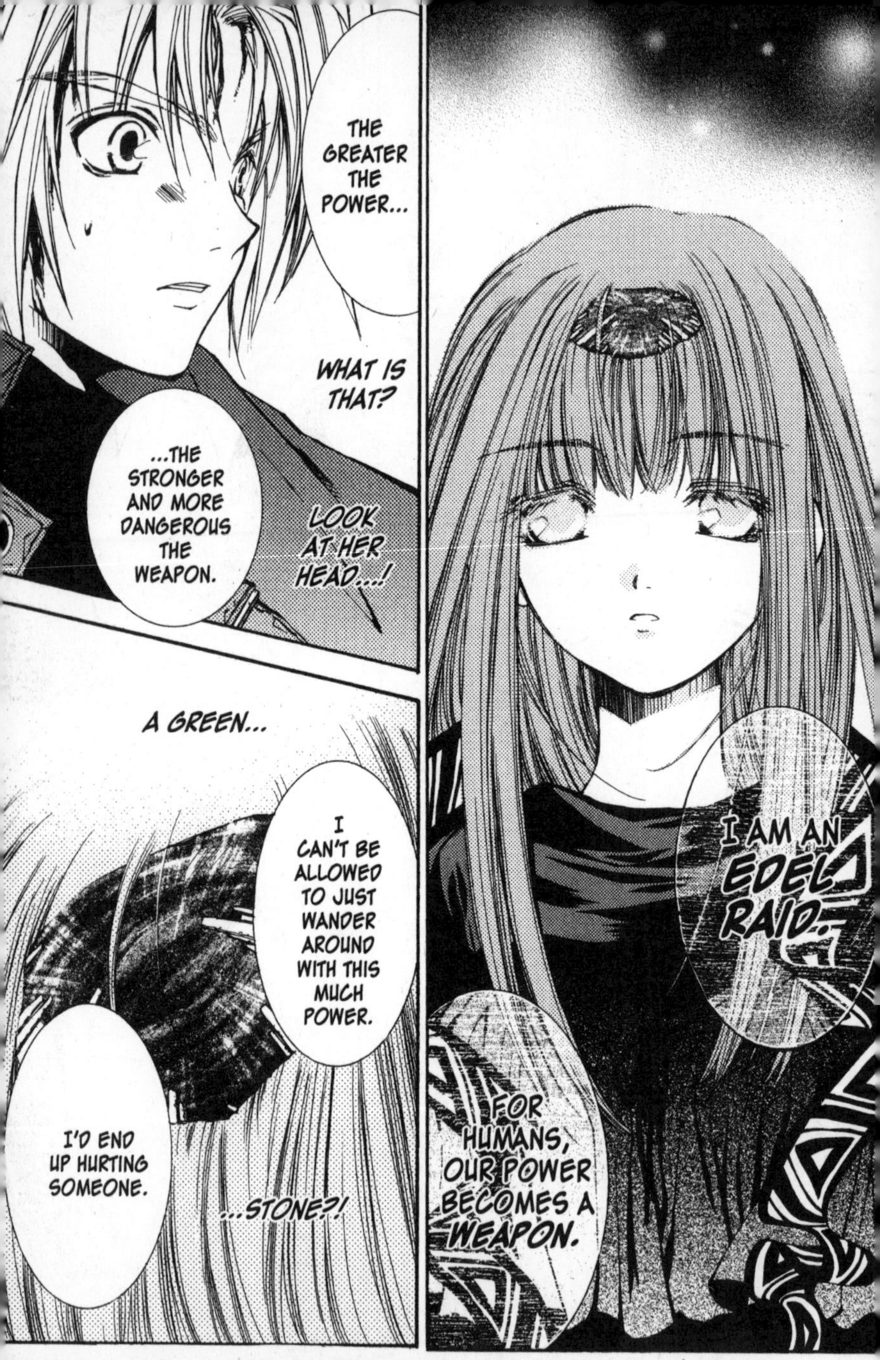
I AM AN EDEL RAID.
FOR HUMANS, OUR POWER BECOMES A WEAPON.
THE GREATER THE POWER...
WHAT IS THAT?
...THE STRONGER AND MORE DANGEROUS THE WEAPON.
LOOK AT HER HEAD...!
A GREEN...
I CAN'T BE ALLOWED TO JUST WANDER AROUND WITH THIS MUCH POWER.
...STONE?!
I'D END UP HURTING SOMEONE.

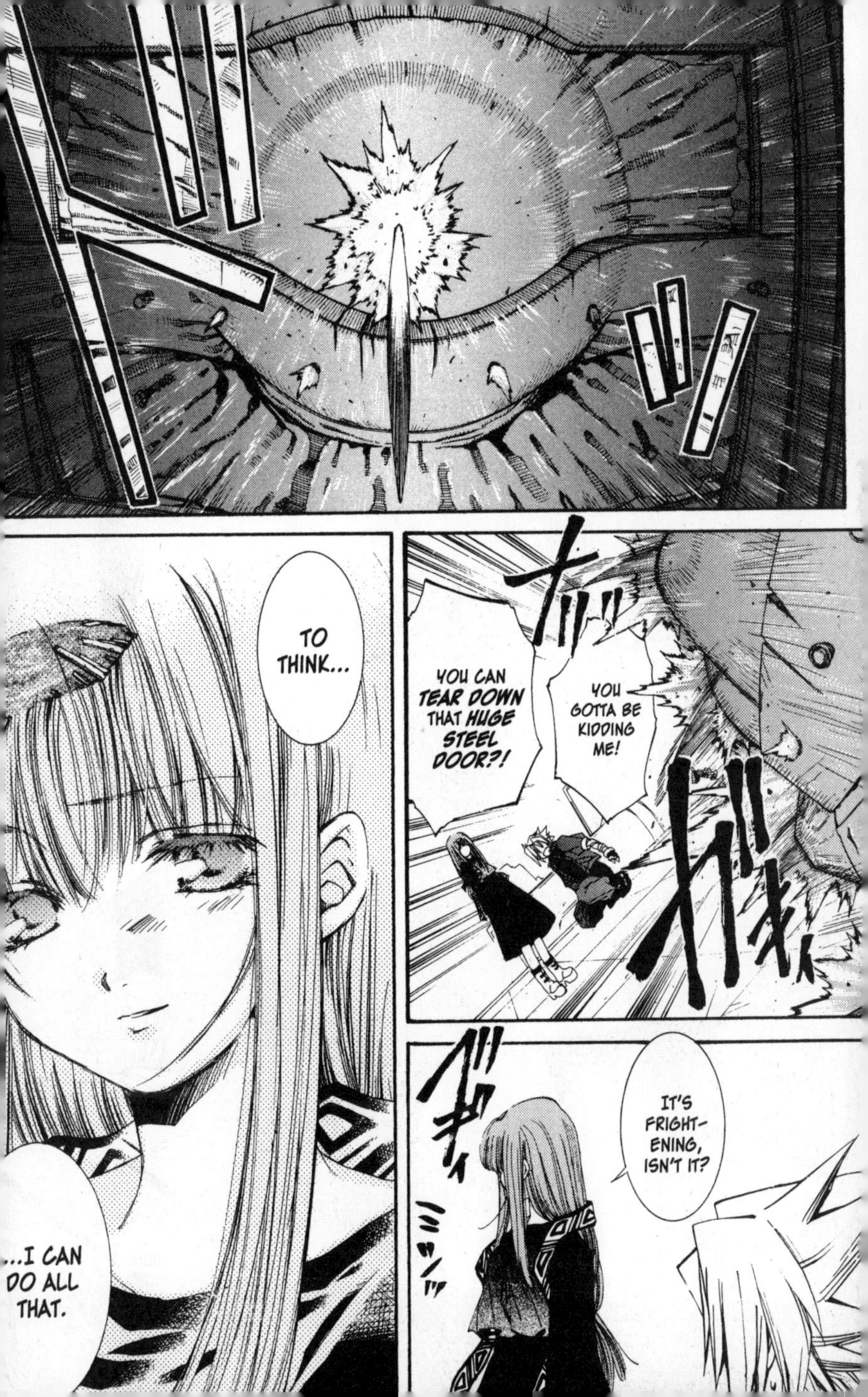
YOU GOTTA BE KIDDING ME!
YOU CAN TEAR DOWN THAT HUGE STEEL DOOR?!
IT'S FRIGHT-ENING, ISN'T IT?
TO THINK...
...I CAN DO ALL THAT.

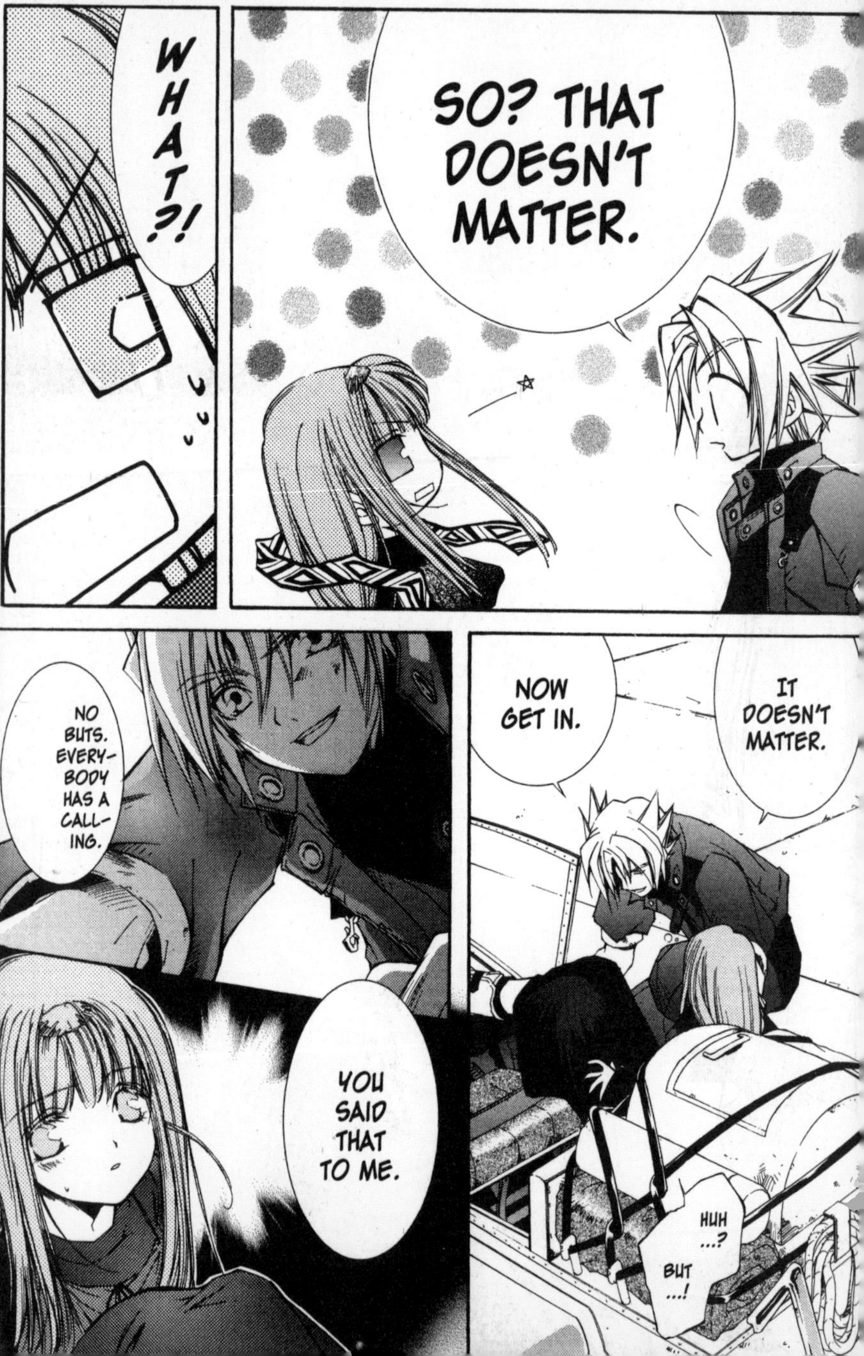
SO? THAT DOESN'T MATTER.
WHAT?!
IT DOESN'T MATTER.
NOW GET IN.
HUH ...?
BUT ...!
NO BUTS. EVERY-BODY HAS A CALL-ING.
YOU SAID THAT TO ME.

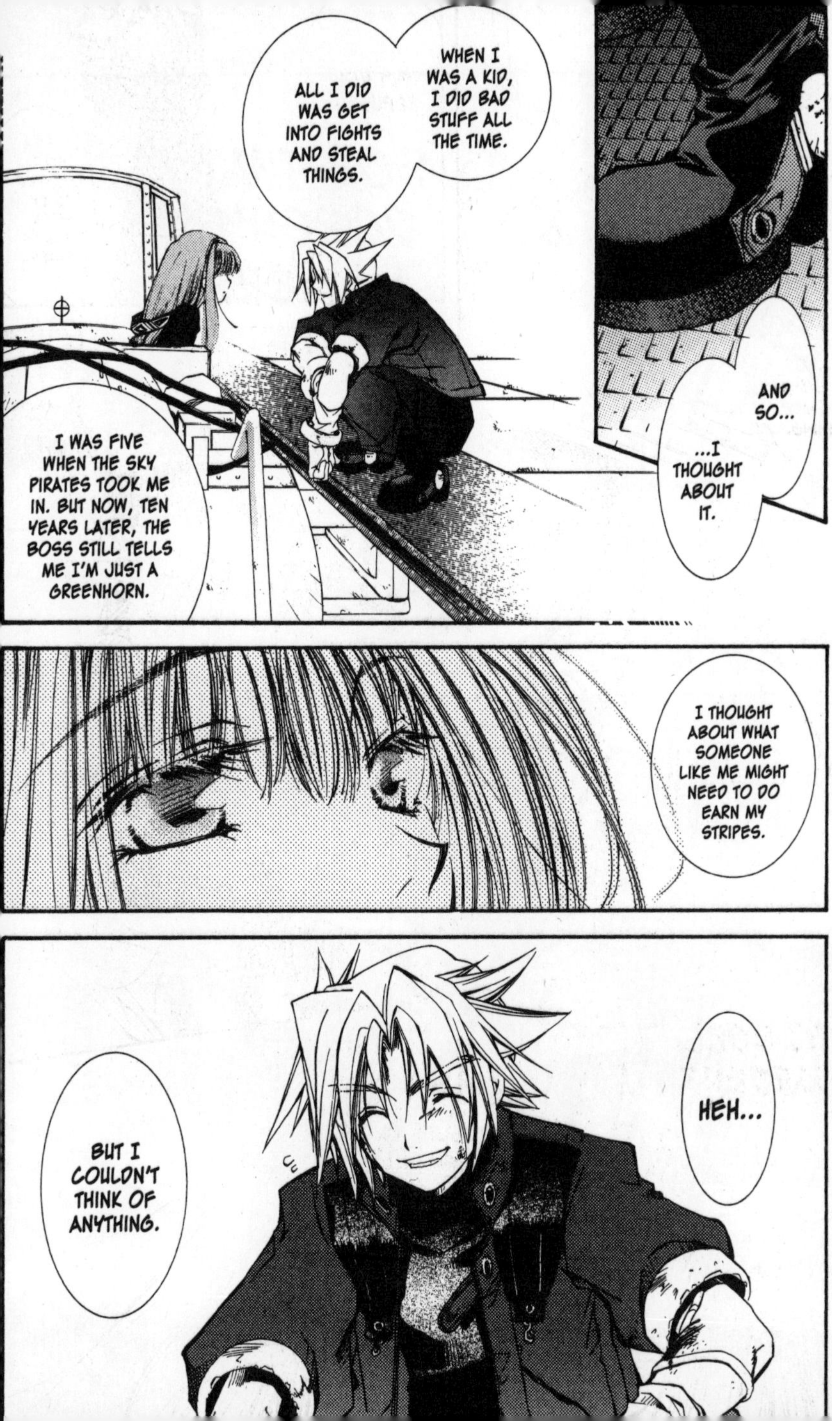
WHEN I WAS A KID, I DID BAD STUFF ALL THE TIME.
ALL I DID WAS GET INTO FIGHTS AND STEAL THINGS.
I WAS FIVE WHEN THE SKY PIRATES TOOK ME IN. BUT NOW, TEN YEARS LATER, THE BOSS STILL TELLS ME I'M JUST A GREENHORN.
AND SO...
...I THOUGHT ABOUT IT.
I THOUGHT ABOUT WHAT SOMEONE LIKE ME MIGHT NEED TO DO EARN MY STRIPES.
HEH...
BUT I COULDN'T THINK OF ANYTHING.

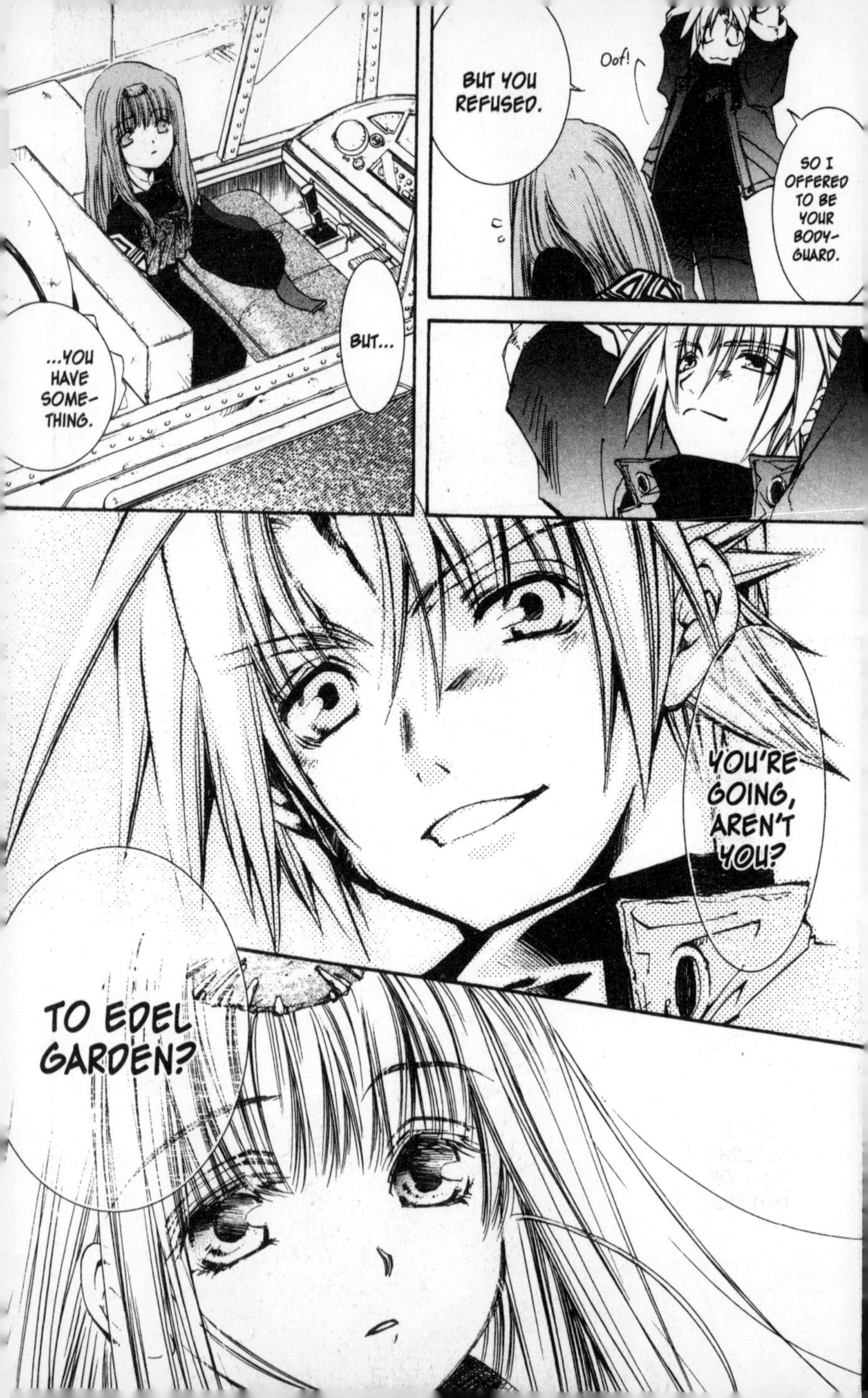

Oof!
SO I OFFERED TO BE YOUR BODY-GUARD.
BUT YOU REFUSED.
BUT...
...YOU HAVE SOMETHING.
YOU'RE GOING, AREN'T YOU?
TO EDEL GARDEN?

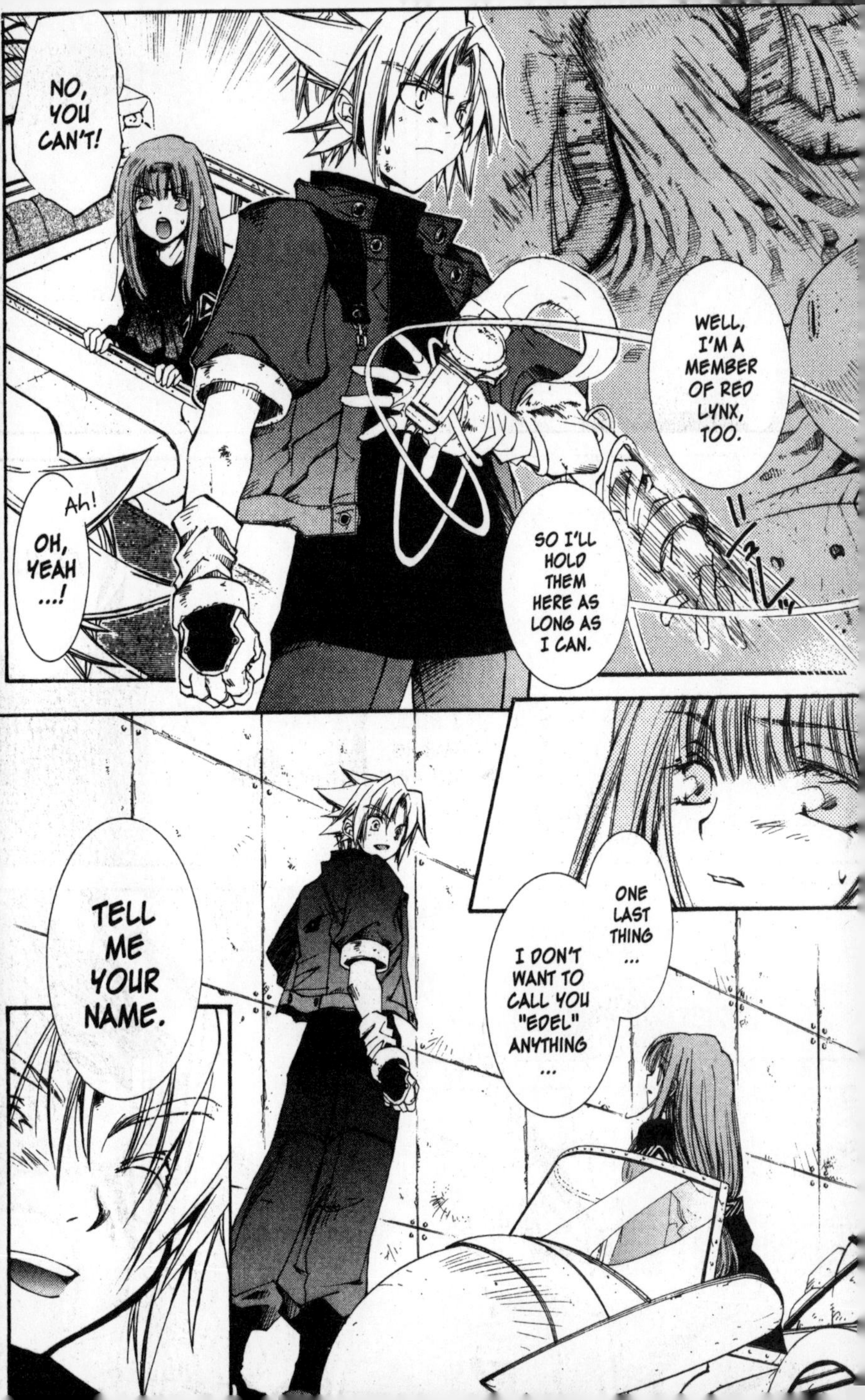
WELL, I'M A MEMBER OF RED LYNX, TOO.
SO I'LL HOLD THEM HERE AS LONG AS I CAN.
NO, YOU CAN'T!
Ah!
OH, YEAH ...!
ONE LAST THING ...
I DON'T WANT TO CALL YOU "EDEL" ANYTHING ...
TELL ME YOUR NAME.

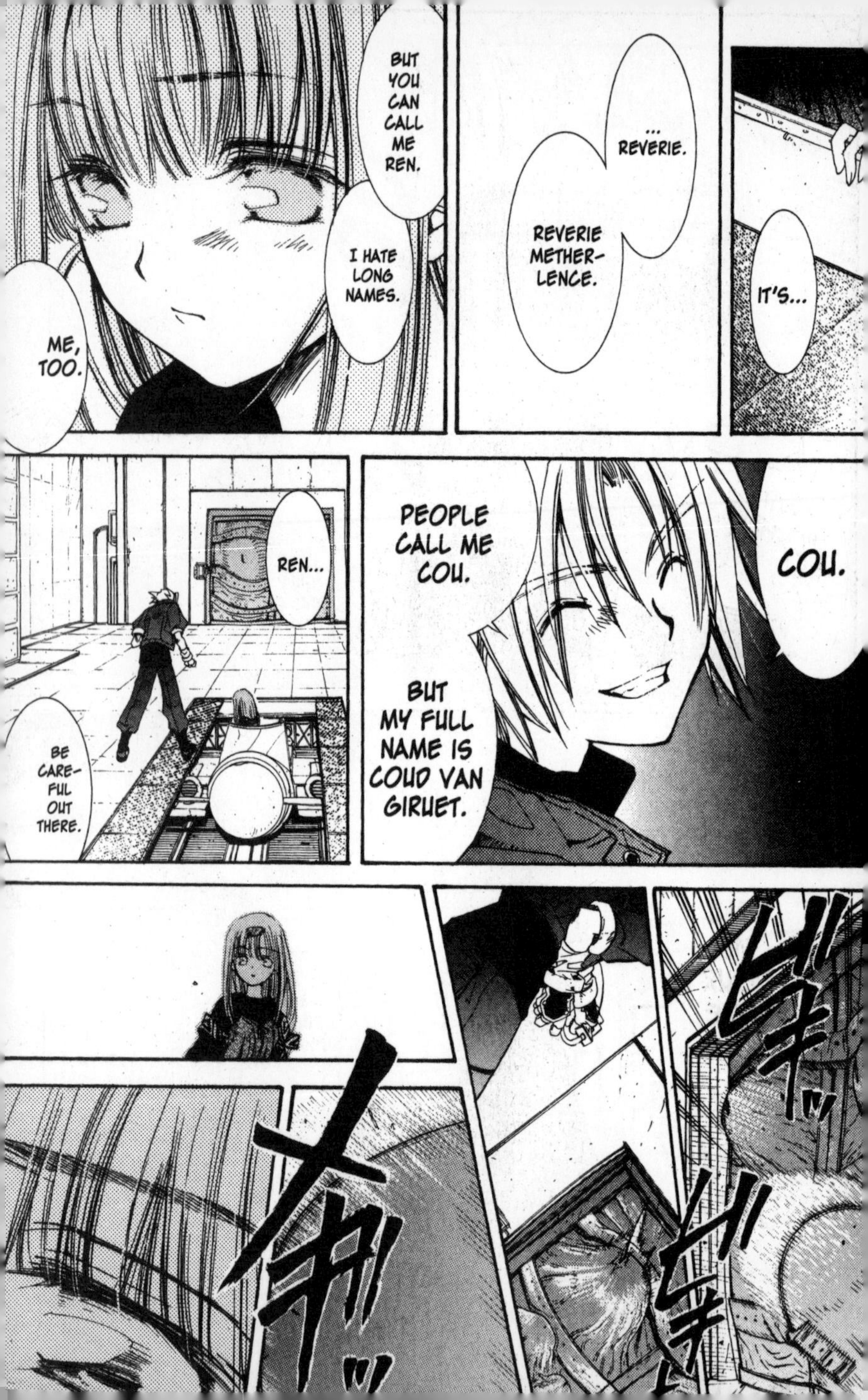
IT'S...
... REVERIE.
REVERIE METHER-LENCE.
BUT YOU CAN CALL ME REN.
I HATE LONG NAMES.
ME, TOO.
COU.
PEOPLE CALL ME COU.
BUT MY FULL NAME IS COUD VAN GIRUET.
REN...
BE CARE-FUL OUT THERE.

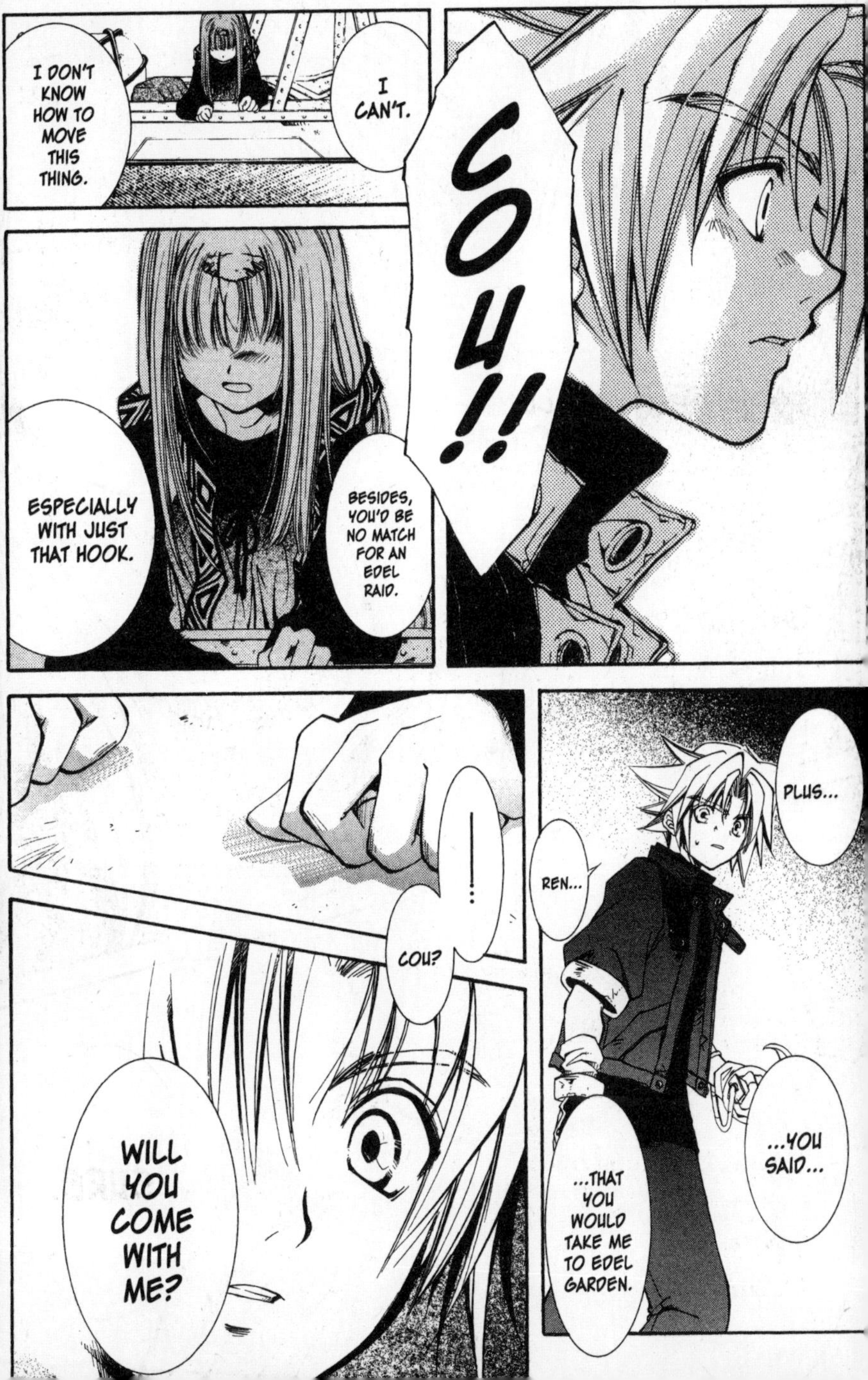
COU!!
I CAN'T.
I DON'T KNOW HOW TO MOVE THIS THING.
BESIDES, YOU'D BE NO MATCH FOR AN EDEL RAID.
ESPECIALLY WITH JUST THAT HOOK.
PLUS...
REN...
...YOU SAID...
...THAT YOU WOULD TAKE ME TO EDEL GARDEN.
—...!
COU?
WILL YOU COME WITH ME?

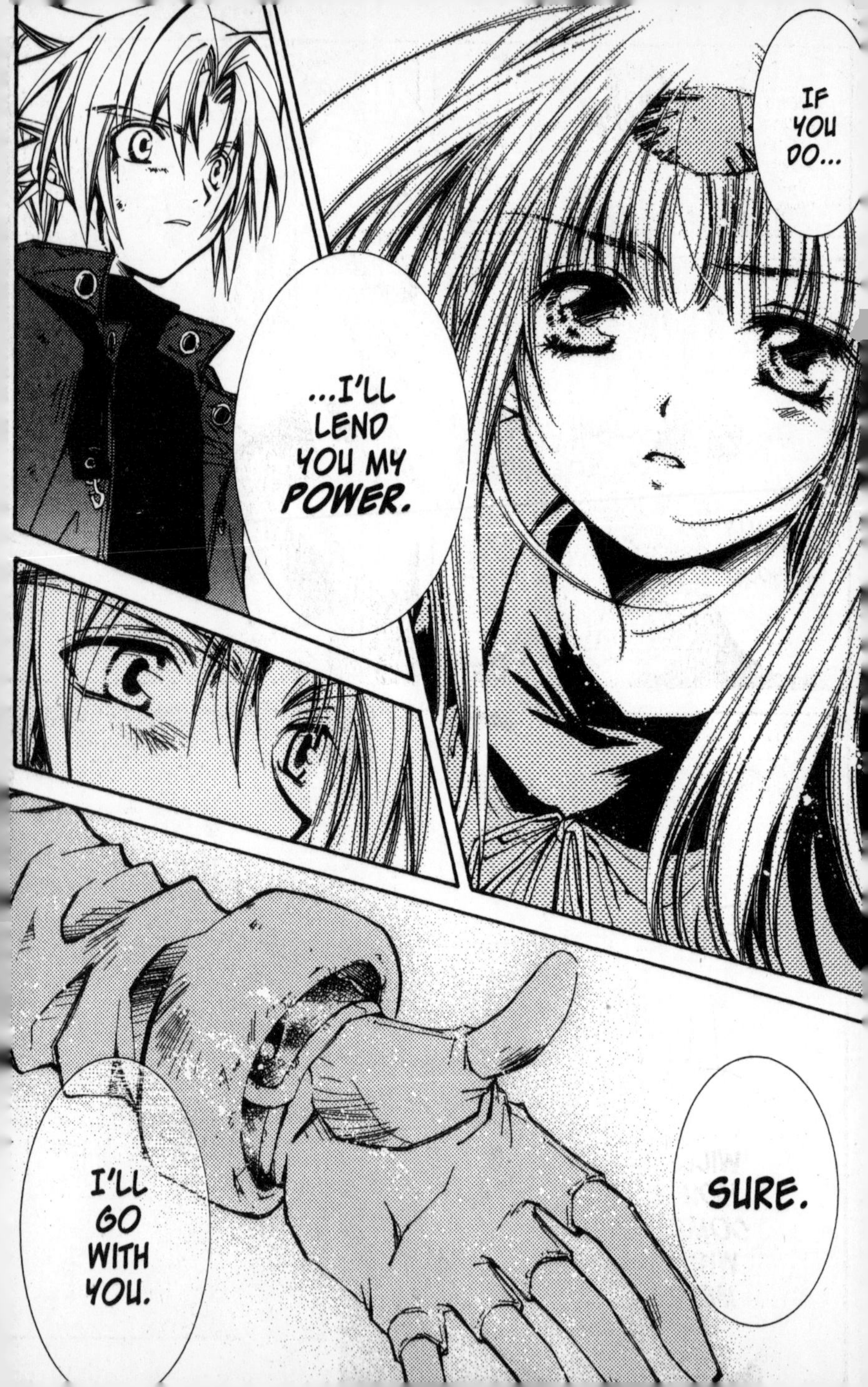
IF YOU DO...
...I'LL LEND YOU MY POWER.
SURE.
I'LL GO WITH YOU.

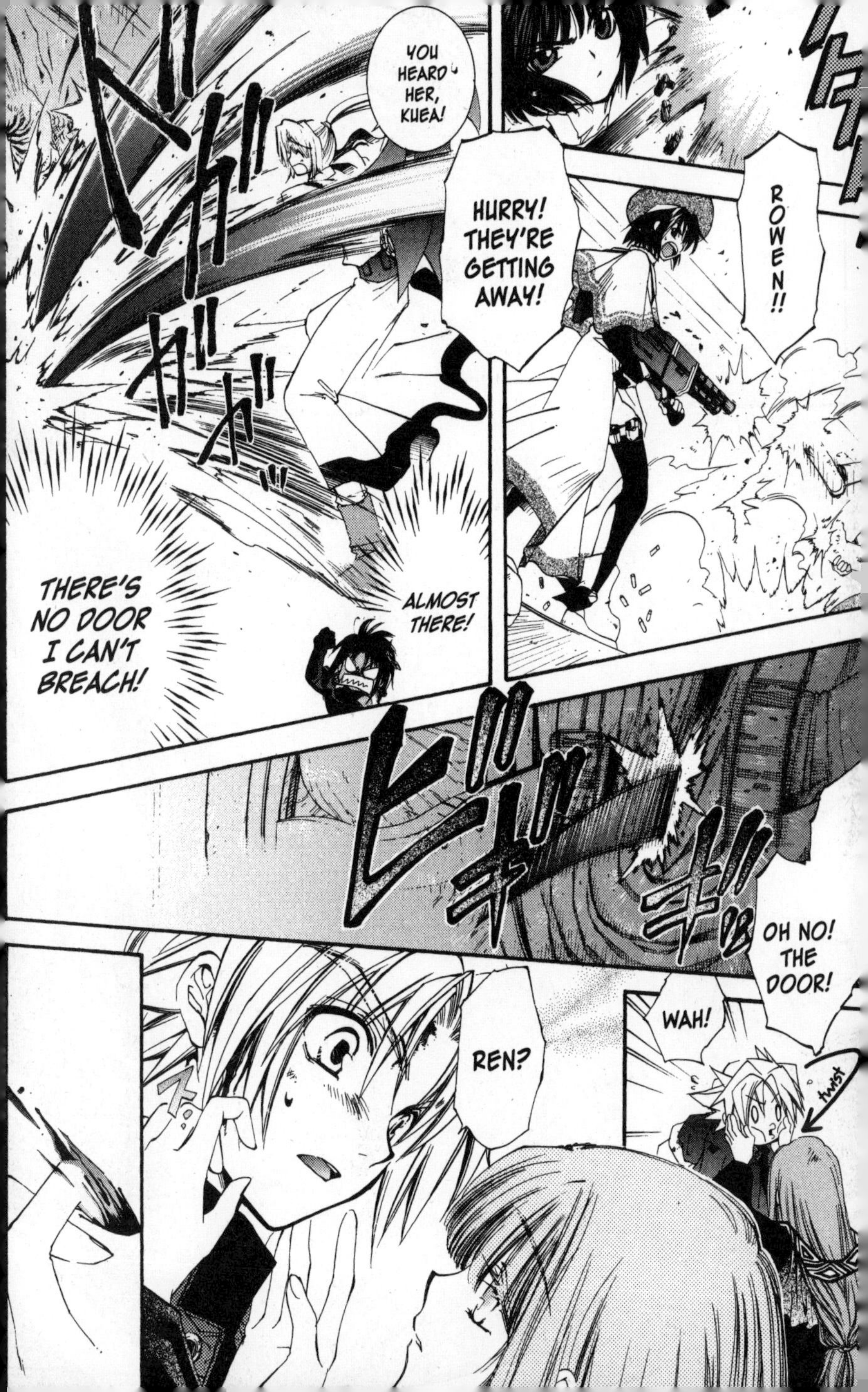
ROWEN!!
HURRY! THEY'RE GETTING AWAY!
YOU HEARD HER, KUEA!
THERE'S NO DOOR I CAN'T BREACH!
ALMOST THERE!
OH NO! THE DOOR!
WAH!
twist
REN?

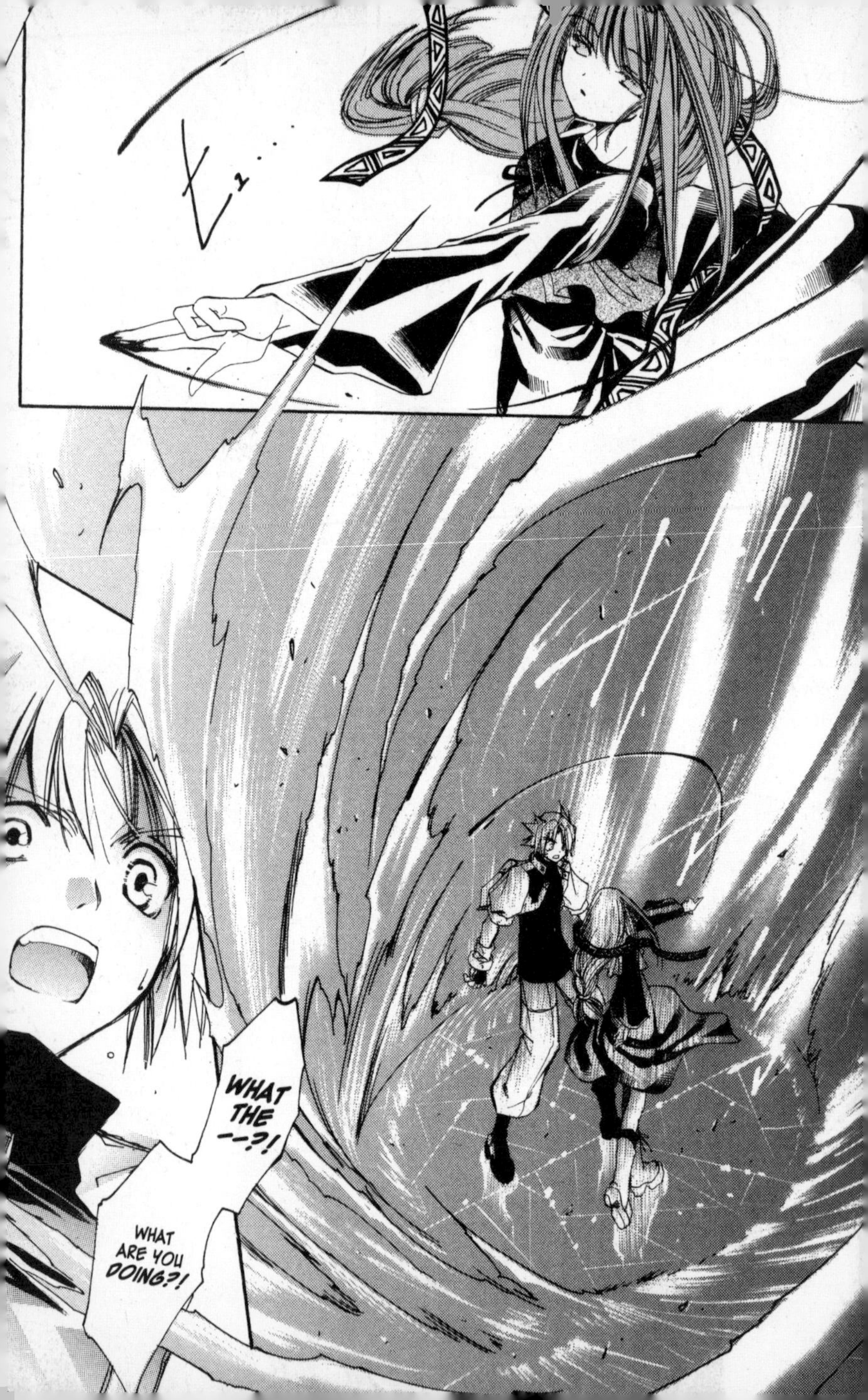
WHAT THE --?!
WHAT ARE YOU DOING?!

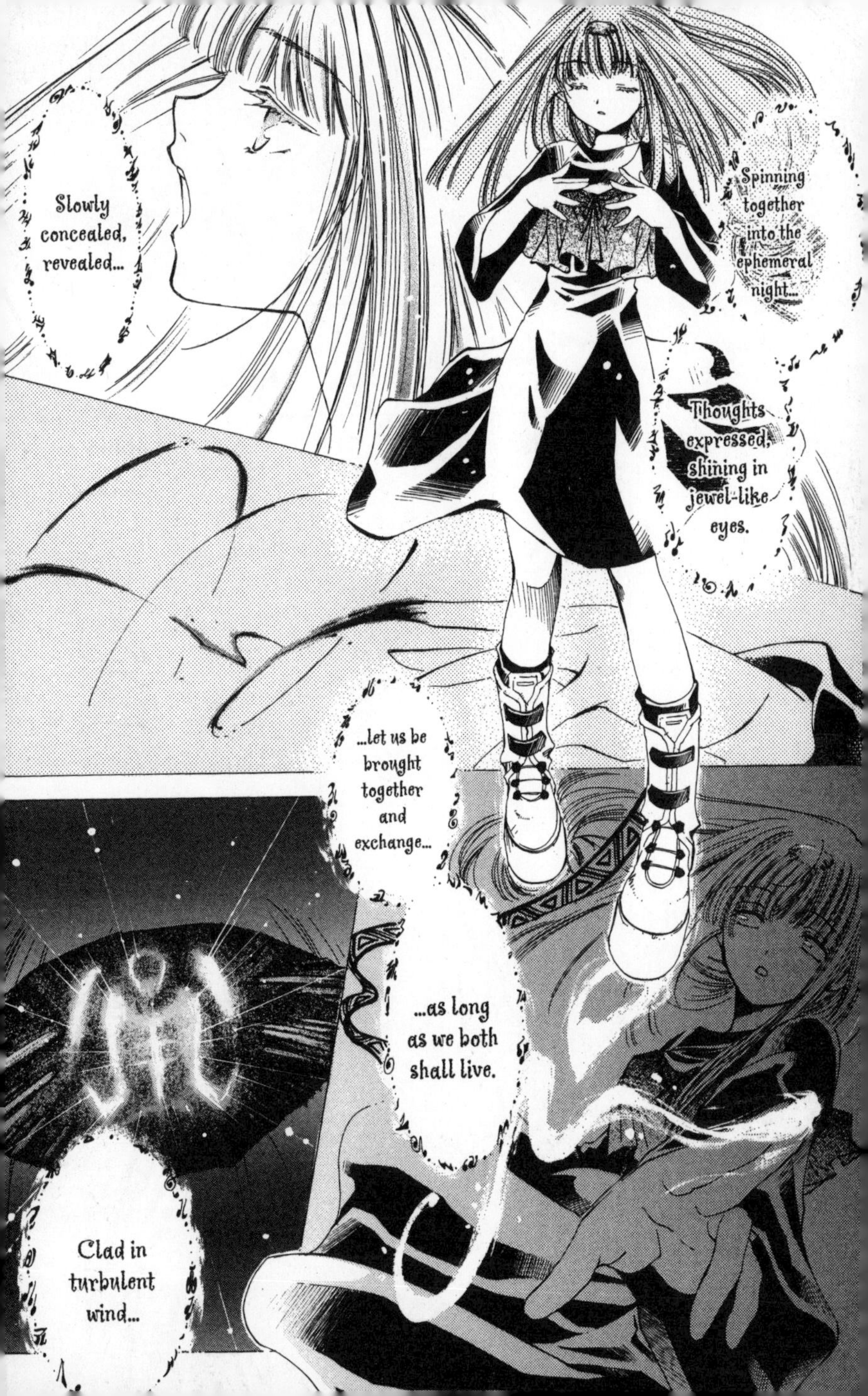

Spinning together into the ephemeral night...
Slowly concealed, revealed...
Thoughts expressed, shining in jewel-like eyes.
...let us be brought together and exchange...
...as long as we both shall live.
Clad in turbulent wind...

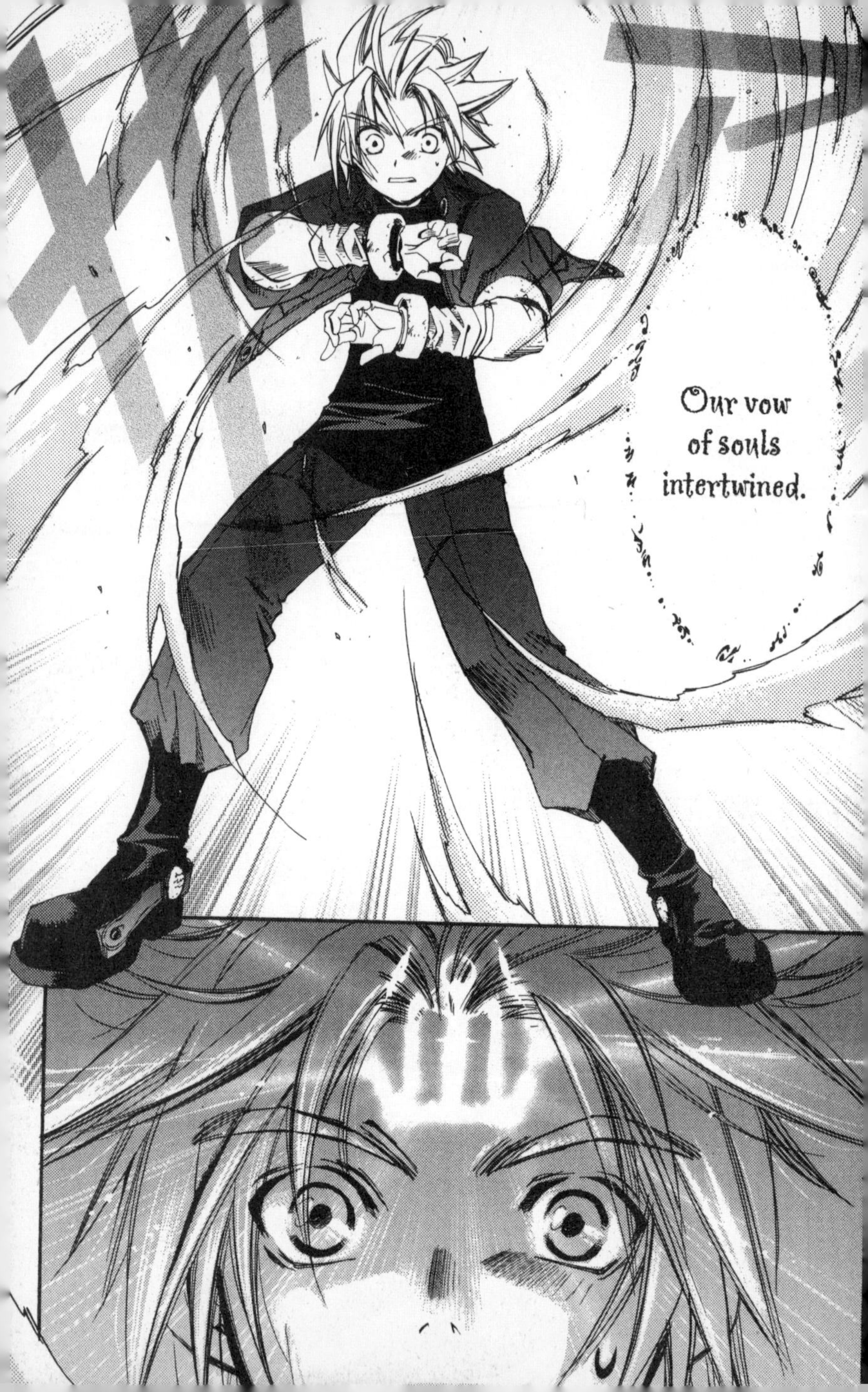
Our vow of souls intertwined.

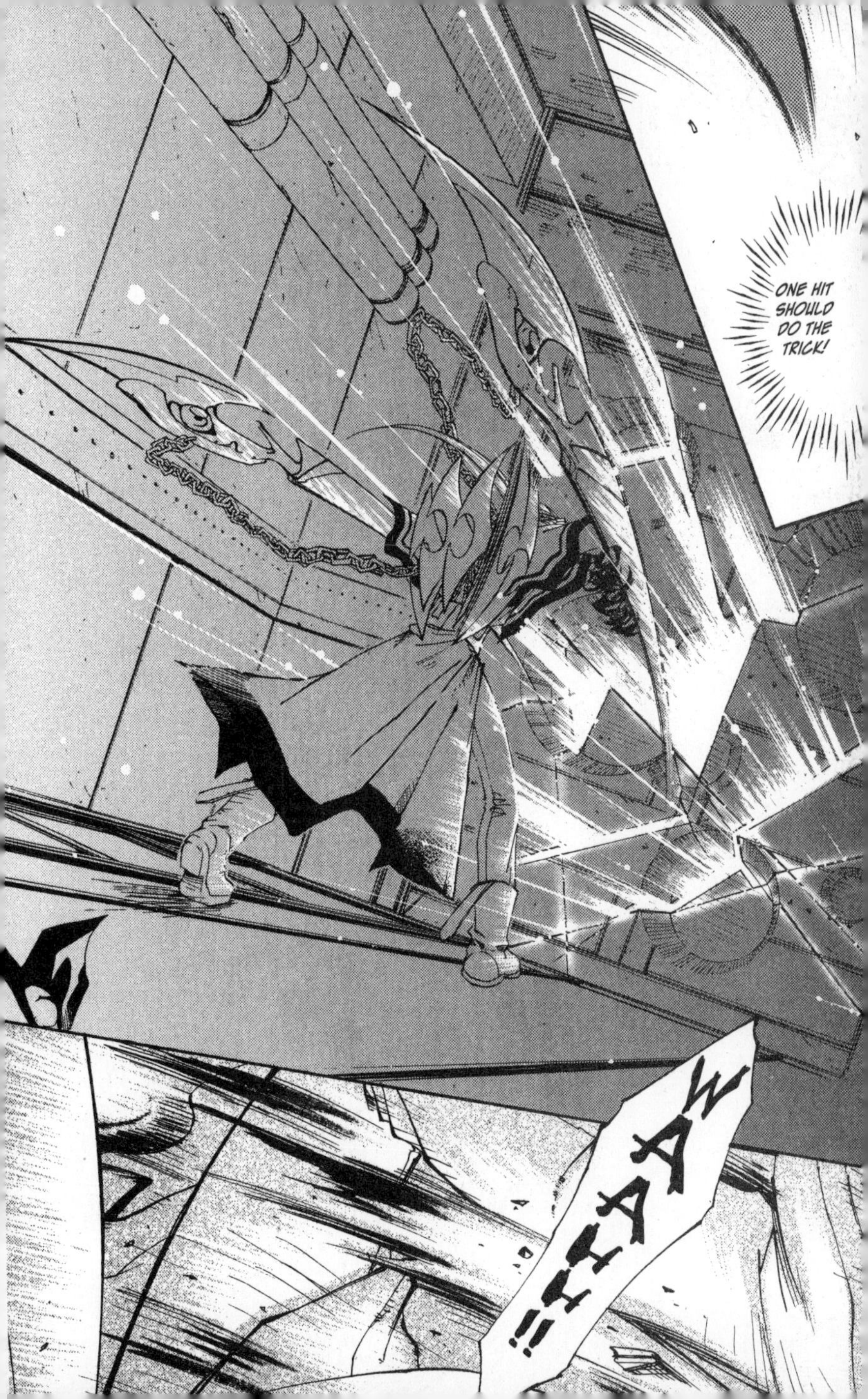
ONE HIT SHOULD DO THE TRICK!
WAAHH!!

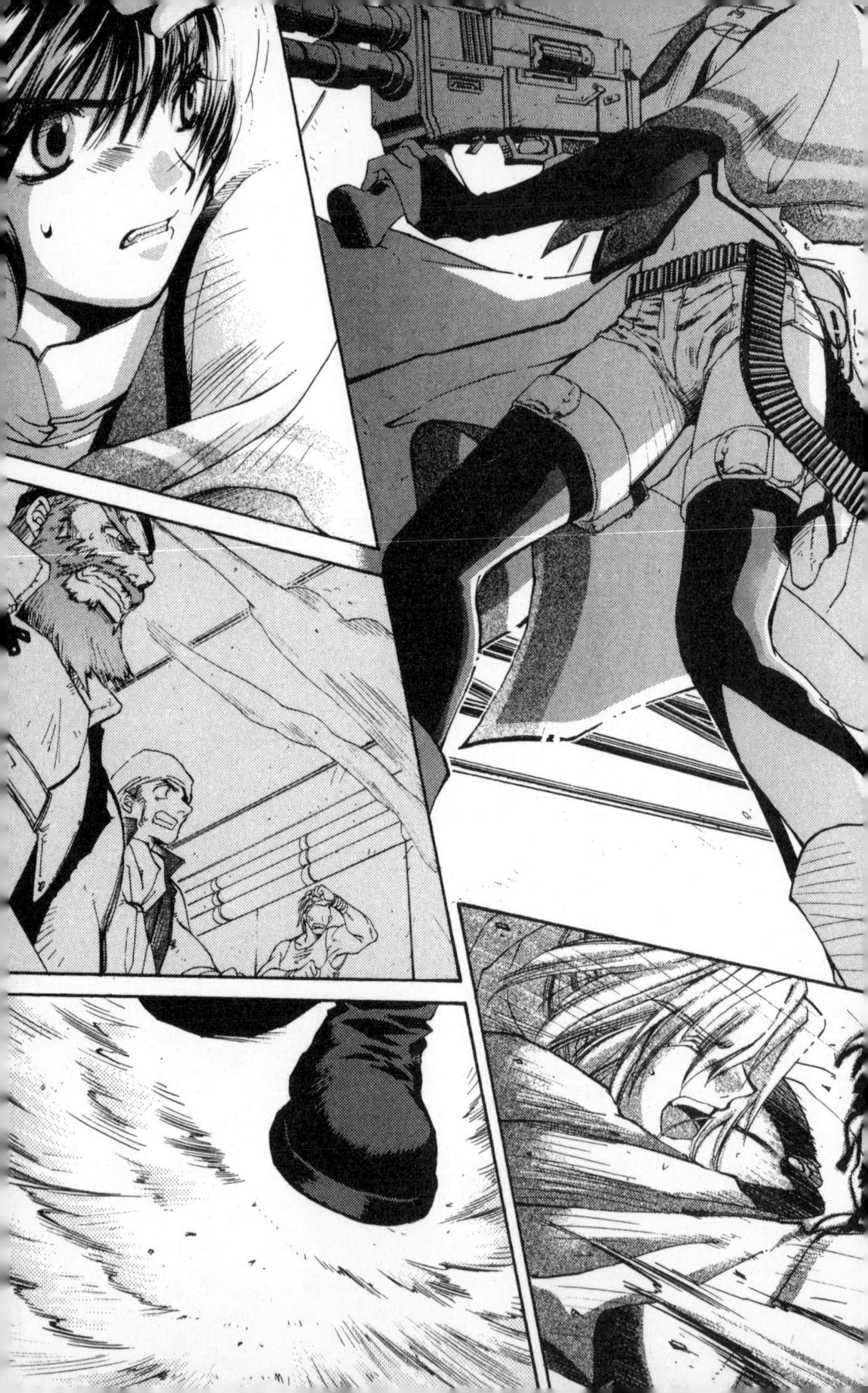

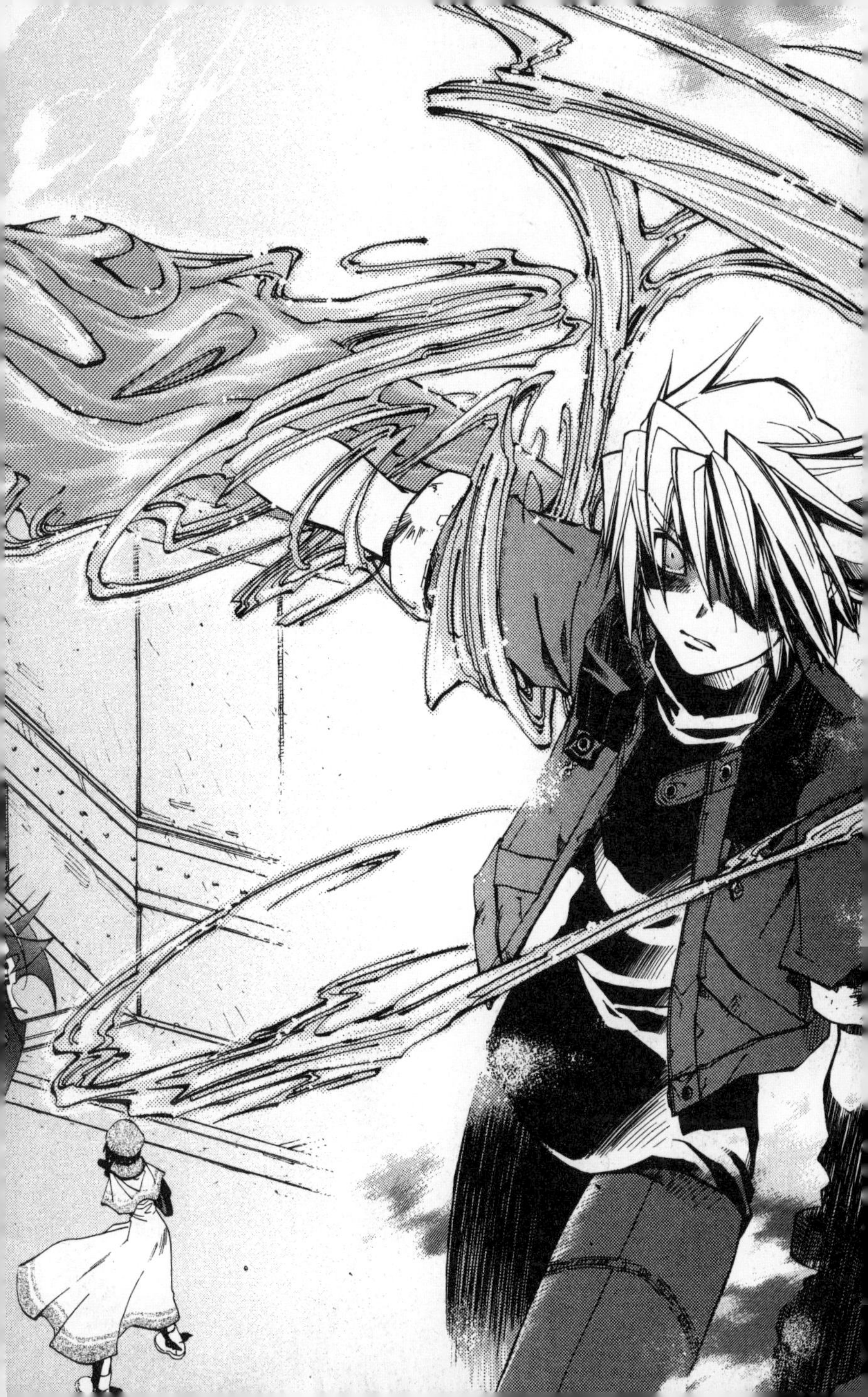

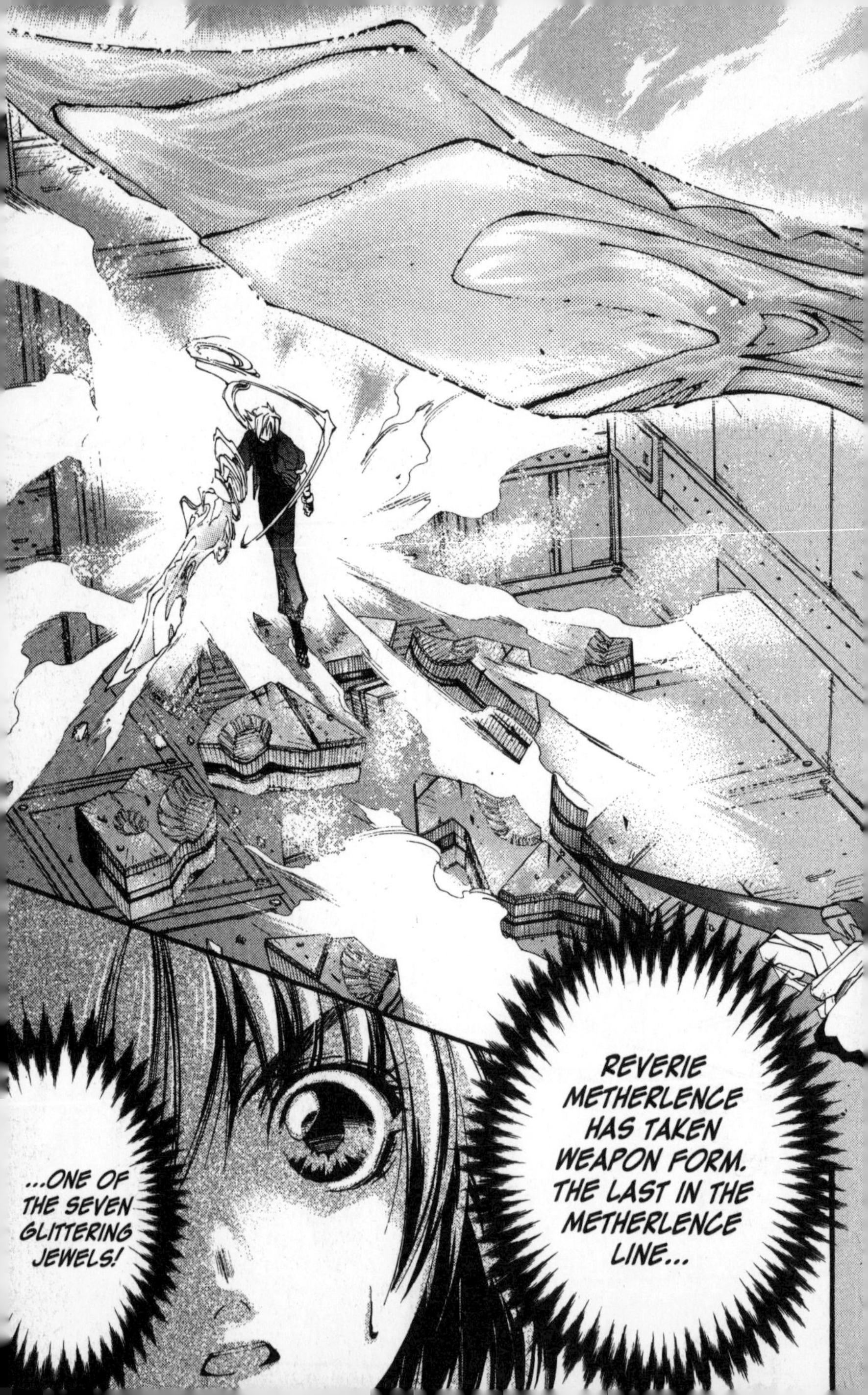
REVERIE METHERLENCE HAS TAKEN WEAPON FORM. THE LAST IN THE METHERLENCE LINE...
...ONE OF THE SEVEN GLITTERING JEWELS!

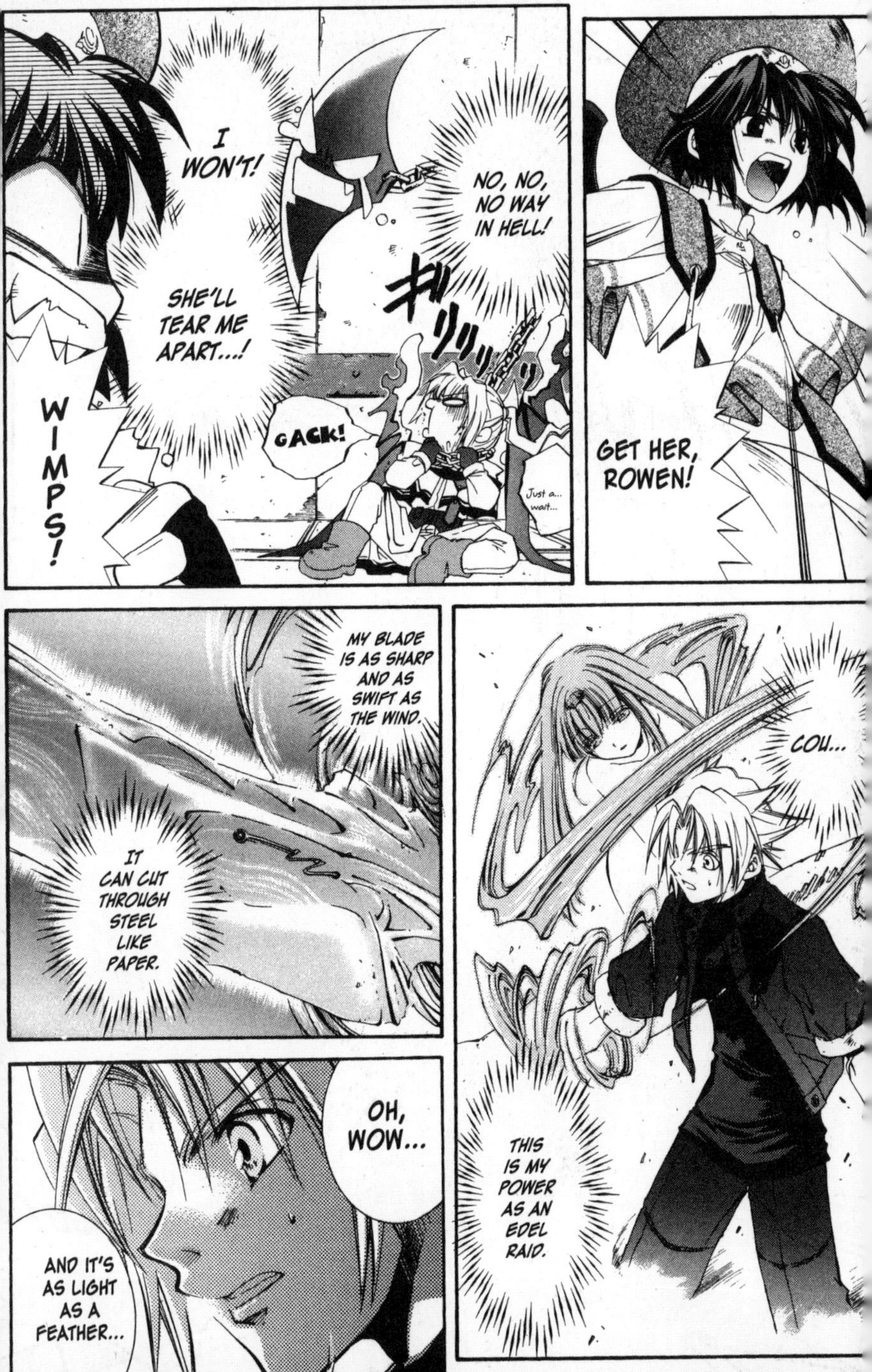
GET HER, ROWEN!
NO, NO, NO WAY IN HELL!
I WON'T!
SHE'LL TEAR ME APART...!
Just a... wait...
GACK!
WIMPS!
COU...
THIS IS MY POWER AS AN EDEL RAID.
MY BLADE IS AS SHARP AND AS SWIFT AS THE WIND.
IT CAN CUT THROUGH STEEL LIKE PAPER.
OH, WOW...
AND IT'S AS LIGHT AS A FEATHER...

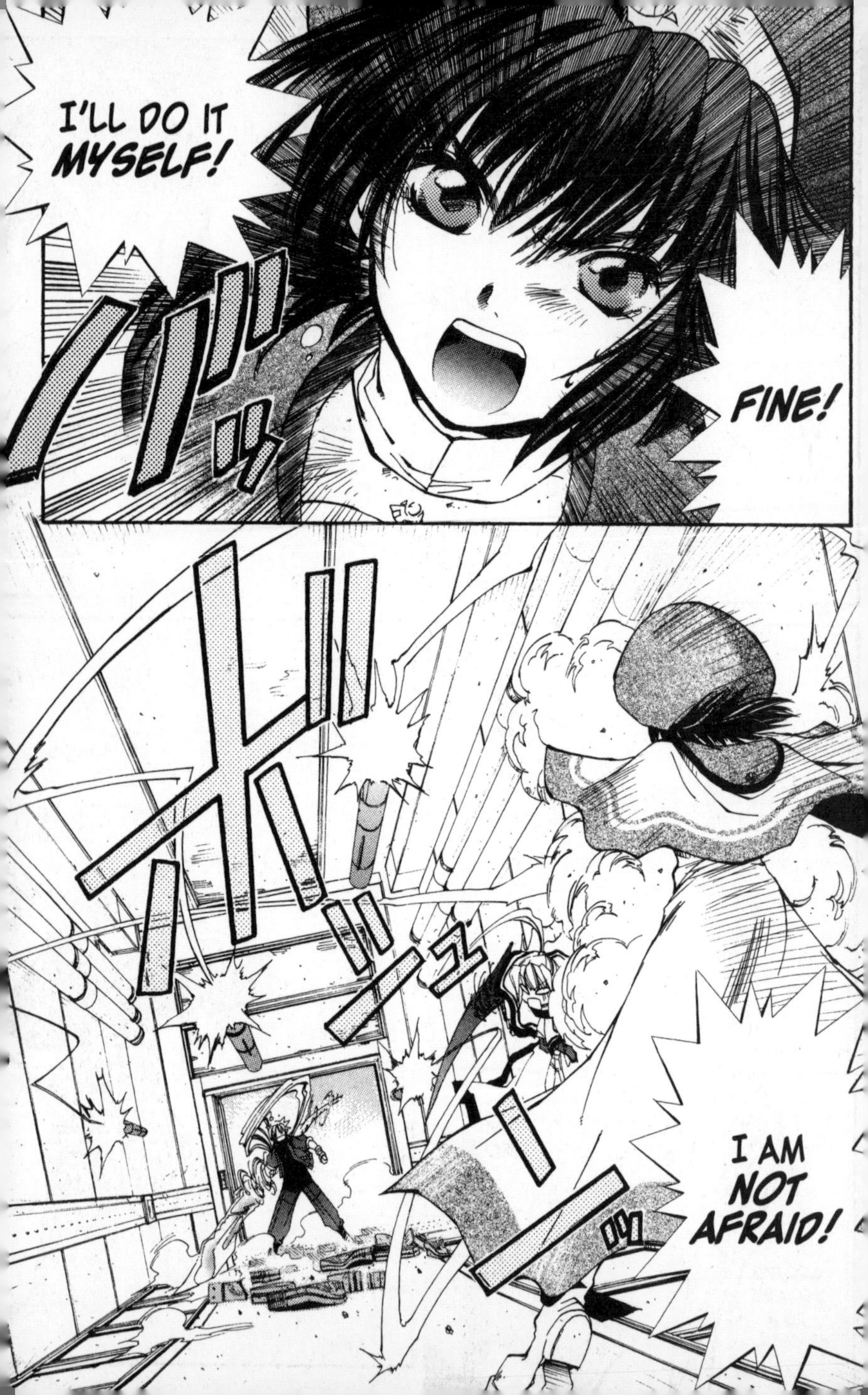
FINE!
I'LL DO IT MYSELF!
I AM NOT AFRAID!

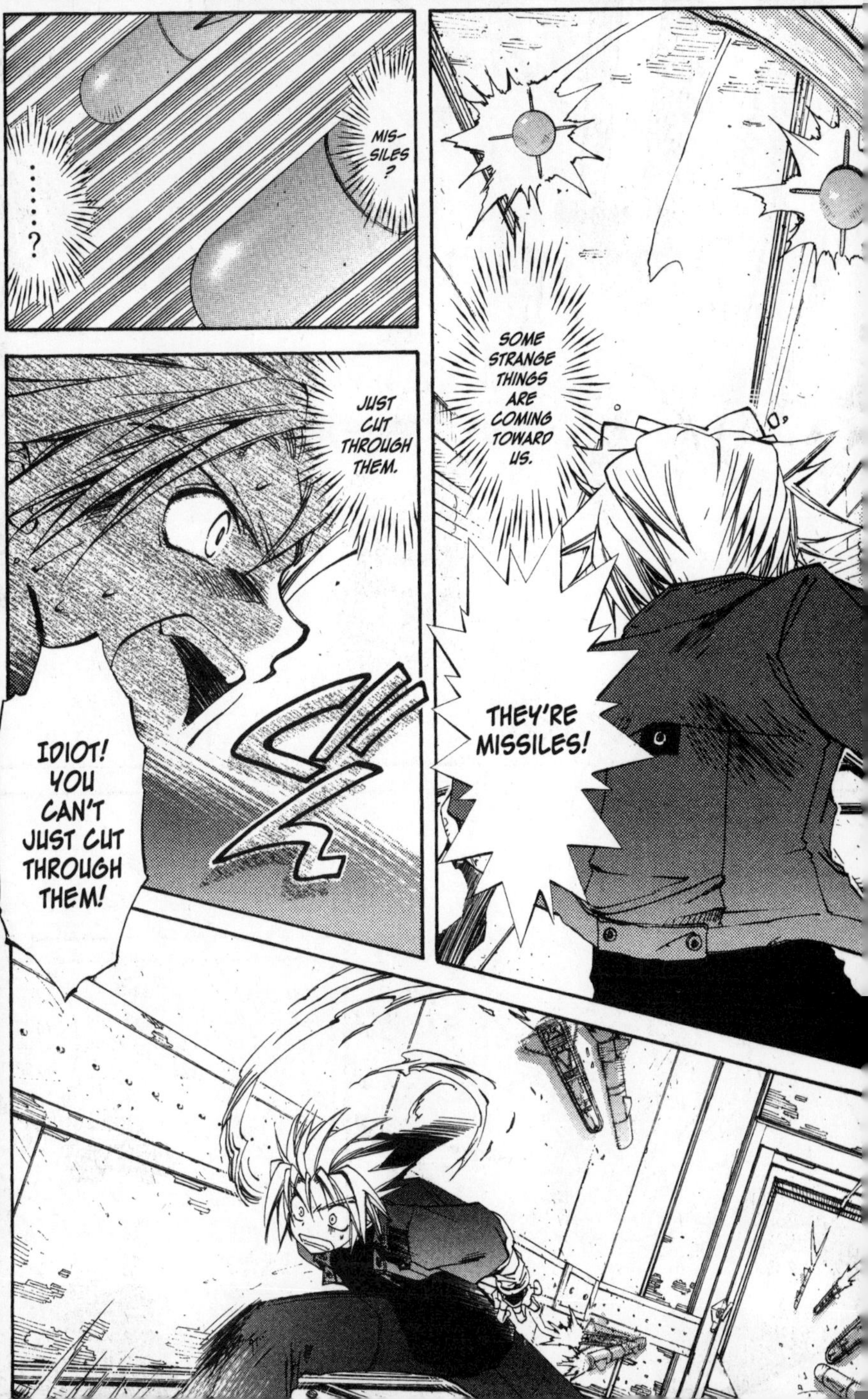
SOME STRANGE THINGS ARE COMING TOWARD US.
THEY'RE MISSILES!
MIS-SILES?
......?
JUST CUT THROUGH THEM.
IDIOT! YOU CAN'T JUST CUT THROUGH THEM!

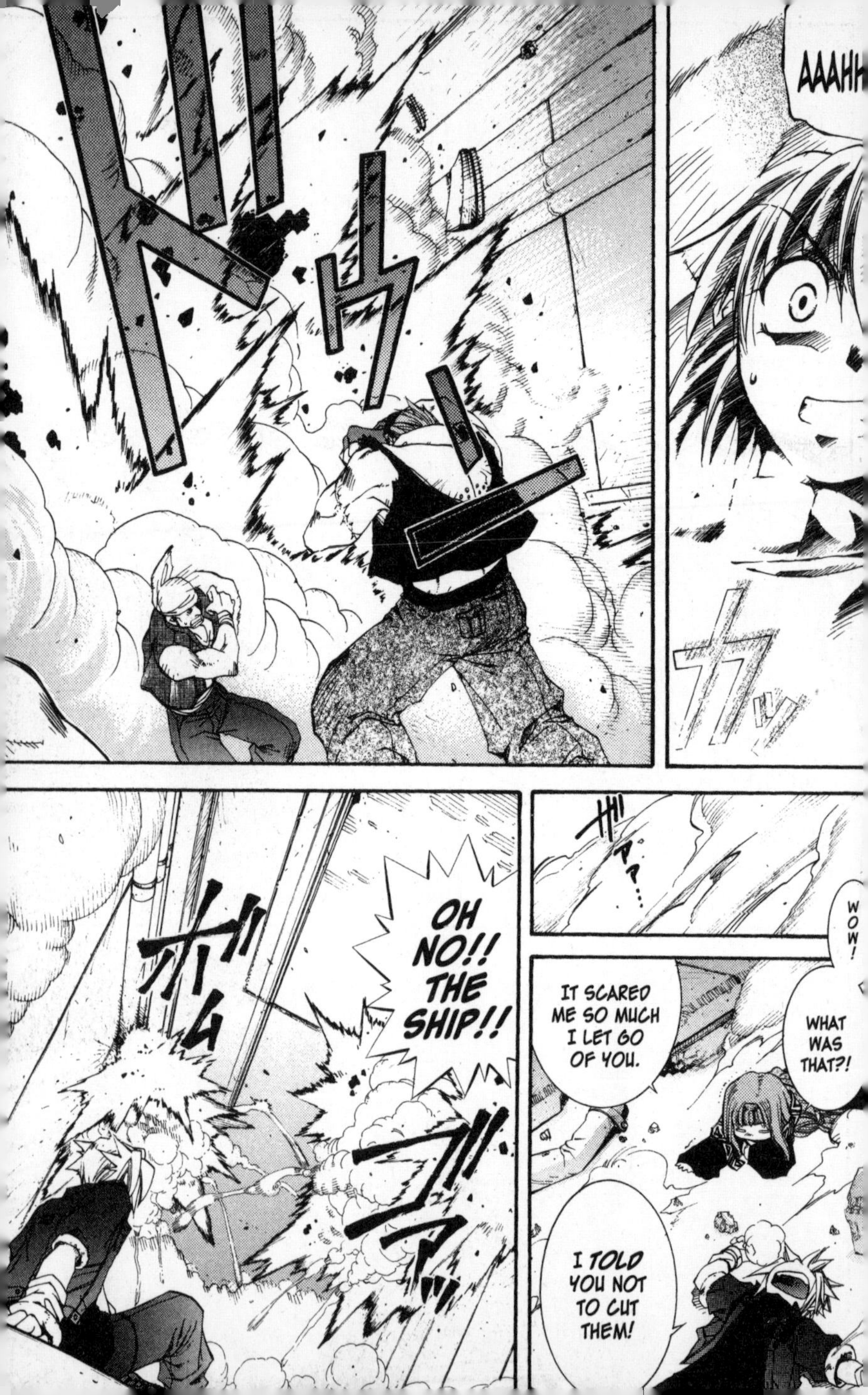
AAAHH
WOW!
WHAT WAS THAT?!
IT SCARED ME SO MUCH I LET GO OF YOU.
I TOLD YOU NOT TO CUT THEM!
OH NO!! THE SHIP!!

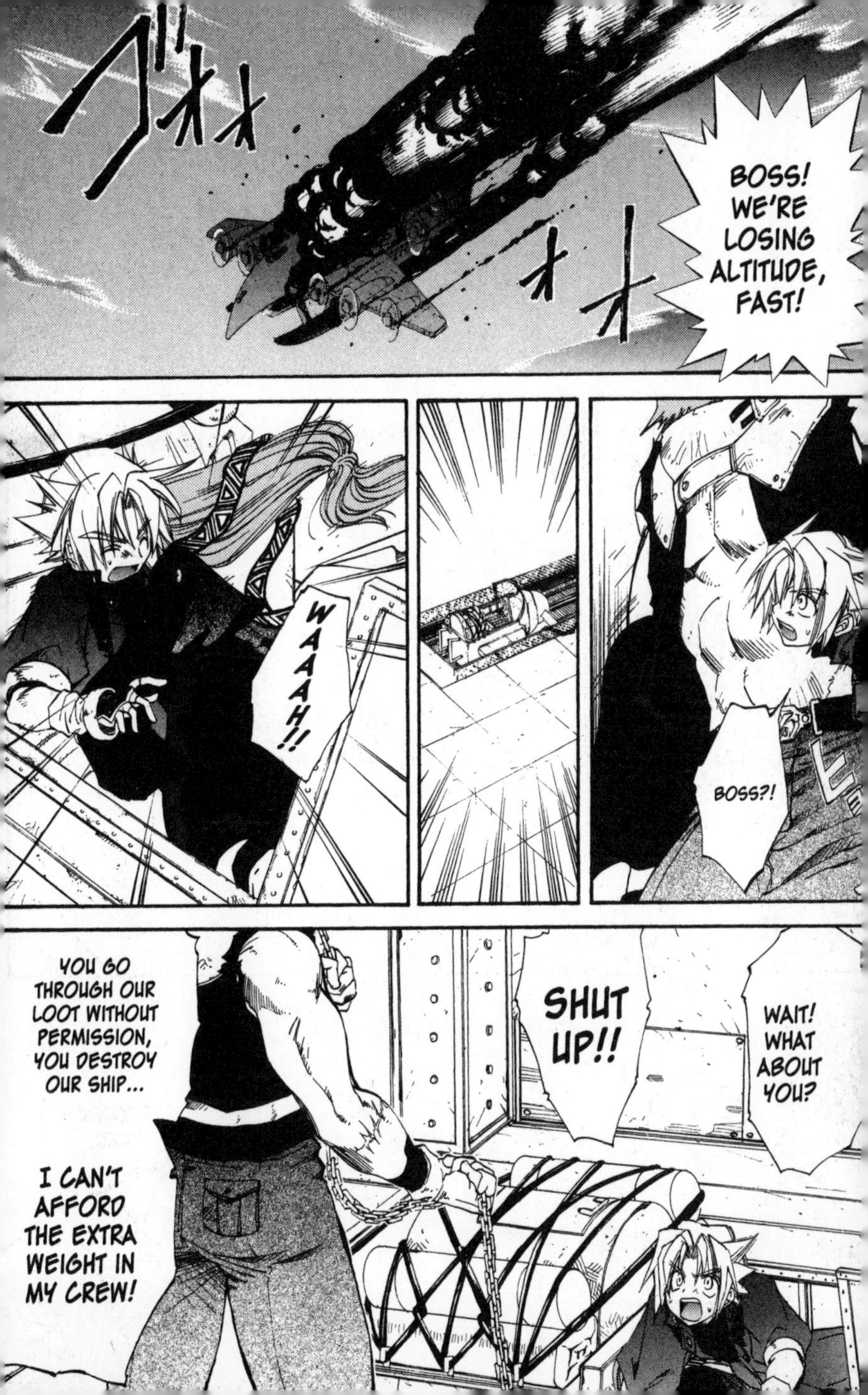
BOSS! WE'RE LOSING ALTITUDE, FAST!
BOSS?!
WAAAAH!!
WAIT! WHAT ABOUT YOU?
SHUT UP!!
YOU GO THROUGH OUR LOOT WITHOUT PERMISSION, YOU DESTROY OUR SHIP...
I CAN'T AFFORD THE EXTRA WEIGHT IN MY CREW!

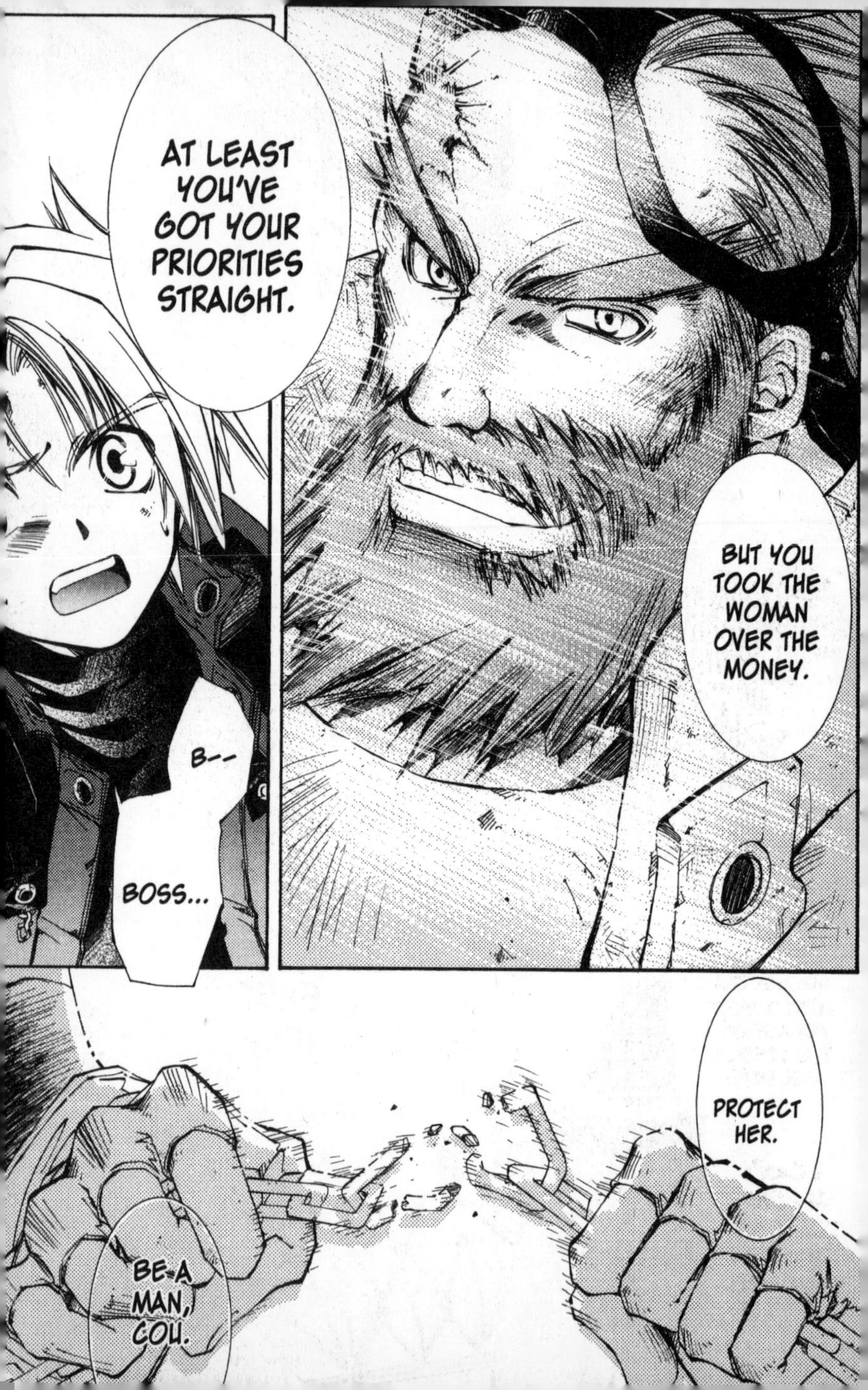
AT LEAST YOU'VE GOT YOUR PRIORITIES STRAIGHT.
BUT YOU TOOK THE WOMAN OVER THE MONEY.
B--
BOSS...
PROTECT HER.
BE A MAN, COU.

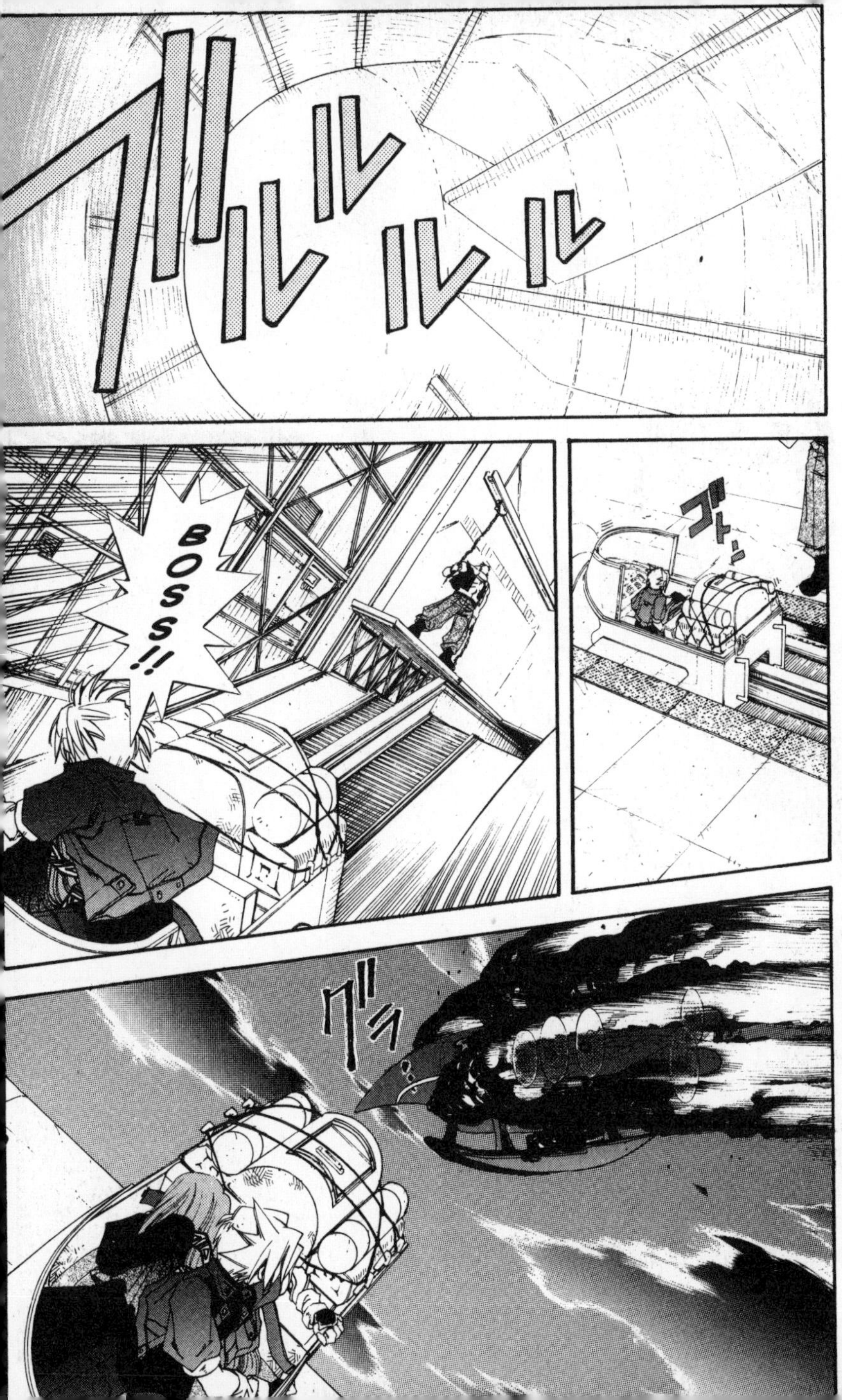
フルルルルル
ゴトッ
BOSS!!
グラ

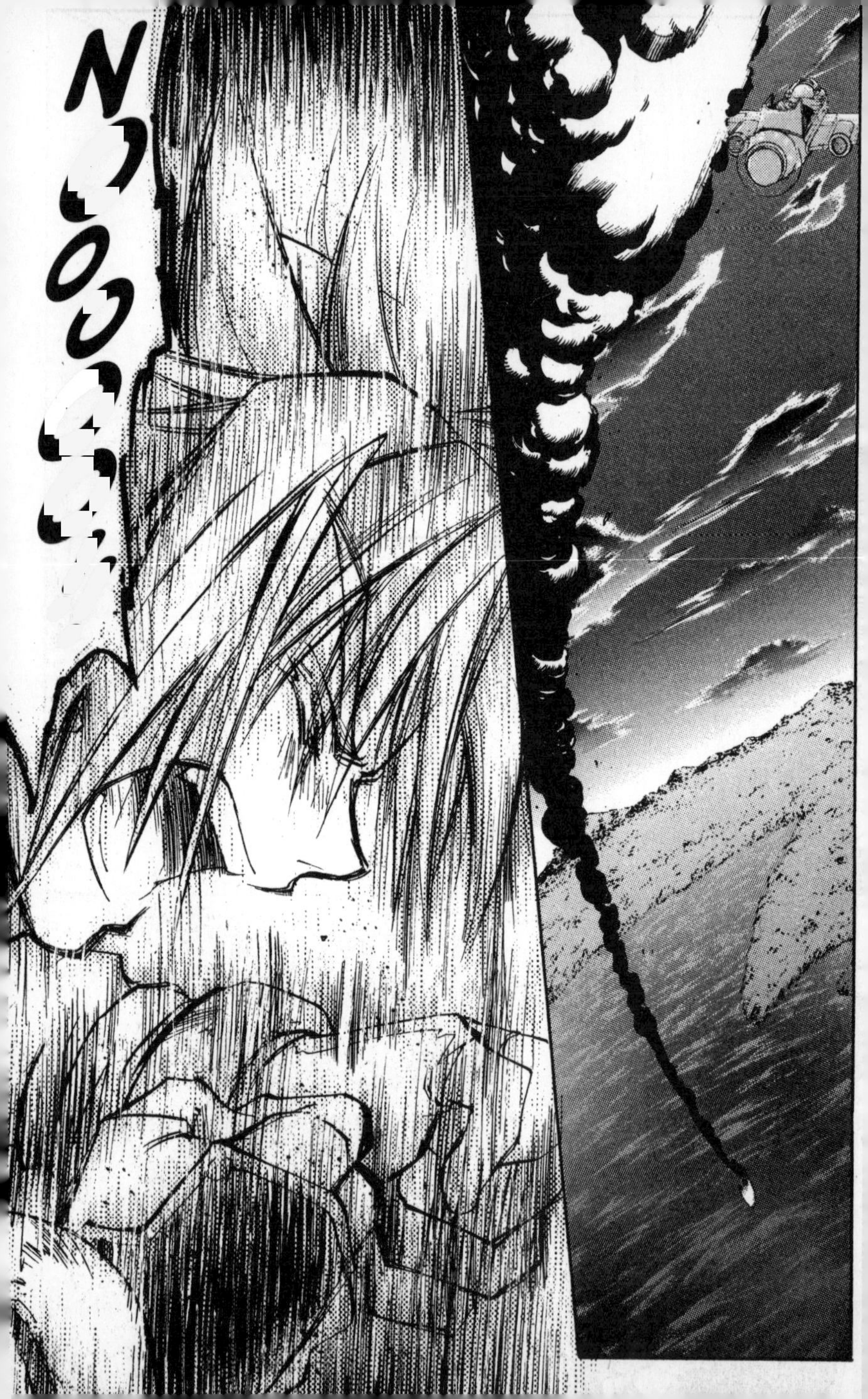
NOOOOO

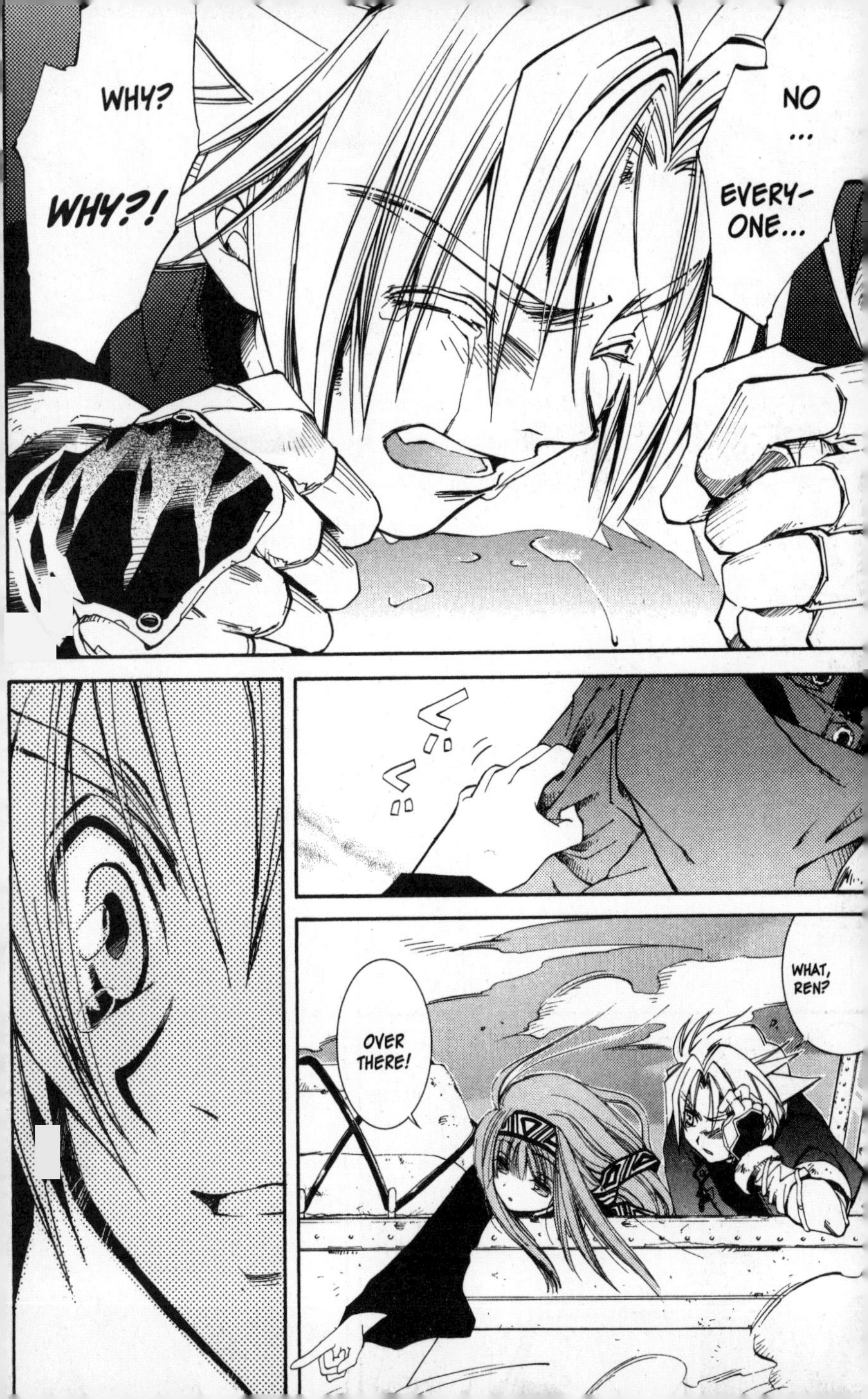
NO ... EVERY-ONE...
WHY?
WHY?!
WHAT, REN?
OVER THERE!

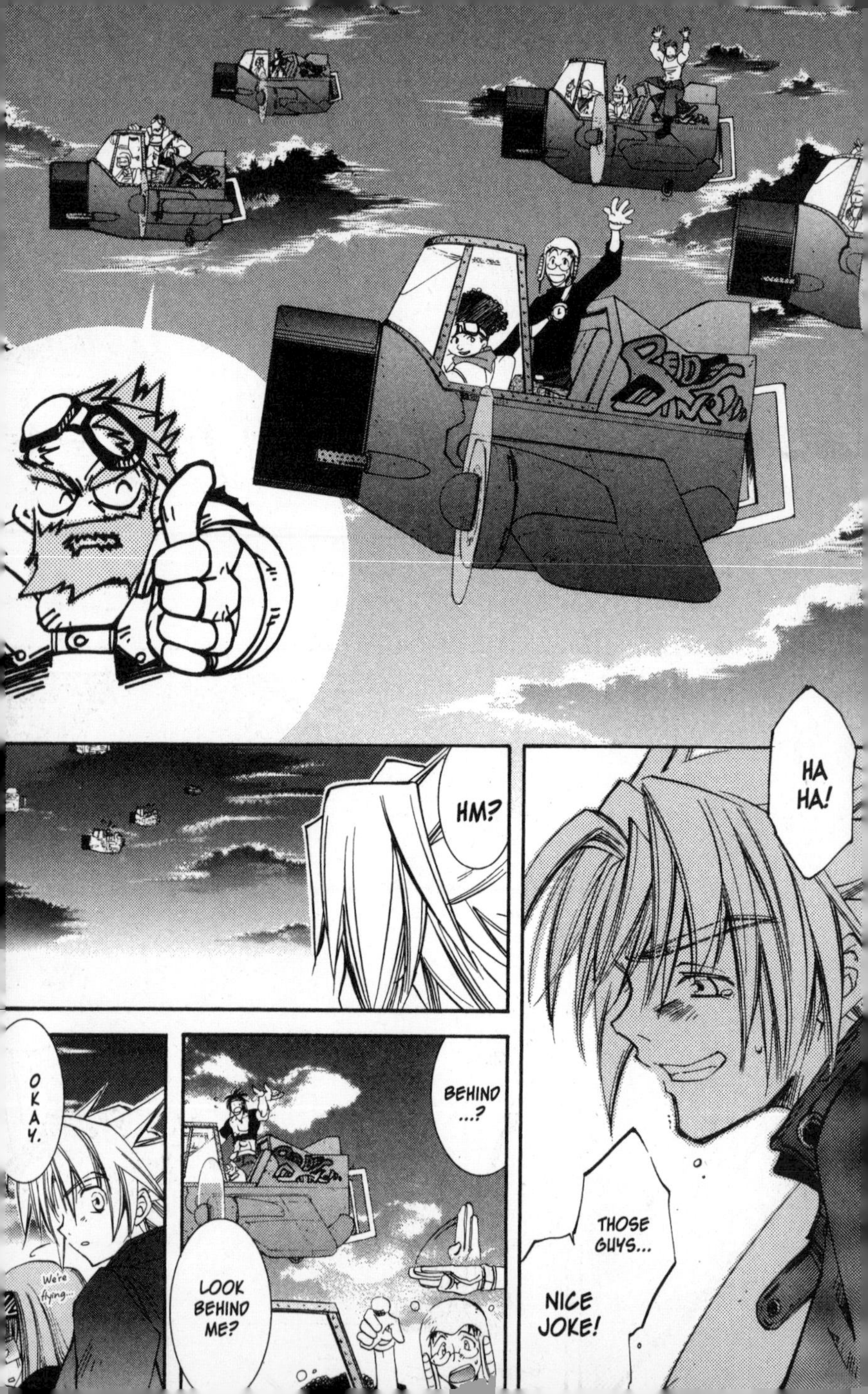
HA HA!
THOSE GUYS...
NICE JOKE!
HM?
BEHIND ...?
LOOK BEHIND ME?
OKAY.
We're flying...

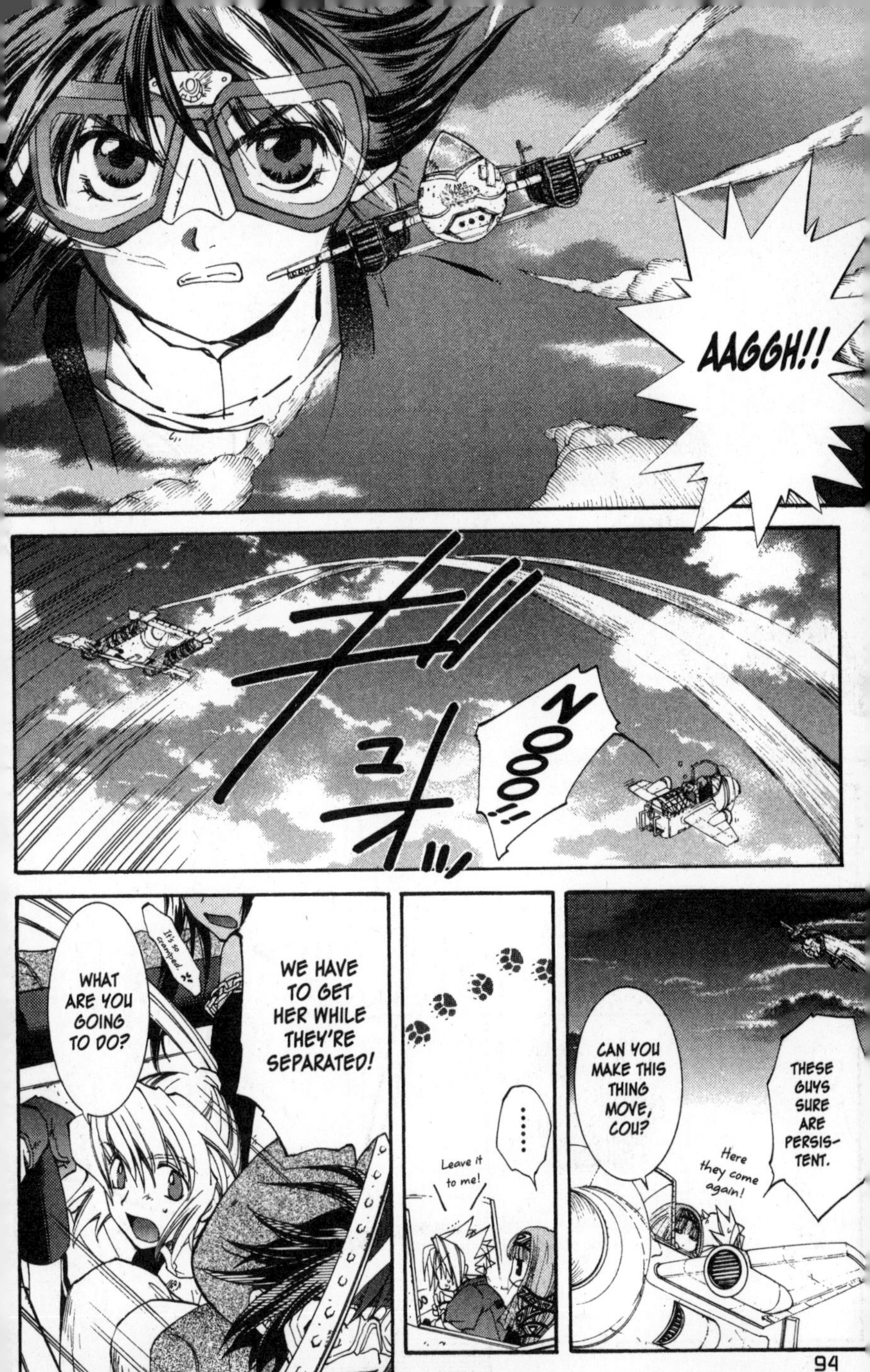
AAGGH!!
NOOOO!!
THESE GUYS SURE ARE PERSIS-TENT.
Here they come again!
CAN YOU MAKE THIS THING MOVE, COU?
......
Leave it to me!
WE HAVE TO GET HER WHILE THEY'RE SEPARATED!
It's so cramped.
WHAT ARE YOU GOING TO DO?

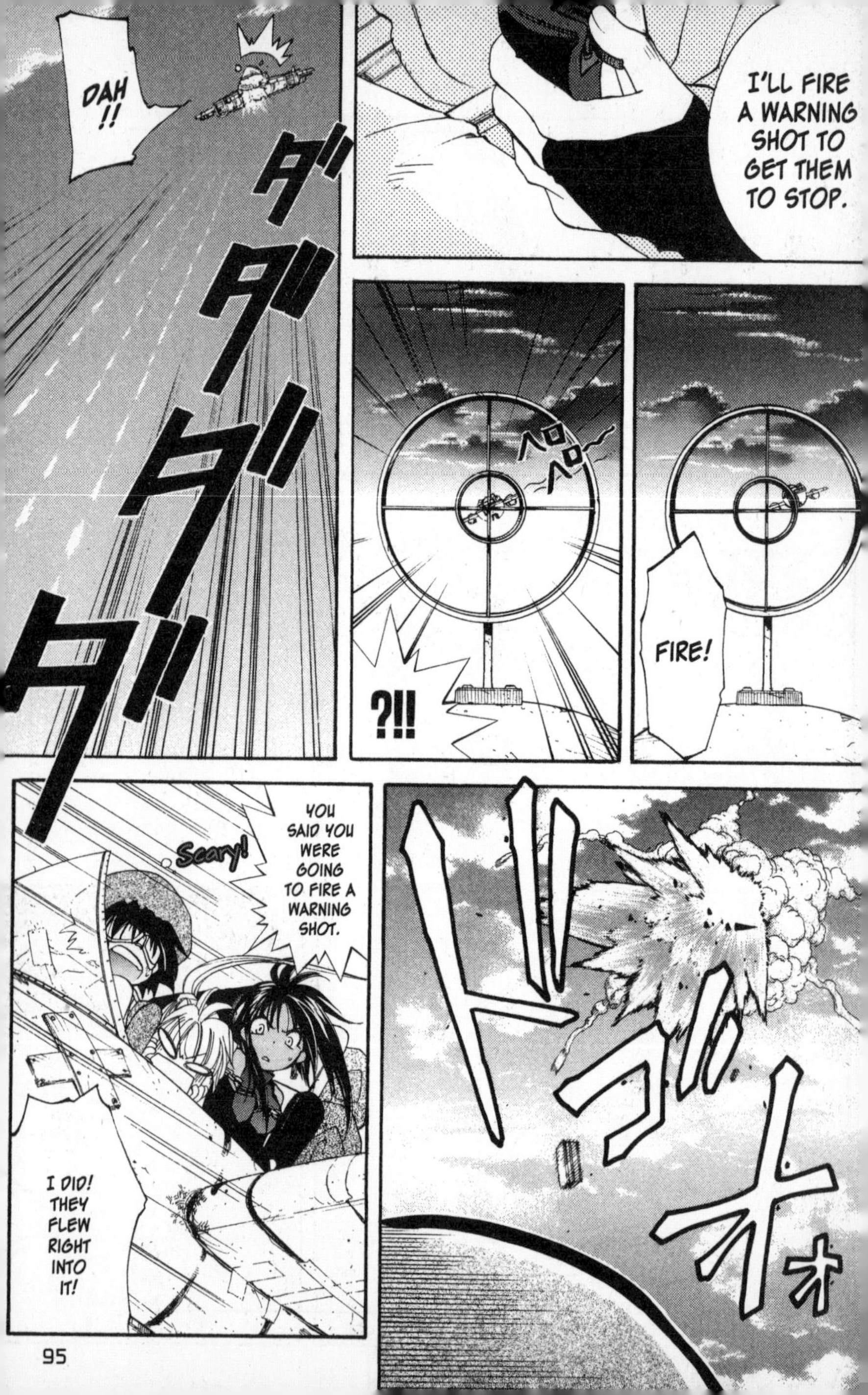
I'LL FIRE A WARNING SHOT TO GET THEM TO STOP.
FIRE!
?!!
DAH !!
YOU SAID YOU WERE GOING TO FIRE A WARNING SHOT.
Scary!
I DID! THEY FLEW RIGHT INTO IT!

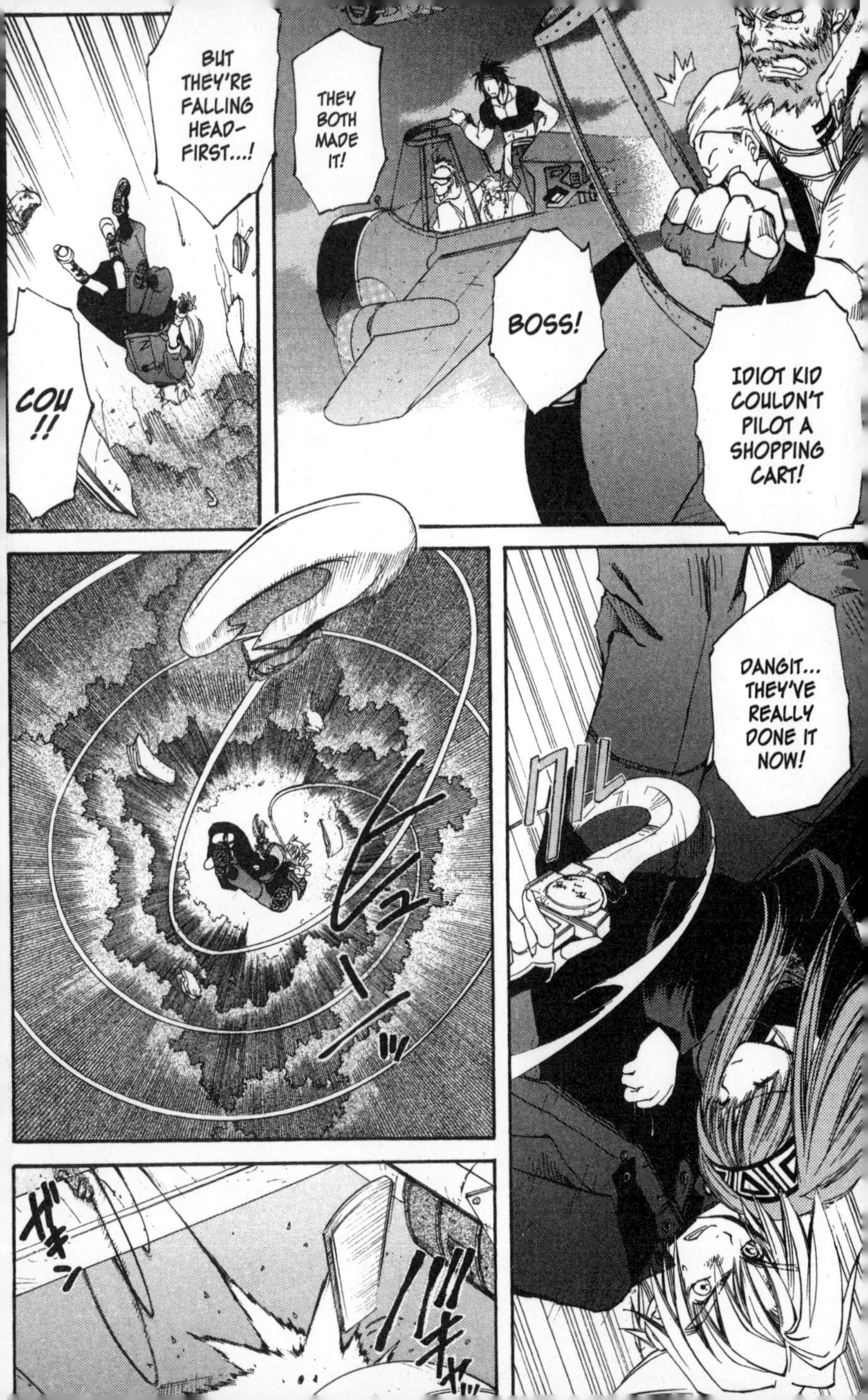
BOSS!
IDIOT KID COULDN'T PILOT A SHOPPING CART!
THEY BOTH MADE IT!
BUT THEY'RE FALLING HEAD-FIRST...!
COU !!
DANGIT... THEY'VE REALLY DONE IT NOW!

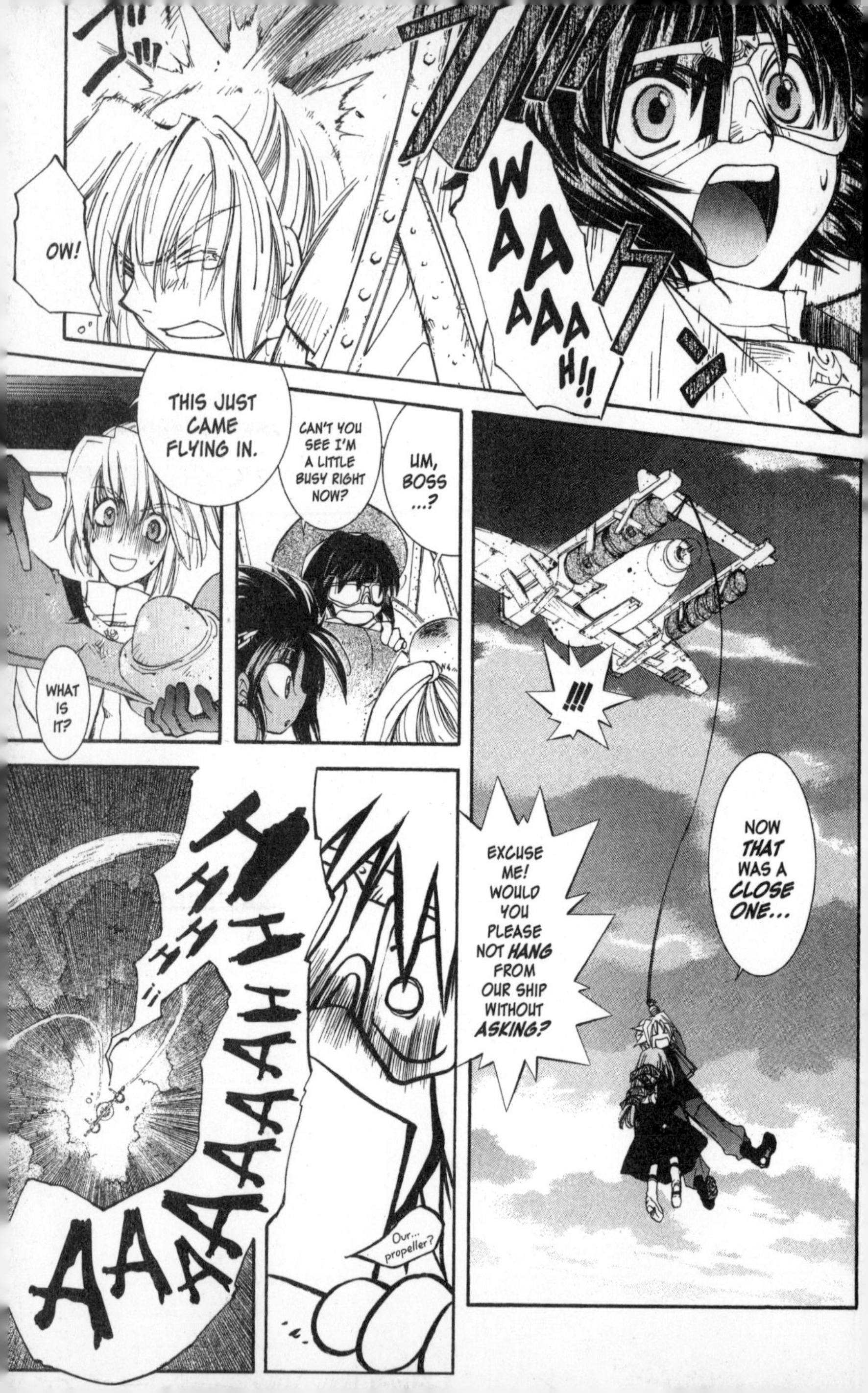
WAAAAAH!!
OW!
!!!
NOW THAT WAS A CLOSE ONE...
UM, BOSS ...?
CAN'T YOU SEE I'M A LITTLE BUSY RIGHT NOW?
THIS JUST CAME FLYING IN.
WHAT IS IT?
EXCUSE ME! WOULD YOU PLEASE NOT HANG FROM OUR SHIP WITHOUT ASKING?
Our... propeller?
AAAAAAAAHHHH!!

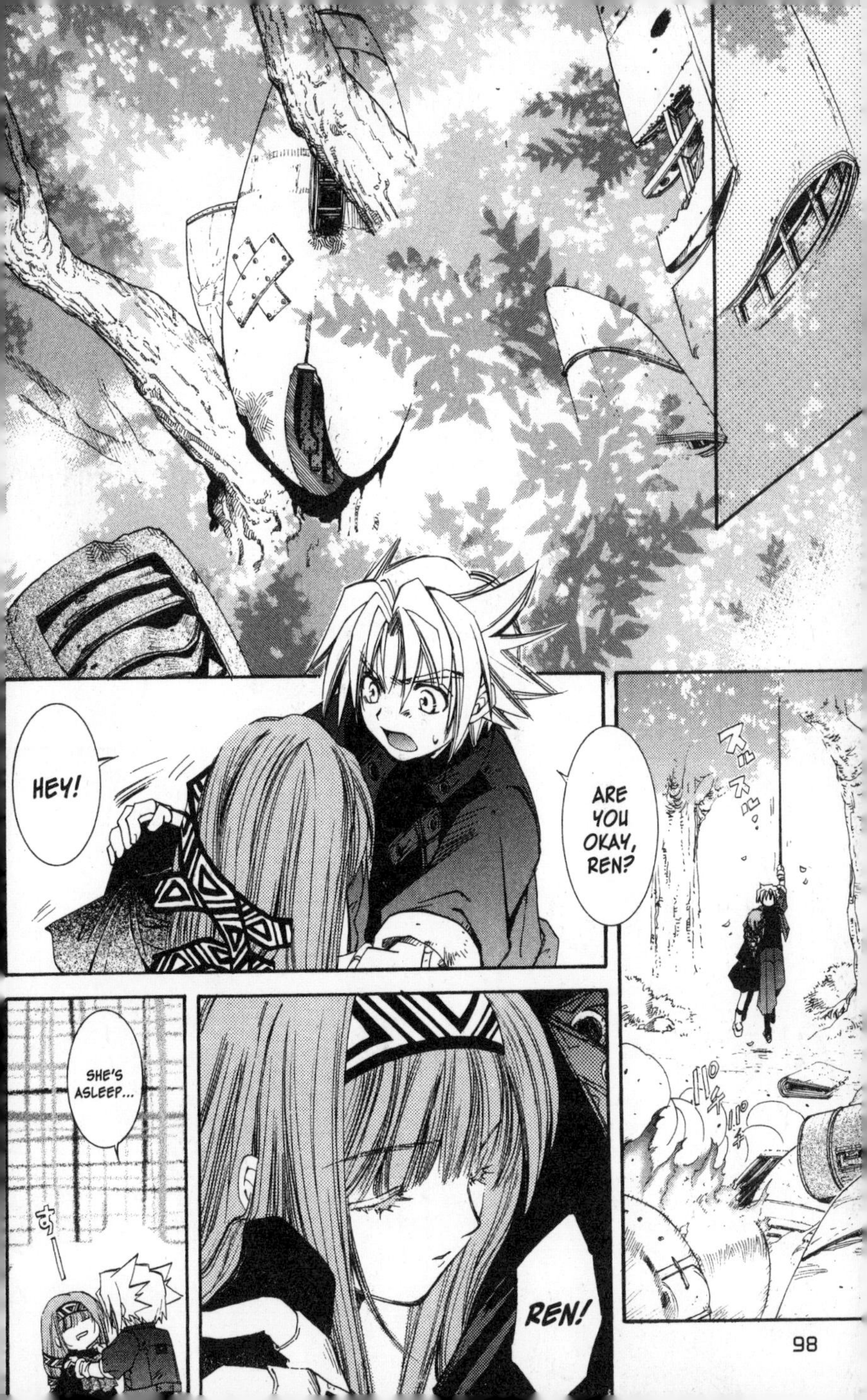
スルスル。
パチパチ
ARE YOU OKAY, REN?
HEY!
REN!
SHE'S ASLEEP...
すー

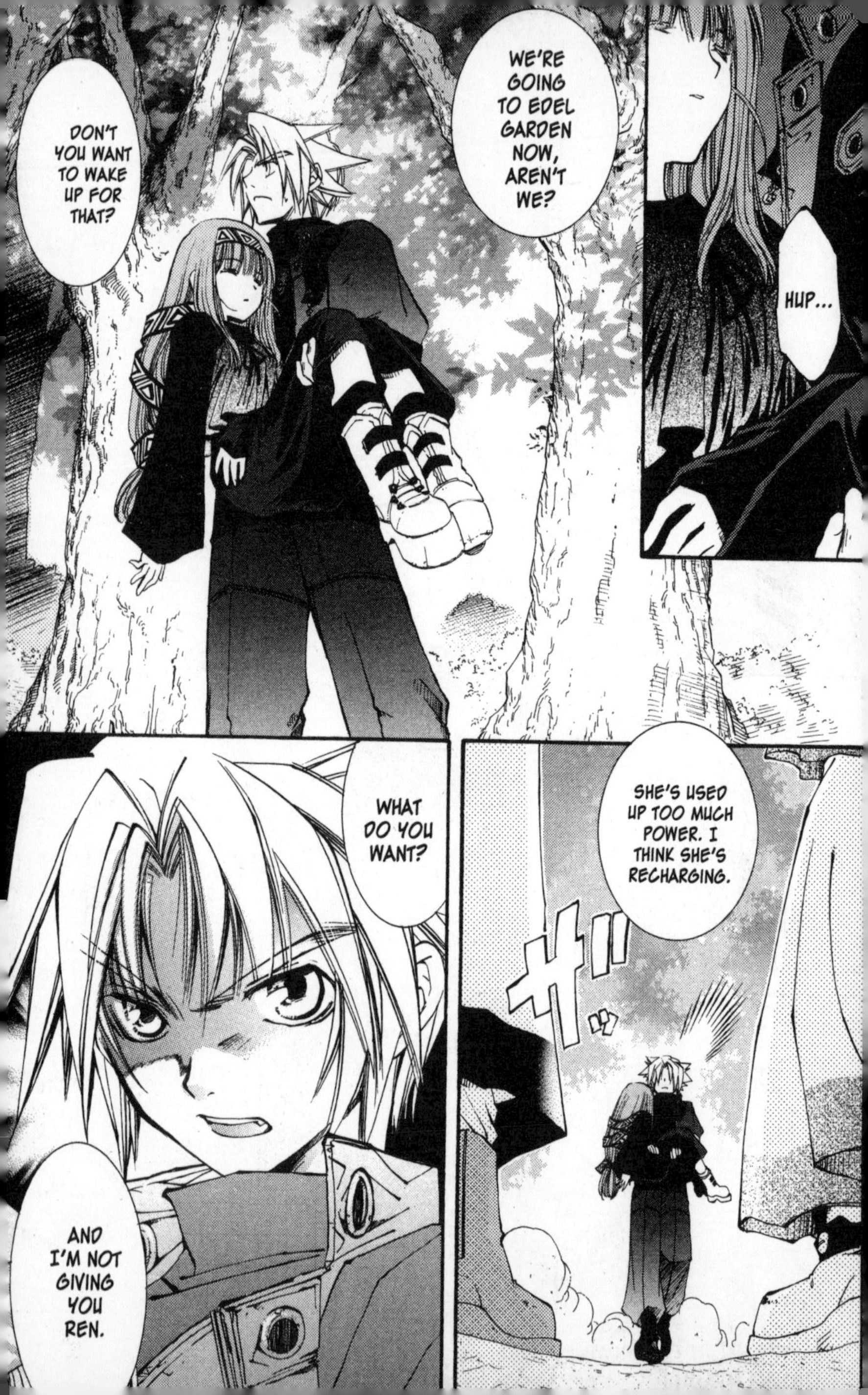
HUP...
WE'RE GOING TO EDEL GARDEN NOW, AREN'T WE?
DON'T YOU WANT TO WAKE UP FOR THAT?
SHE'S USED UP TOO MUCH POWER. I THINK SHE'S RECHARGING.
WHAT DO YOU WANT?
AND I'M NOT GIVING YOU REN.

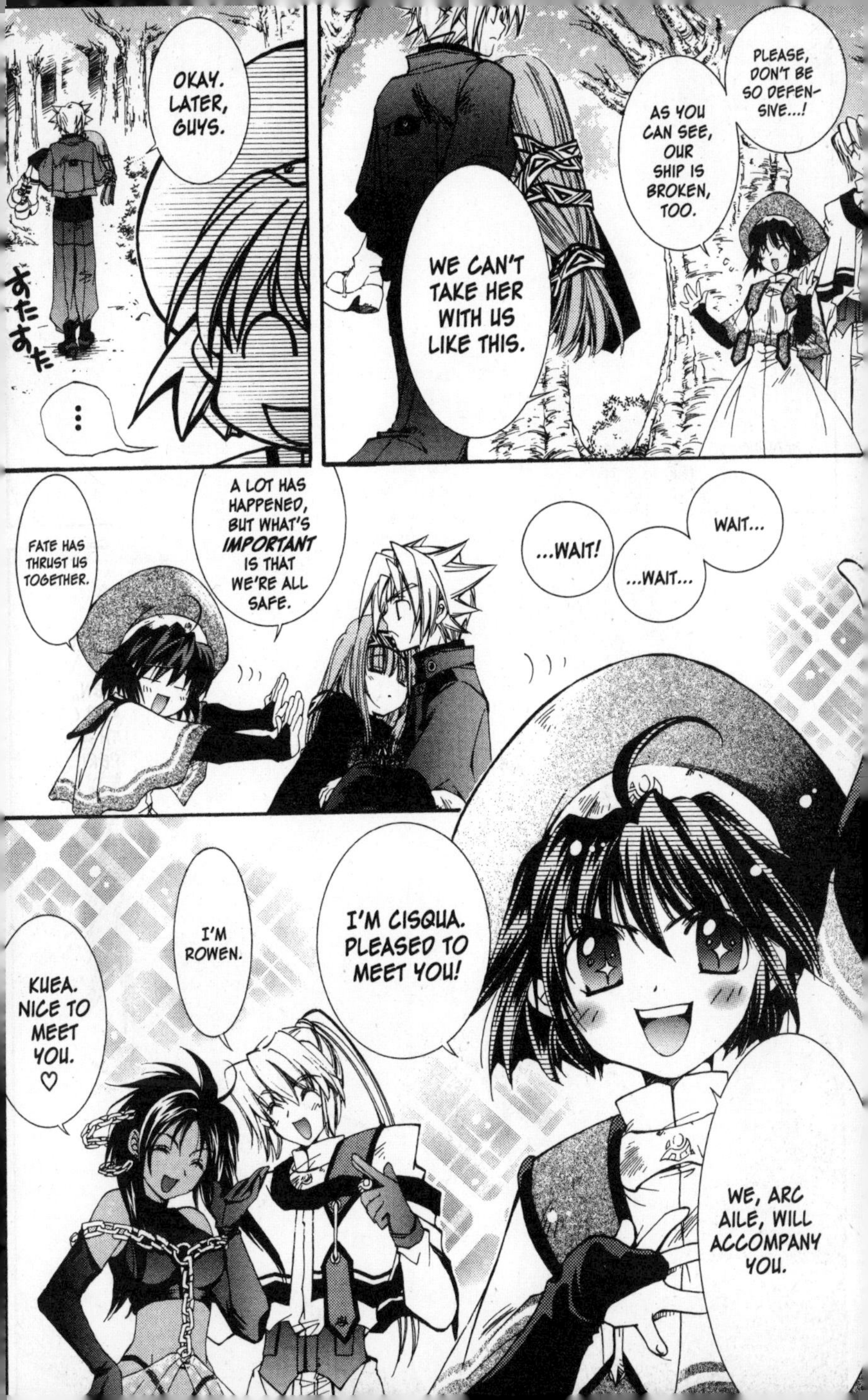
PLEASE, DON'T BE SO DEFENSIVE...!
AS YOU CAN SEE, OUR SHIP IS BROKEN, TOO.
WE CAN'T TAKE HER WITH US LIKE THIS.
OKAY. LATER, GUYS.
すたすた
...
WAIT...
...WAIT...
...WAIT!
A LOT HAS HAPPENED, BUT WHAT'S *IMPORTANT* IS THAT WE'RE ALL SAFE.
FATE HAS THRUST US TOGETHER.
WE, ARC AILE, WILL ACCOMPANY YOU.
I'M CISQUA. PLEASED TO MEET YOU!
I'M ROWEN.
KUEA. NICE TO MEET YOU. ♡

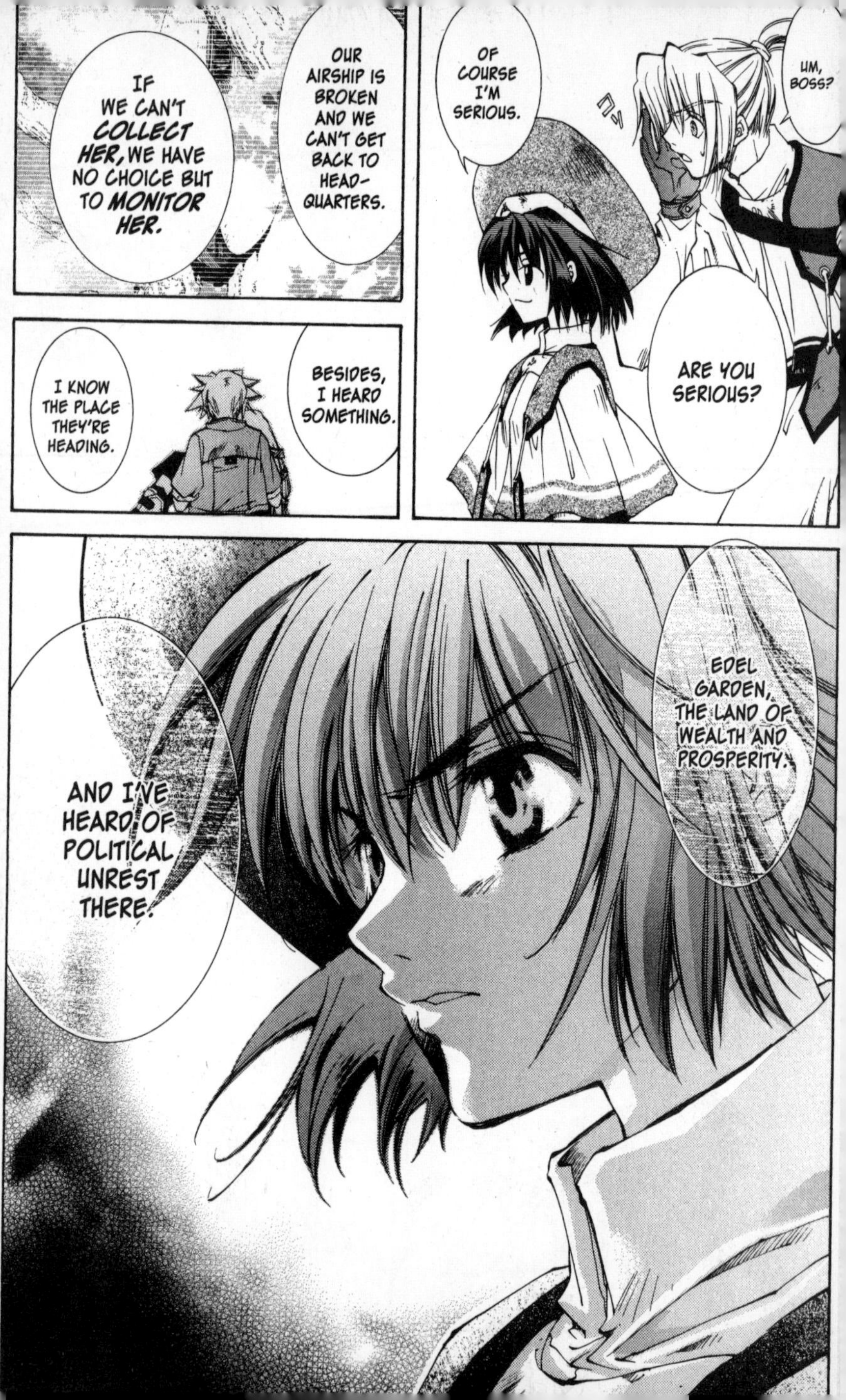
UM, BOSS?
ARE YOU SERIOUS?
OF COURSE I'M SERIOUS.
OUR AIRSHIP IS BROKEN AND WE CAN'T GET BACK TO HEAD-QUARTERS.
IF WE CAN'T COLLECT HER, WE HAVE NO CHOICE BUT TO MONITOR HER.
BESIDES, I HEARD SOMETHING.
I KNOW THE PLACE THEY'RE HEADING.
EDEL GARDEN, THE LAND OF WEALTH AND PROSPERITY.
AND I'VE HEARD OF POLITICAL UNREST THERE.

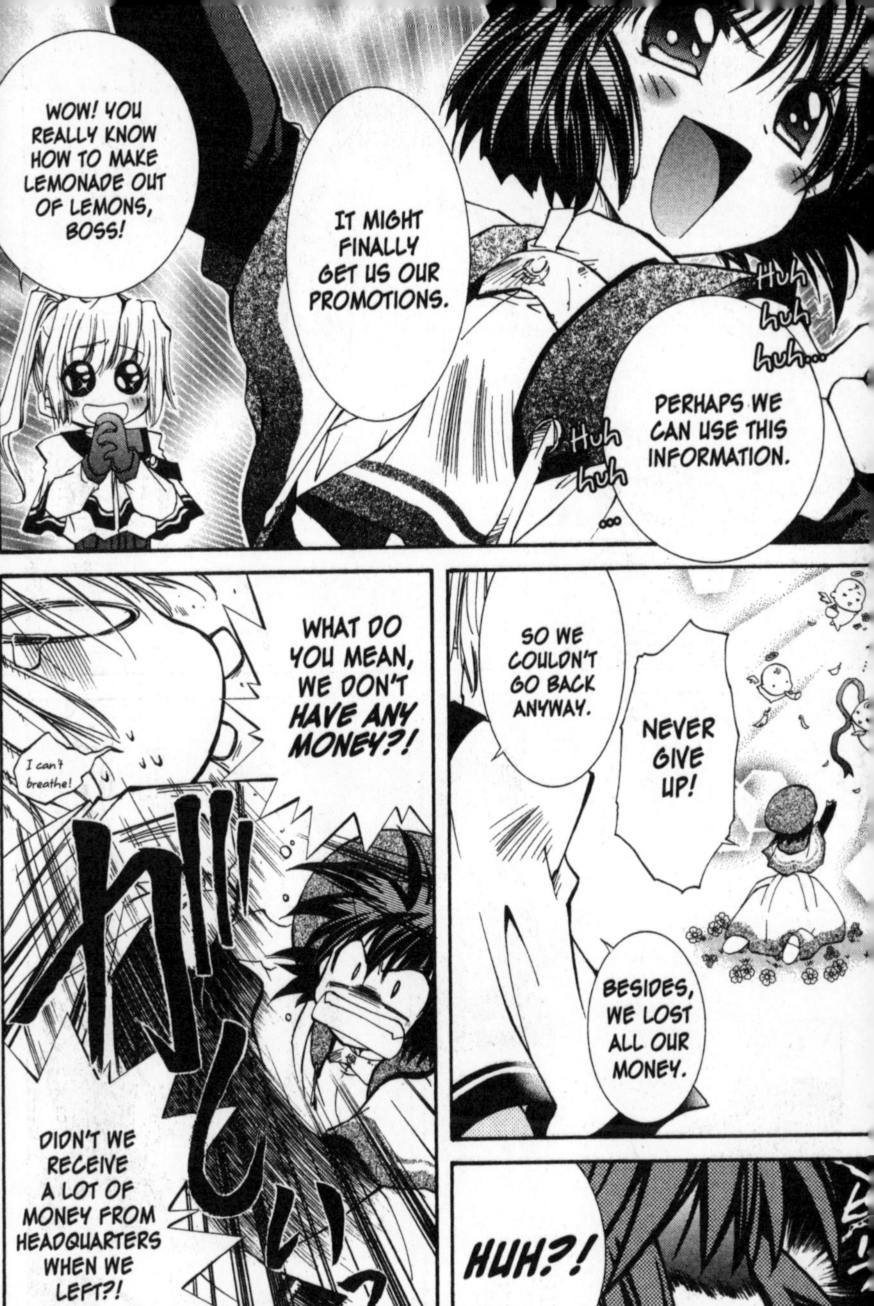
Huh huh huh...
PERHAPS WE CAN USE THIS INFORMATION.
Huh huh ...
IT MIGHT FINALLY GET US OUR PROMOTIONS.
WOW! YOU REALLY KNOW HOW TO MAKE LEMONADE OUT OF LEMONS, BOSS!
NEVER GIVE UP!
SO WE COULDN'T GO BACK ANYWAY.
BESIDES, WE LOST ALL OUR MONEY.
HUH?!
WHAT DO YOU MEAN, WE DON'T HAVE ANY MONEY?!
I can't breathe!
DIDN'T WE RECEIVE A LOT OF MONEY FROM HEADQUARTERS WHEN WE LEFT?!

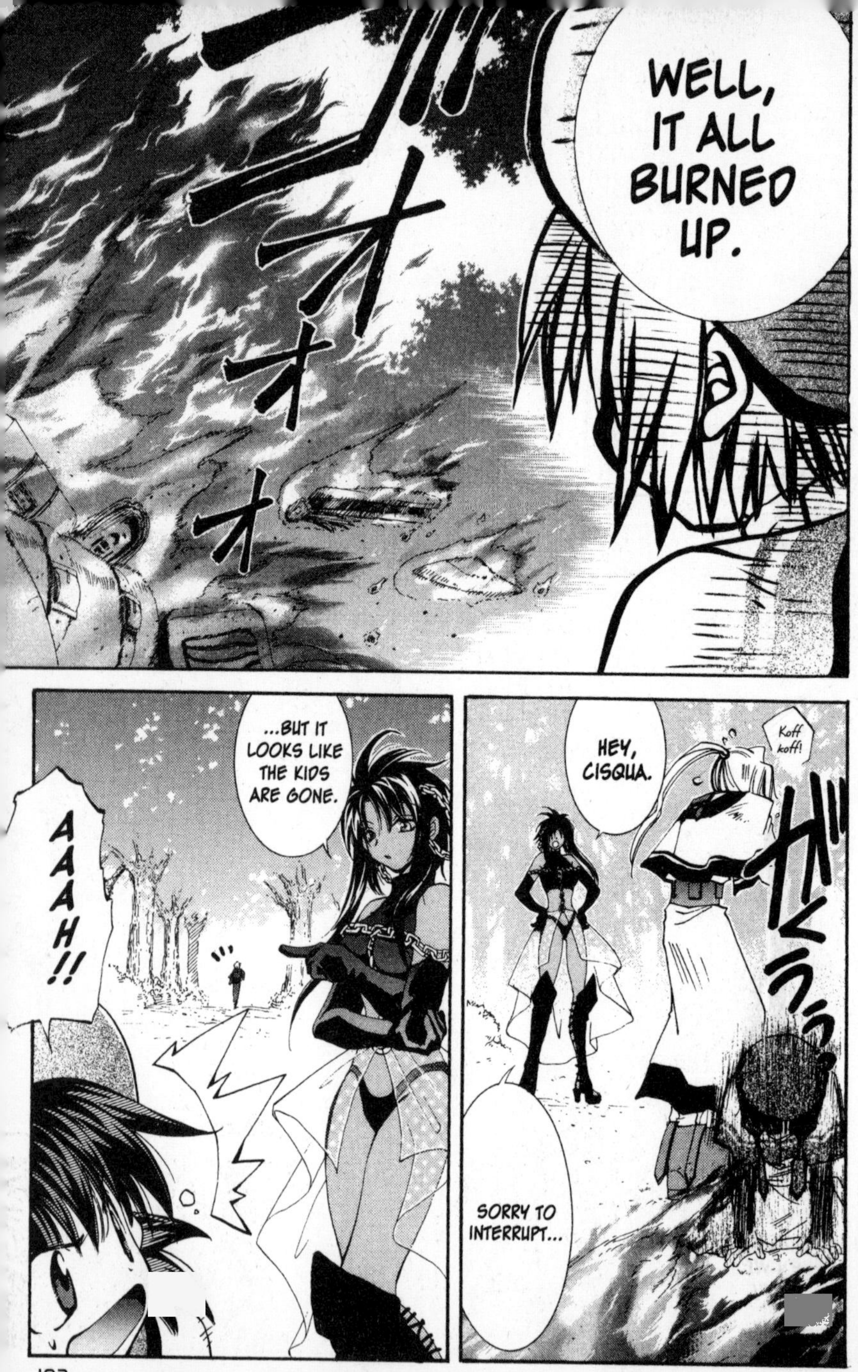
WELL, IT ALL BURNED UP.
HEY, CISQUA.
Koff koff!
SORRY TO INTERRUPT...
...BUT IT LOOKS LIKE THE KIDS ARE GONE.
AAAAH!!

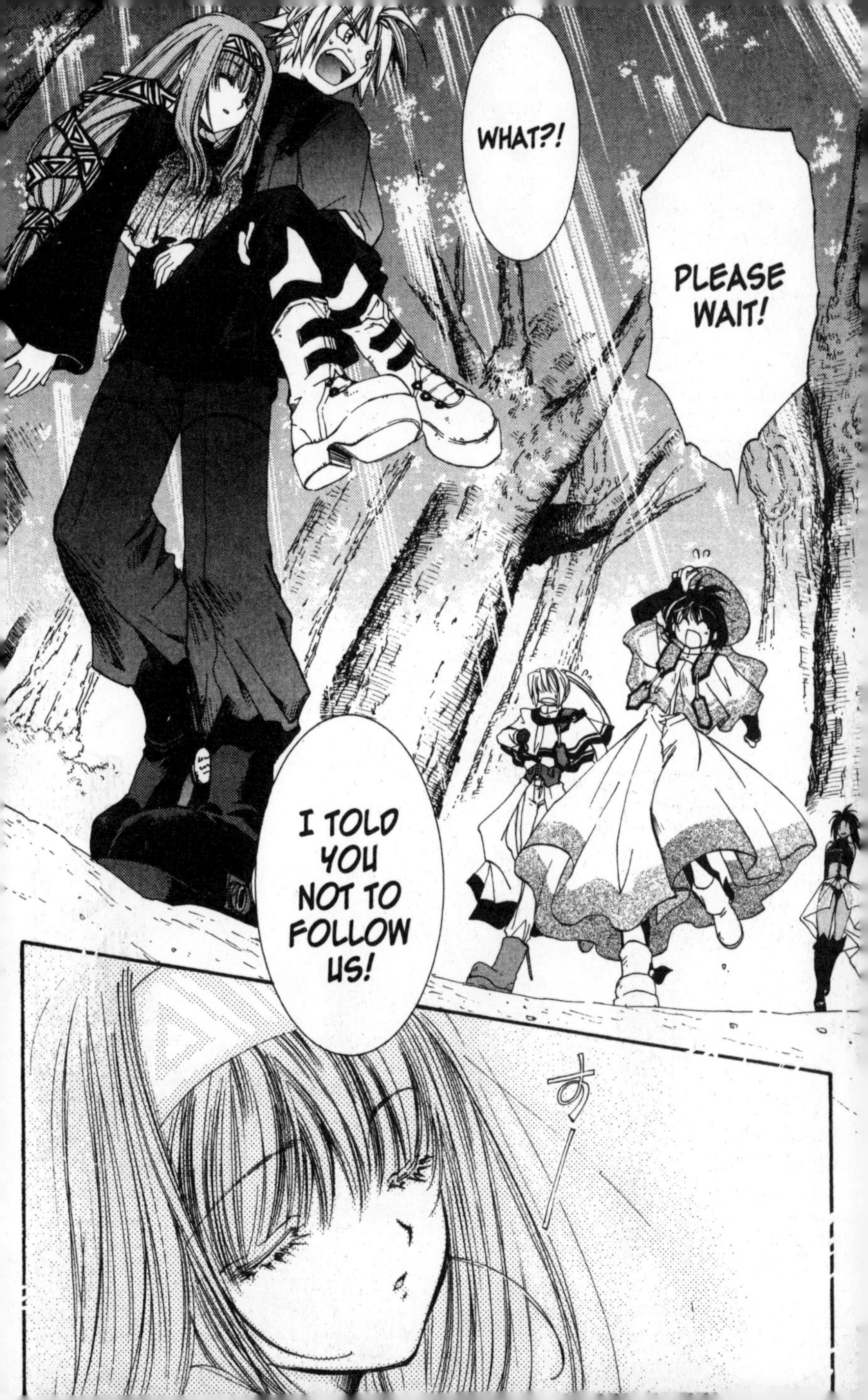
PLEASE WAIT!
WHAT?!
I TOLD YOU NOT TO FOLLOW US!
あ

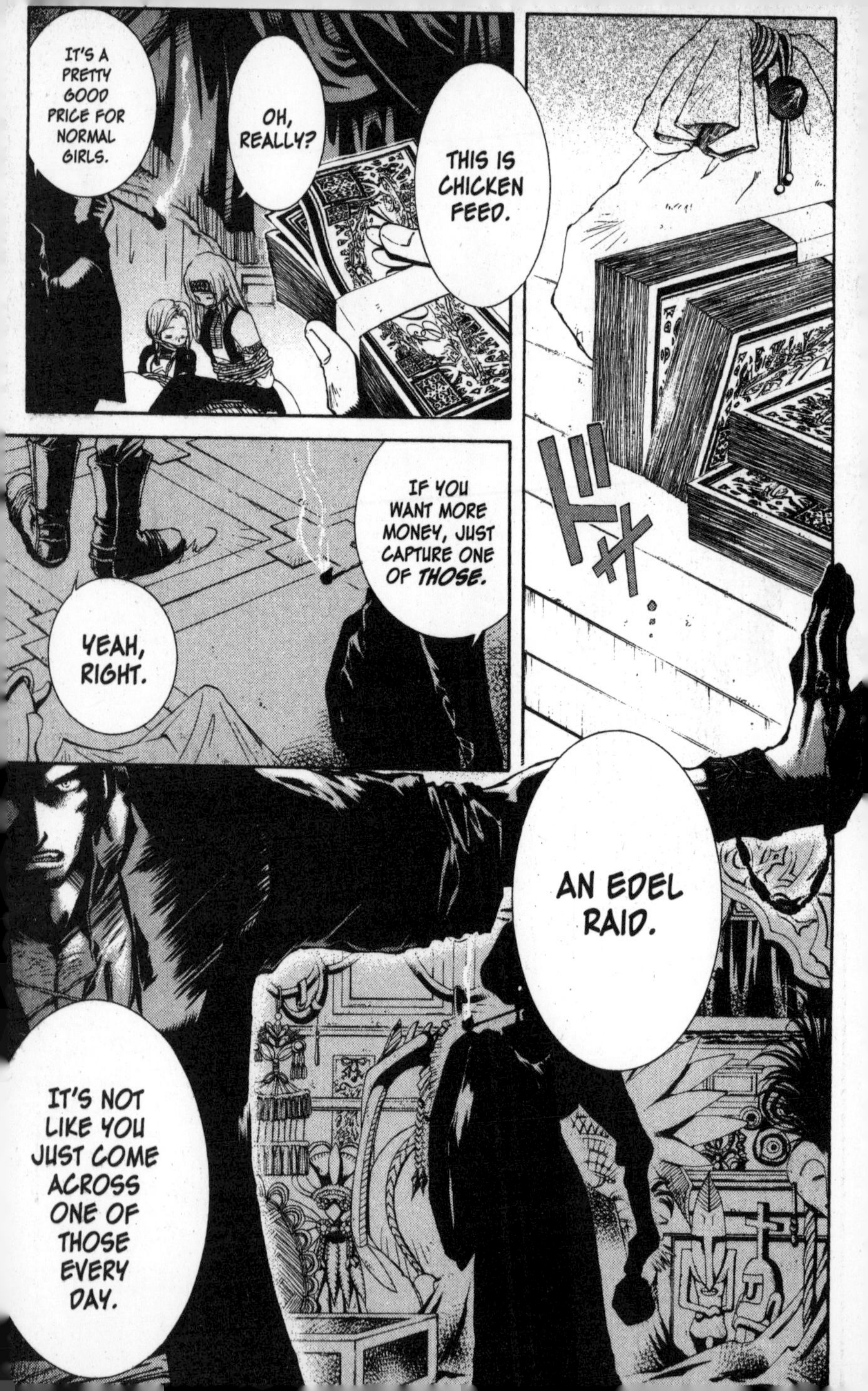
ドッ
THIS IS CHICKEN FEED.
OH, REALLY?
IT'S A PRETTY GOOD PRICE FOR NORMAL GIRLS.
IF YOU WANT MORE MONEY, JUST CAPTURE ONE OF *THOSE.*
YEAH, RIGHT.
AN EDEL RAID.
IT'S NOT LIKE YOU JUST COME ACROSS ONE OF THOSE EVERY DAY.

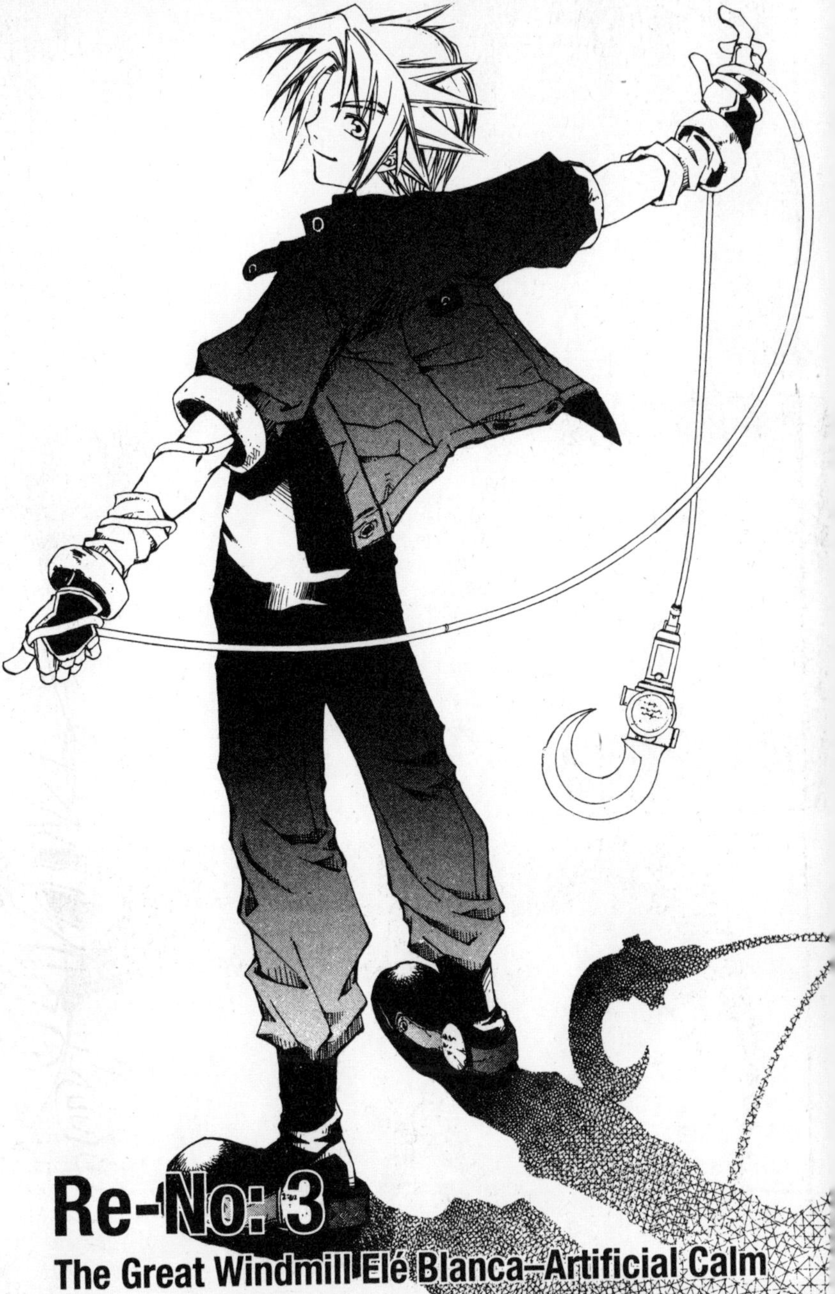

Re-No: 3

The Great Windmill Elé Blanca–Artificial Calm

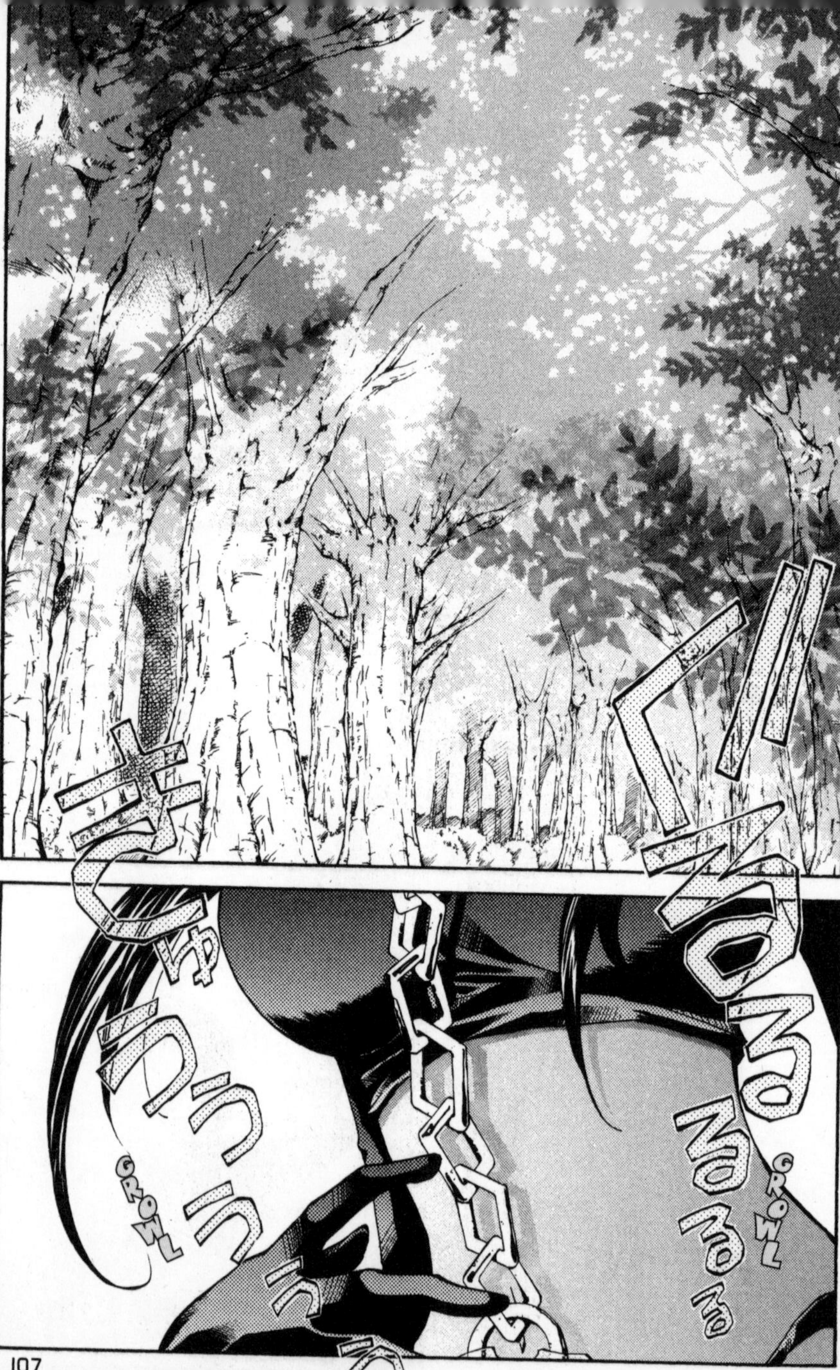
GROWL
GROWL

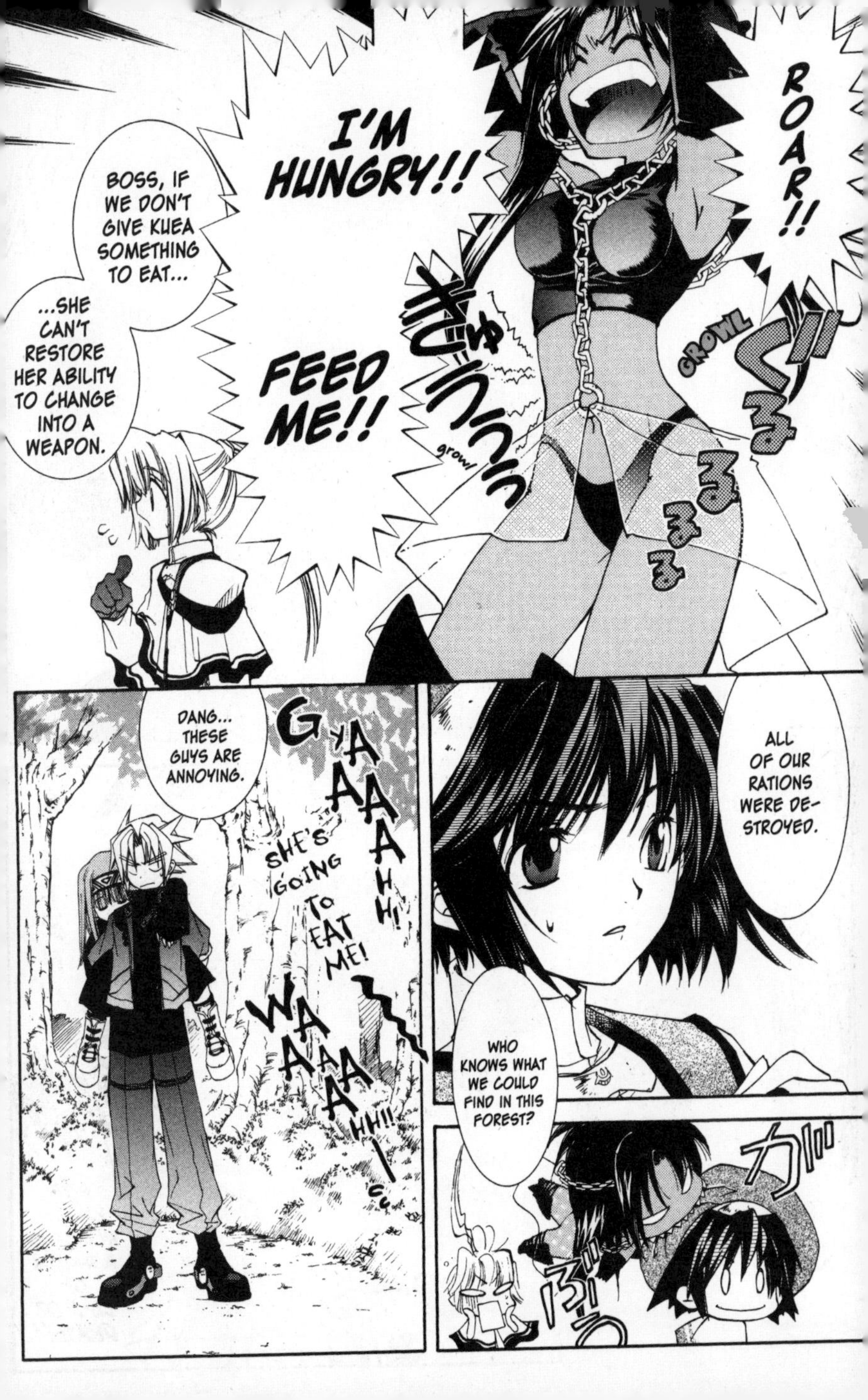
ROAR!!
I'M HUNGRY!!
FEED ME!!
growl
GROWL
BOSS, IF WE DON'T GIVE KUEA SOMETHING TO EAT...
...SHE CAN'T RESTORE HER ABILITY TO CHANGE INTO A WEAPON.
ALL OF OUR RATIONS WERE DE-STROYED.
WHO KNOWS WHAT WE COULD FIND IN THIS FOREST?
DANG... THESE GUYS ARE ANNOYING.
GYAAAAHH!
SHE'S GOING TO EAT ME!
WAAAAAHH!!

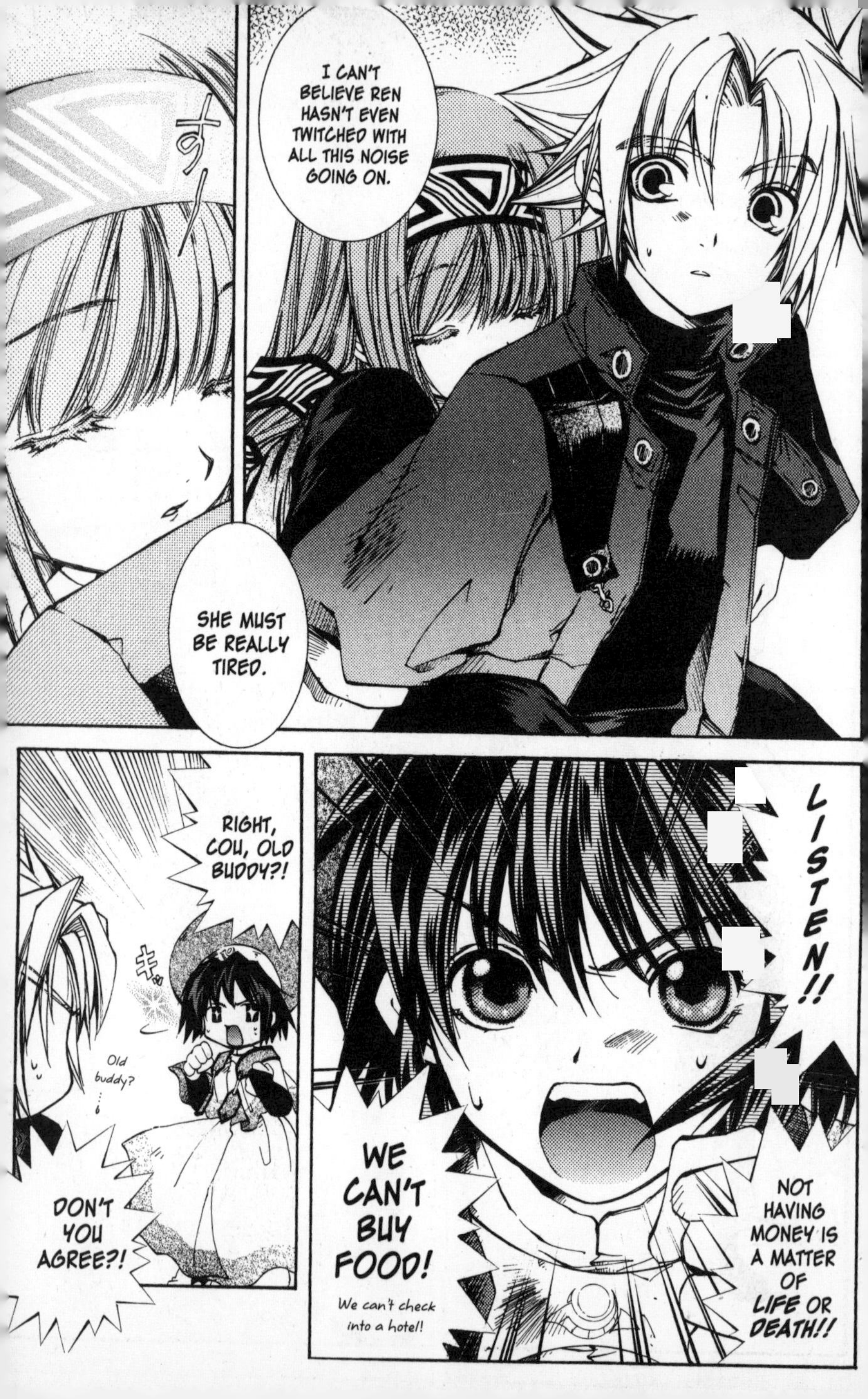
I CAN'T BELIEVE REN HASN'T EVEN TWITCHED WITH ALL THIS NOISE GOING ON.
SHE MUST BE REALLY TIRED.
すぅ
LISTEN!!
NOT HAVING MONEY IS A MATTER OF LIFE OR DEATH!!
WE CAN'T BUY FOOD!
We can't check into a hotel!
RIGHT, COU, OLD BUDDY?!
キッ
Old buddy?
DON'T YOU AGREE?!

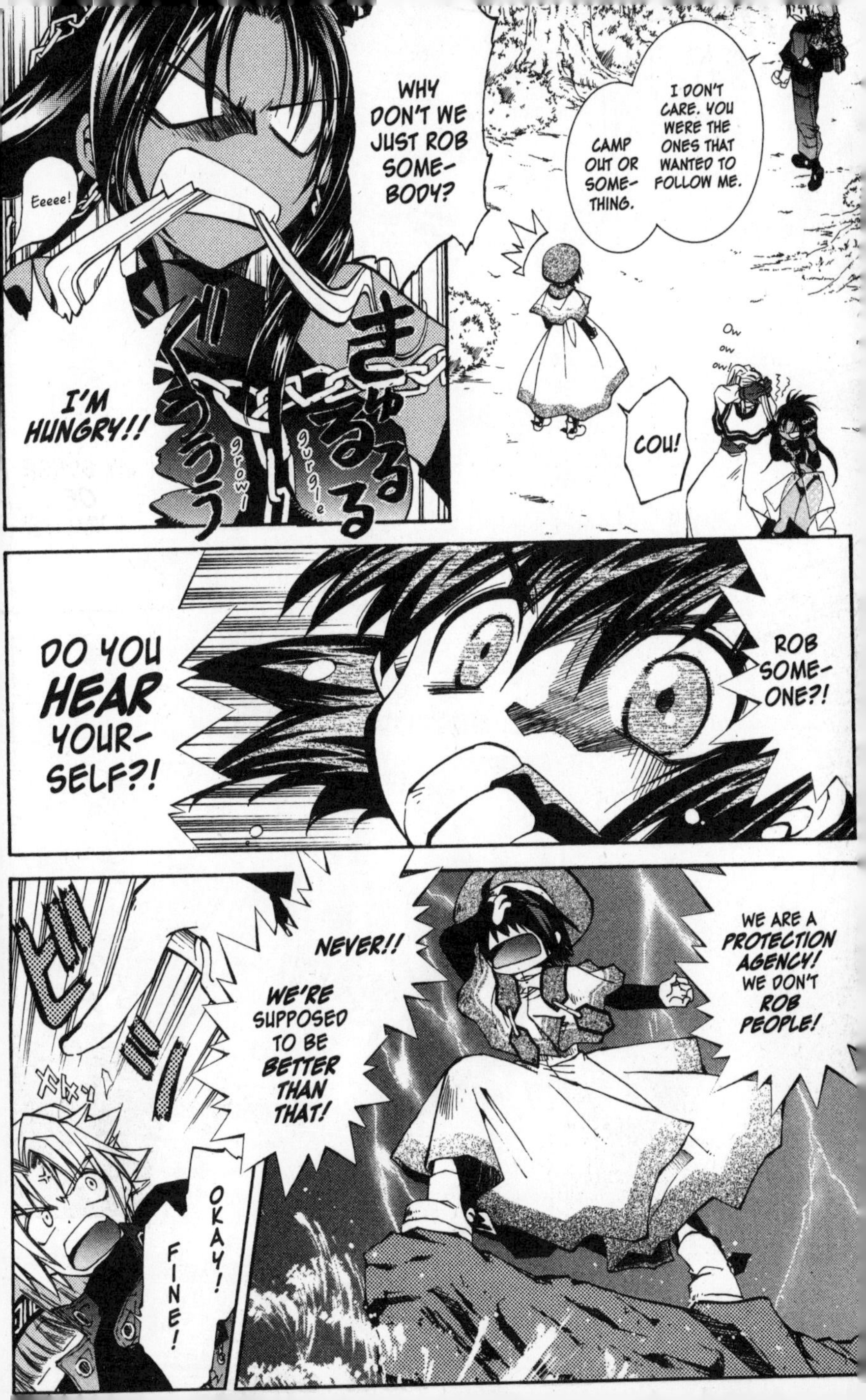
I DON'T CARE. YOU WERE THE ONES THAT WANTED TO FOLLOW ME.
CAMP OUT OR SOMETHING.
Ow ow ow!
COU!
WHY DON'T WE JUST ROB SOMEBODY?
Eeeee!
きゅるるる
gurgle
growl
I'M HUNGRY!!
ROB SOMEONE?!
DO YOU HEAR YOURSELF?!
WE ARE A PROTECTION AGENCY! WE DON'T ROB PEOPLE!
NEVER!!
WE'RE SUPPOSED TO BE BETTER THAN THAT!
OKAY! FINE!

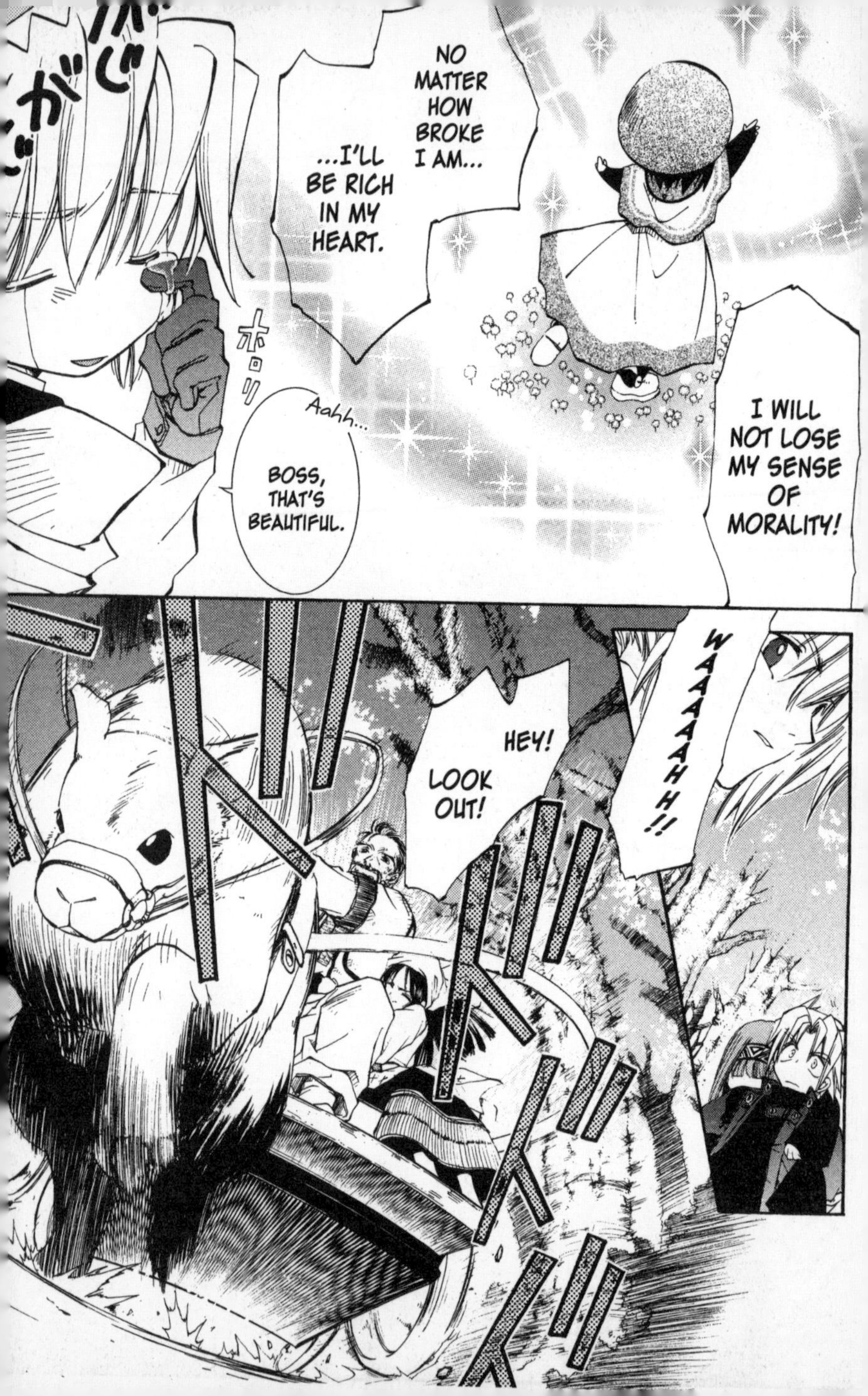

NO MATTER HOW BROKE I AM...
...I'LL BE RICH IN MY HEART.
I WILL NOT LOSE MY SENSE OF MORALITY!
Aahh...
BOSS, THAT'S BEAUTIFUL.
WAAAAAAHH!!
HEY!
LOOK OUT!

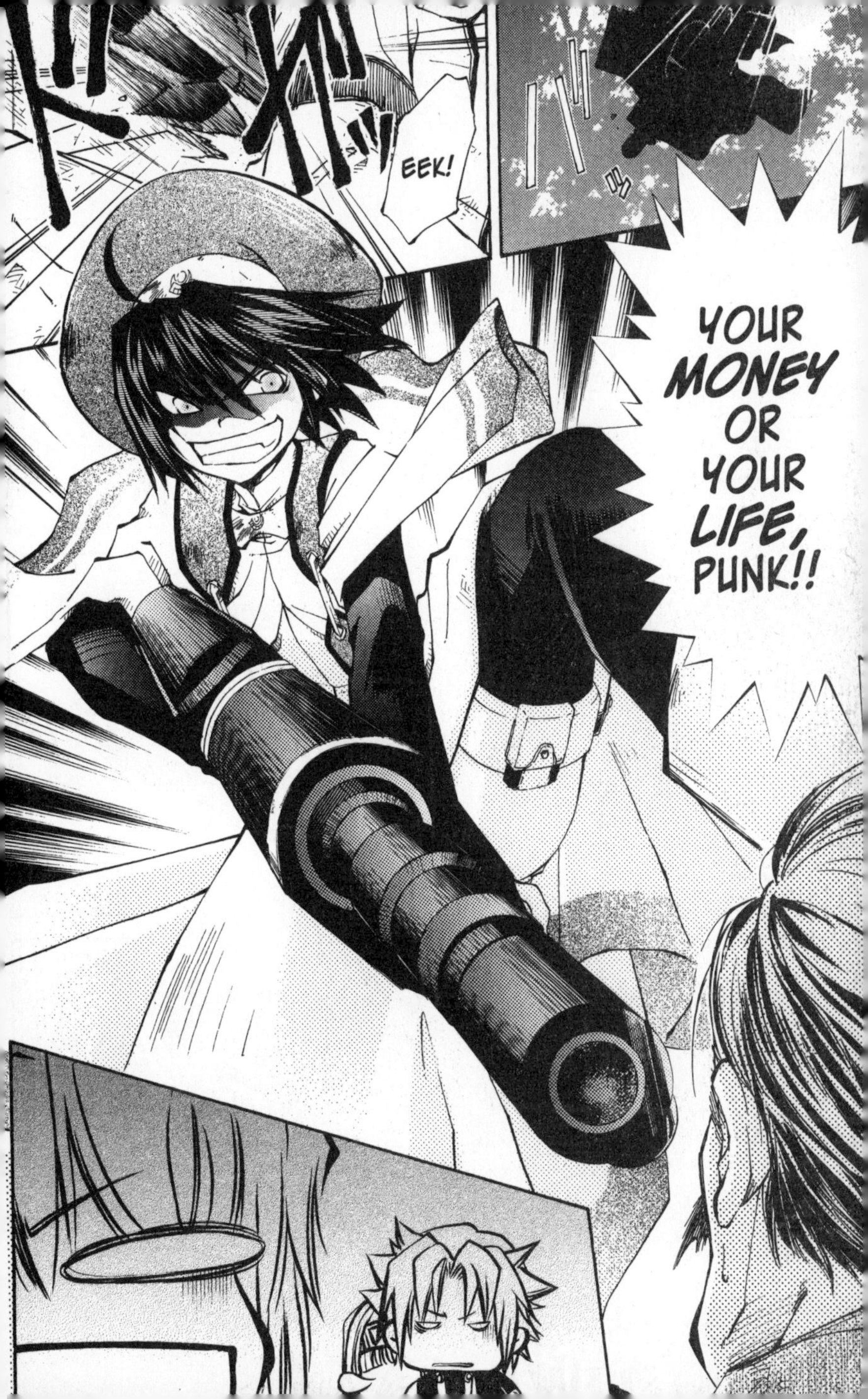
EEK!
YOUR MONEY OR YOUR LIFE, PUNK!!

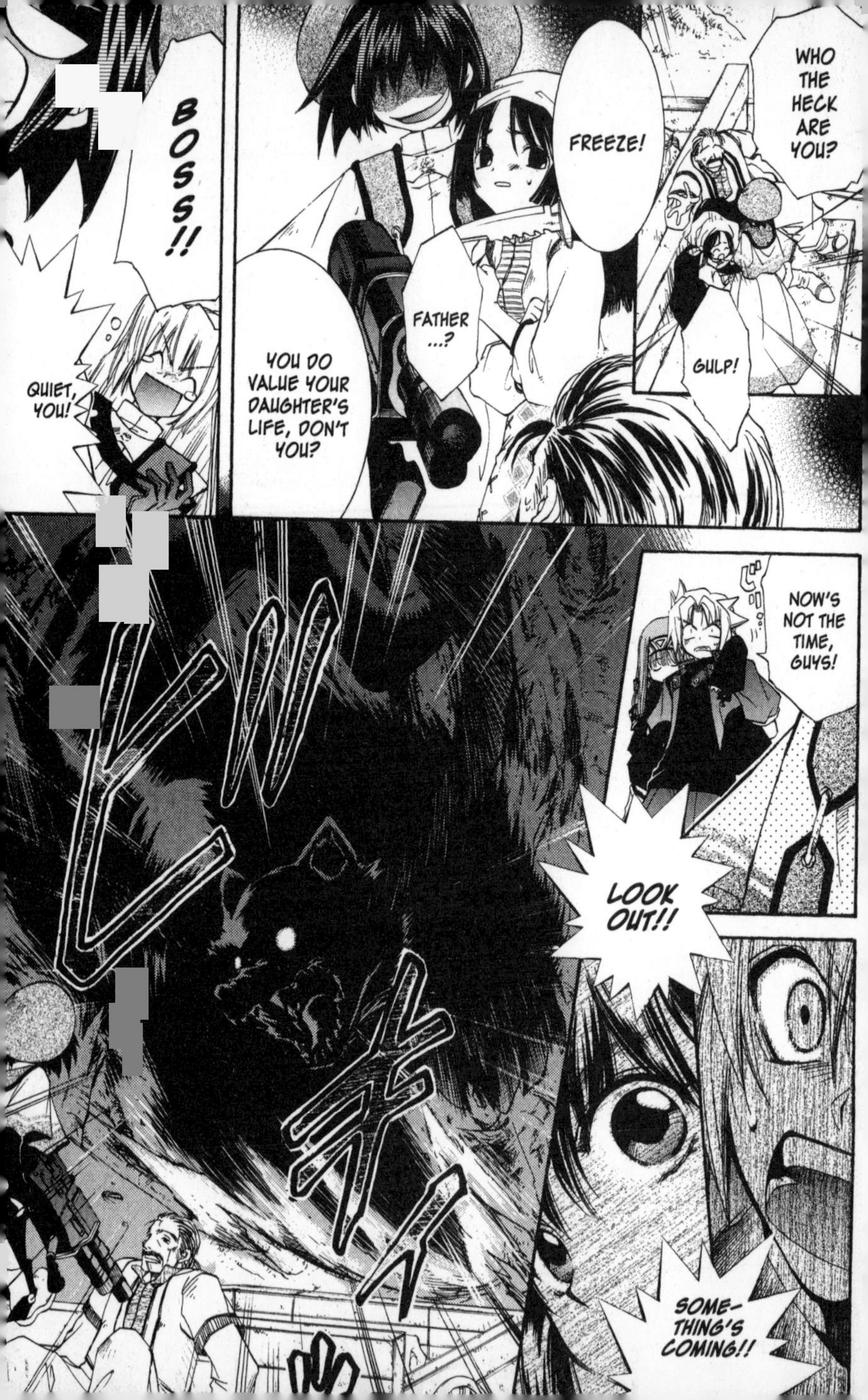
WHO THE HECK ARE YOU?
GULP!
FREEZE!
FATHER ...?
YOU DO VALUE YOUR DAUGHTER'S LIFE, DON'T YOU?
BOSS!!
QUIET, YOU!
NOW'S NOT THE TIME, GUYS!
LOOK OUT!!
SOME-THING'S COMING!!

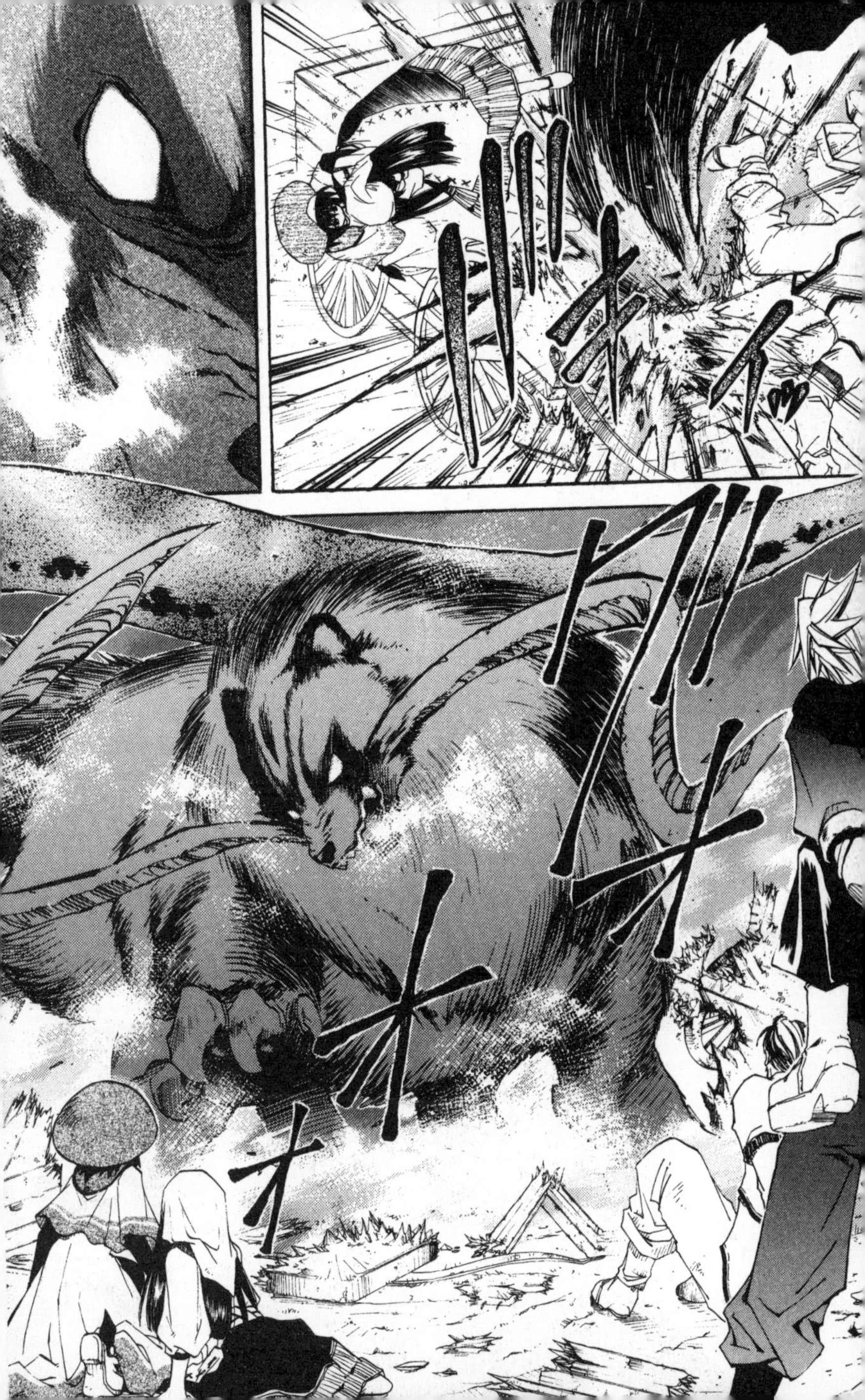
ガオオオ

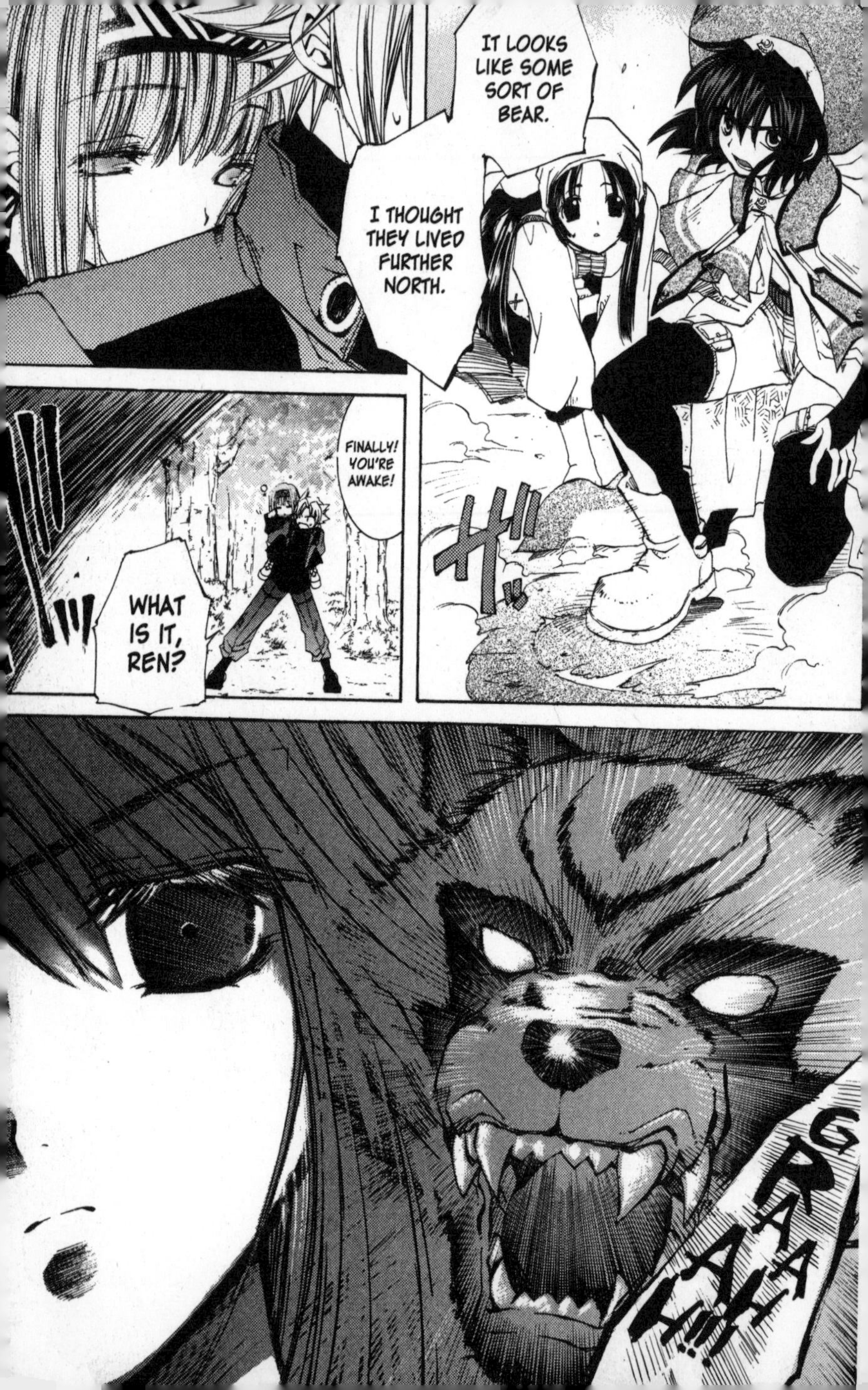
IT LOOKS LIKE SOME SORT OF BEAR.
I THOUGHT THEY LIVED FURTHER NORTH.
FINALLY! YOU'RE AWAKE!
WHAT IS IT, REN?
GRAAAH!!!

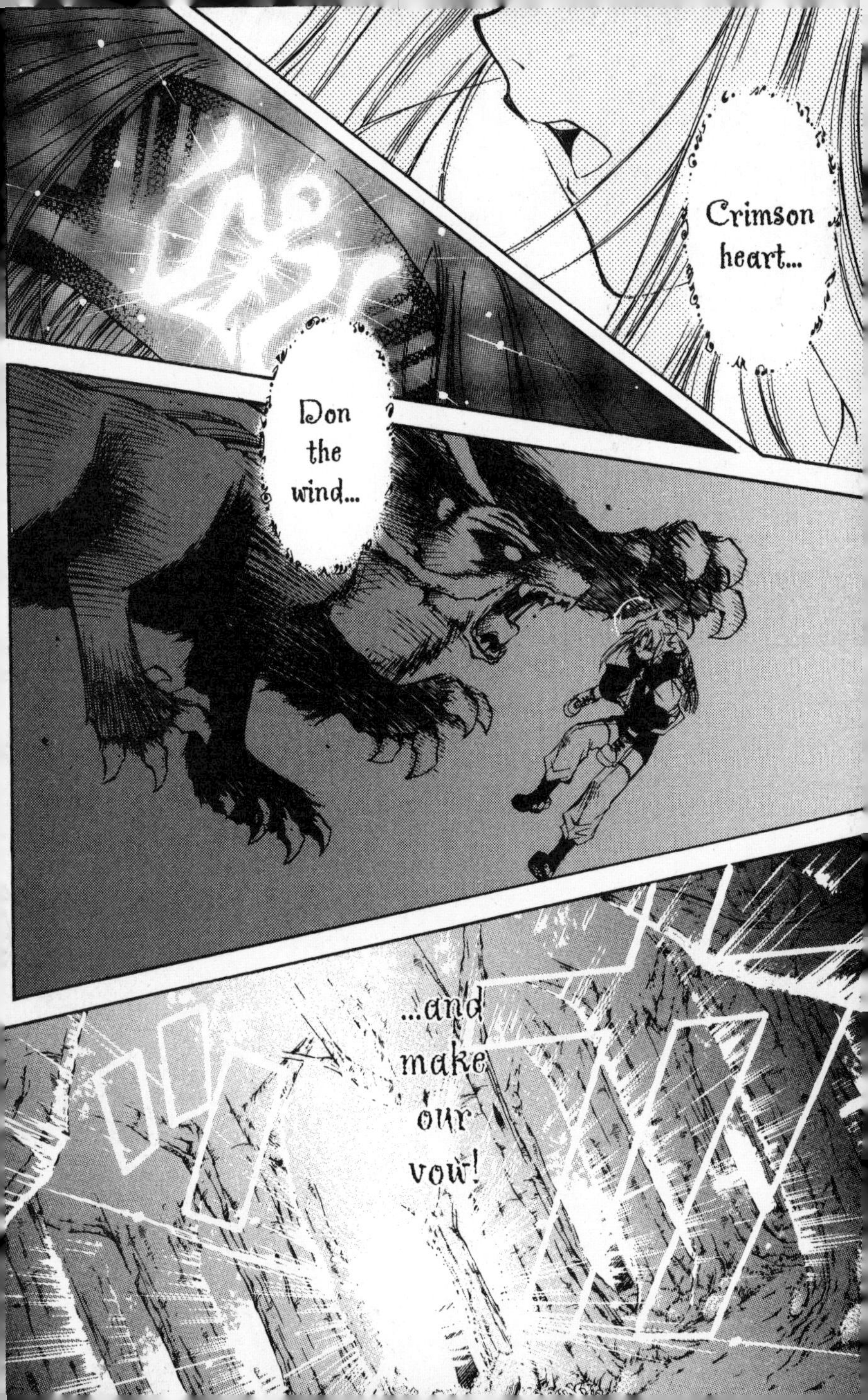
Crimson heart...
Don the wind...
...and make our vow!

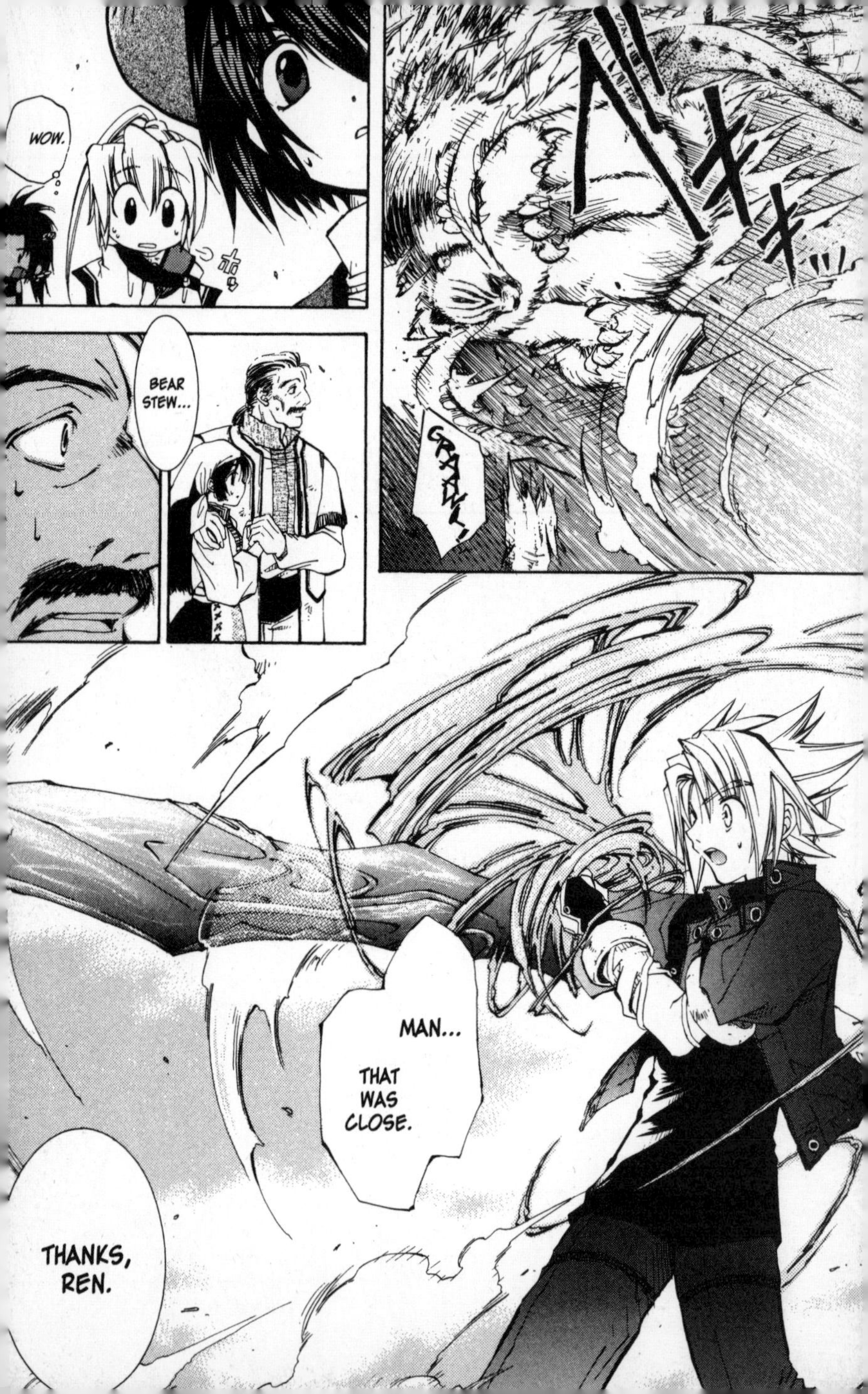
GRAAWL!
WOW.
BEAR STEW...
MAN...
THAT WAS CLOSE.
THANKS, REN.

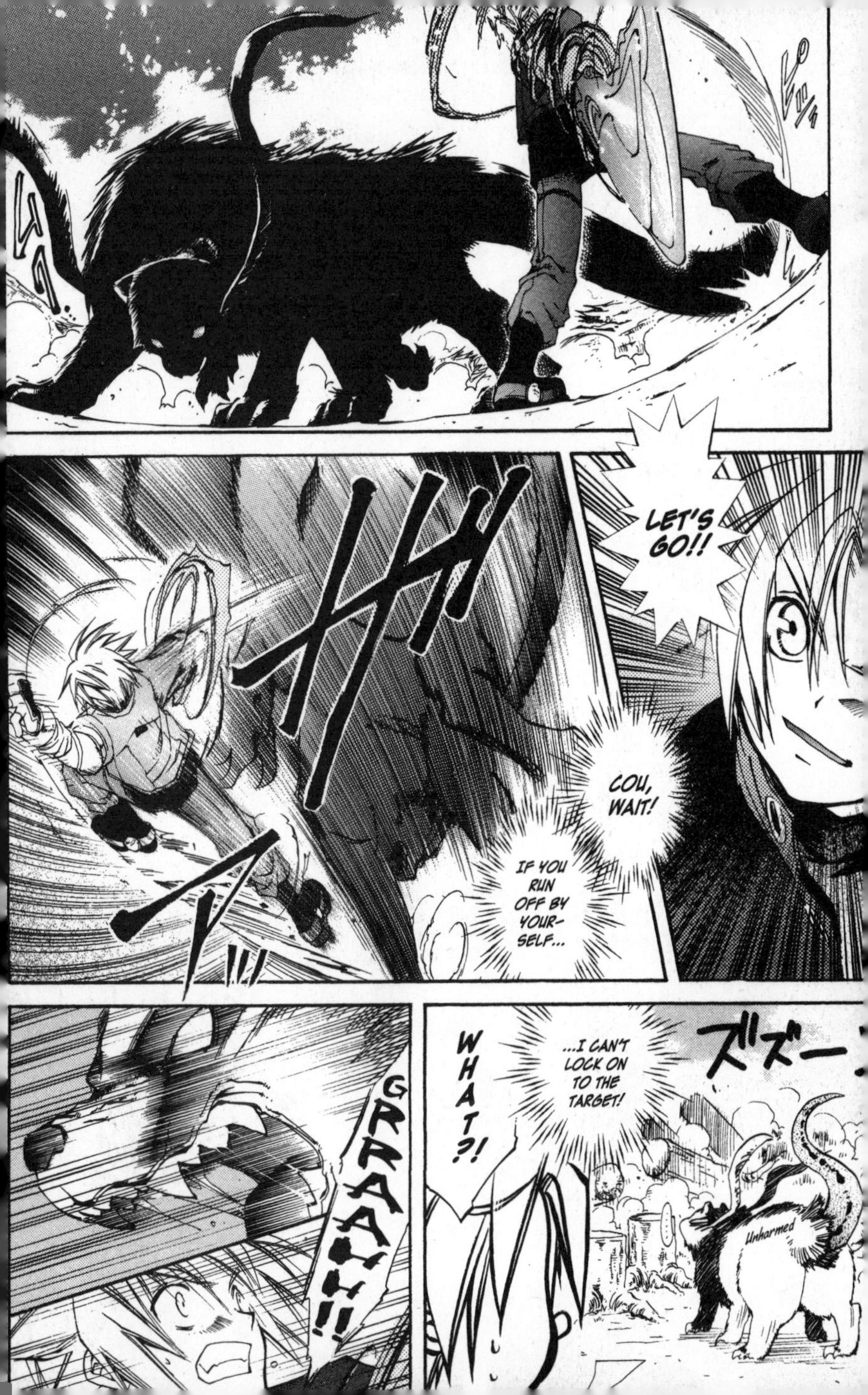
LET'S GO!!
COU, WAIT!
IF YOU RUN OFF BY YOUR-SELF...
...I CAN'T LOCK ON TO THE TARGET!
WHAT?!
Unharmed
GRRAAAH!!

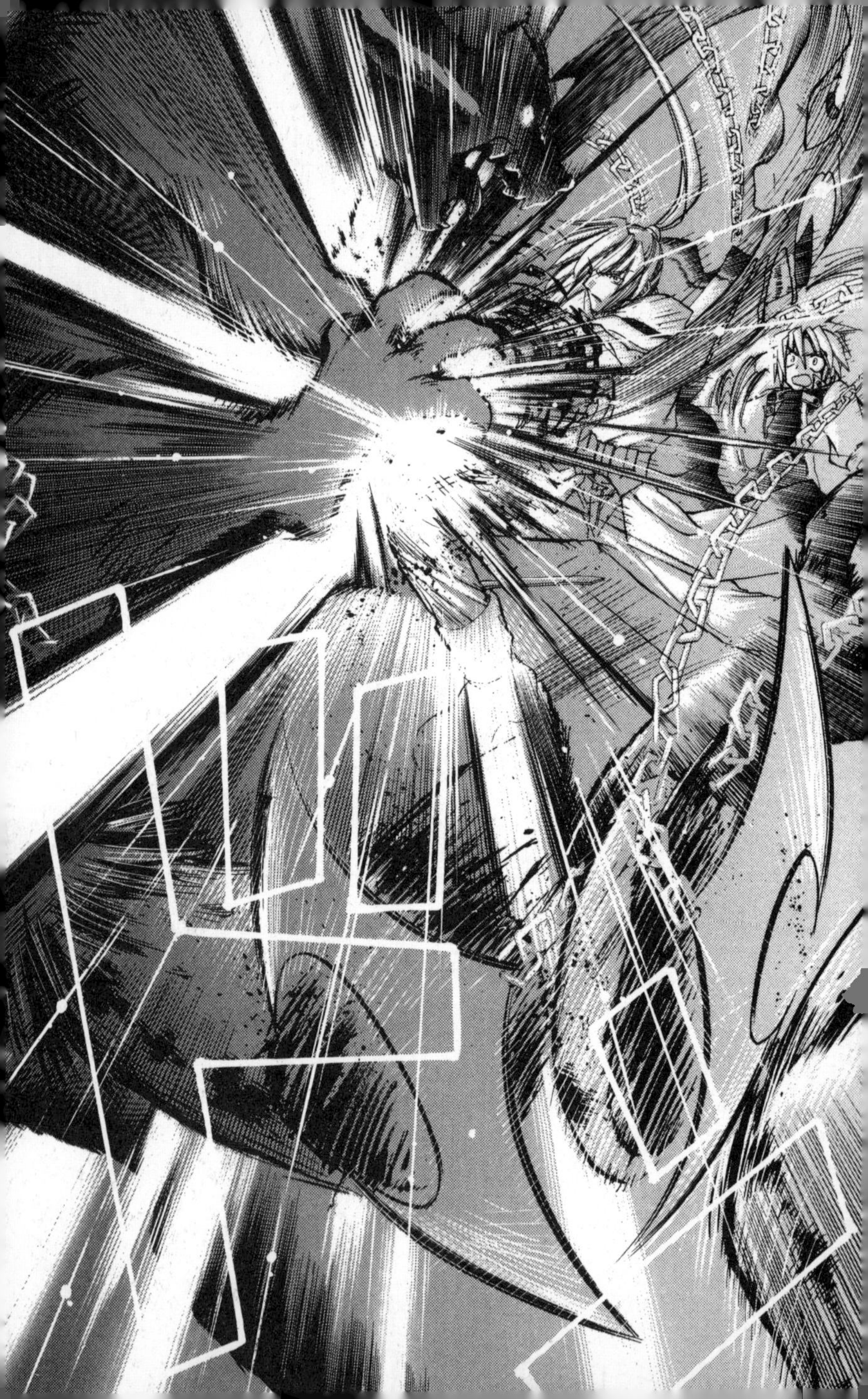

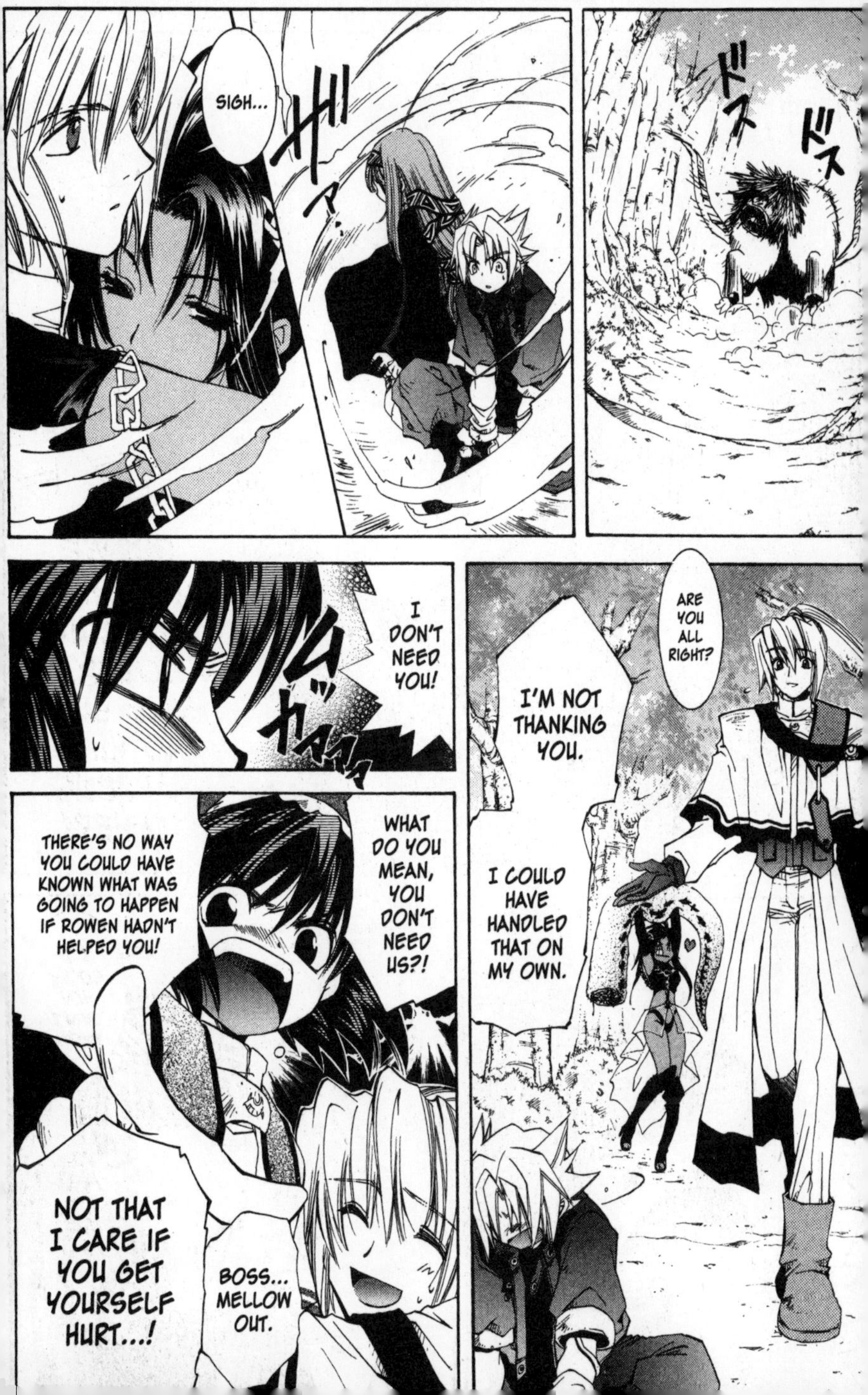
ドス
ドス
SIGH...
ARE YOU ALL RIGHT?
I'M NOT THANKING YOU.
I COULD HAVE HANDLED THAT ON MY OWN.
I DON'T NEED YOU!
WHAT DO YOU MEAN, YOU DON'T NEED US?!
THERE'S NO WAY YOU COULD HAVE KNOWN WHAT WAS GOING TO HAPPEN IF ROWEN HADN'T HELPED YOU!
NOT THAT I CARE IF YOU GET YOURSELF HURT...!
BOSS... MELLOW OUT.

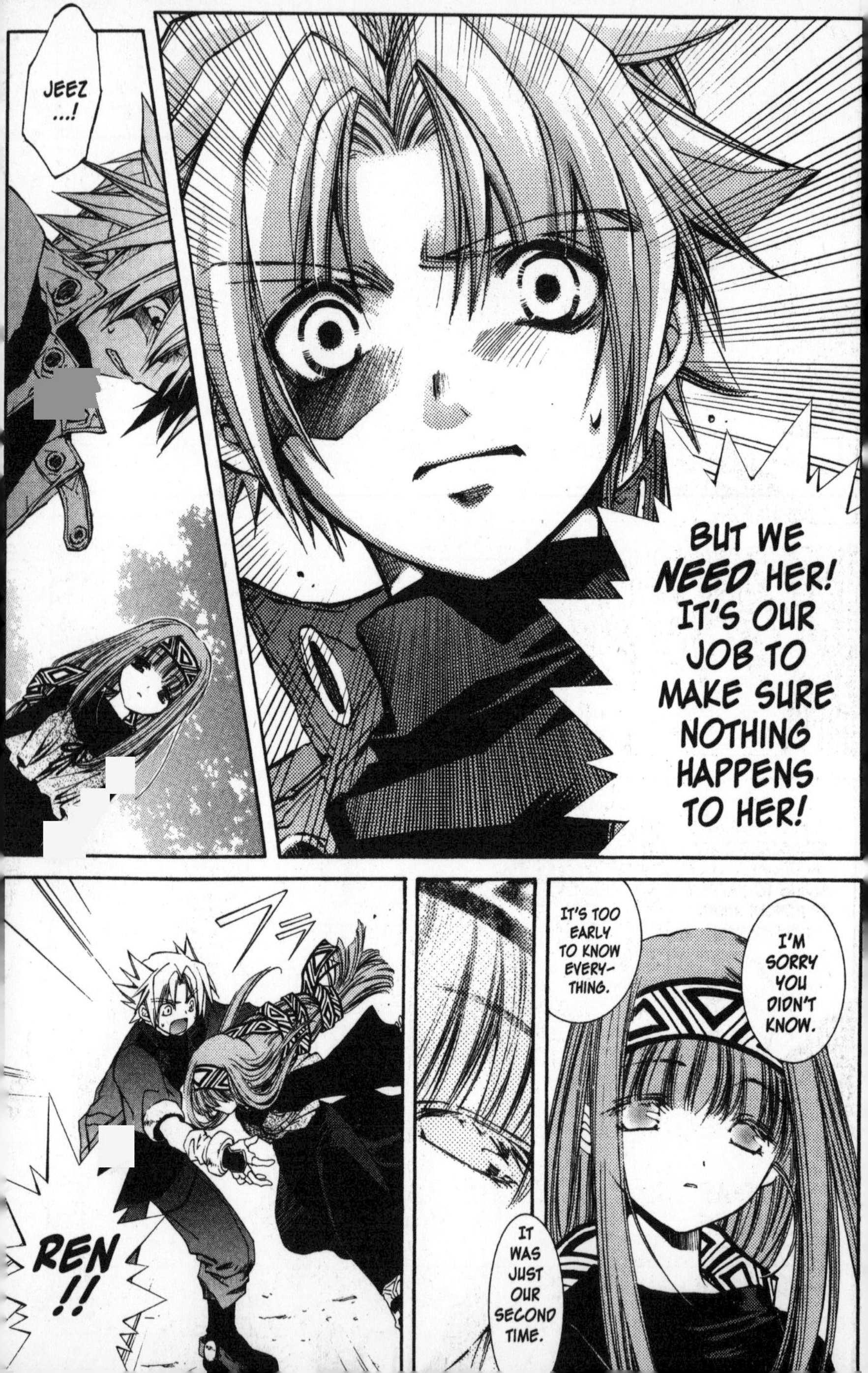
BUT WE NEED HER! IT'S OUR JOB TO MAKE SURE NOTHING HAPPENS TO HER!
JEEZ ...!
I'M SORRY YOU DIDN'T KNOW.
IT'S TOO EARLY TO KNOW EVERY-THING.
IT WAS JUST OUR SECOND TIME.
REN!!

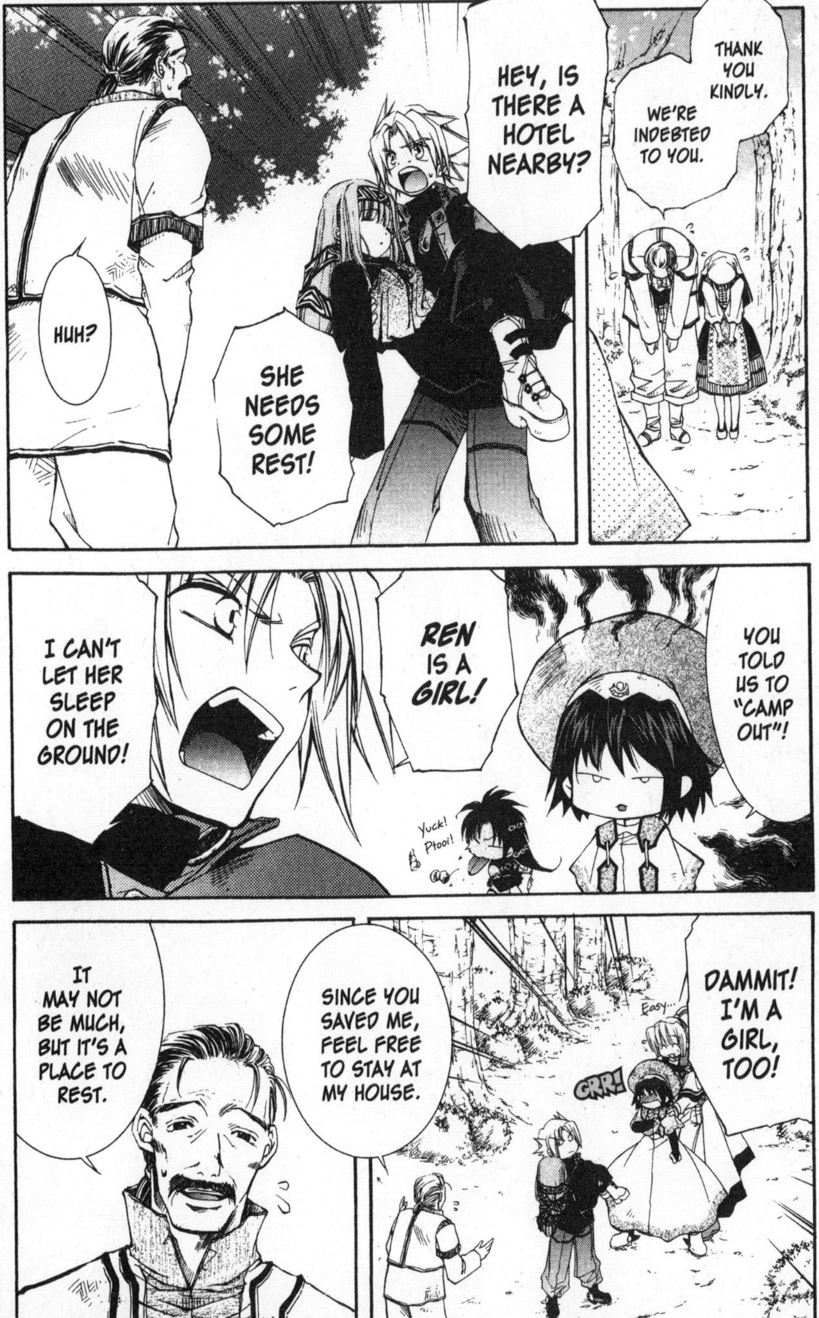
THANK YOU KINDLY.
WE'RE INDEBTED TO YOU.
HEY, IS THERE A HOTEL NEARBY?
SHE NEEDS SOME REST!
HUH?
YOU TOLD US TO "CAMP OUT"!
REN IS A GIRL!
I CAN'T LET HER SLEEP ON THE GROUND!
Yuck! Ptooi!
DAMMIT! I'M A GIRL, TOO!
Easy...
GRR!
SINCE YOU SAVED ME, FEEL FREE TO STAY AT MY HOUSE.
IT MAY NOT BE MUCH, BUT IT'S A PLACE TO REST.

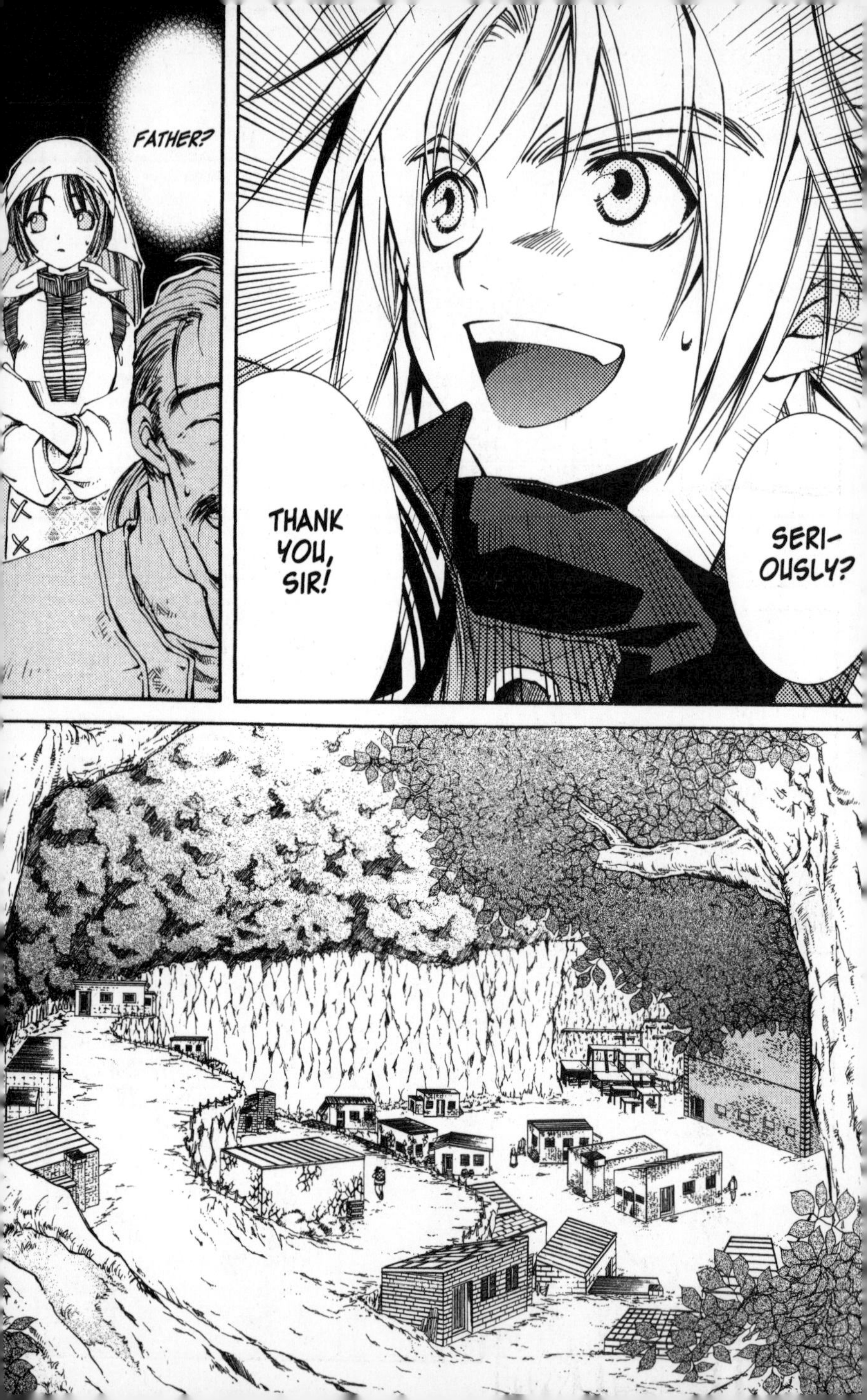
SERI-OUSLY?
THANK YOU, SIR!
FATHER?

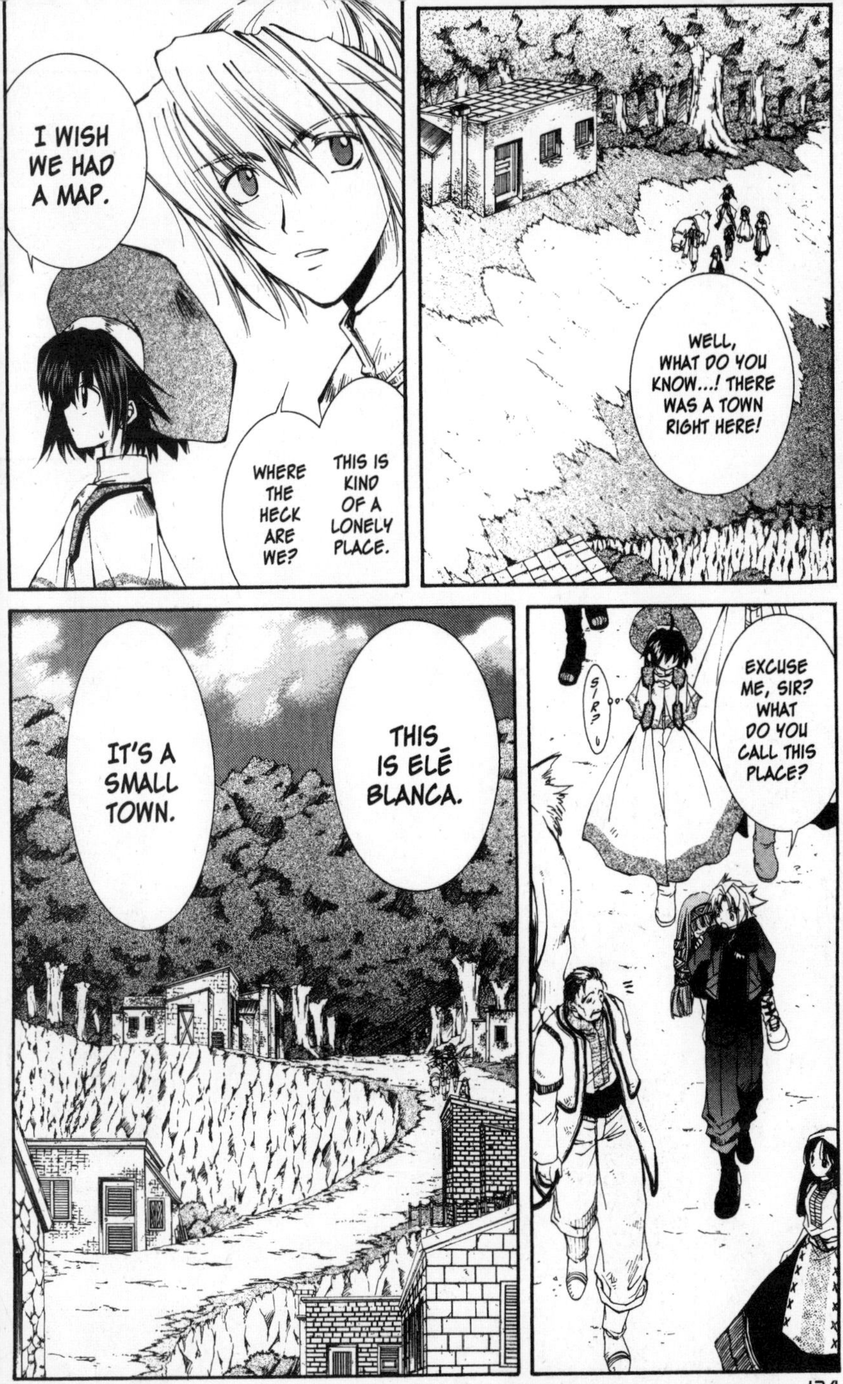
WELL, WHAT DO YOU KNOW...! THERE WAS A TOWN RIGHT HERE!
I WISH WE HAD A MAP.
THIS IS KIND OF A LONELY PLACE.
WHERE THE HECK ARE WE?
EXCUSE ME, SIR? WHAT DO YOU CALL THIS PLACE?
SIR?..
THIS IS ELĒ BLANCA.
IT'S A SMALL TOWN.

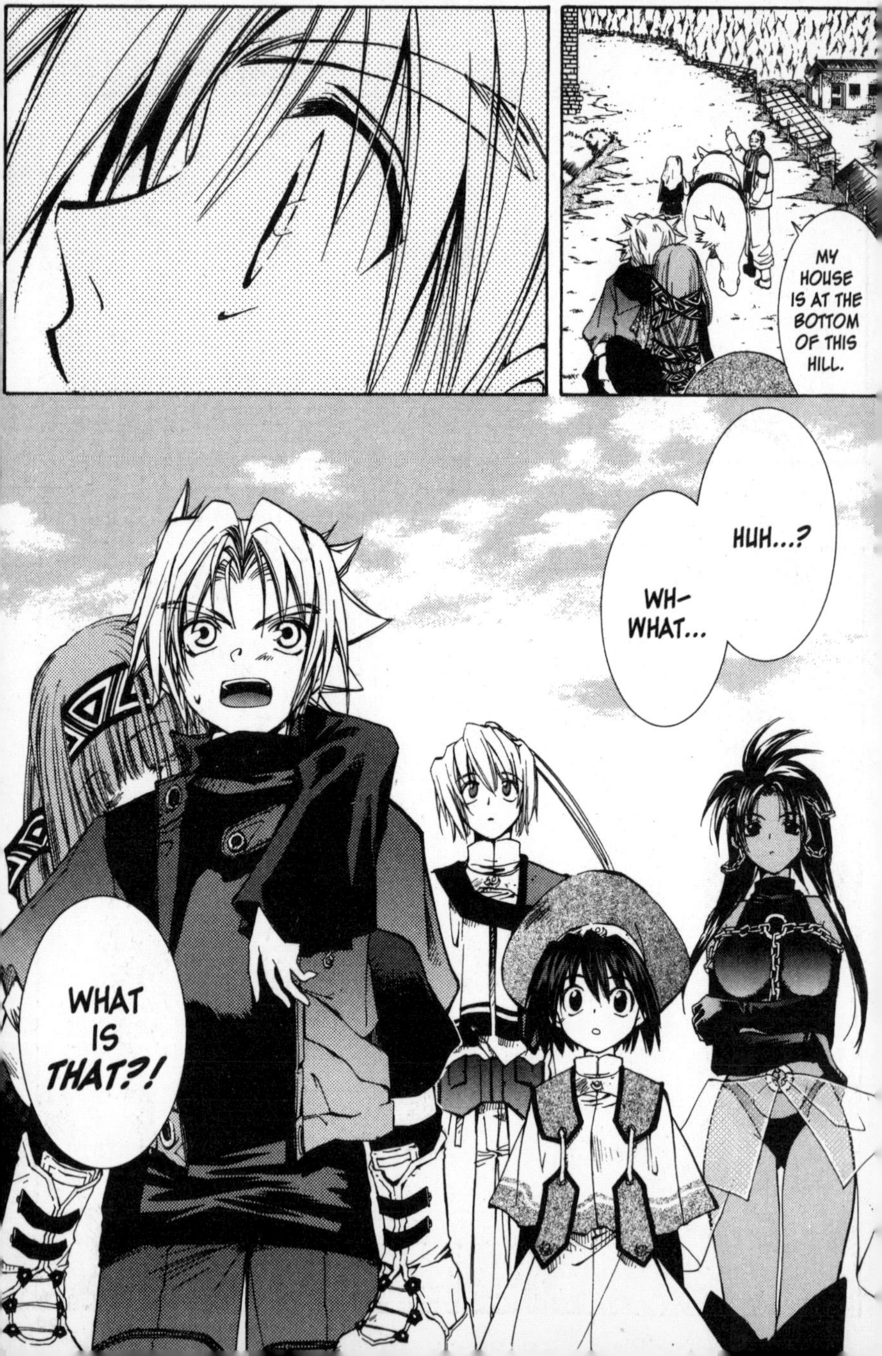
MY HOUSE IS AT THE BOTTOM OF THIS HILL.
HUH...?
WH- WHAT...
WHAT IS THAT?!

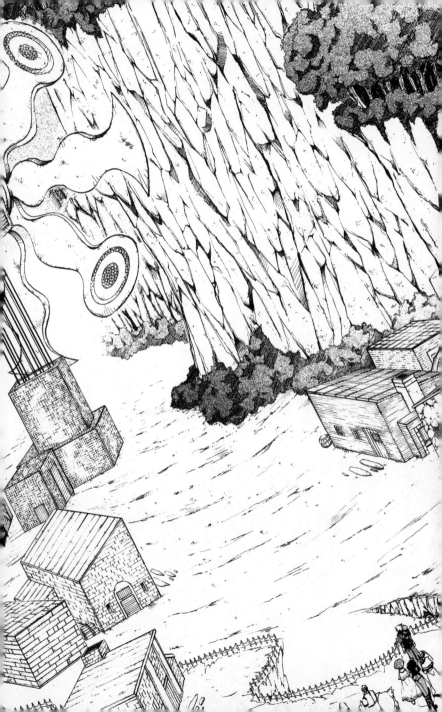

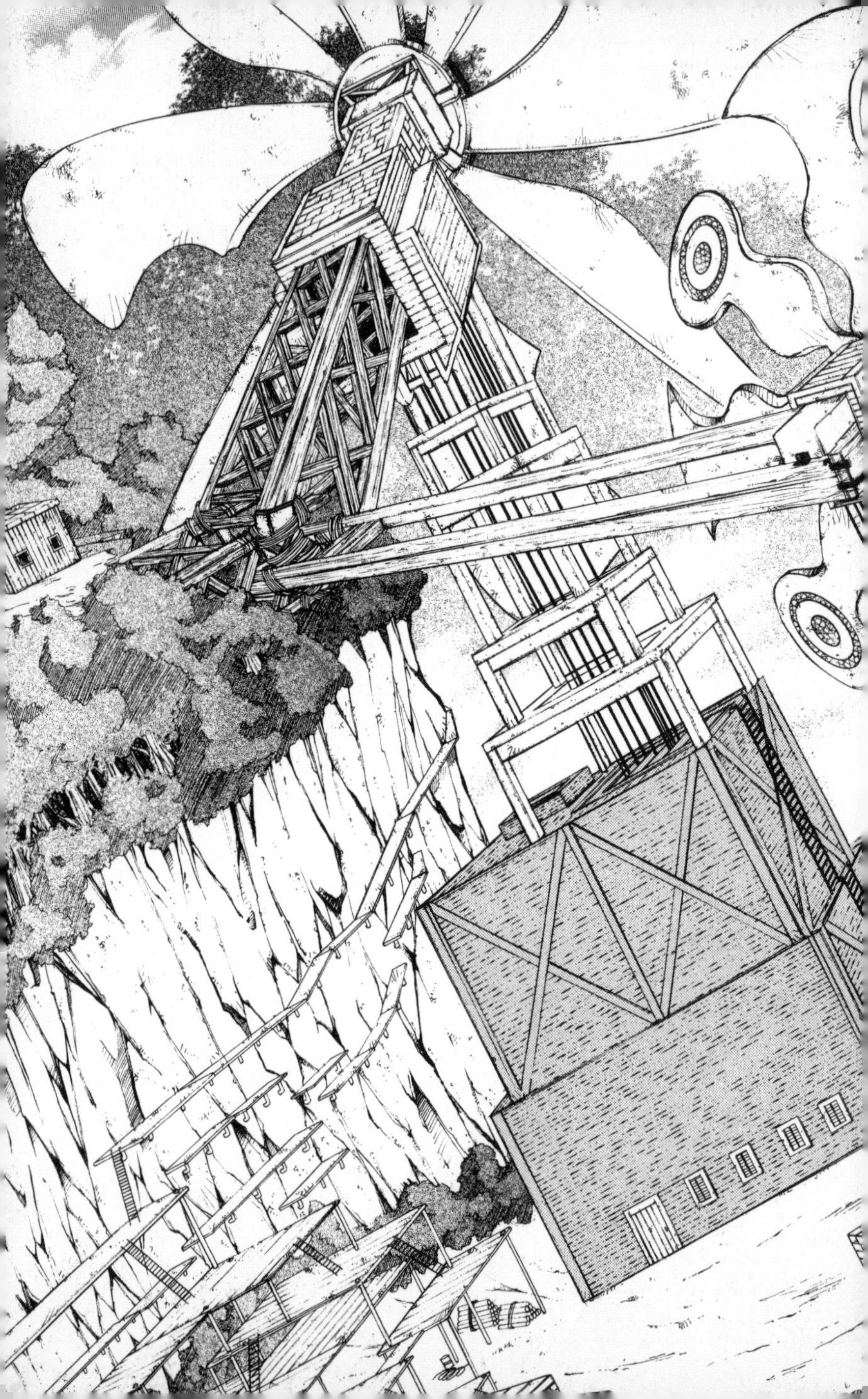

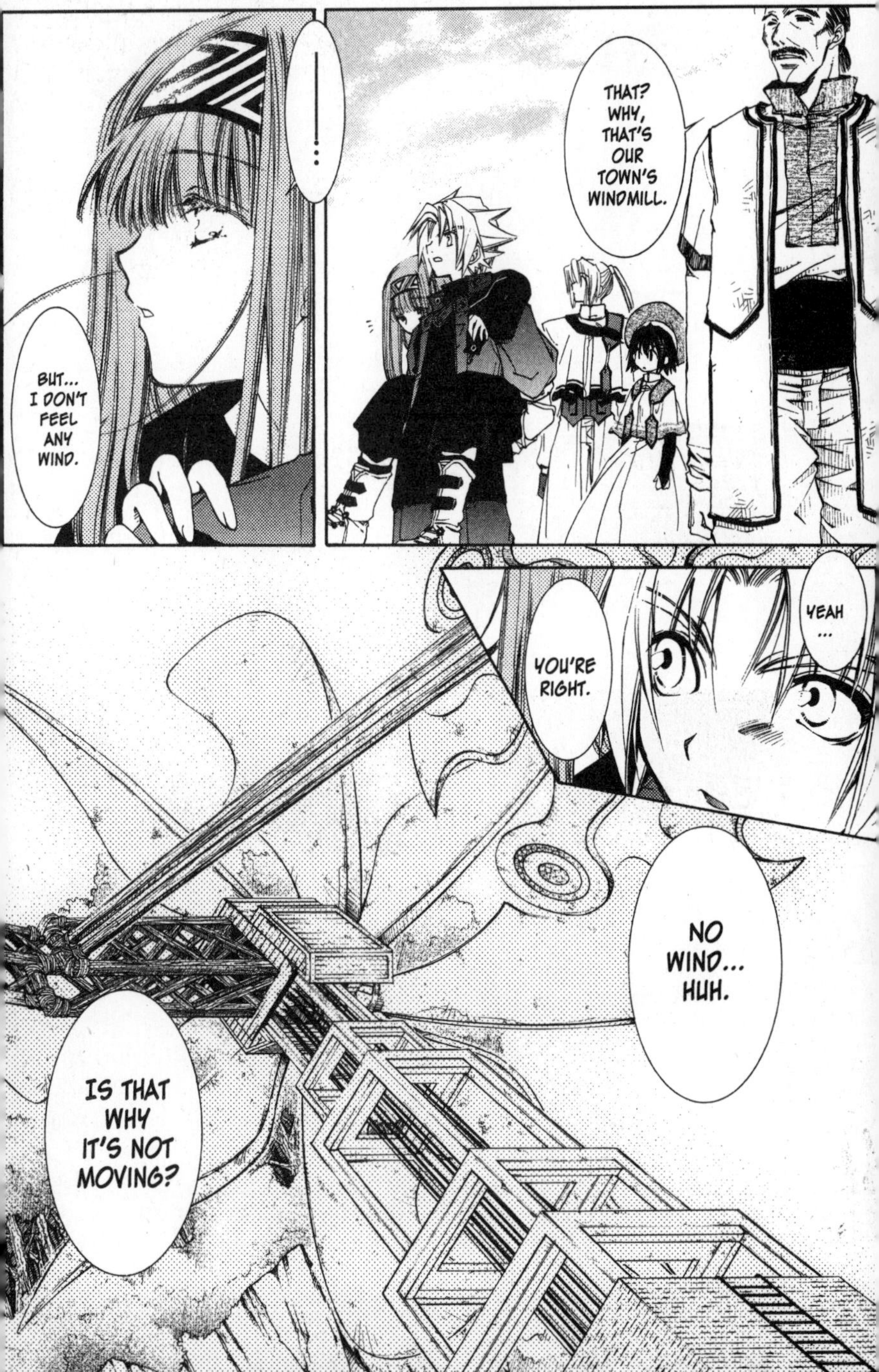
THAT? WHY, THAT'S OUR TOWN'S WINDMILL.
......
BUT... I DON'T FEEL ANY WIND.
YEAH...
YOU'RE RIGHT.
NO WIND... HUH.
IS THAT WHY IT'S NOT MOVING?

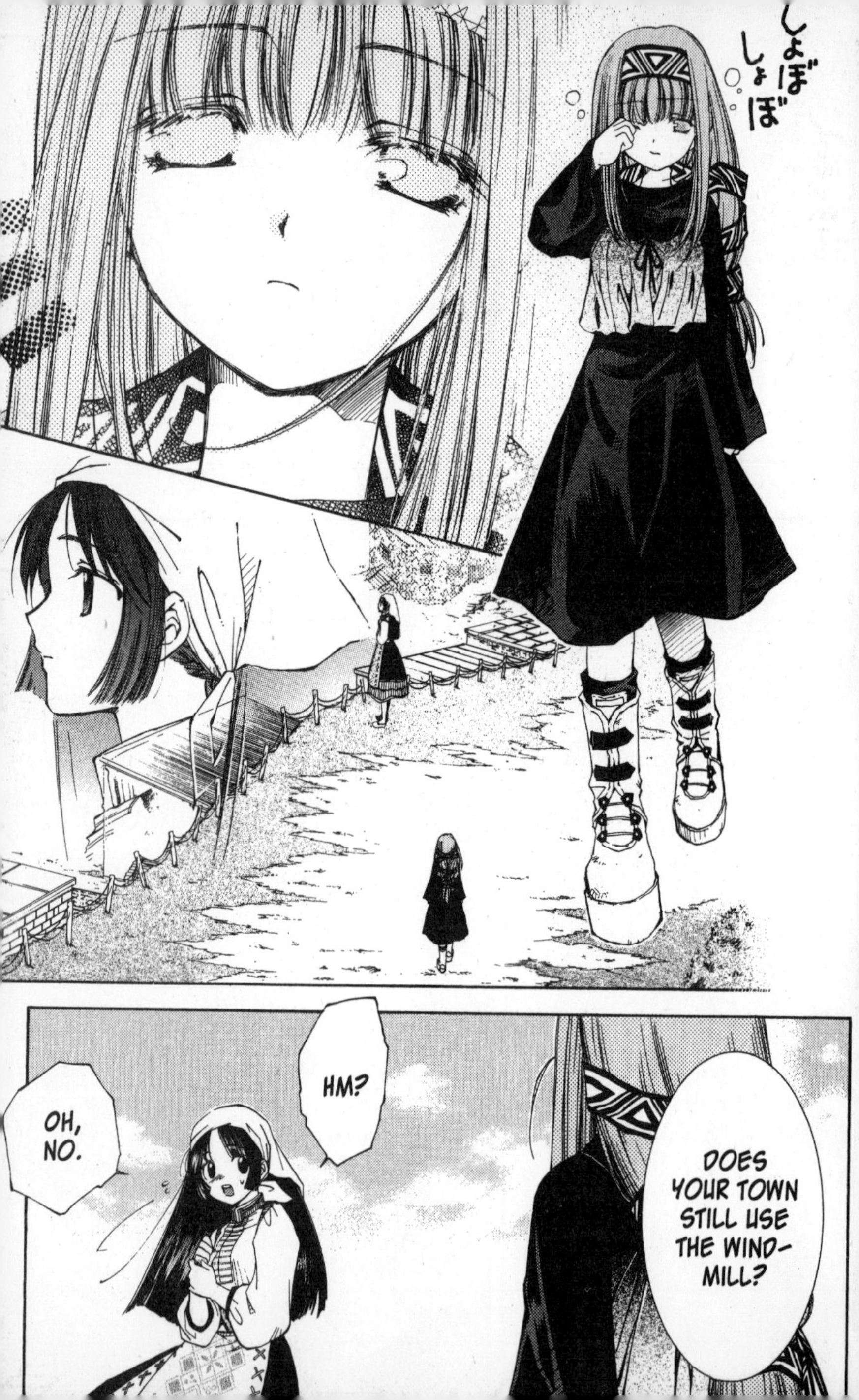
しょぼしょぼ
DOES YOUR TOWN STILL USE THE WIND-MILL?
HM?
OH, NO.

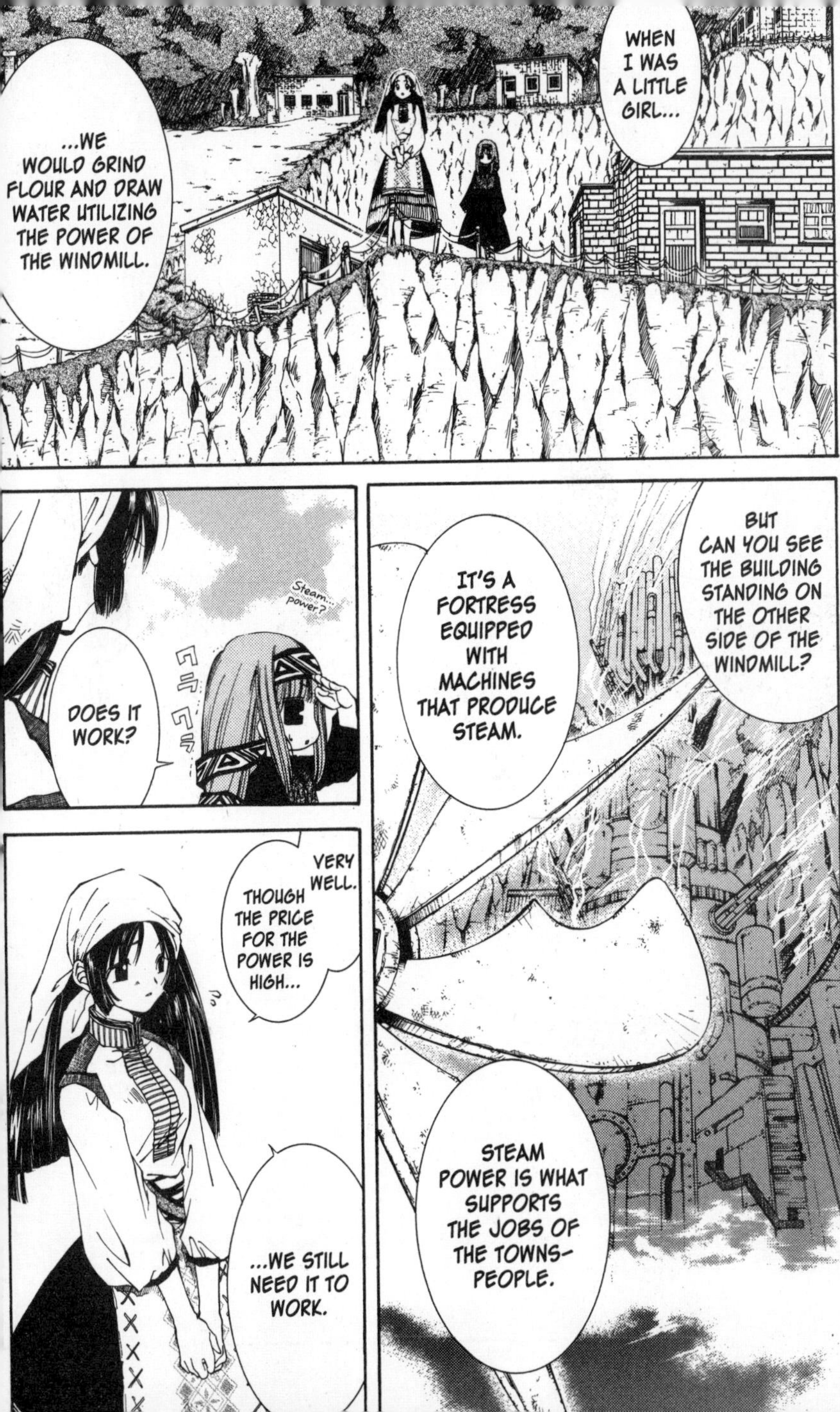

WHEN I WAS A LITTLE GIRL...
...WE WOULD GRIND FLOUR AND DRAW WATER UTILIZING THE POWER OF THE WINDMILL.
BUT CAN YOU SEE THE BUILDING STANDING ON THE OTHER SIDE OF THE WINDMILL?
IT'S A FORTRESS EQUIPPED WITH MACHINES THAT PRODUCE STEAM.
STEAM POWER IS WHAT SUPPORTS THE JOBS OF THE TOWNS-PEOPLE.
Steam... power?
DOES IT WORK?
VERY WELL.
THOUGH THE PRICE FOR THE POWER IS HIGH...
...WE STILL NEED IT TO WORK.

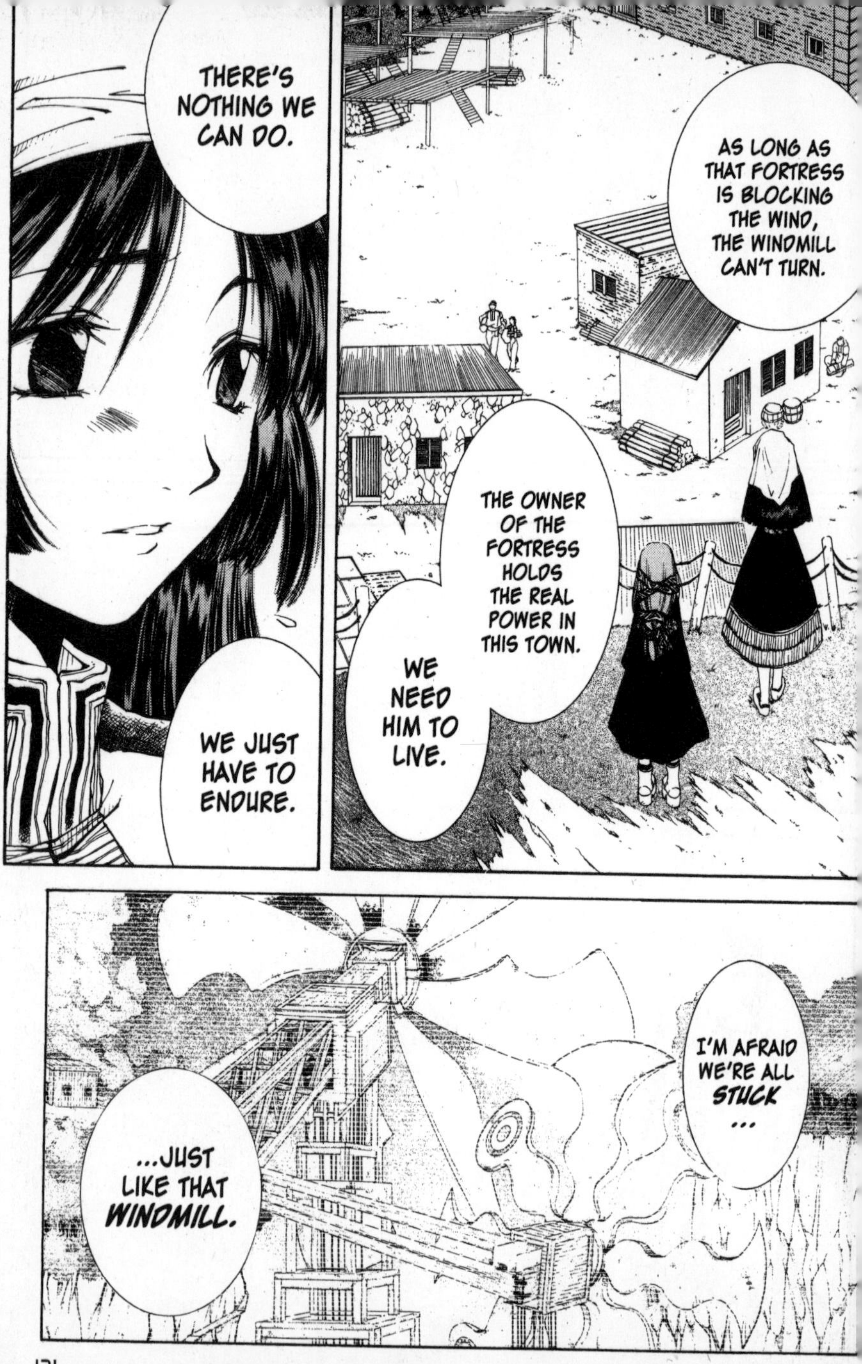
AS LONG AS THAT FORTRESS IS BLOCKING THE WIND, THE WINDMILL CAN'T TURN.
THE OWNER OF THE FORTRESS HOLDS THE REAL POWER IN THIS TOWN.
WE NEED HIM TO LIVE.
THERE'S NOTHING WE CAN DO.
WE JUST HAVE TO ENDURE.
I'M AFRAID WE'RE ALL ***STUCK*** ...
...JUST LIKE THAT ***WINDMILL.***

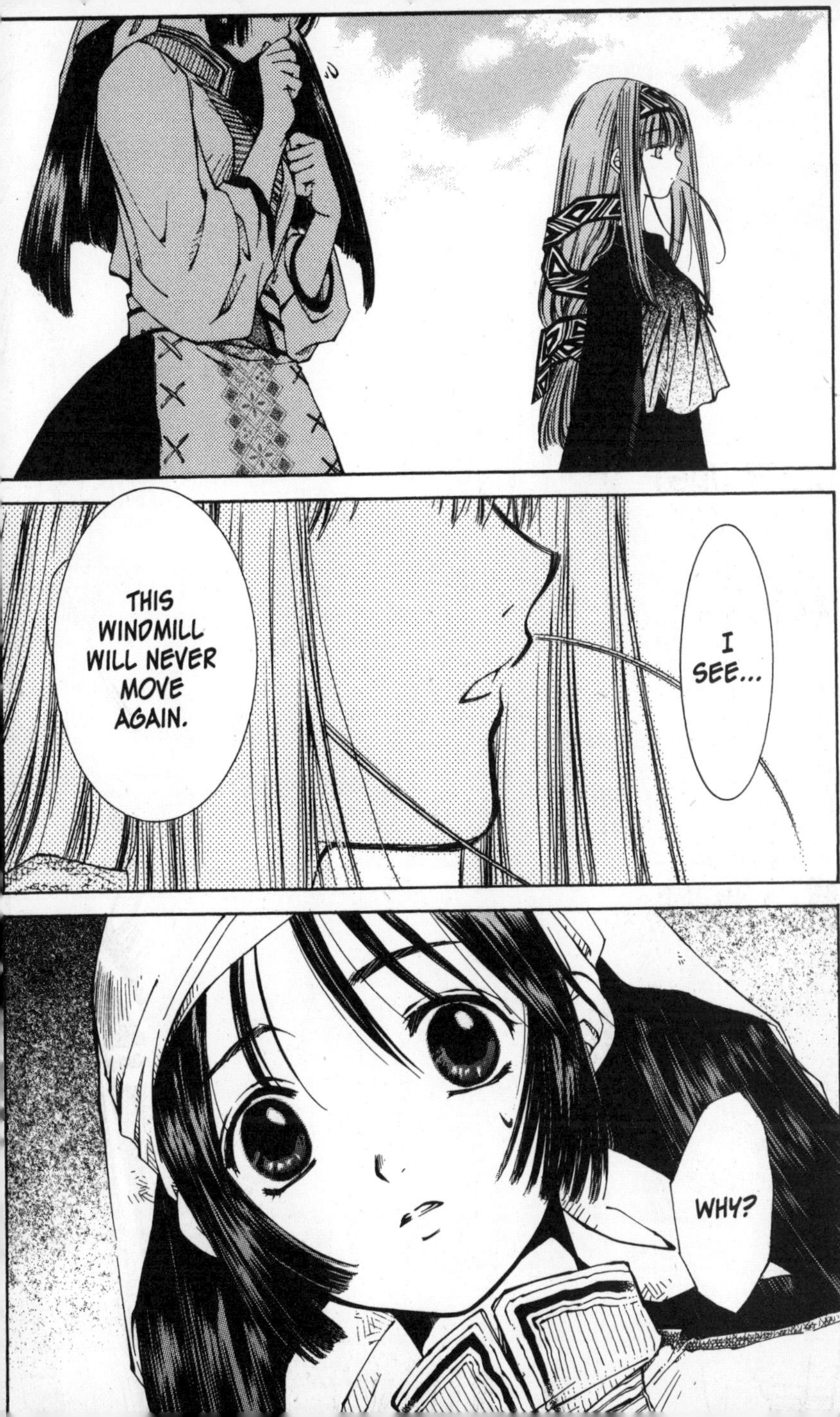
I SEE...
THIS WINDMILL WILL NEVER MOVE AGAIN.
WHY?

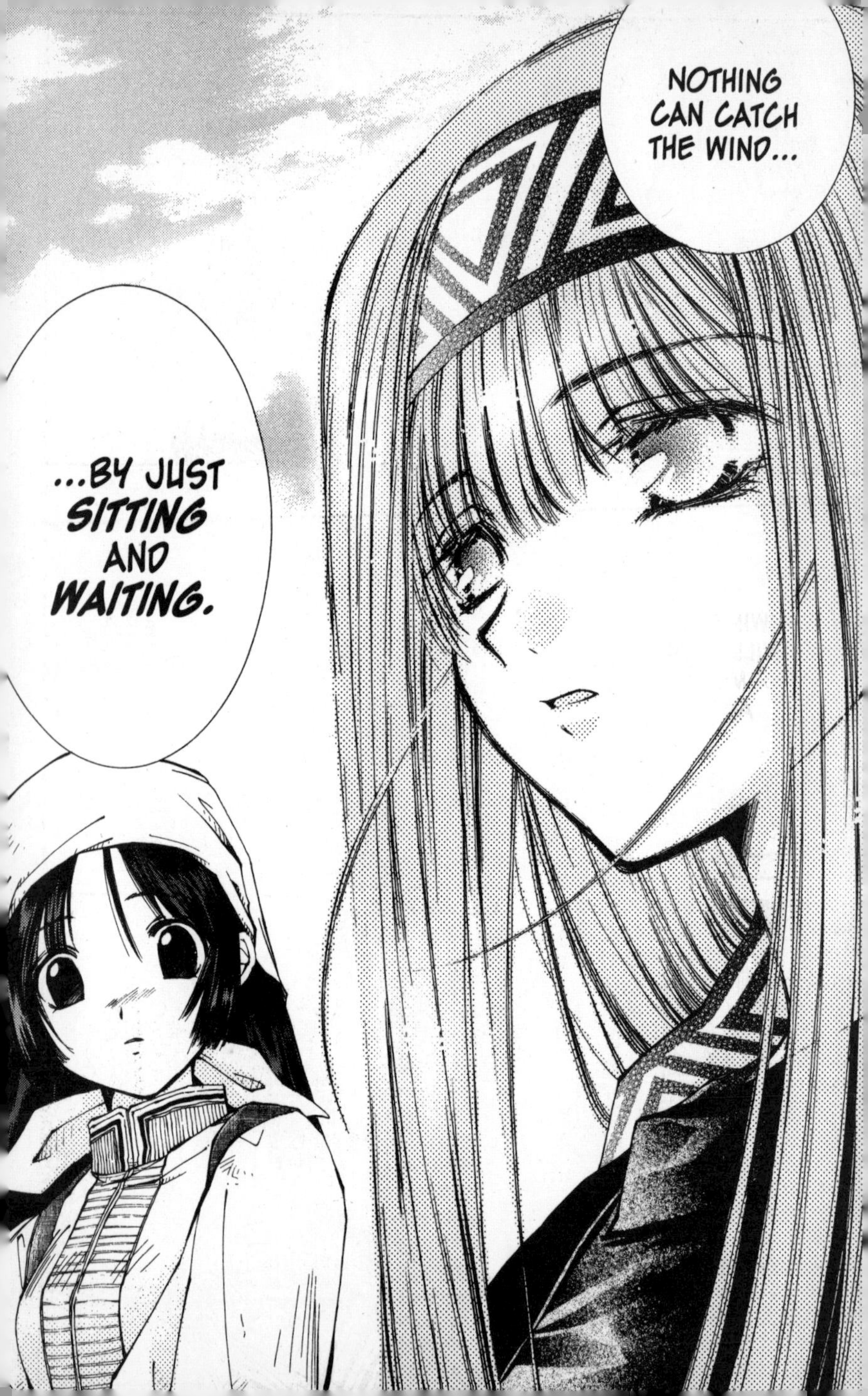
NOTHING CAN CATCH THE WIND...
...BY JUST SITTING AND WAITING.

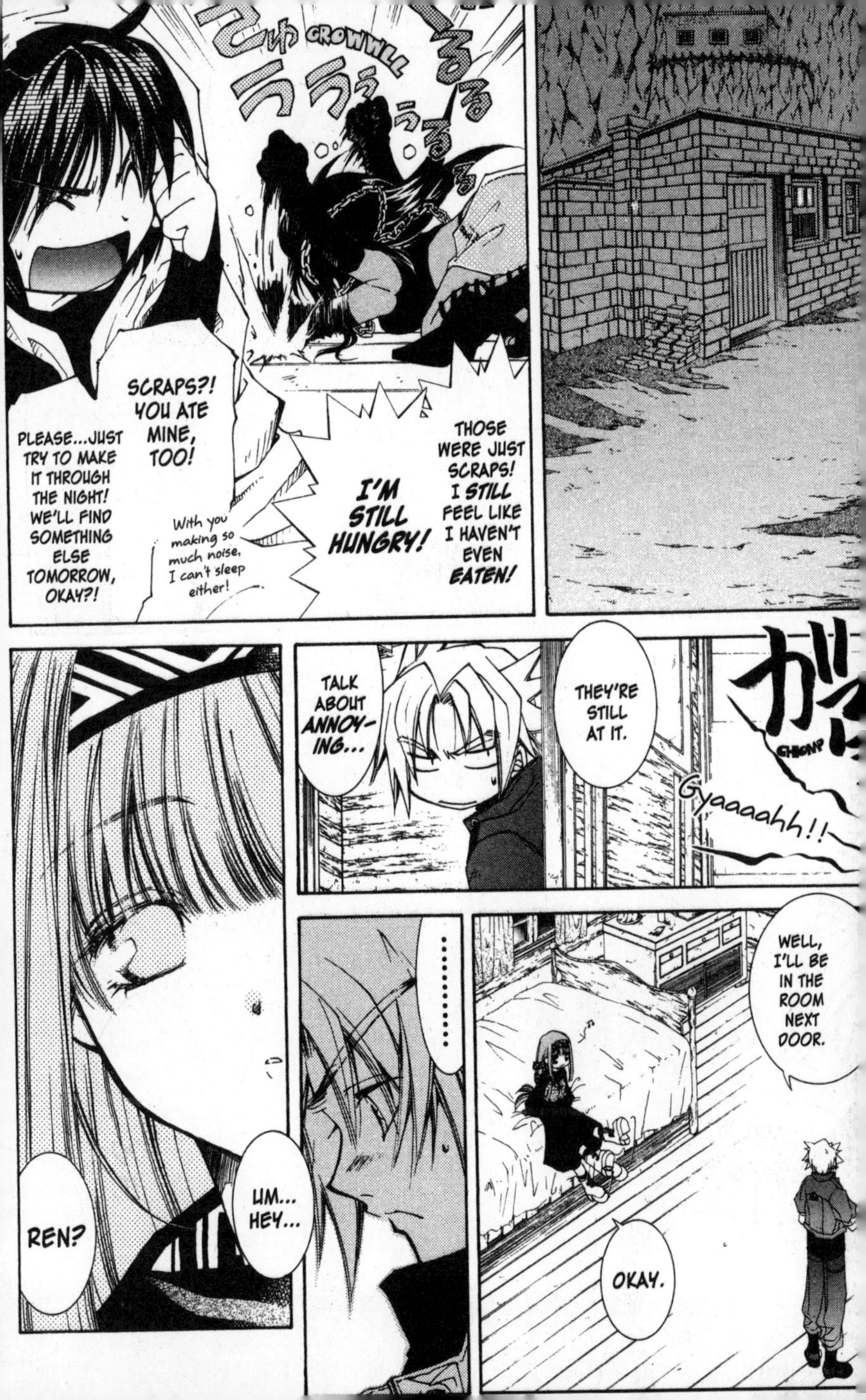

GROWWLL
THOSE WERE JUST SCRAPS! I STILL FEEL LIKE I HAVEN'T EVEN EATEN!
I'M STILL HUNGRY!
SCRAPS?! YOU ATE MINE, TOO!
With you making so much noise, I can't sleep either!
PLEASE...JUST TRY TO MAKE IT THROUGH THE NIGHT! WE'LL FIND SOMETHING ELSE TOMORROW, OKAY?!
CHOMP
Gyaaaaahh!!
THEY'RE STILL AT IT.
TALK ABOUT ANNOYING...
WELL, I'LL BE IN THE ROOM NEXT DOOR.
OKAY.
......
UM... HEY...
REN?

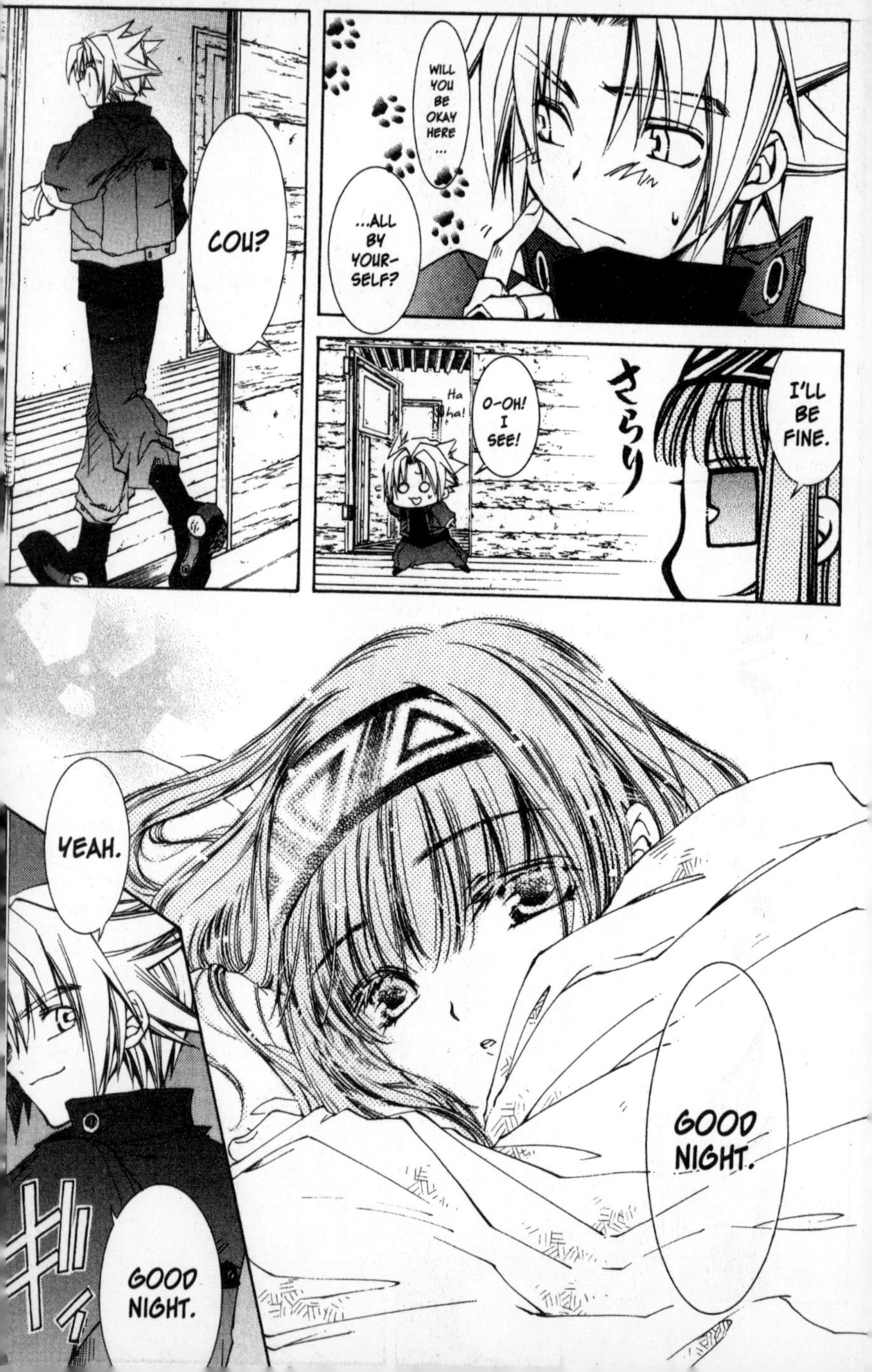

WILL YOU BE OKAY HERE...
...ALL BY YOURSELF?
I'LL BE FINE.
さらり
O-OH! I SEE!
Ha ha!
COU?
GOOD NIGHT.
YEAH.
GOOD NIGHT.
ギィ

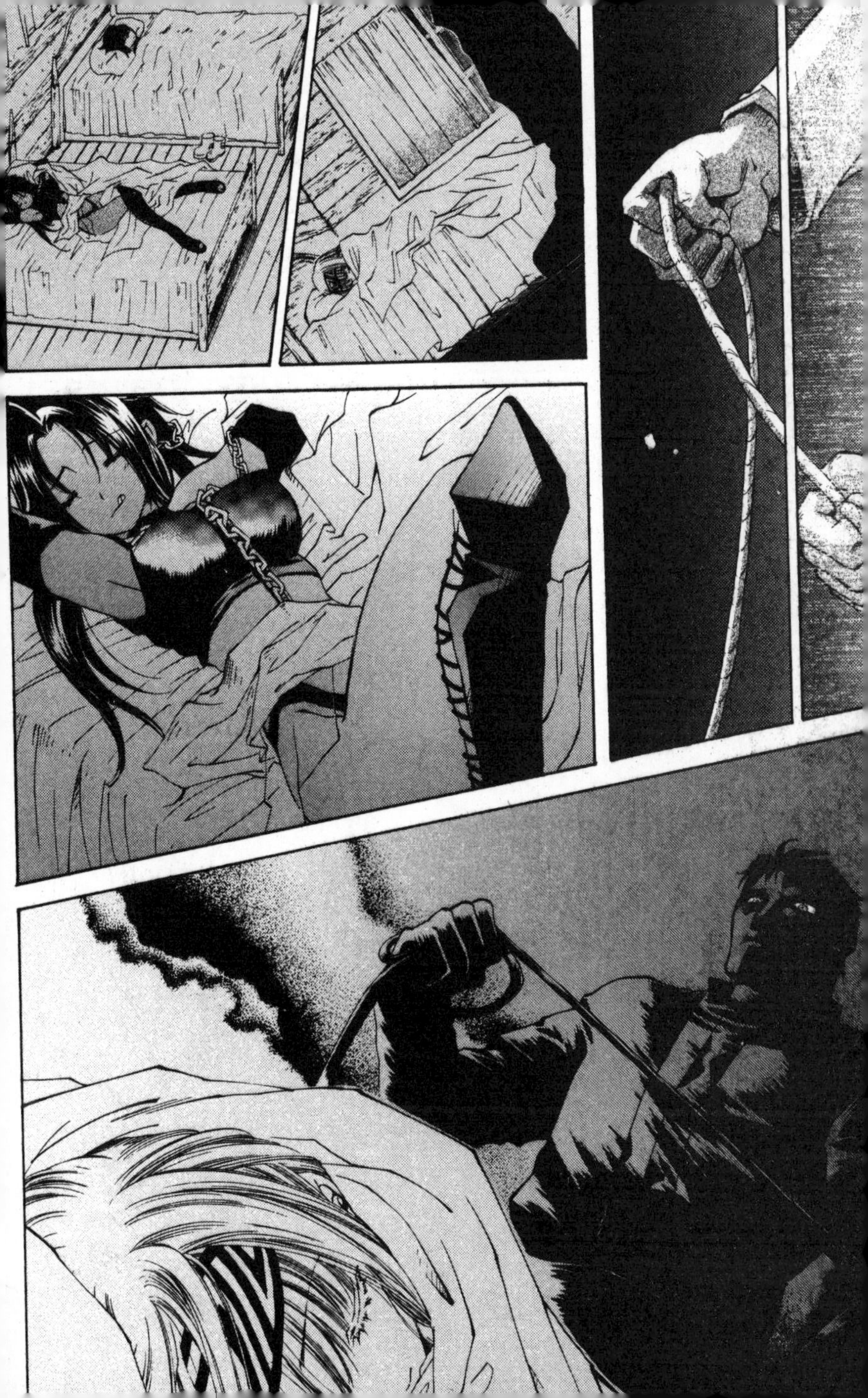

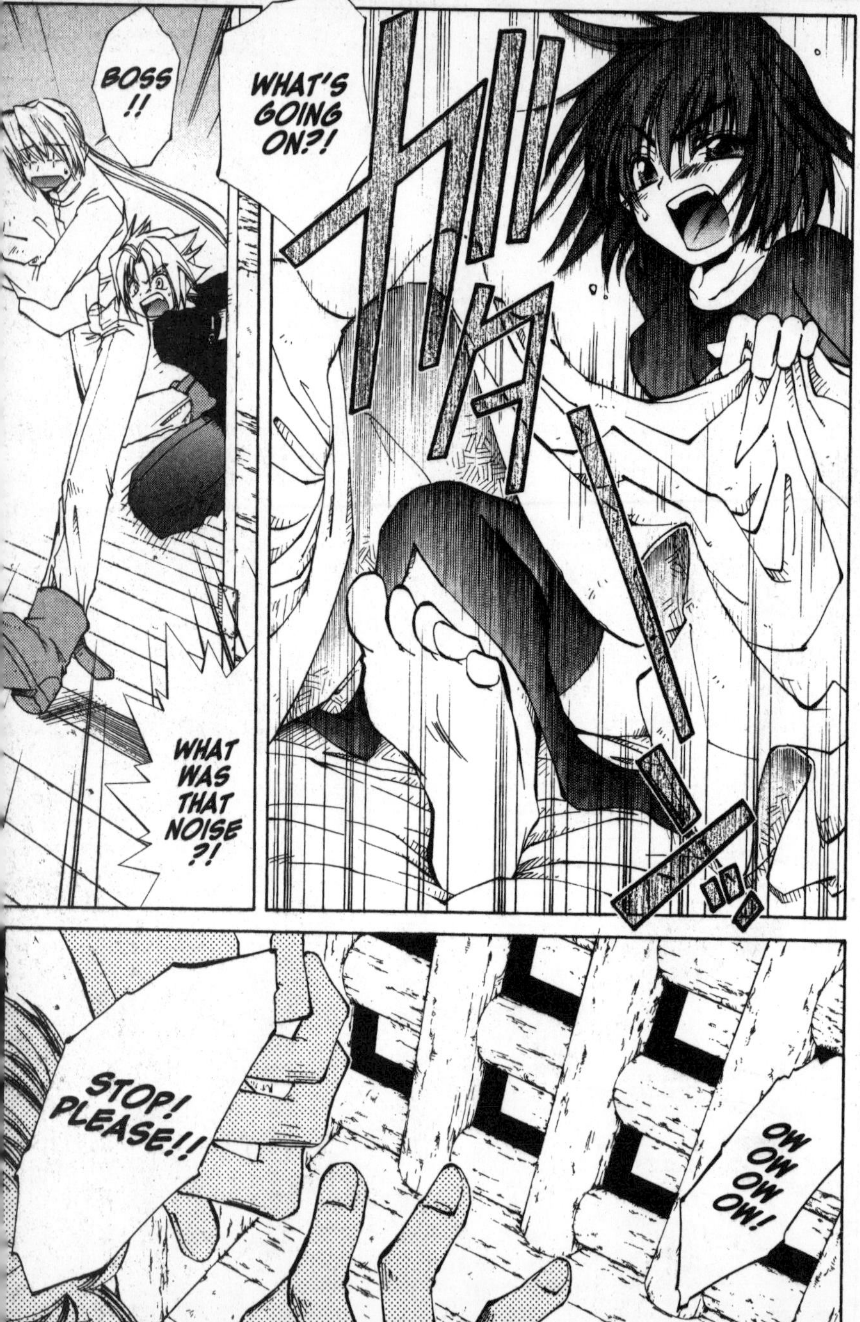
WHAT'S GOING ON?!
BOSS!!
WHAT WAS THAT NOISE?!
OW OW OW OW!
STOP! PLEASE!!

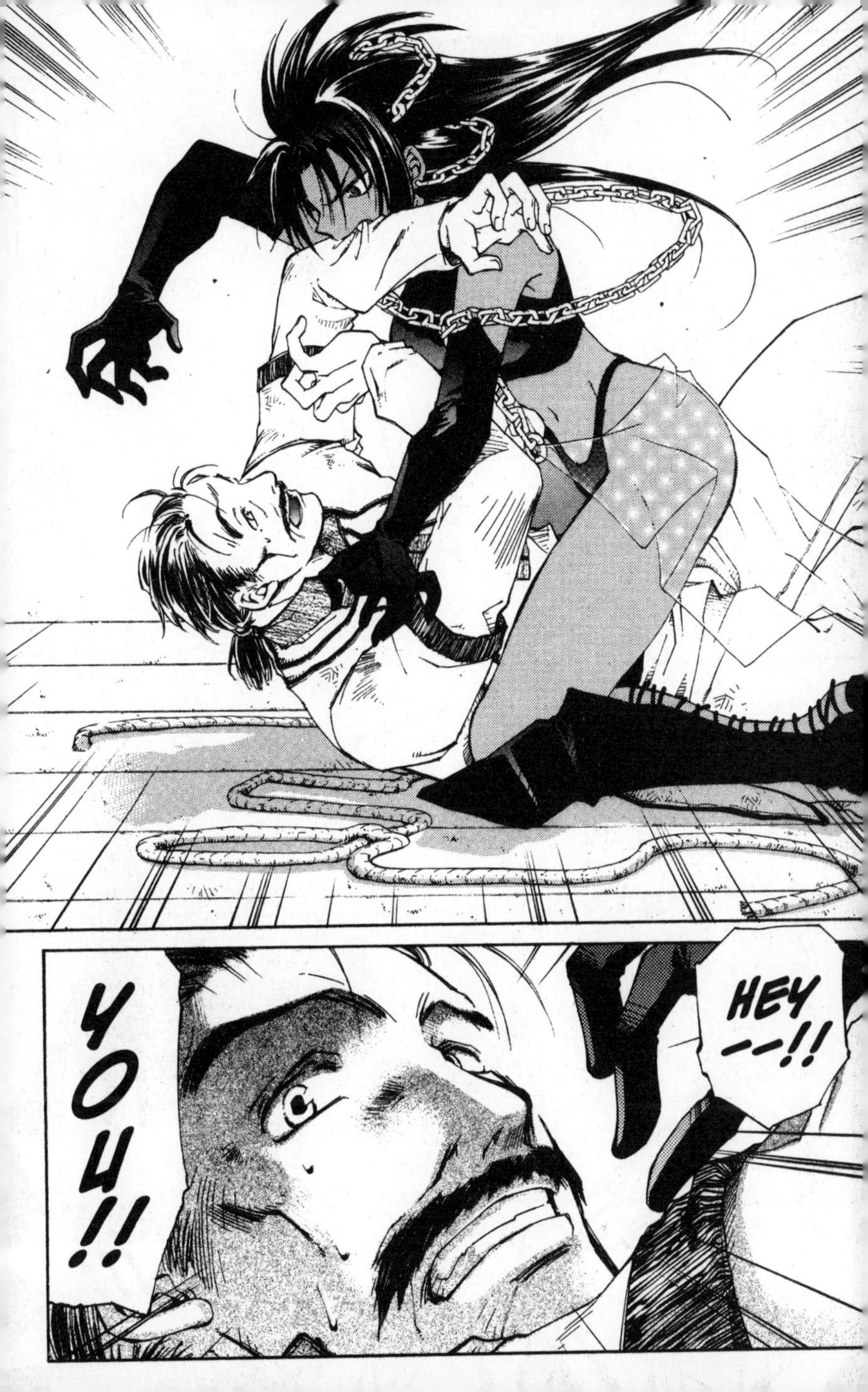
HEY
--!!
YOU!!

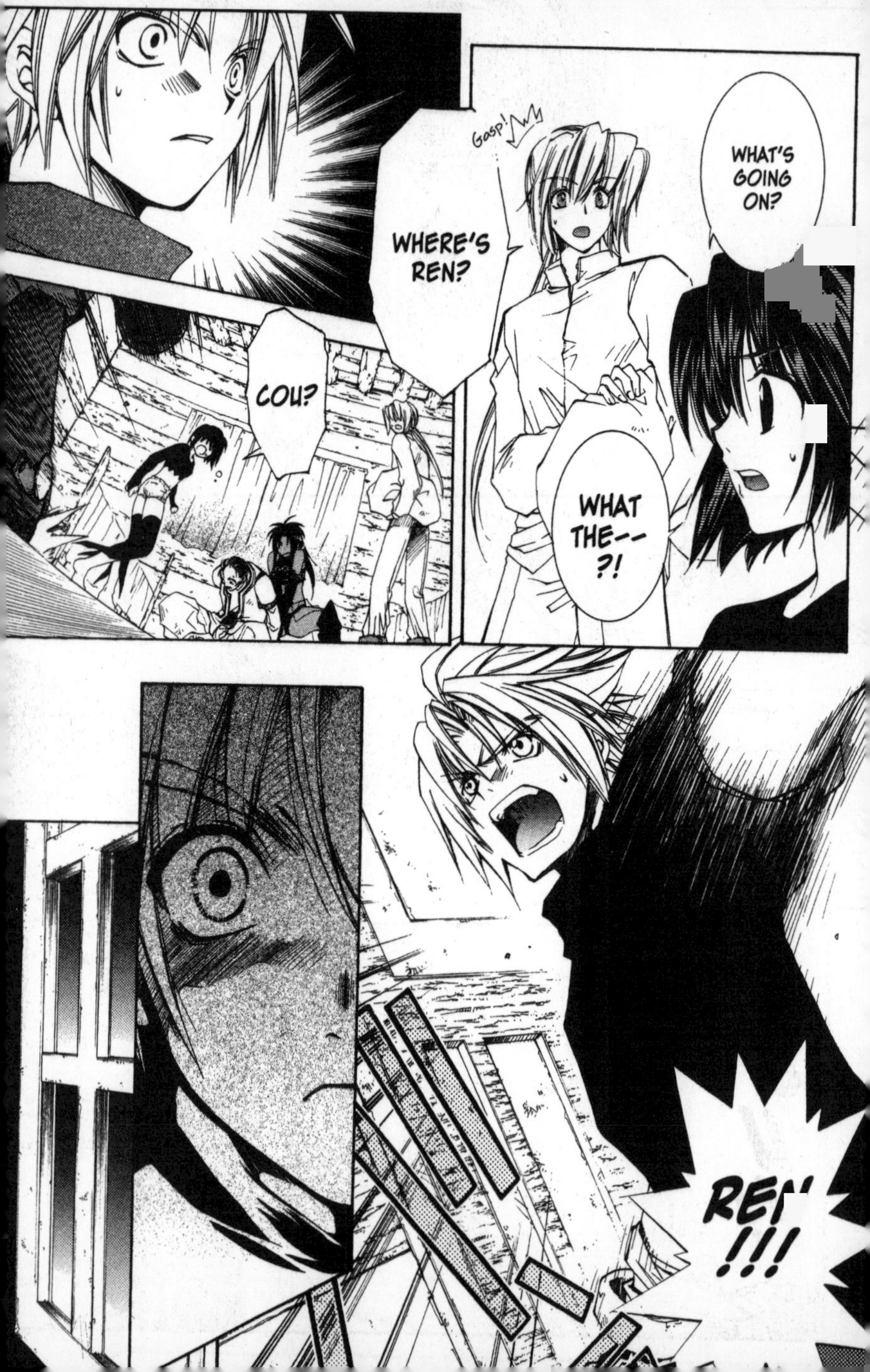
WHAT'S GOING ON?
Gasp!
WHERE'S REN?
WHAT THE--?!
COU?
REN!!!

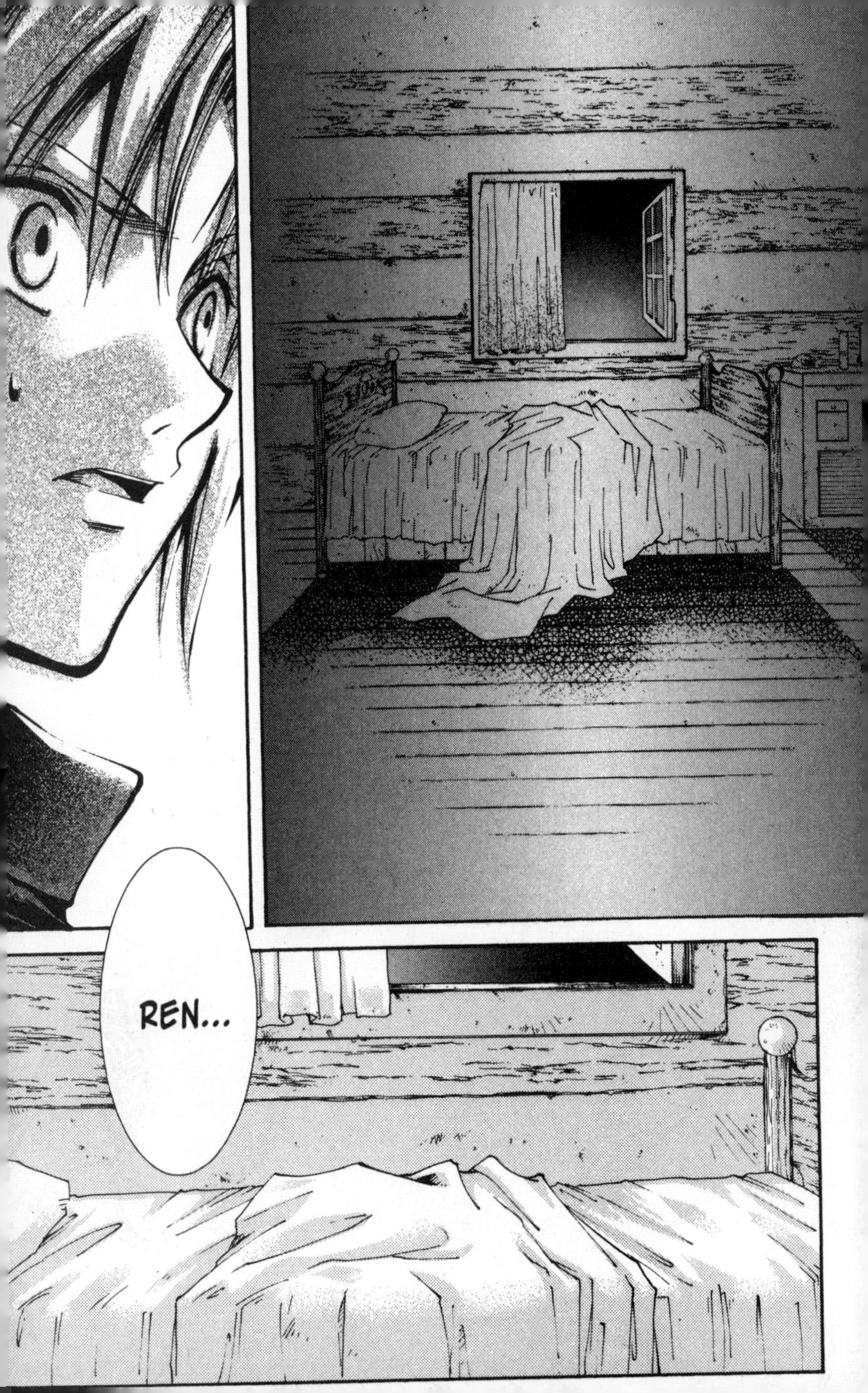
REN...

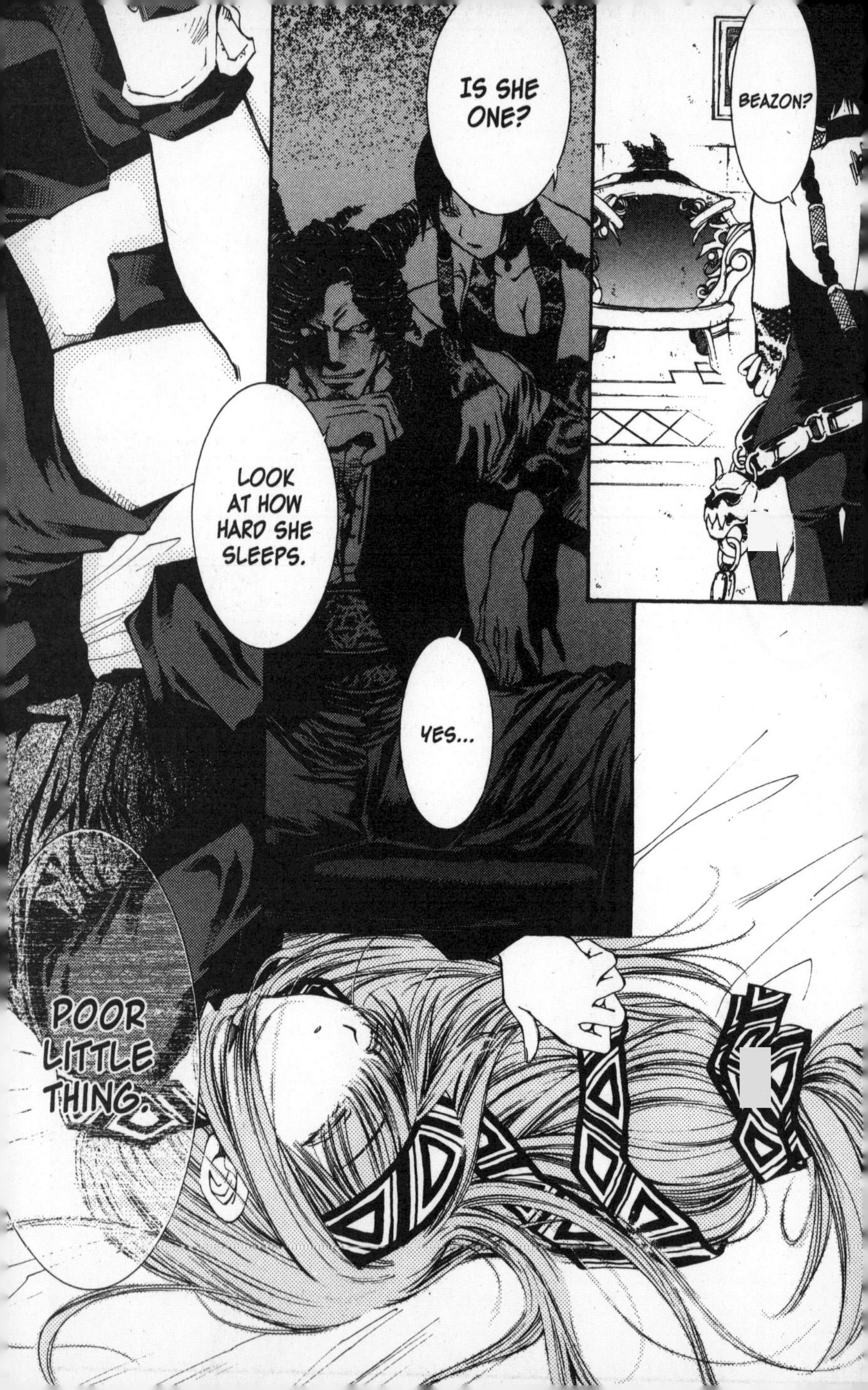
BEAZON?
IS SHE ONE?
LOOK AT HOW HARD SHE SLEEPS.
YES...
POOR LITTLE THING.

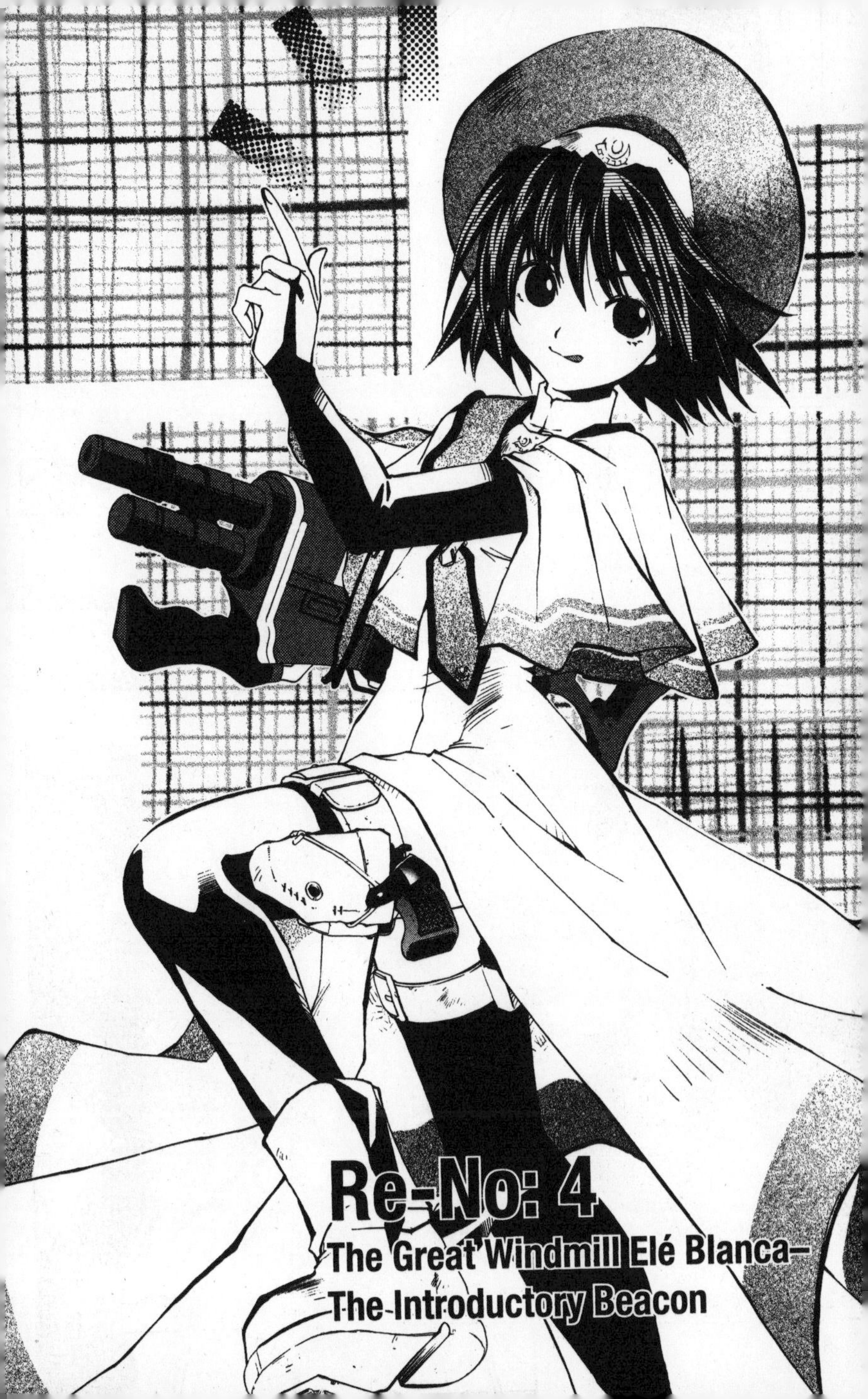
Re-No: 4
The Great Windmill Elé Blanca–
The Introductory Beacon

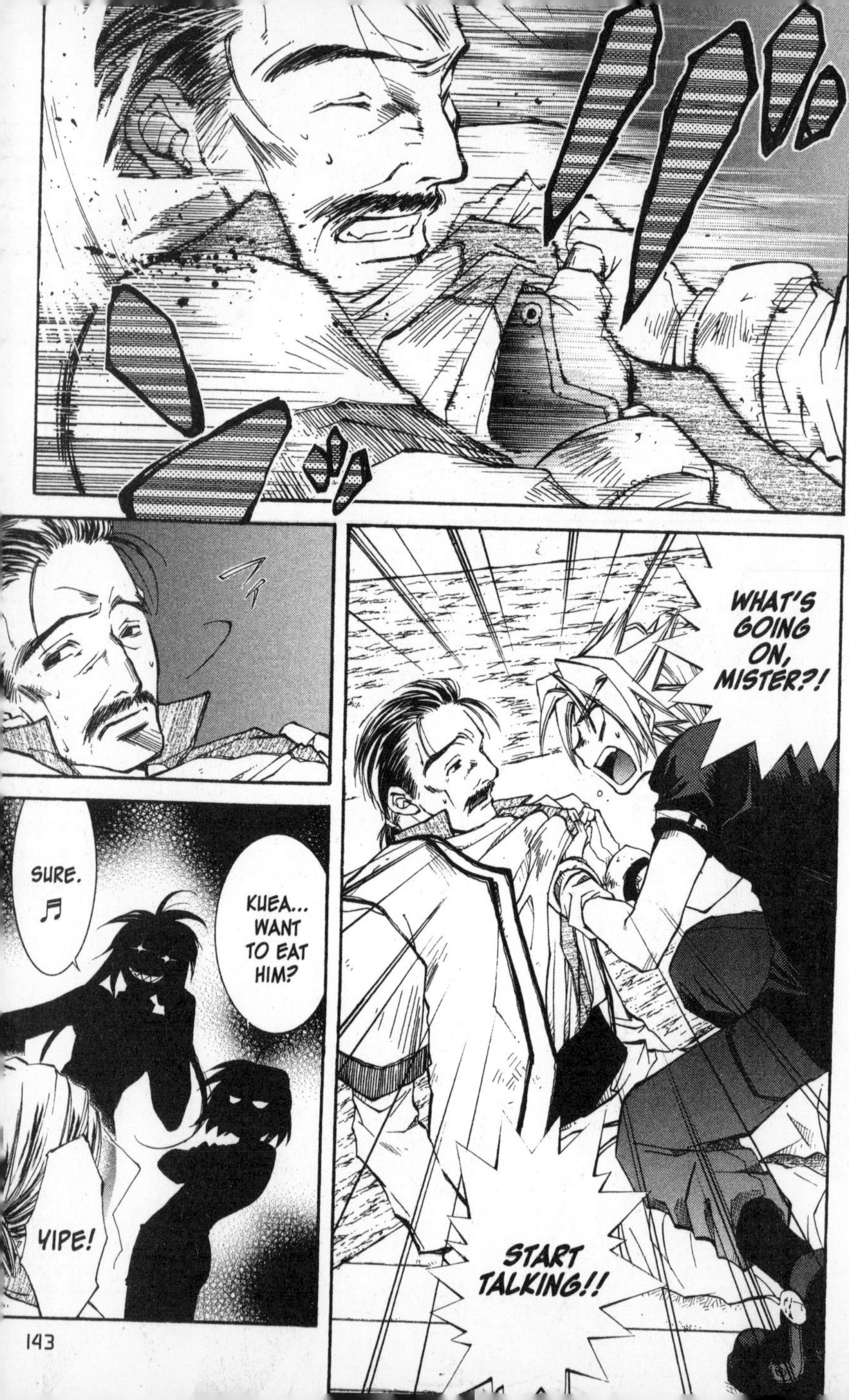
WHAT'S GOING ON, MISTER?!
START TALKING!!
KUEA... WANT TO EAT HIM?
SURE. ♬
YIPE!

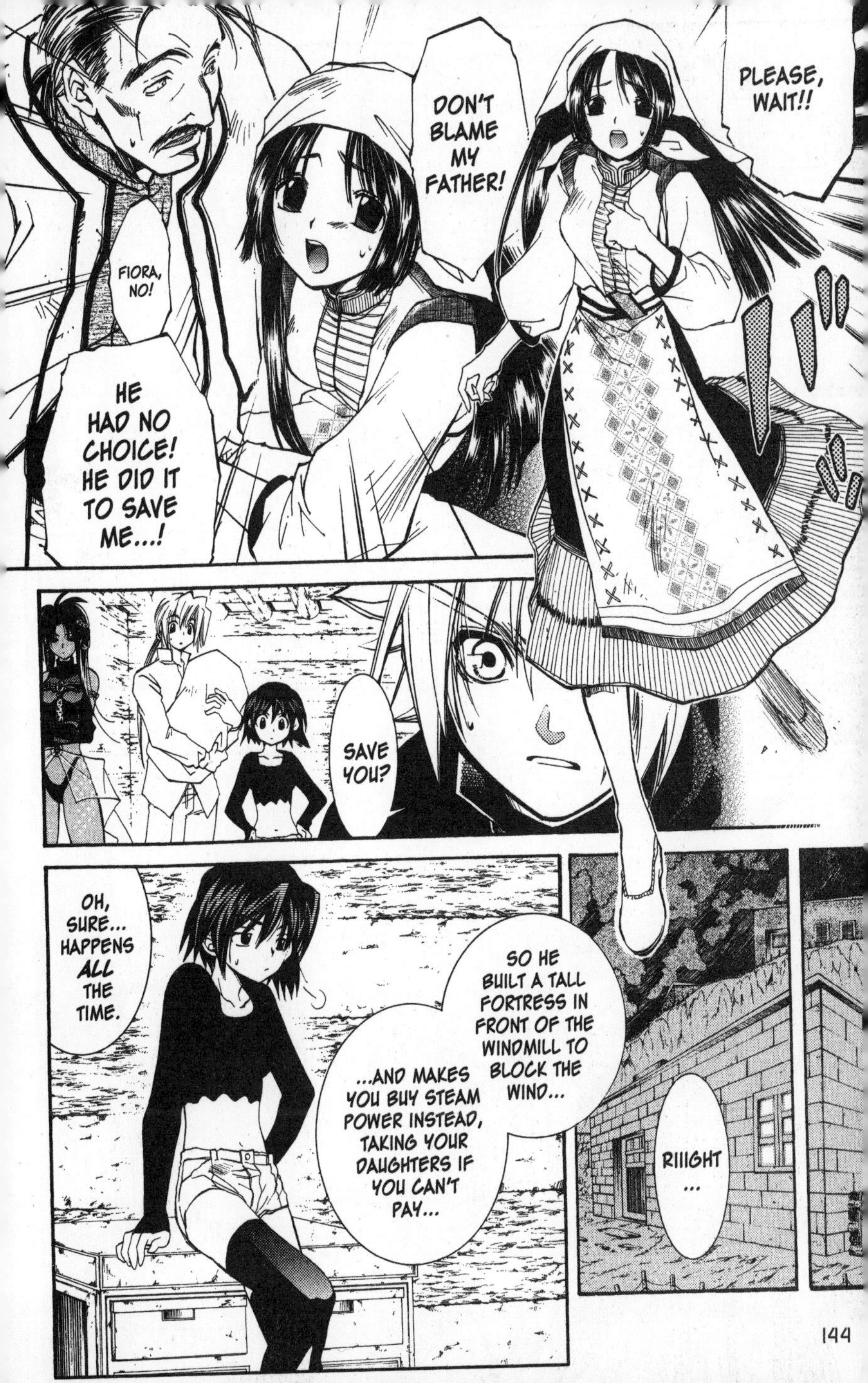
PLEASE, WAIT!!
DON'T BLAME MY FATHER!
FIORA, NO!
HE HAD NO CHOICE! HE DID IT TO SAVE ME...!
SAVE YOU?
RIIIGHT ...
SO HE BUILT A TALL FORTRESS IN FRONT OF THE WINDMILL TO BLOCK THE WIND...
...AND MAKES YOU BUY STEAM POWER INSTEAD, TAKING YOUR DAUGHTERS IF YOU CAN'T PAY...
OH, SURE... HAPPENS ALL THE TIME.

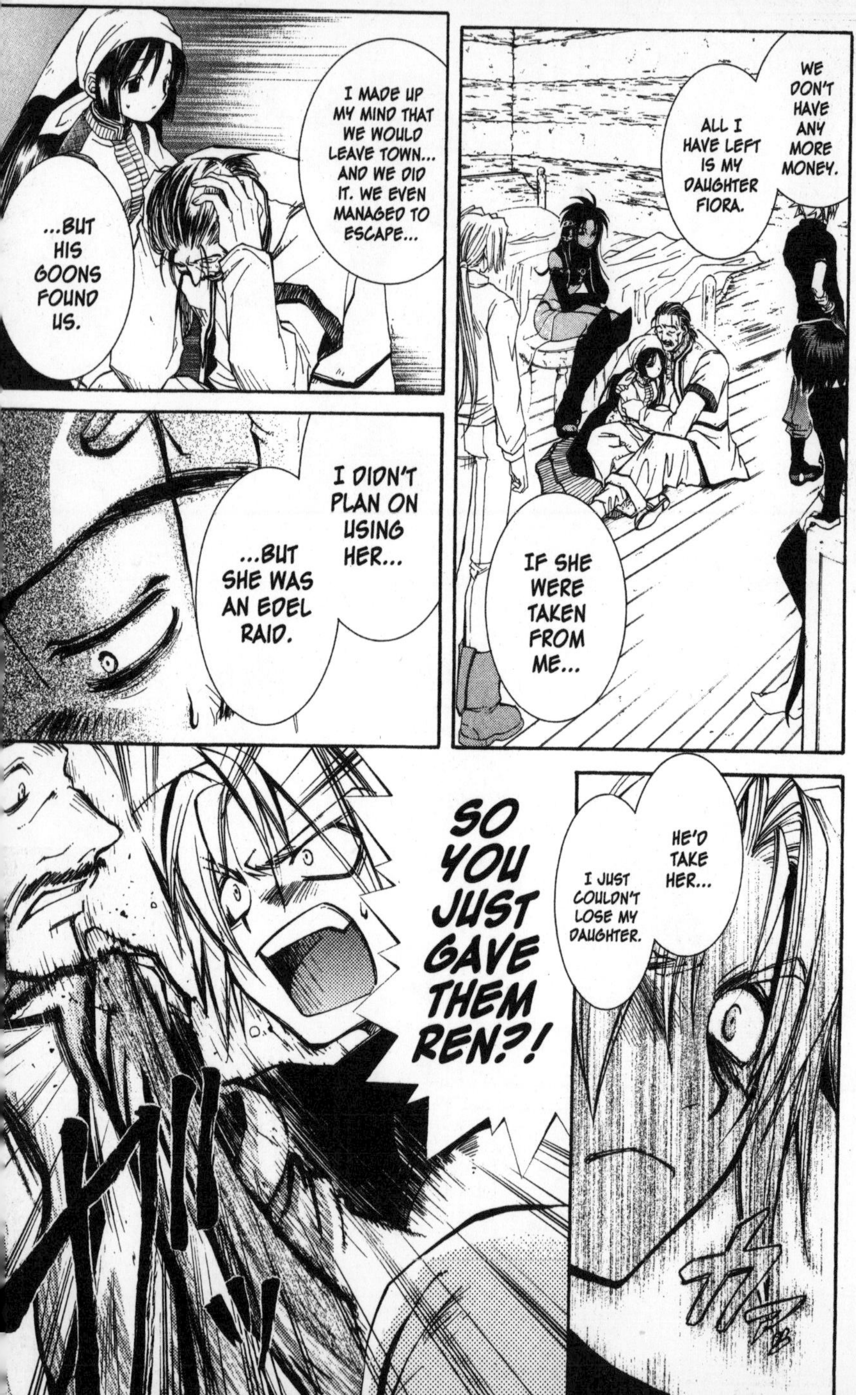
WE DON'T HAVE ANY MORE MONEY.
ALL I HAVE LEFT IS MY DAUGHTER FIORA.
IF SHE WERE TAKEN FROM ME...
I MADE UP MY MIND THAT WE WOULD LEAVE TOWN... AND WE DID IT. WE EVEN MANAGED TO ESCAPE...
...BUT HIS GOONS FOUND US.
I DIDN'T PLAN ON USING HER...
...BUT SHE WAS AN EDEL RAID.
HE'D TAKE HER...
I JUST COULDN'T LOSE MY DAUGHTER.
SO YOU JUST GAVE THEM REN?!

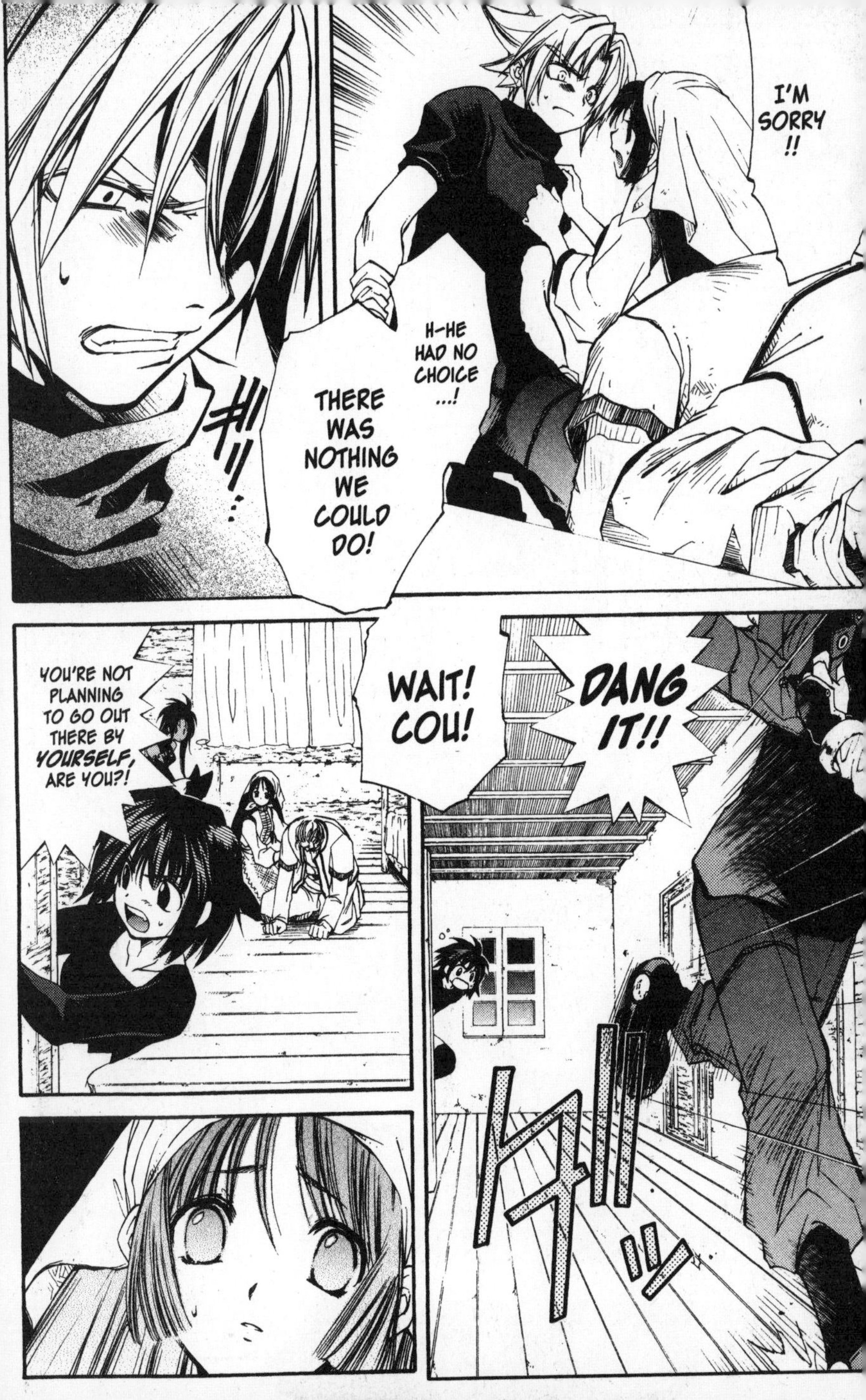
I'M SORRY!!
H-HE HAD NO CHOICE ...!
THERE WAS NOTHING WE COULD DO!
DANG IT!!
WAIT! COU!
YOU'RE NOT PLANNING TO GO OUT THERE BY *YOURSELF*, ARE YOU?!

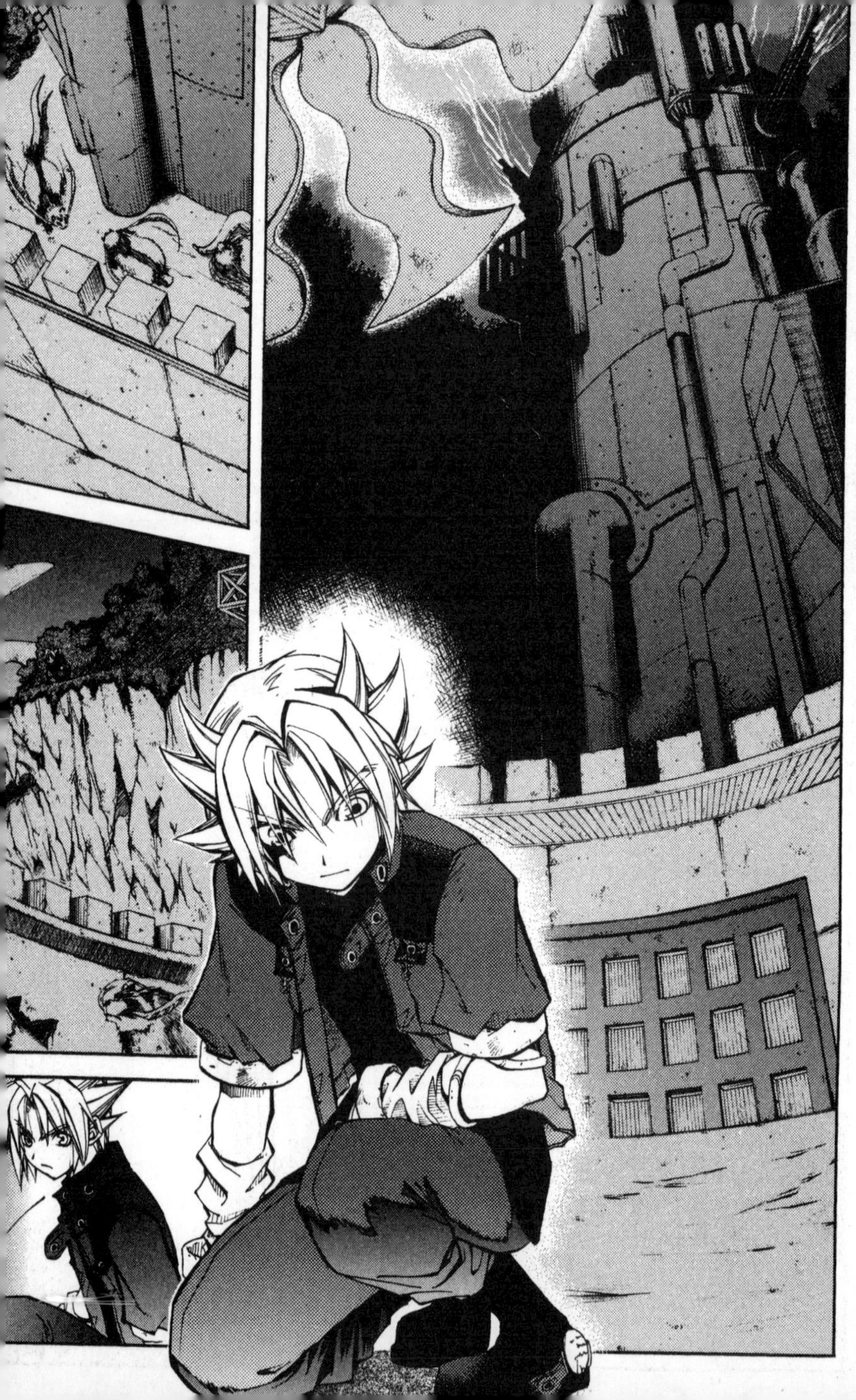

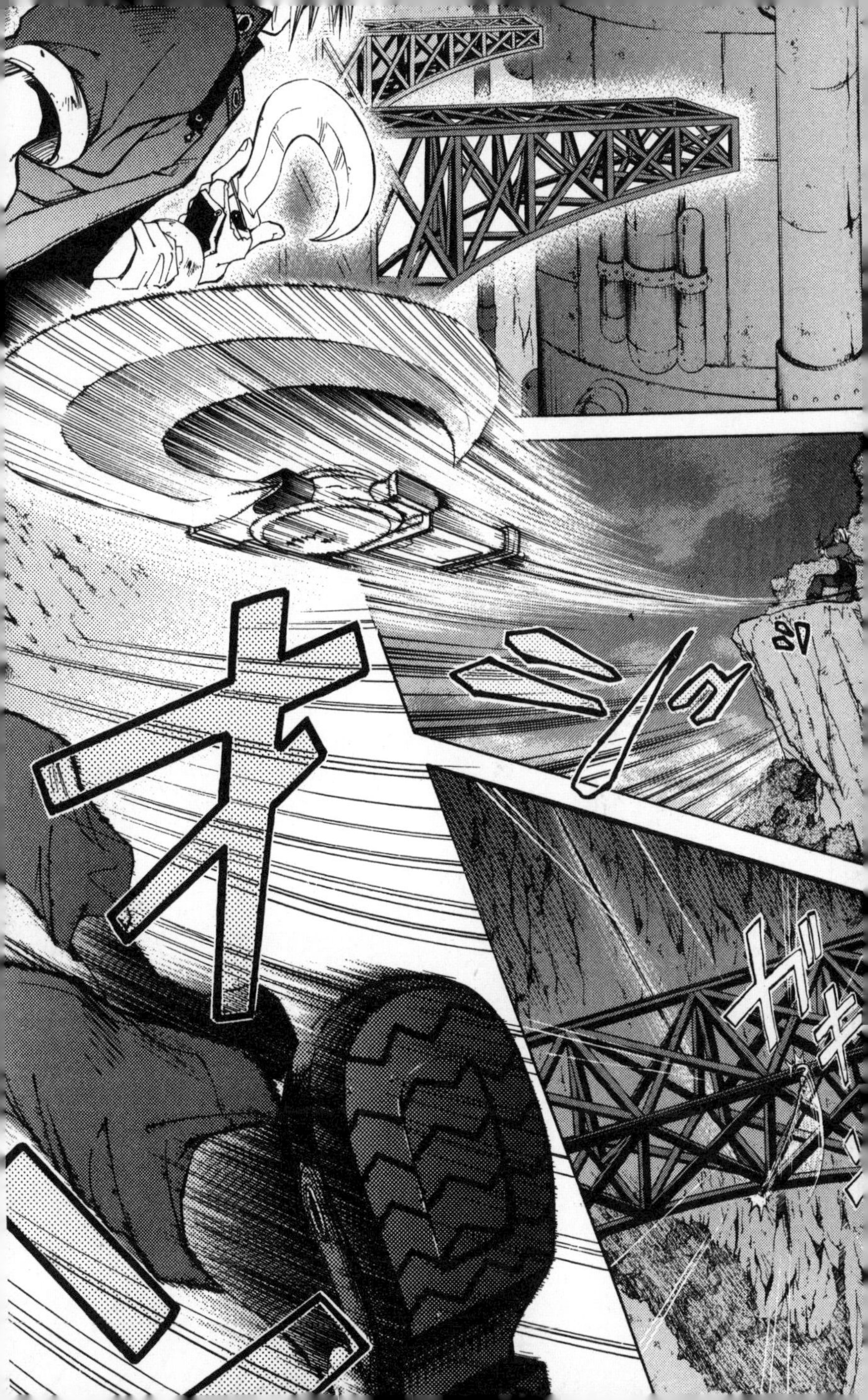
オ
ガキ

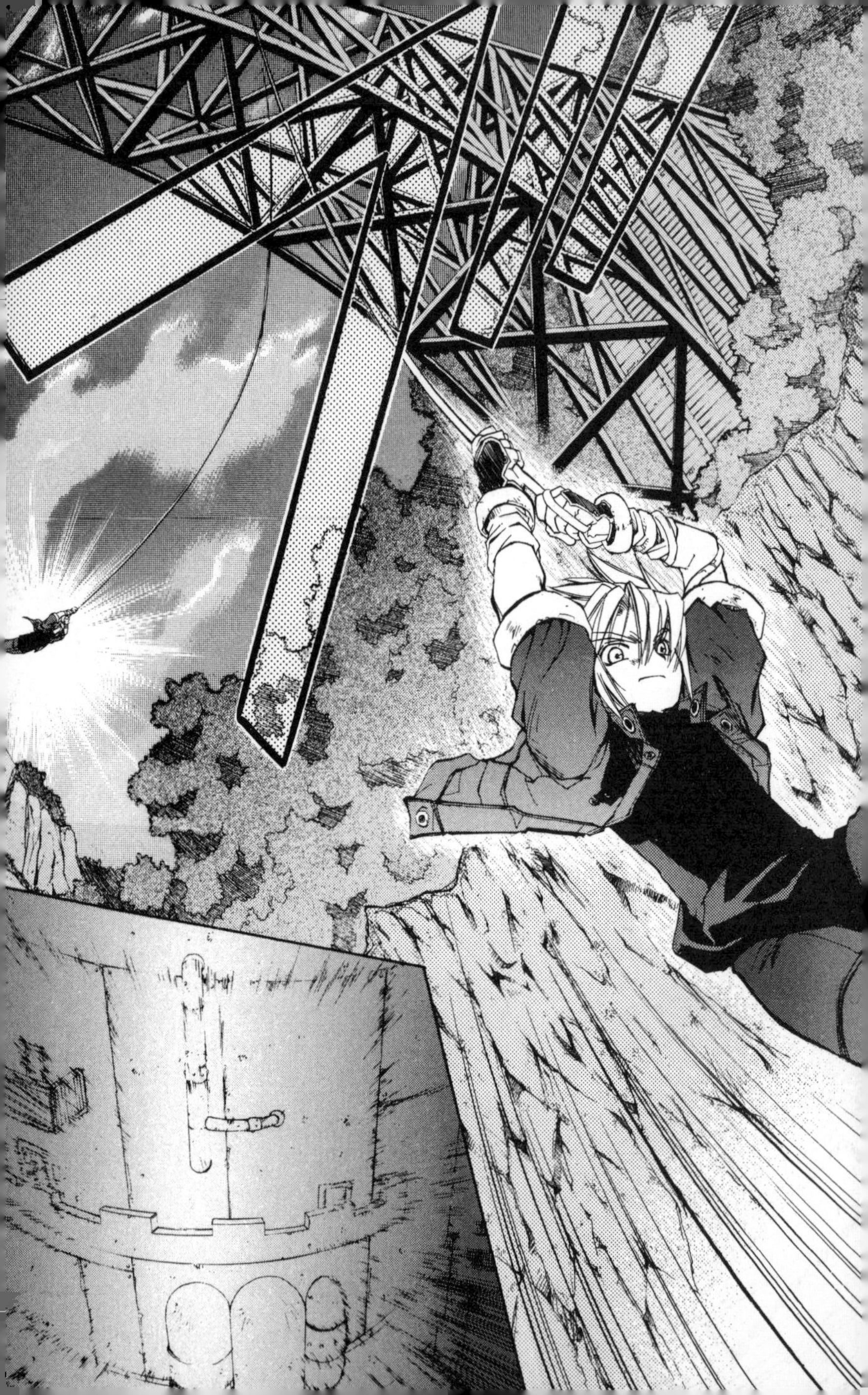

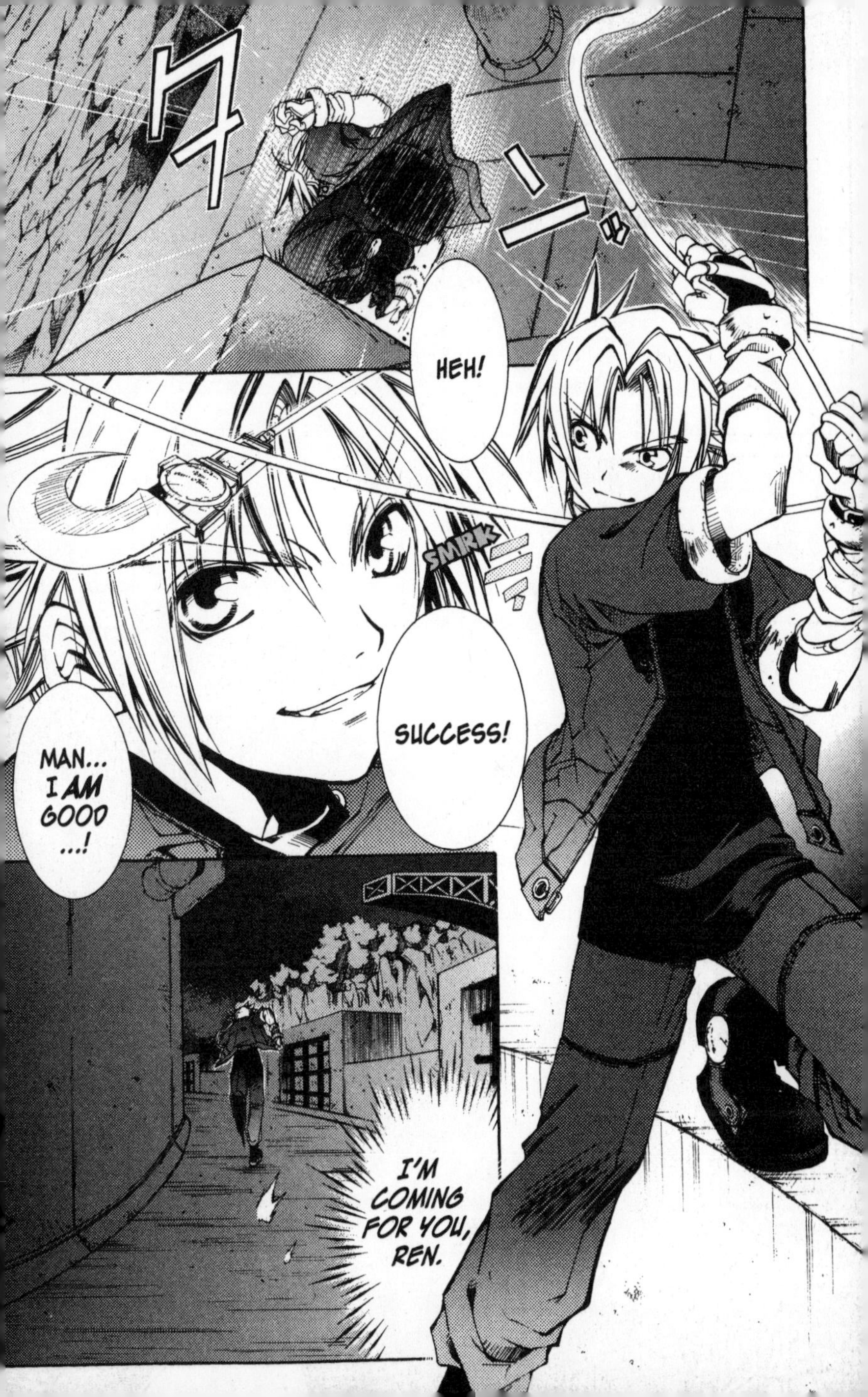
HEH!
SMRK
SUCCESS!
MAN... I AM GOOD ...!
I'M COMING FOR YOU, REN.

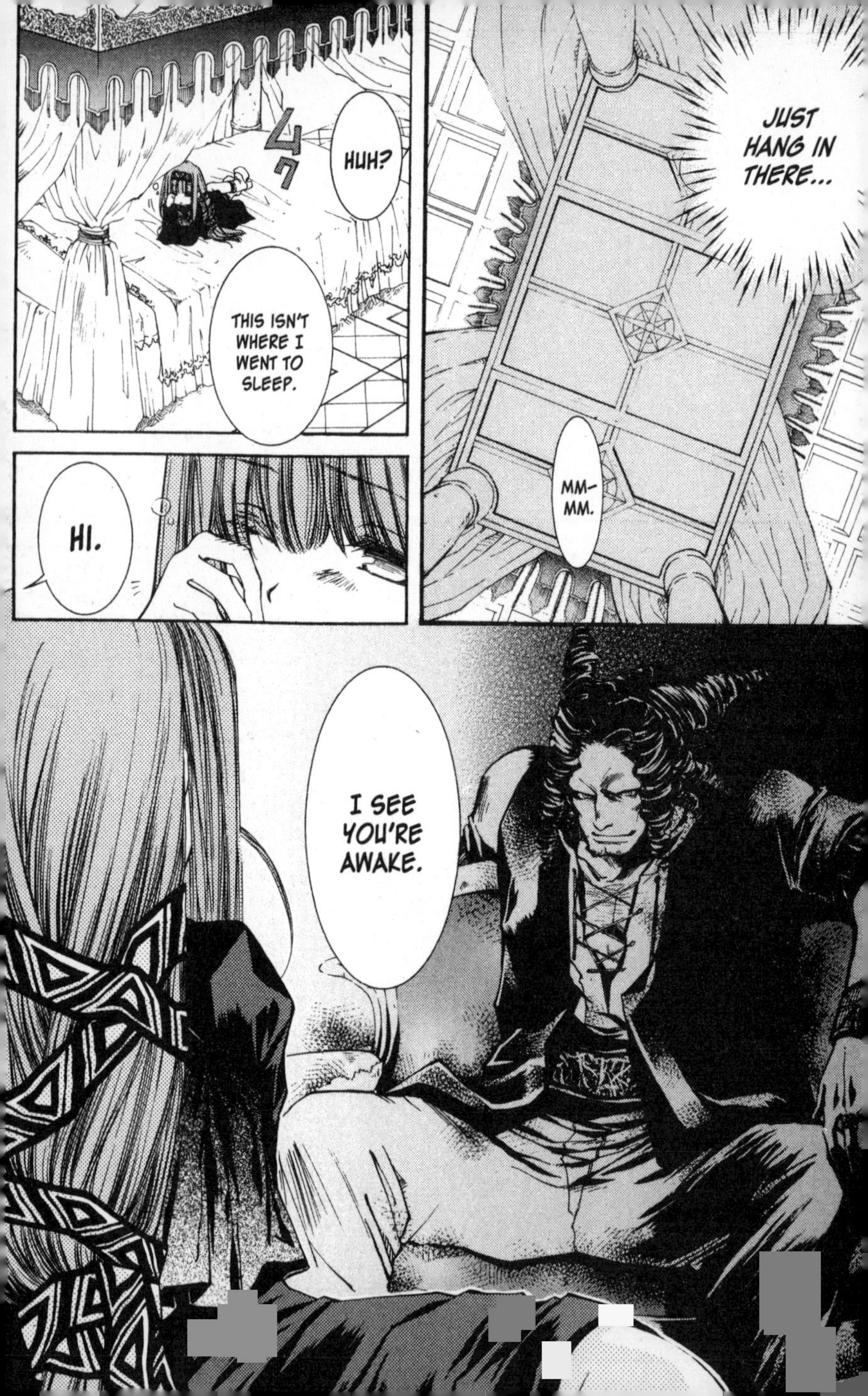
JUST HANG IN THERE...
MM-MM.
ムク
HUH?
THIS ISN'T WHERE I WENT TO SLEEP.
HI.
I SEE YOU'RE AWAKE.

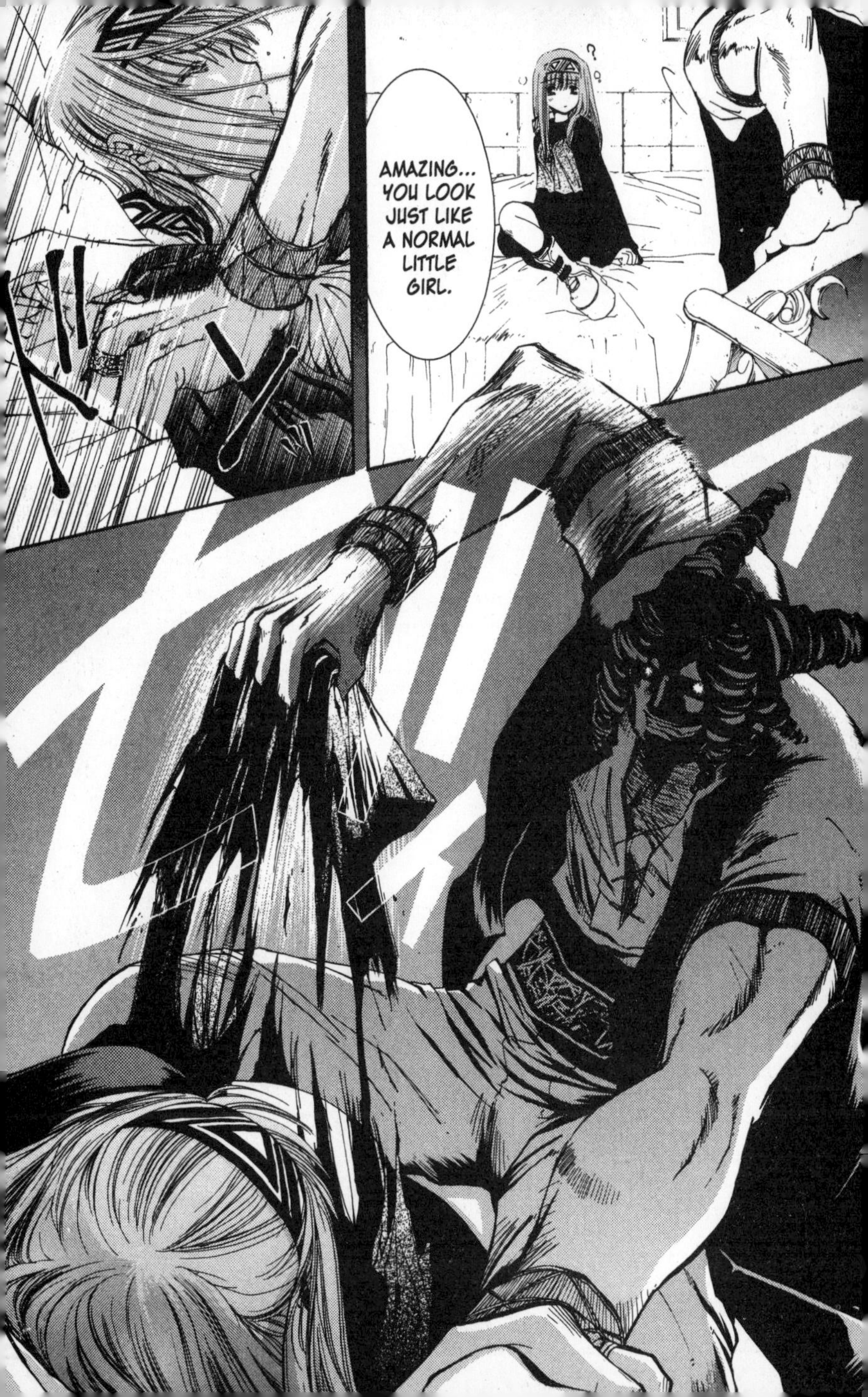
AMAZING... YOU LOOK JUST LIKE A NORMAL LITTLE GIRL.

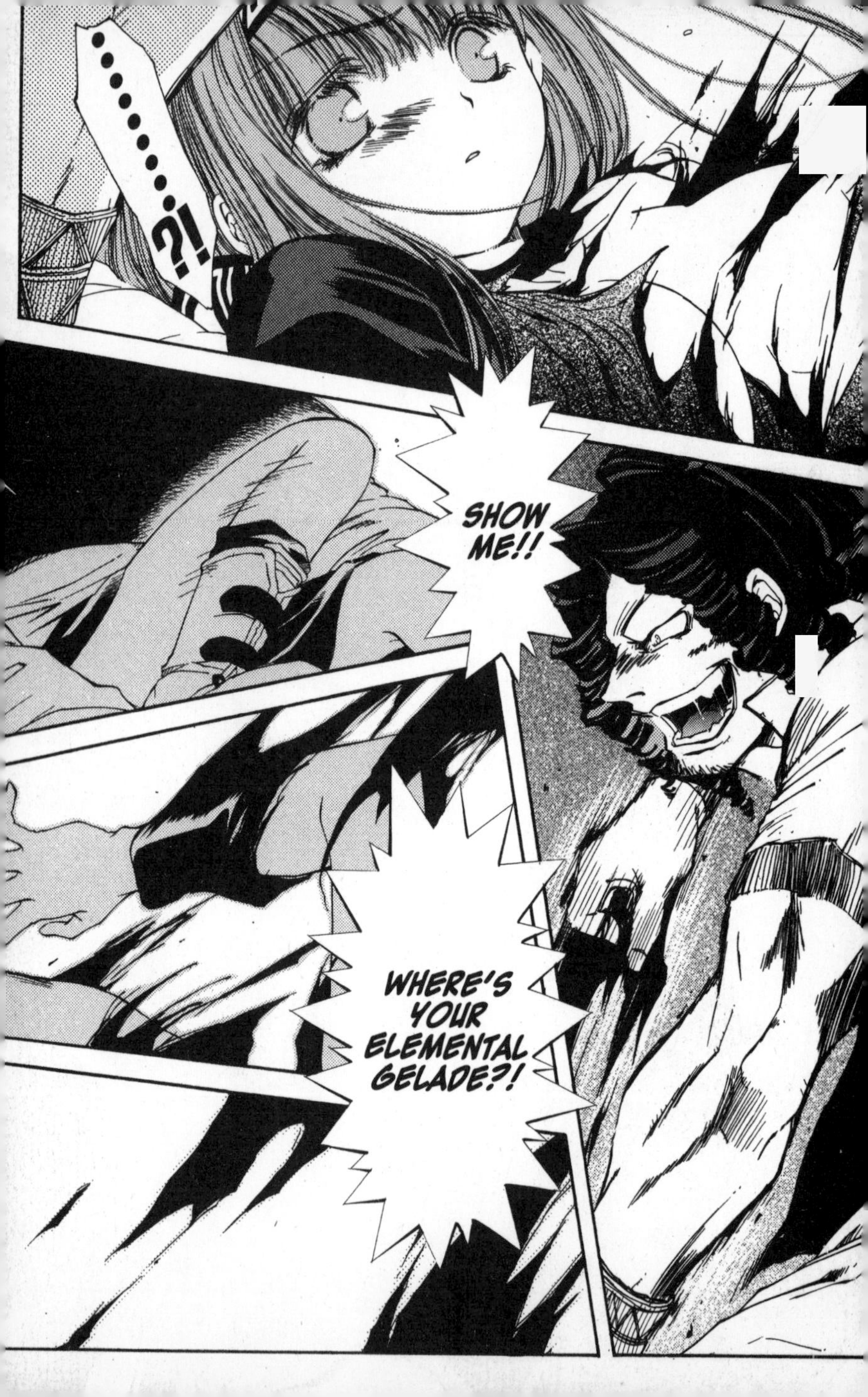
......?!
SHOW ME!!
WHERE'S YOUR ELEMENTAL GELADE?!

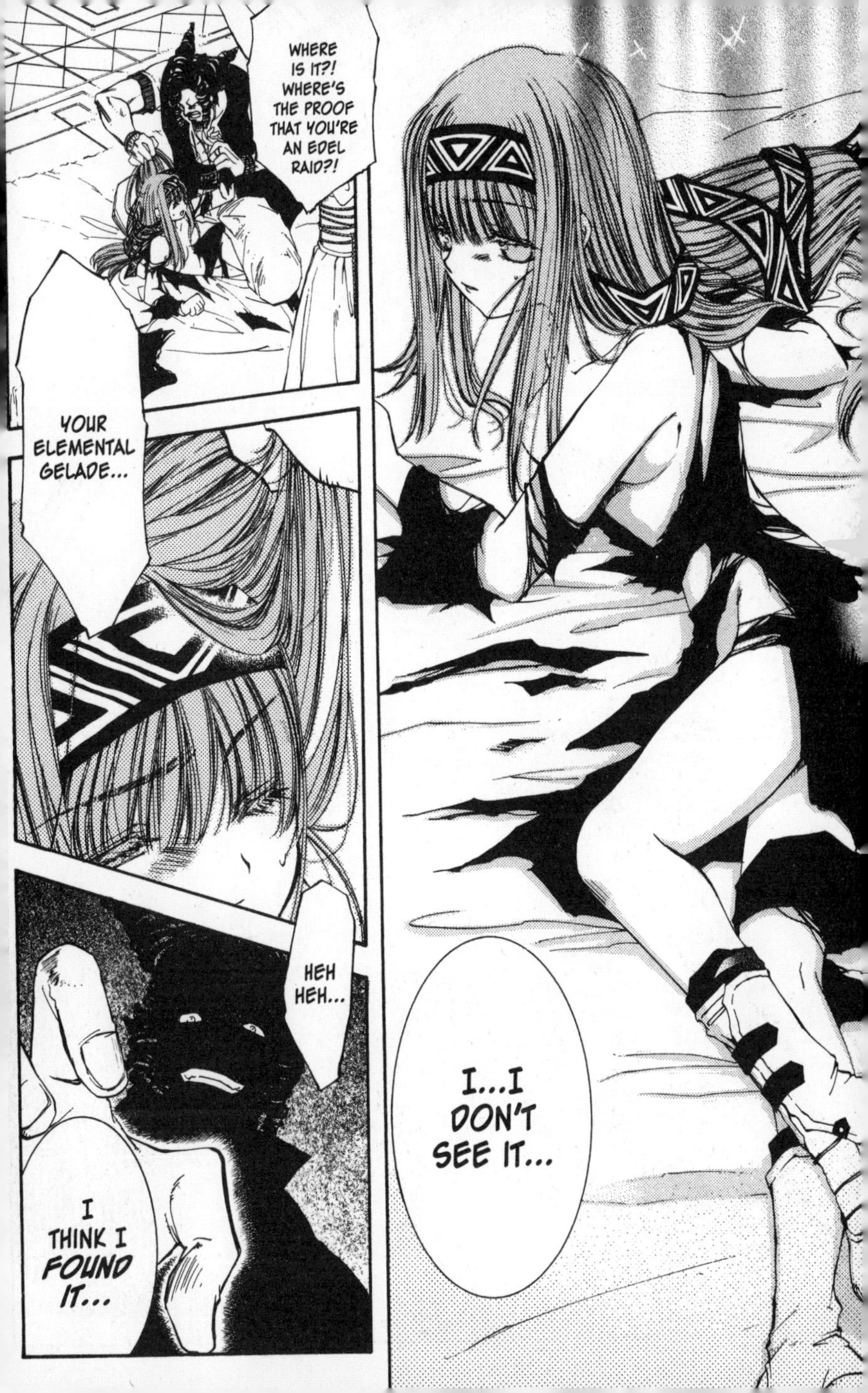
I...I DON'T SEE IT...
WHERE IS IT?! WHERE'S THE PROOF THAT YOU'RE AN EDEL RAID?!
YOUR ELEMENTAL GELADE...
HEH HEH...
I THINK I *FOUND* IT...

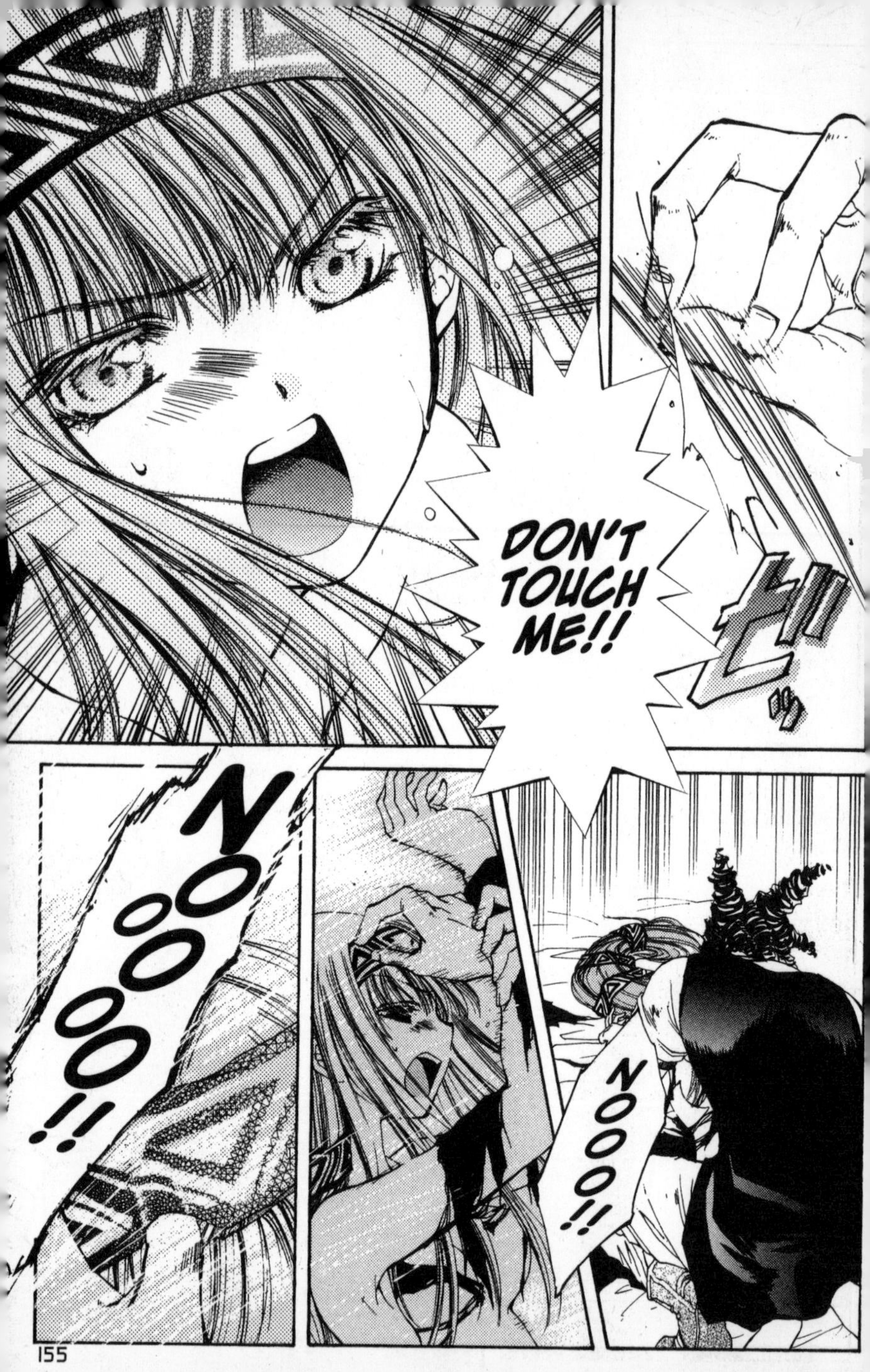
DON'T TOUCH ME!!
NOOOO!!
NOOOOOO!!

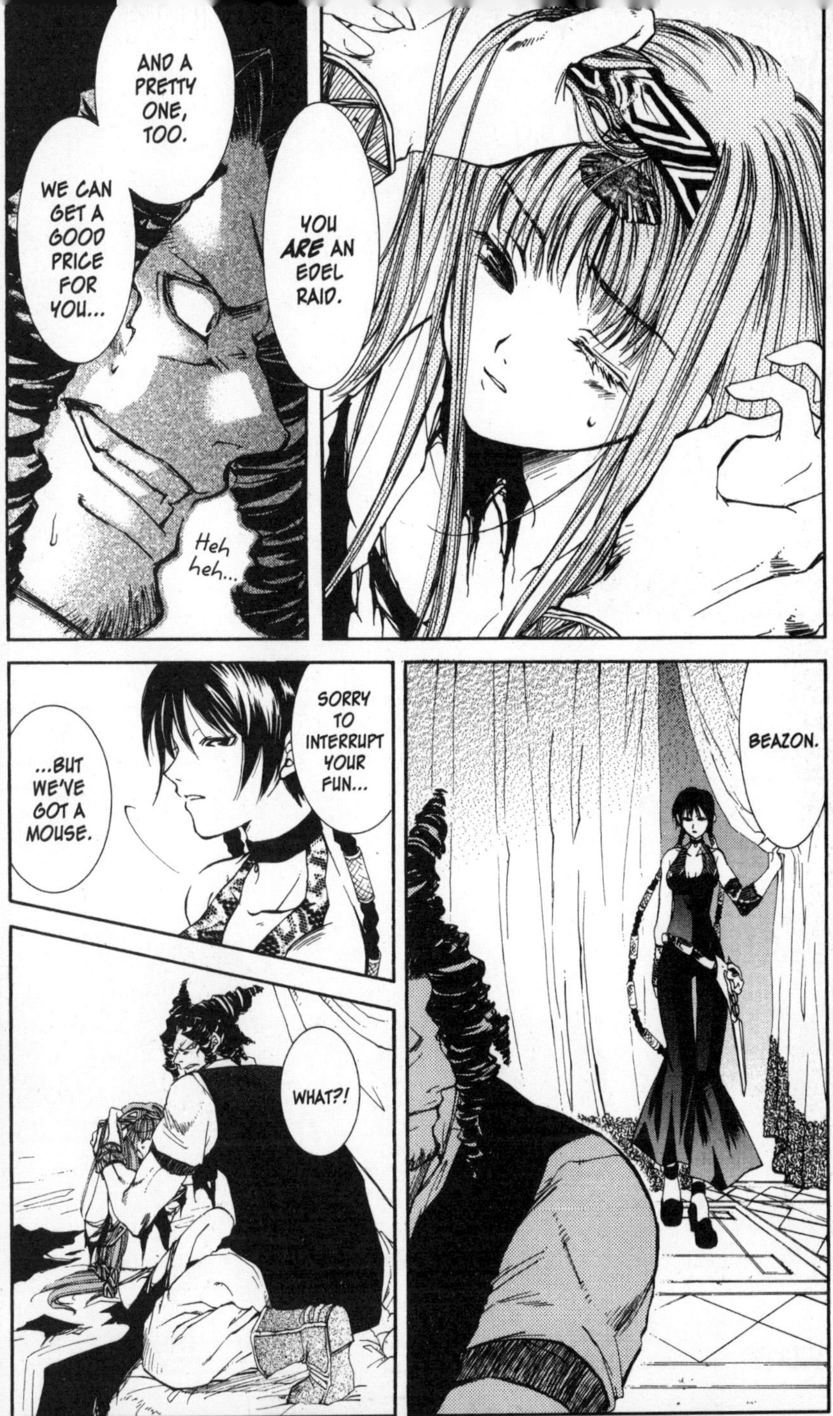
YOU ARE AN EDEL RAID.
AND A PRETTY ONE, TOO.
WE CAN GET A GOOD PRICE FOR YOU...
Heh heh...
BEAZON.
SORRY TO INTERRUPT YOUR FUN...
...BUT WE'VE GOT A MOUSE.
WHAT?!

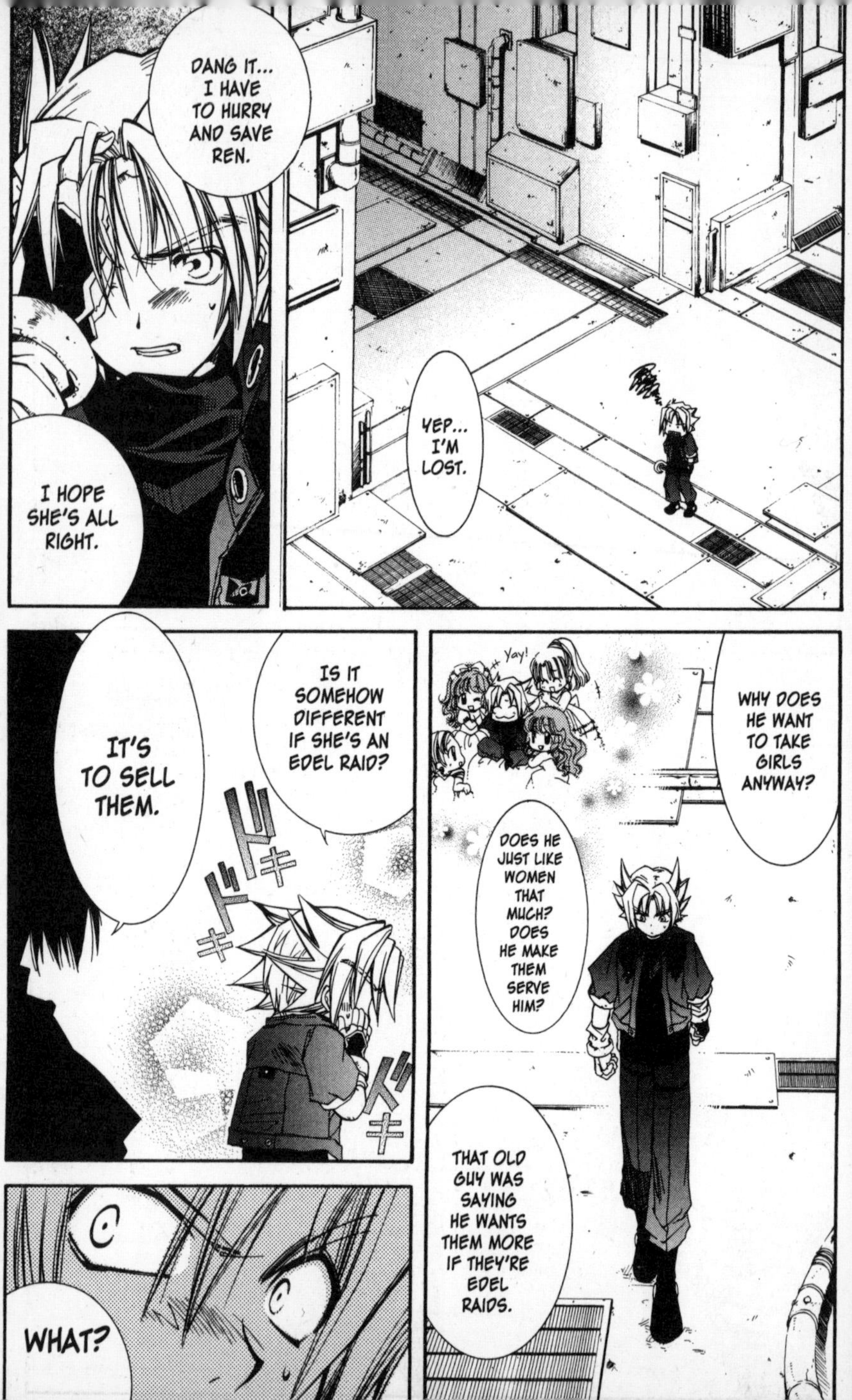
YEP... I'M LOST.
DANG IT... I HAVE TO HURRY AND SAVE REN.
I HOPE SHE'S ALL RIGHT.
WHY DOES HE WANT TO TAKE GIRLS ANYWAY?
Yay!
DOES HE JUST LIKE WOMEN THAT MUCH? DOES HE MAKE THEM SERVE HIM?
THAT OLD GUY WAS SAYING HE WANTS THEM MORE IF THEY'RE EDEL RAIDS.
IS IT SOMEHOW DIFFERENT IF SHE'S AN EDEL RAID?
IT'S TO SELL THEM.
WHAT?

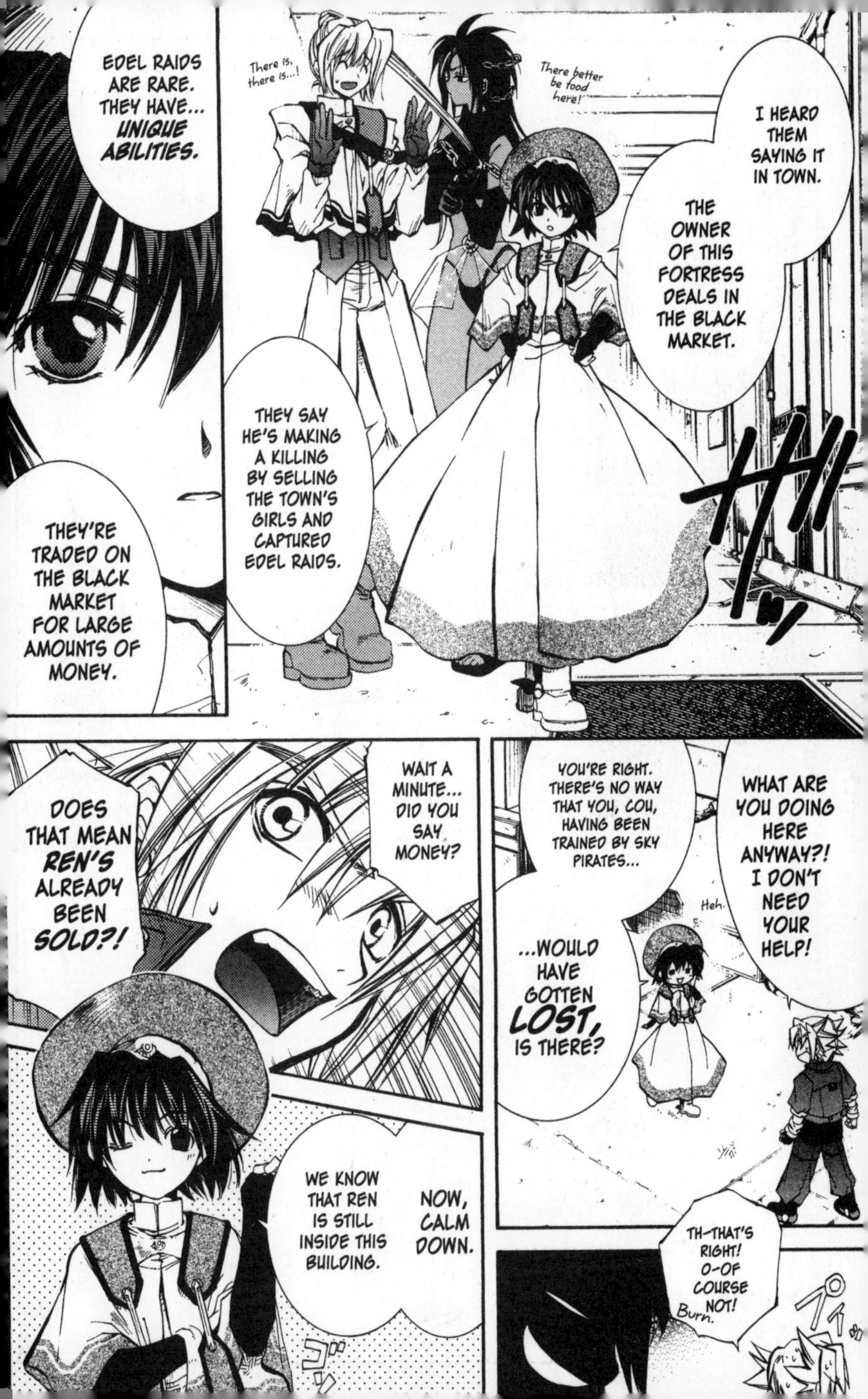
I HEARD THEM SAYING IT IN TOWN.
THE OWNER OF THIS FORTRESS DEALS IN THE BLACK MARKET.
There better be food here!
There is, there is...!
THEY SAY HE'S MAKING A KILLING BY SELLING THE TOWN'S GIRLS AND CAPTURED EDEL RAIDS.
EDEL RAIDS ARE RARE. THEY HAVE... UNIQUE ABILITIES.
THEY'RE TRADED ON THE BLACK MARKET FOR LARGE AMOUNTS OF MONEY.
WHAT ARE YOU DOING HERE ANYWAY?! I DON'T NEED YOUR HELP!
YOU'RE RIGHT. THERE'S NO WAY THAT YOU, COU, HAVING BEEN TRAINED BY SKY PIRATES...
Heh.
...WOULD HAVE GOTTEN LOST, IS THERE?
TH-THAT'S RIGHT! O-OF COURSE NOT!
Burn.
WAIT A MINUTE... DID YOU SAY MONEY?
DOES THAT MEAN REN'S ALREADY BEEN SOLD?!
NOW, CALM DOWN.
WE KNOW THAT REN IS STILL INSIDE THIS BUILDING.

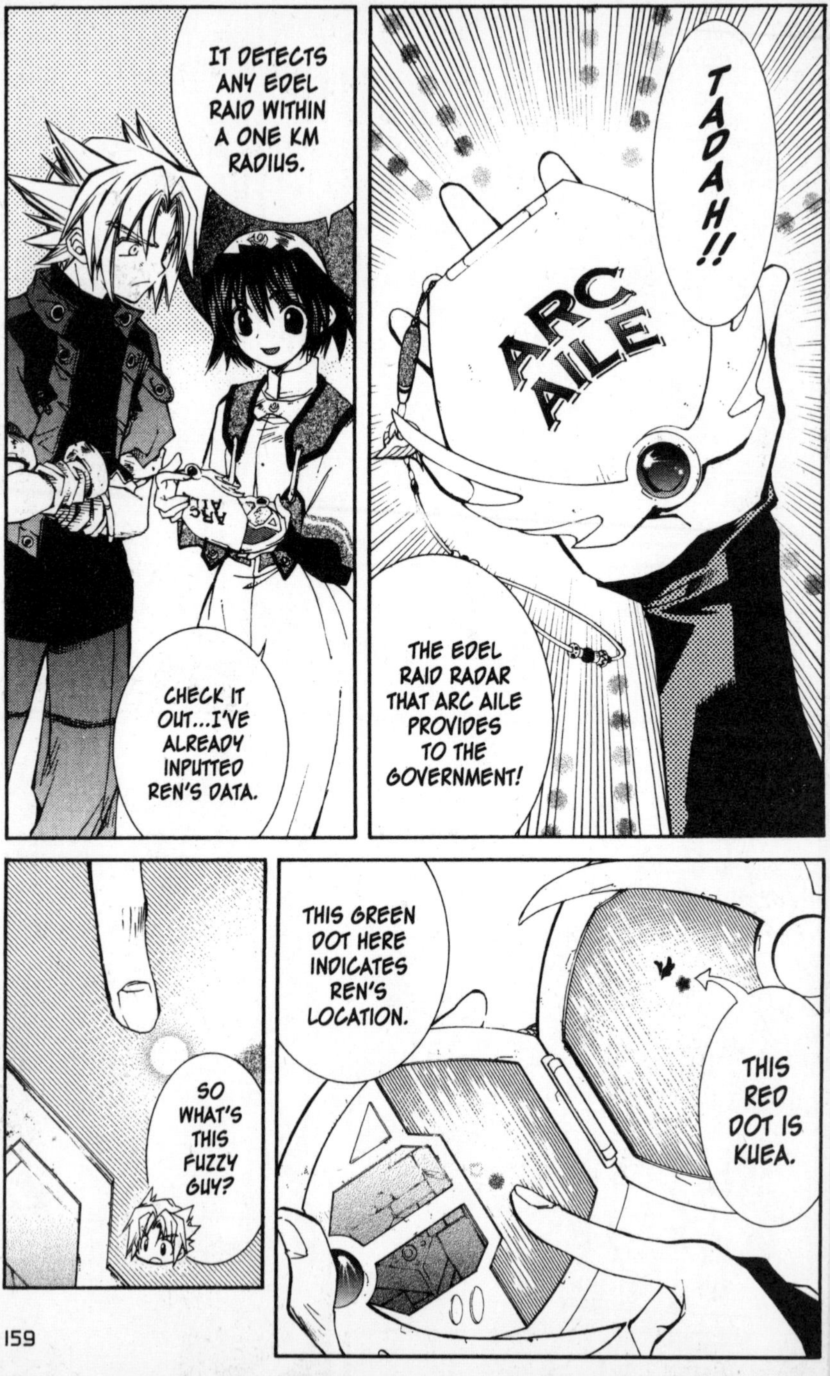
TADAH!!
ARC AILE
THE EDEL RAID RADAR THAT ARC AILE PROVIDES TO THE GOVERNMENT!
IT DETECTS ANY EDEL RAID WITHIN A ONE KM RADIUS.
CHECK IT OUT...I'VE ALREADY INPUTTED REN'S DATA.
ARC AILE
THIS GREEN DOT HERE INDICATES REN'S LOCATION.
THIS RED DOT IS KUEA.
SO WHAT'S THIS FUZZY GUY?

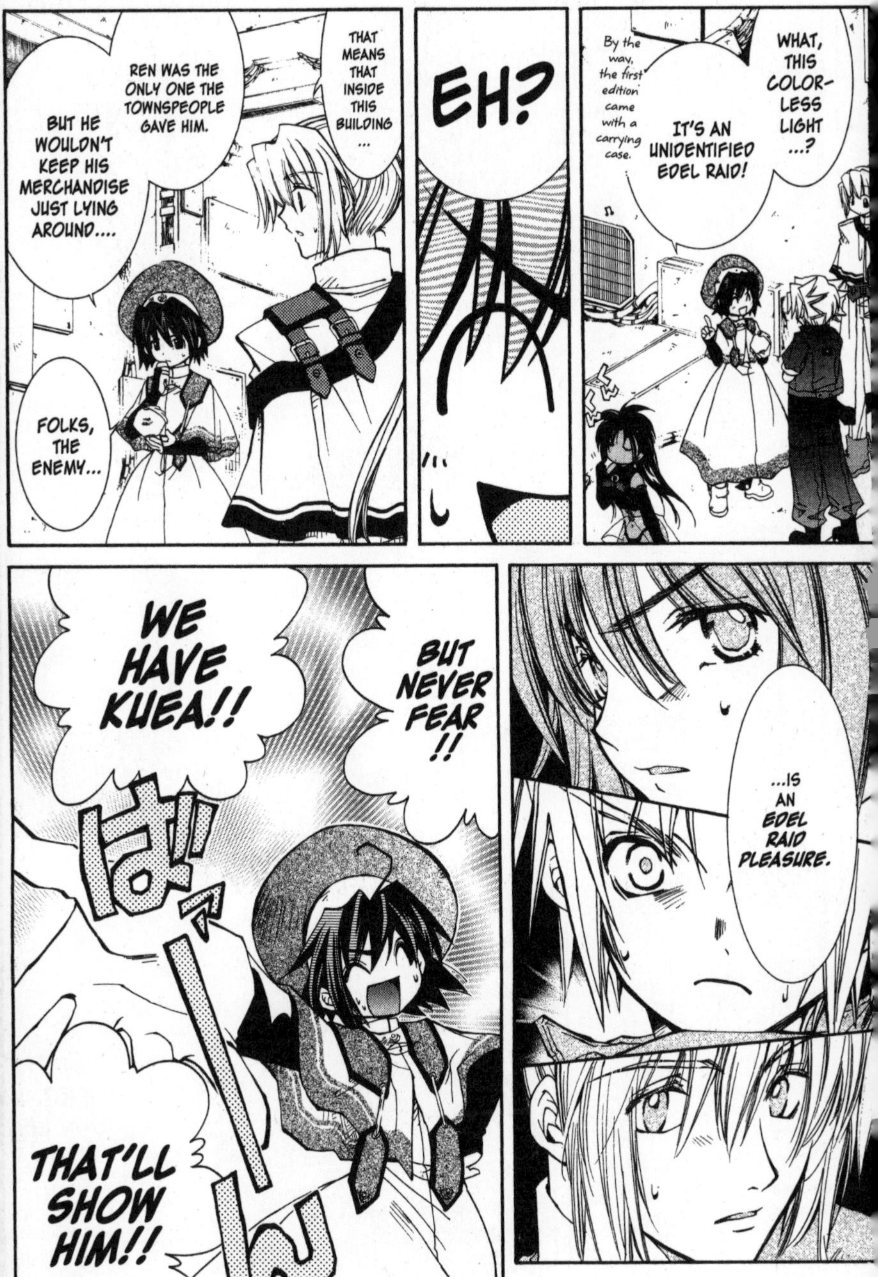
WHAT, THIS COLOR-LESS LIGHT ...?
IT'S AN UNIDENTIFIED EDEL RAID!
By the way, the first edition came with a carrying case.
EH?
THAT MEANS THAT INSIDE THIS BUILDING ...
REN WAS THE ONLY ONE THE TOWNSPEOPLE GAVE HIM.
BUT HE WOULDN'T KEEP HIS MERCHANDISE JUST LYING AROUND....
FOLKS, THE ENEMY...
...IS AN EDEL RAID PLEASURE.
BUT NEVER FEAR!!
WE HAVE KUEA!!
ばーん
THAT'LL SHOW HIM!!

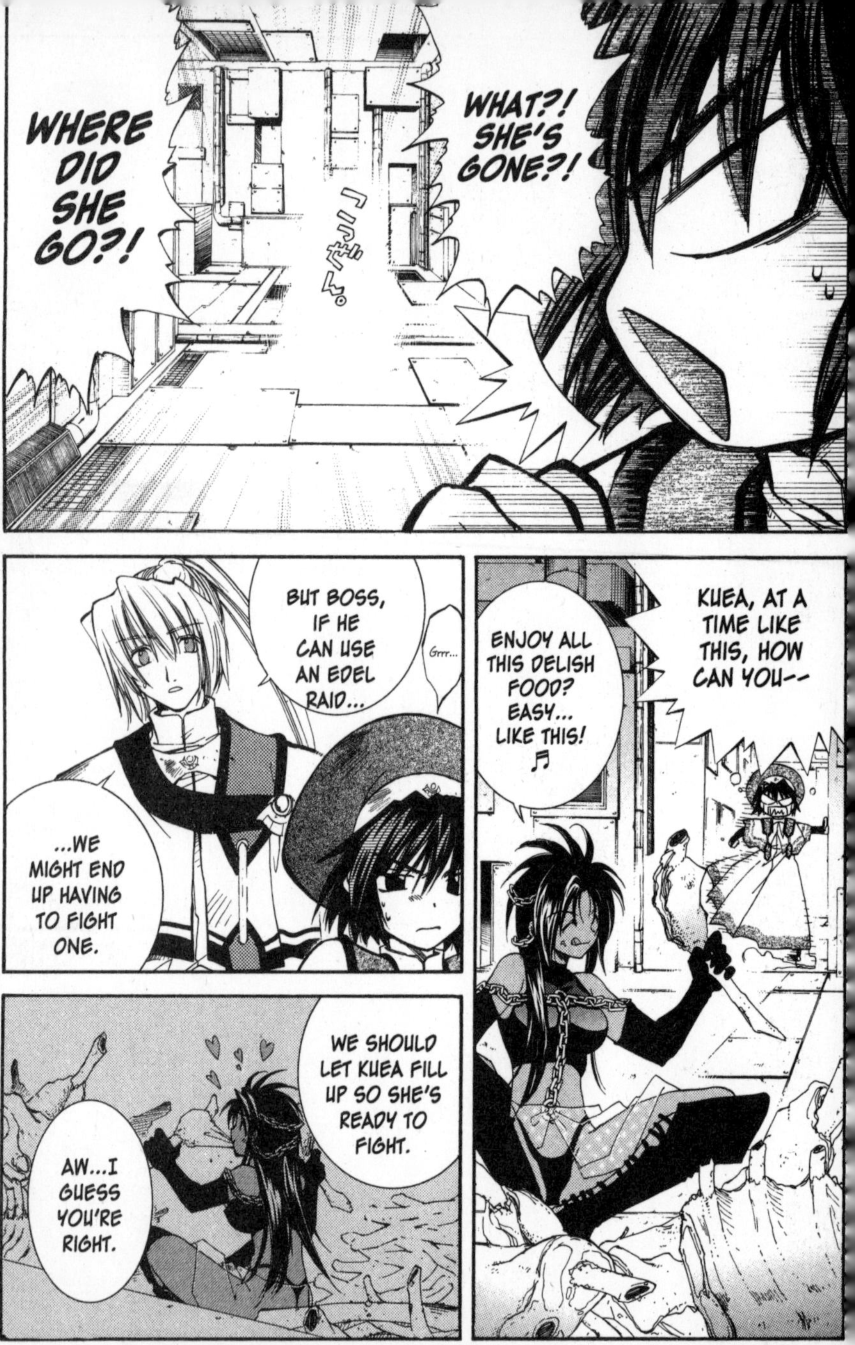
WHAT?! SHE'S GONE?!
こつぜん。
WHERE DID SHE GO?!
KUEA, AT A TIME LIKE THIS, HOW CAN YOU--
ENJOY ALL THIS DELISH FOOD? EASY... LIKE THIS! ♪
BUT BOSS, IF HE CAN USE AN EDEL RAID...
Grrr...
...WE MIGHT END UP HAVING TO FIGHT ONE.
WE SHOULD LET KUEA FILL UP SO SHE'S READY TO FIGHT.
AW...I GUESS YOU'RE RIGHT.

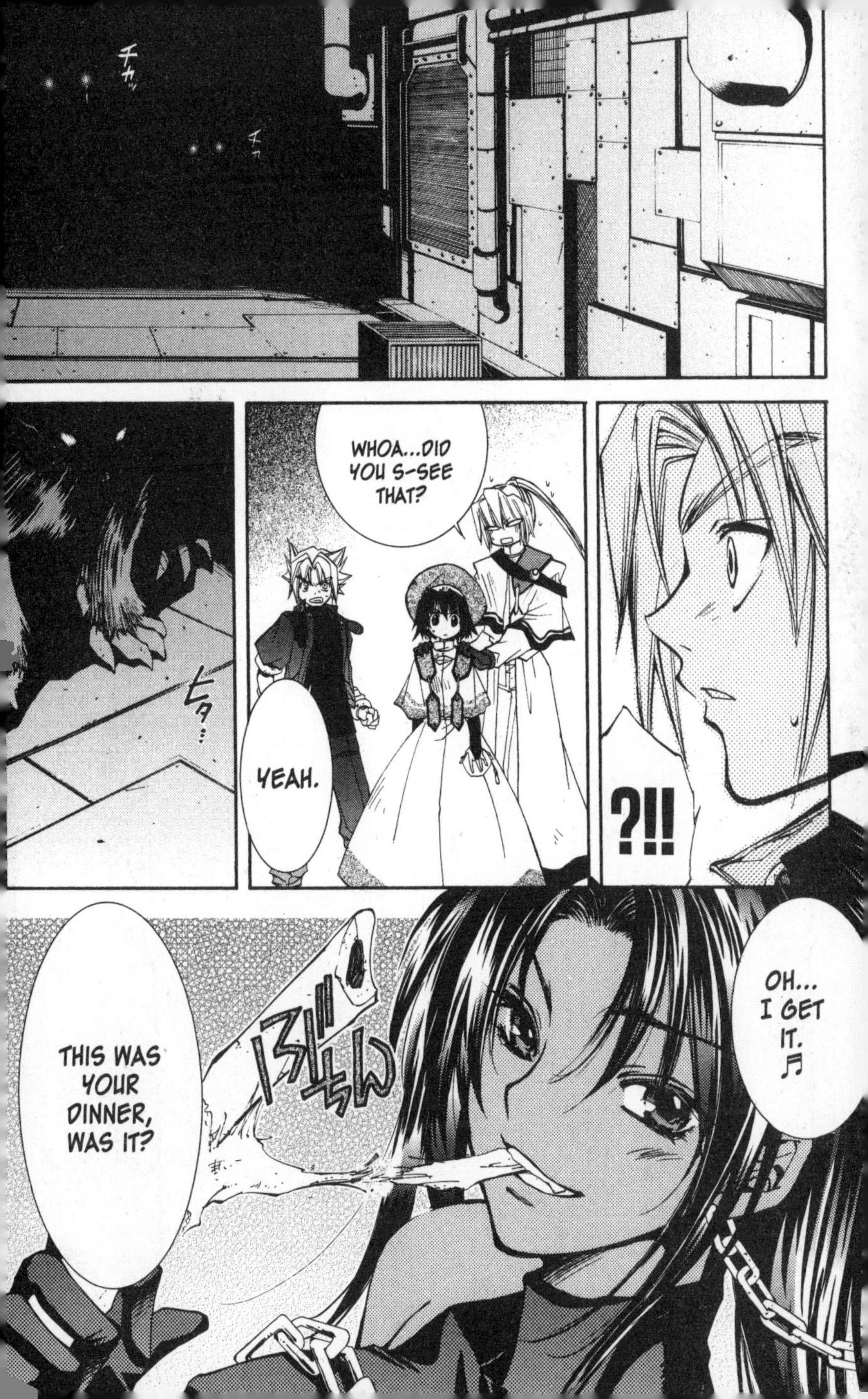
チカッ
チカ
?!!
WHOA...DID YOU S-SEE THAT?
YEAH.
OH... I GET IT. ♪
THIS WAS YOUR DINNER, WAS IT?

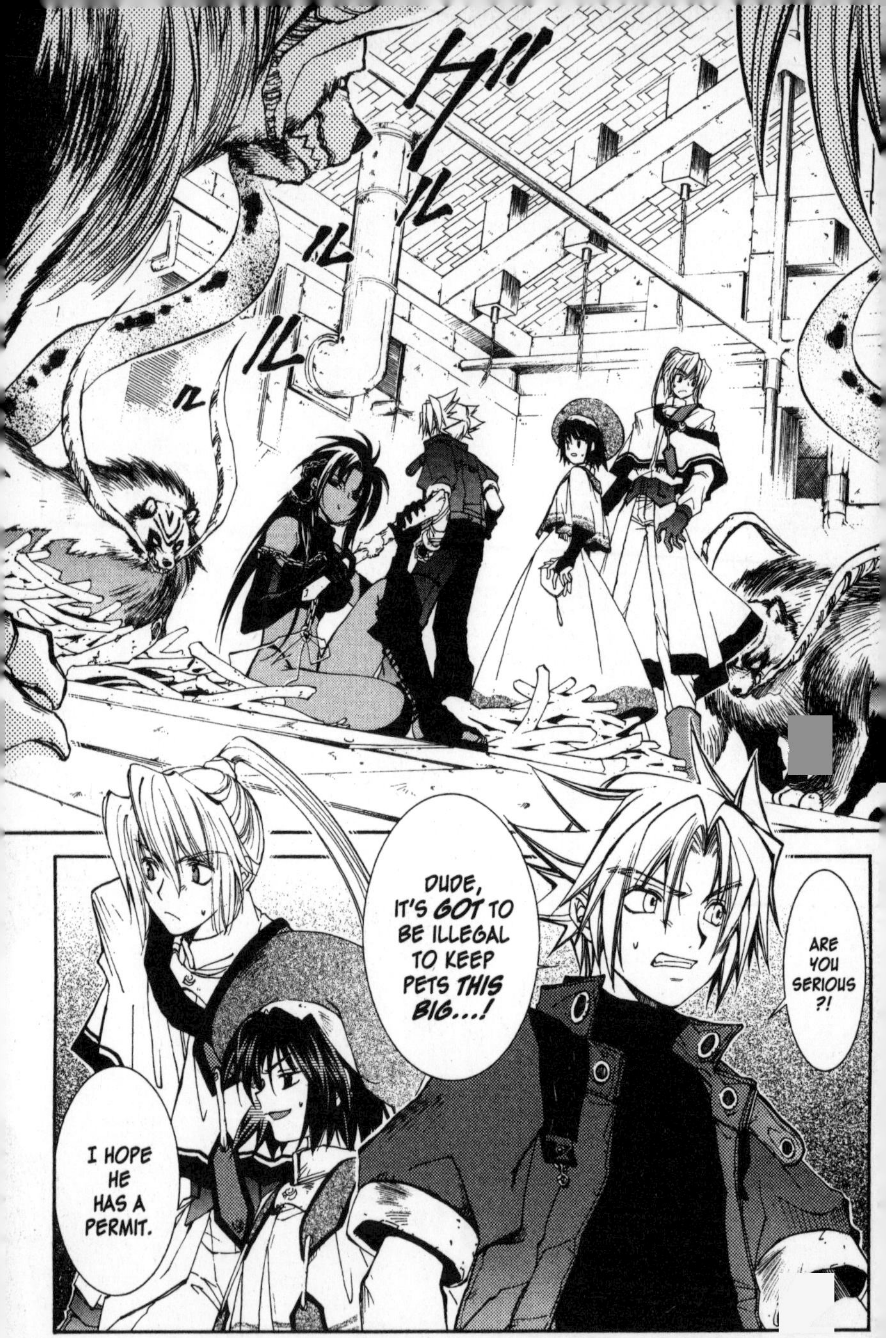
グルルルル
ARE YOU SERIOUS?!
DUDE, IT'S ***GOT*** TO BE ILLEGAL TO KEEP PETS ***THIS BIG...!***
I HOPE HE HAS A PERMIT.

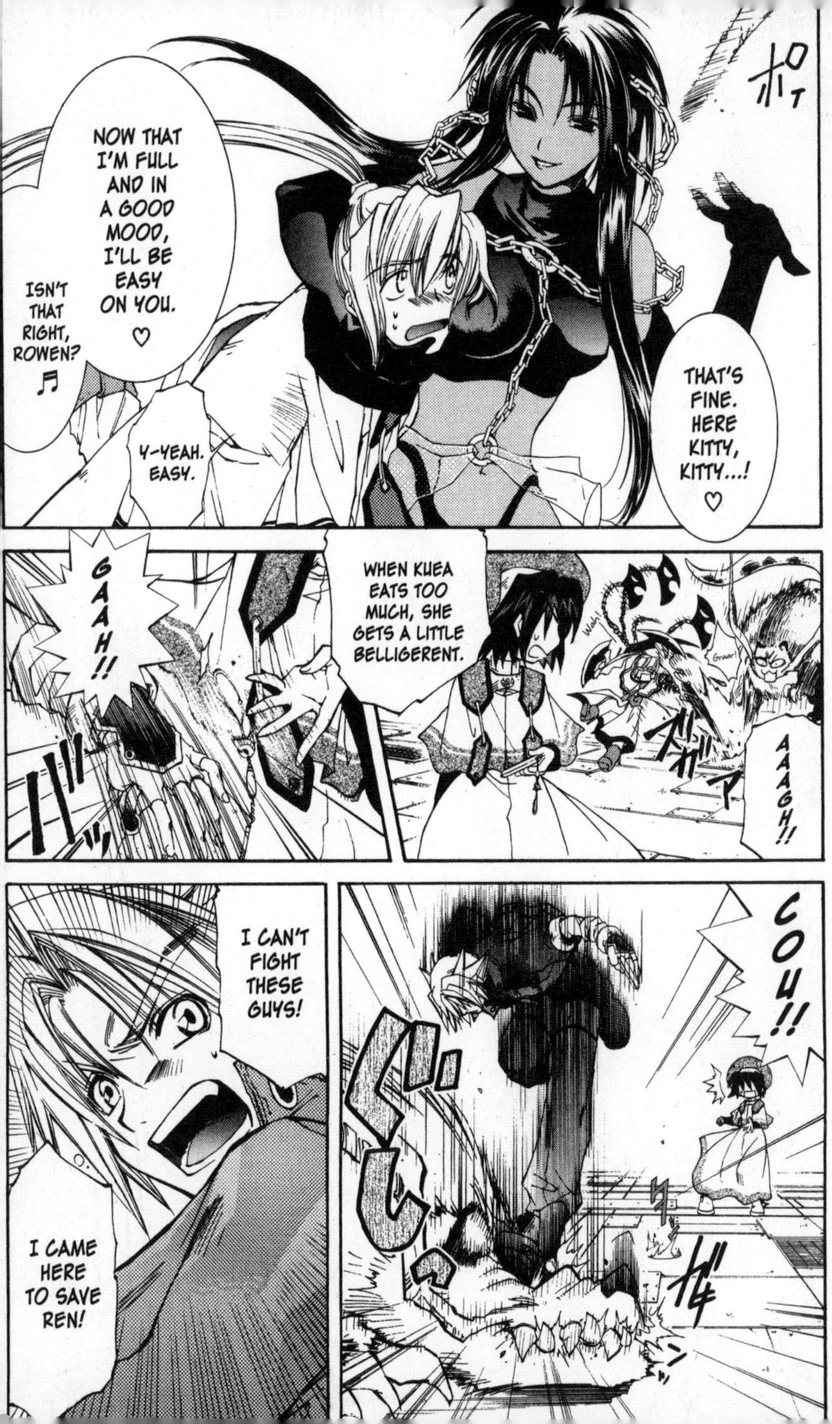
NOW THAT I'M FULL AND IN A GOOD MOOD, I'LL BE EASY ON YOU. ♡
ISN'T THAT RIGHT, ROWEN? ♫
Y-YEAH. EASY.
THAT'S FINE. HERE KITTY, KITTY...! ♡
WHEN KUEA EATS TOO MUCH, SHE GETS A LITTLE BELLIGERENT.
Wah!
Graar!
AAAGH!!
GAAH!!
COU!!
I CAN'T FIGHT THESE GUYS!
I CAME HERE TO SAVE REN!

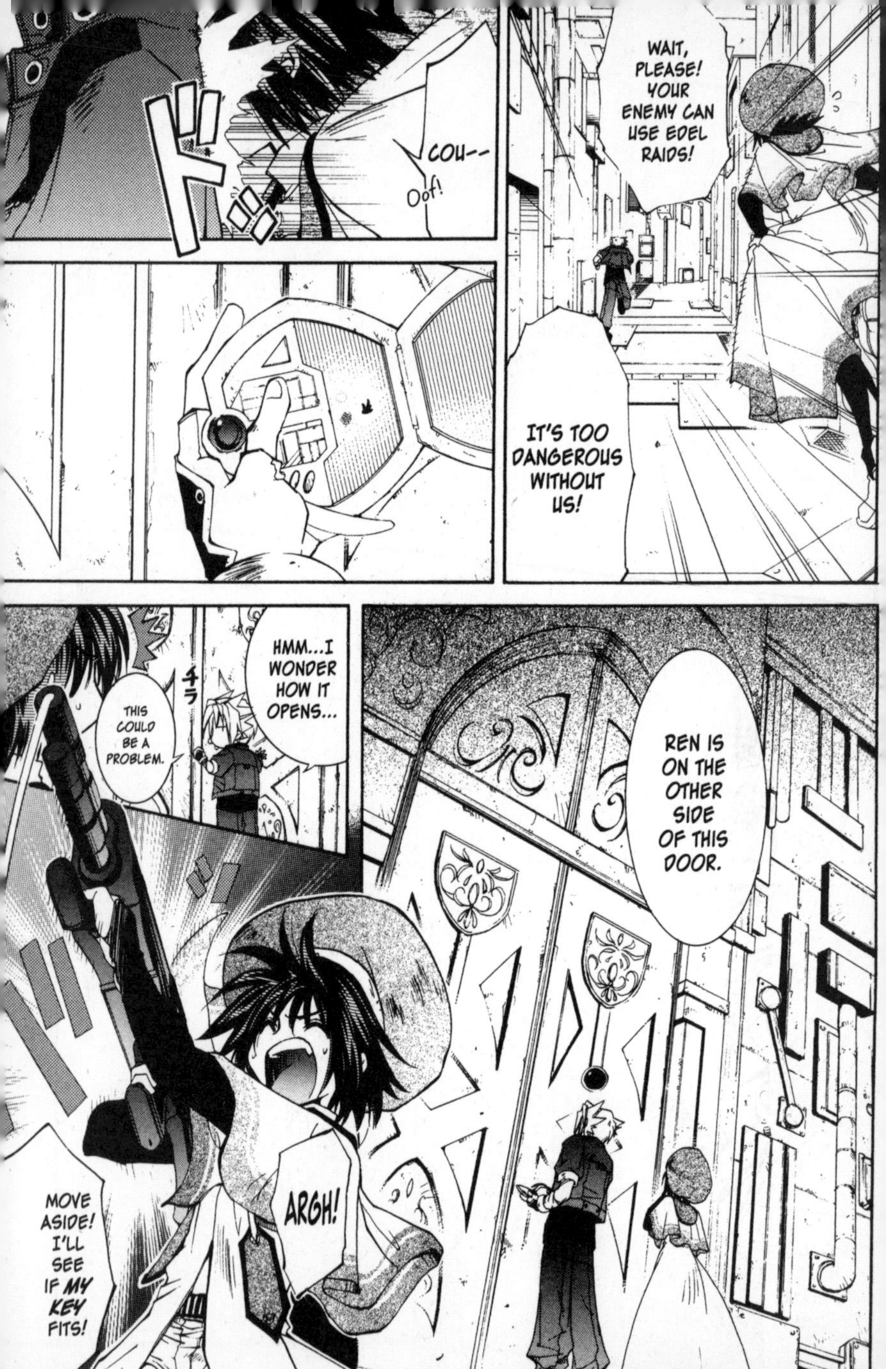
WAIT, PLEASE! YOUR ENEMY CAN USE EDEL RAIDS!
IT'S TOO DANGEROUS WITHOUT US!
COU--
Oof!
REN IS ON THE OTHER SIDE OF THIS DOOR.
HMM...I WONDER HOW IT OPENS...
チラ
THIS COULD BE A PROBLEM.
ARGH!
MOVE ASIDE! I'LL SEE IF *MY KEY* FITS!

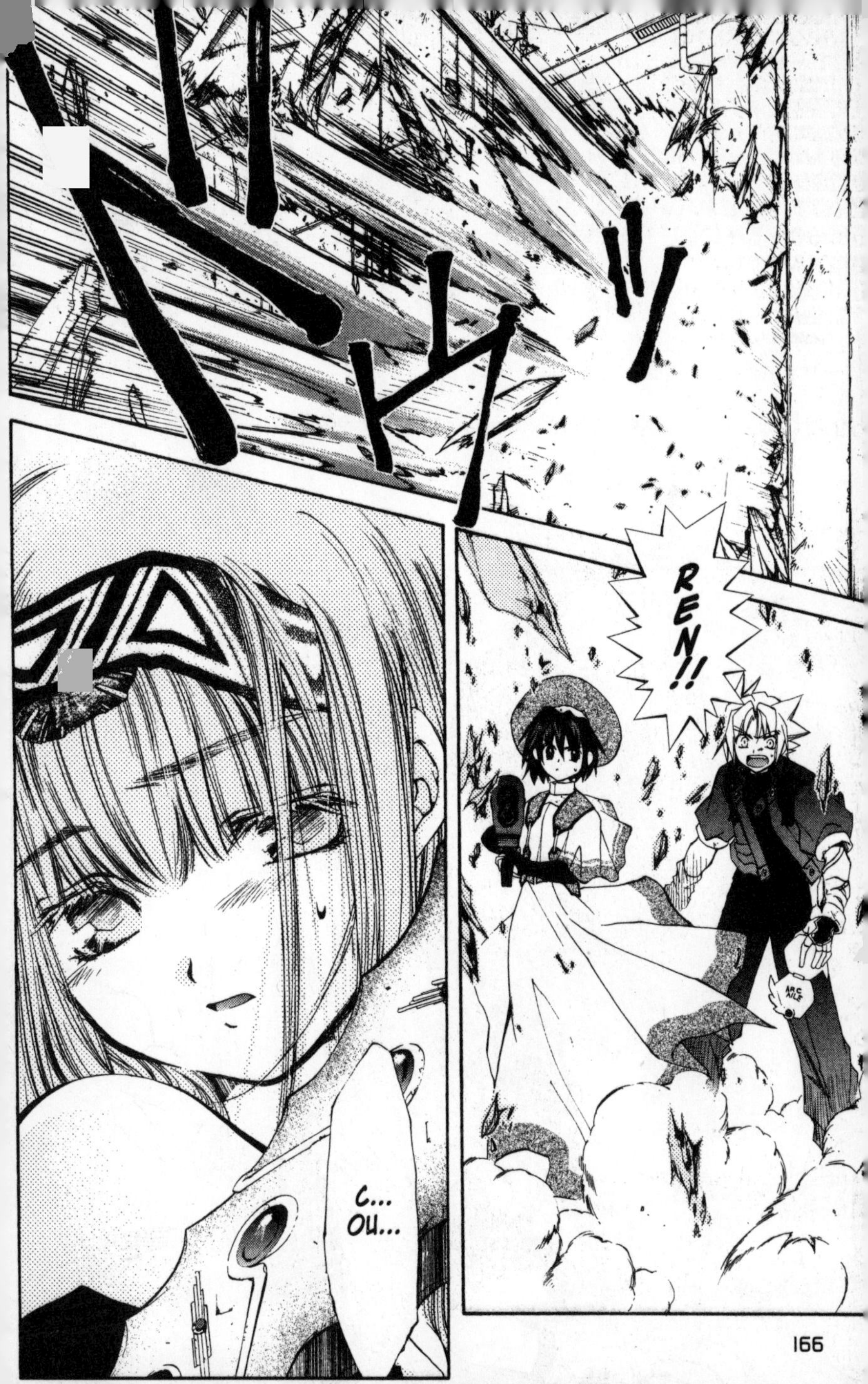
REN!!
C...
OU...

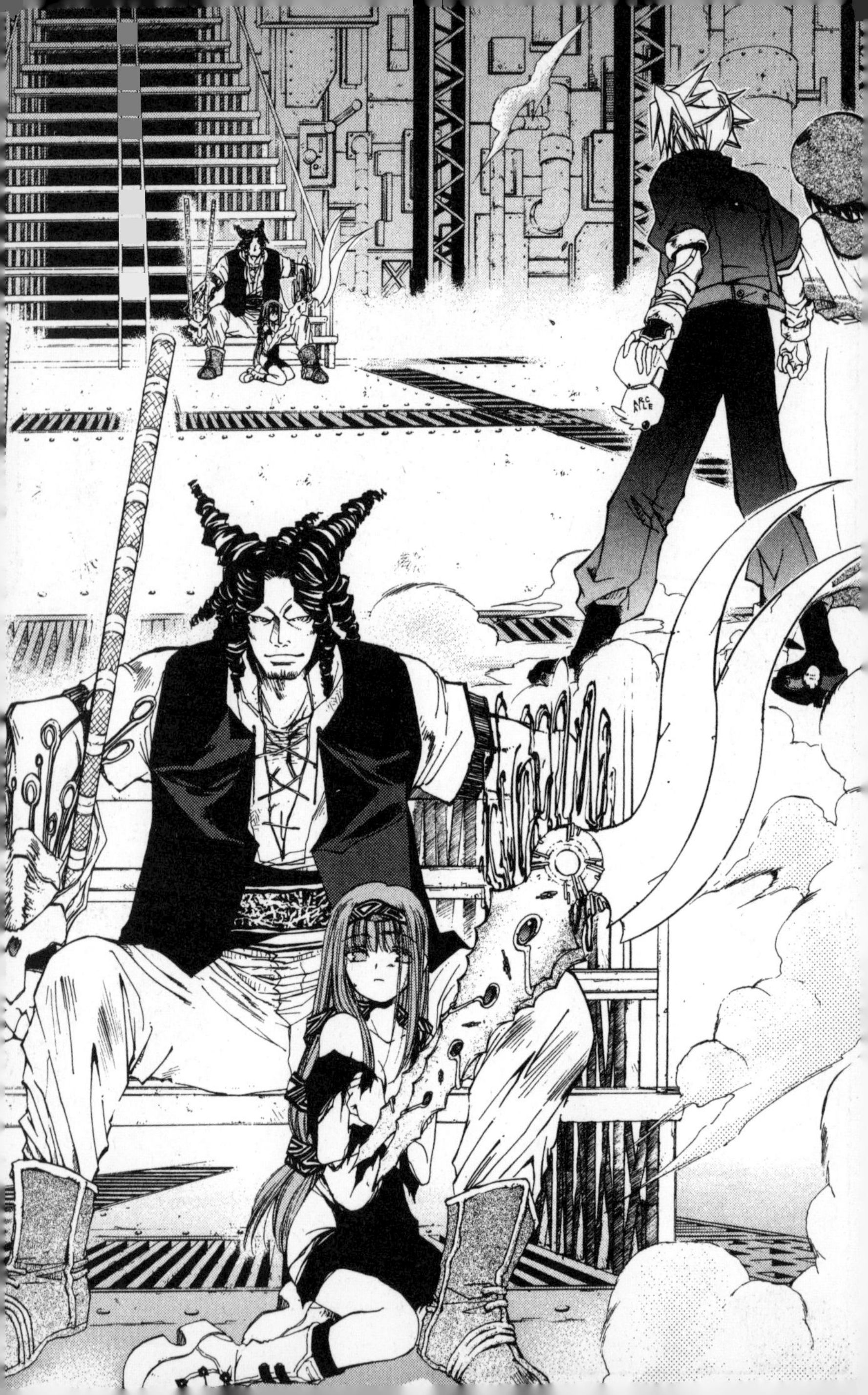
ARC AILE

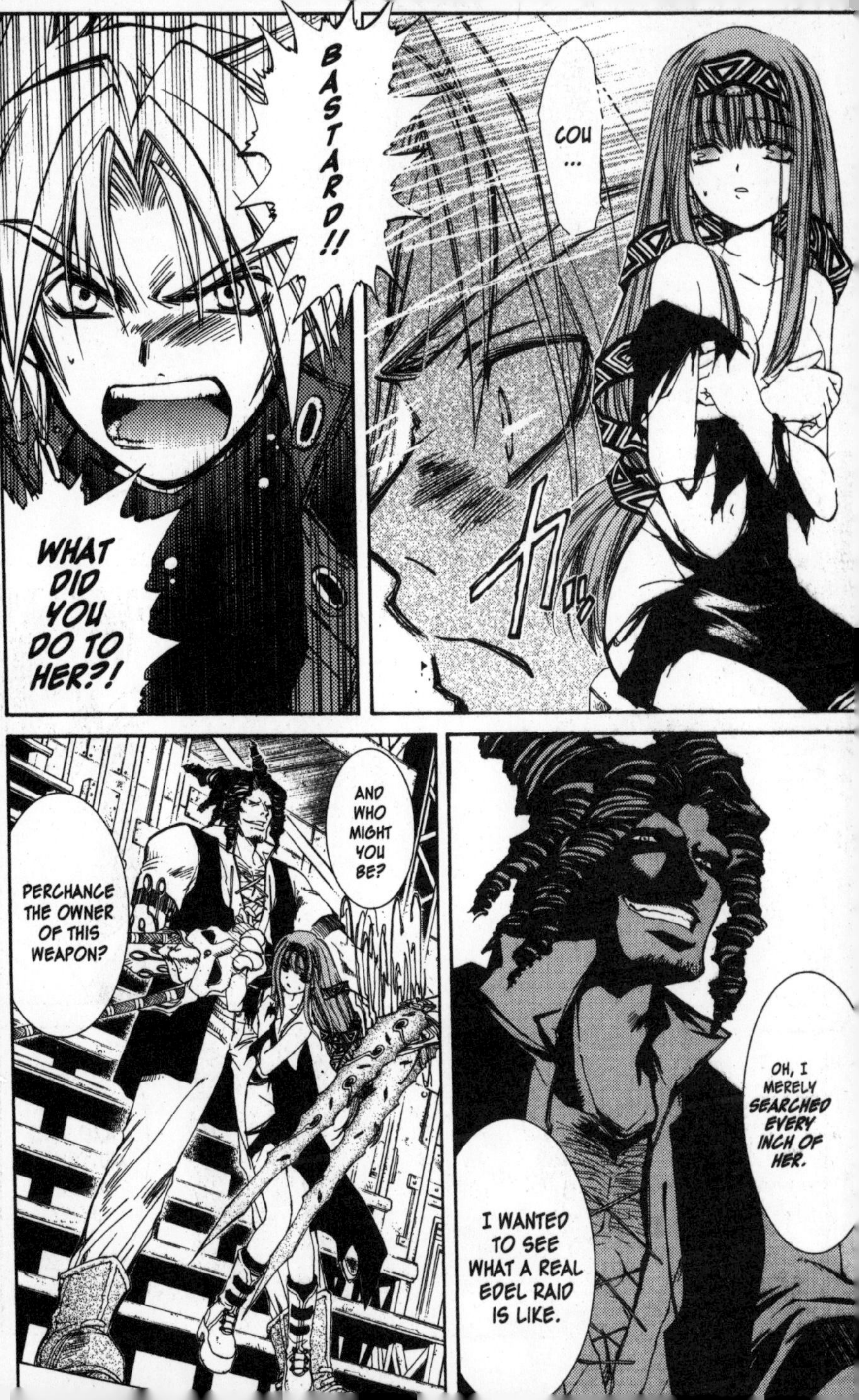
COU ...
BASTARD!!
WHAT DID YOU DO TO HER?!
OH, I MERELY SEARCHED EVERY INCH OF HER.
I WANTED TO SEE WHAT A REAL EDEL RAID IS LIKE.
AND WHO MIGHT YOU BE?
PERCHANCE THE OWNER OF THIS WEAPON?

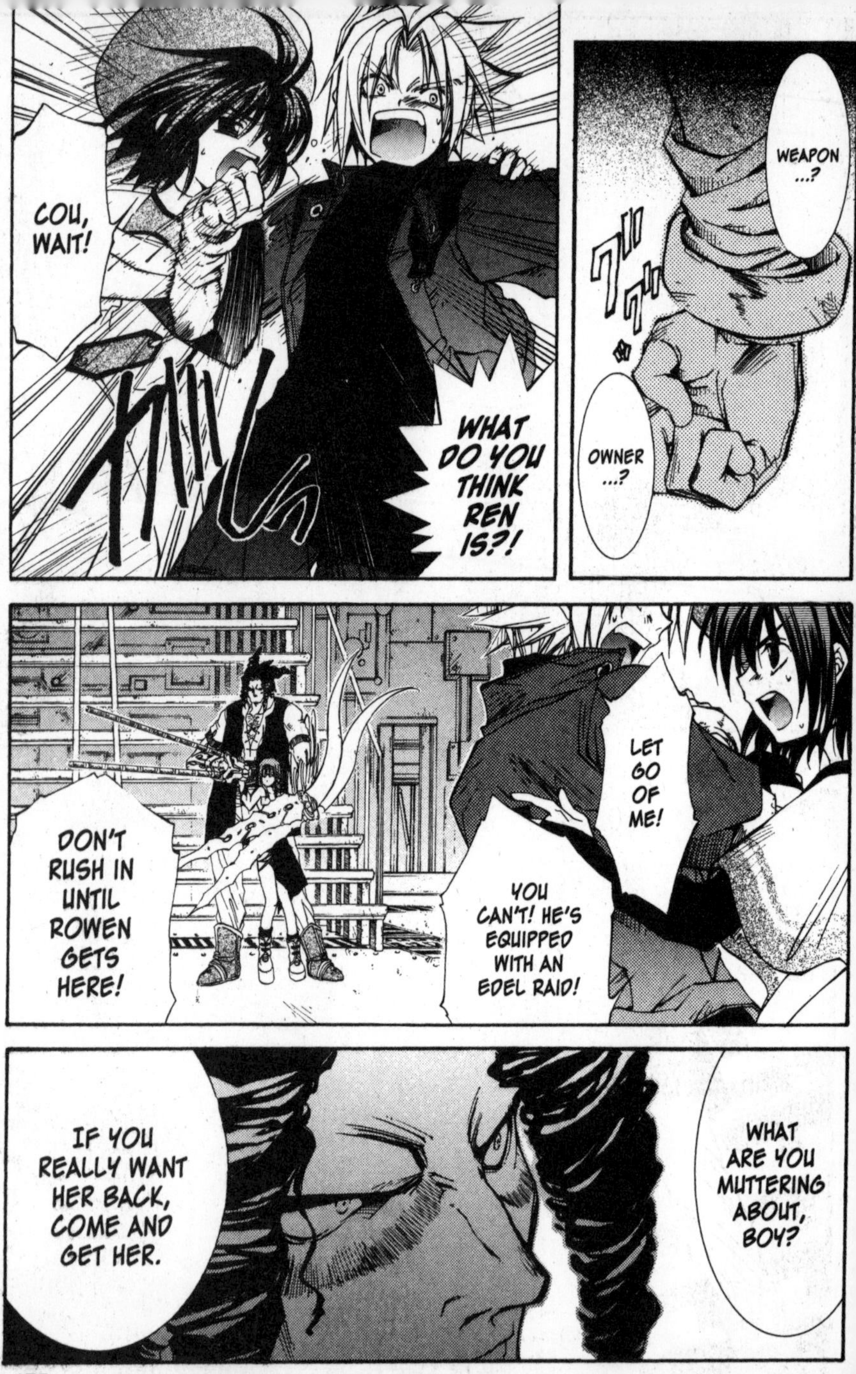
WEAPON ...?
OWNER ...?
WHAT DO YOU THINK REN IS?!
COU, WAIT!
LET GO OF ME!
YOU CAN'T! HE'S EQUIPPED WITH AN EDEL RAID!
DON'T RUSH IN UNTIL ROWEN GETS HERE!
WHAT ARE YOU MUTTERING ABOUT, BOY?
IF YOU REALLY WANT HER BACK, COME AND GET HER.

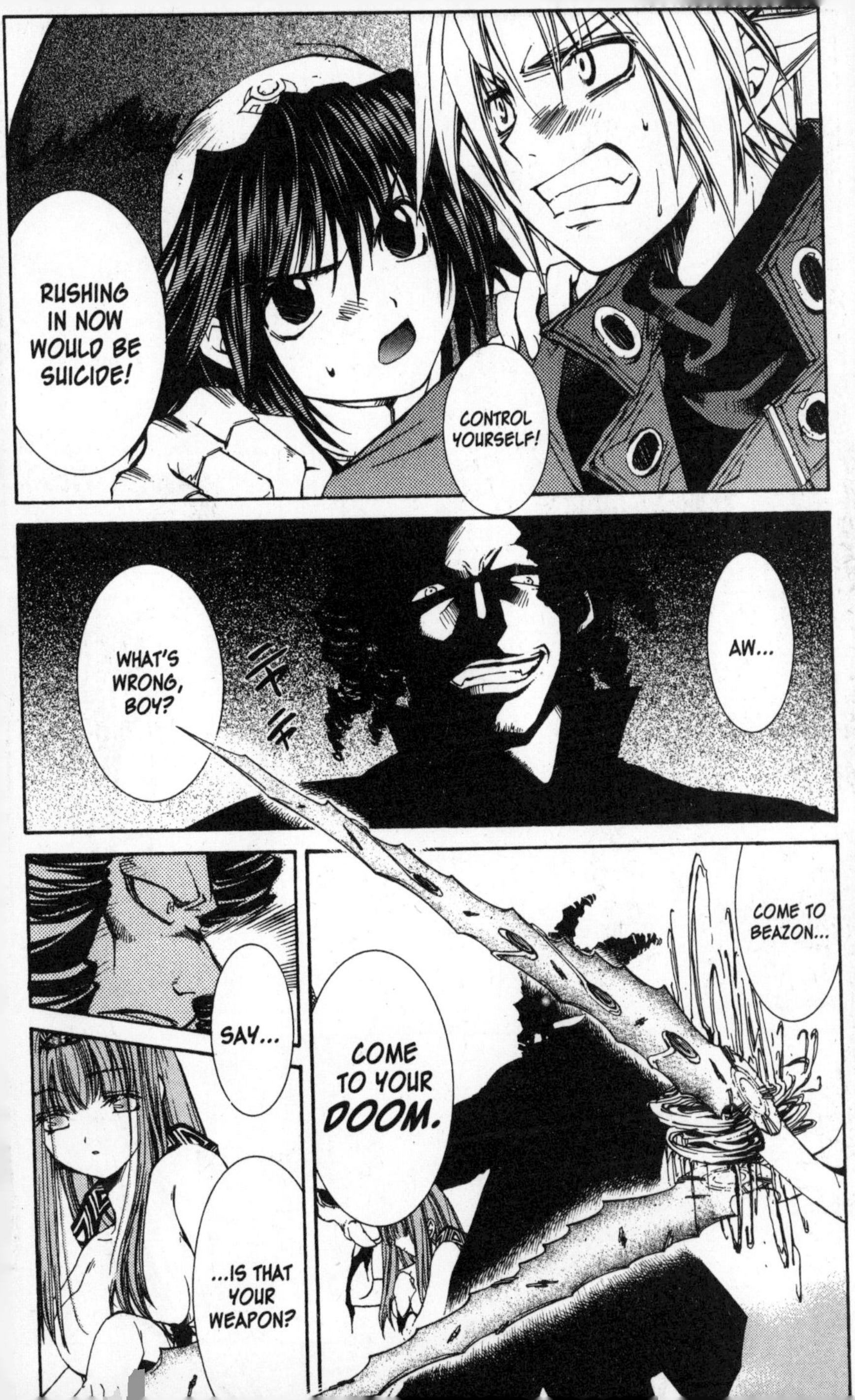
CONTROL YOURSELF!
RUSHING IN NOW WOULD BE SUICIDE!
AW...
WHAT'S WRONG, BOY?
COME TO BEAZON...
COME TO YOUR DOOM.
SAY...
...IS THAT YOUR WEAPON?

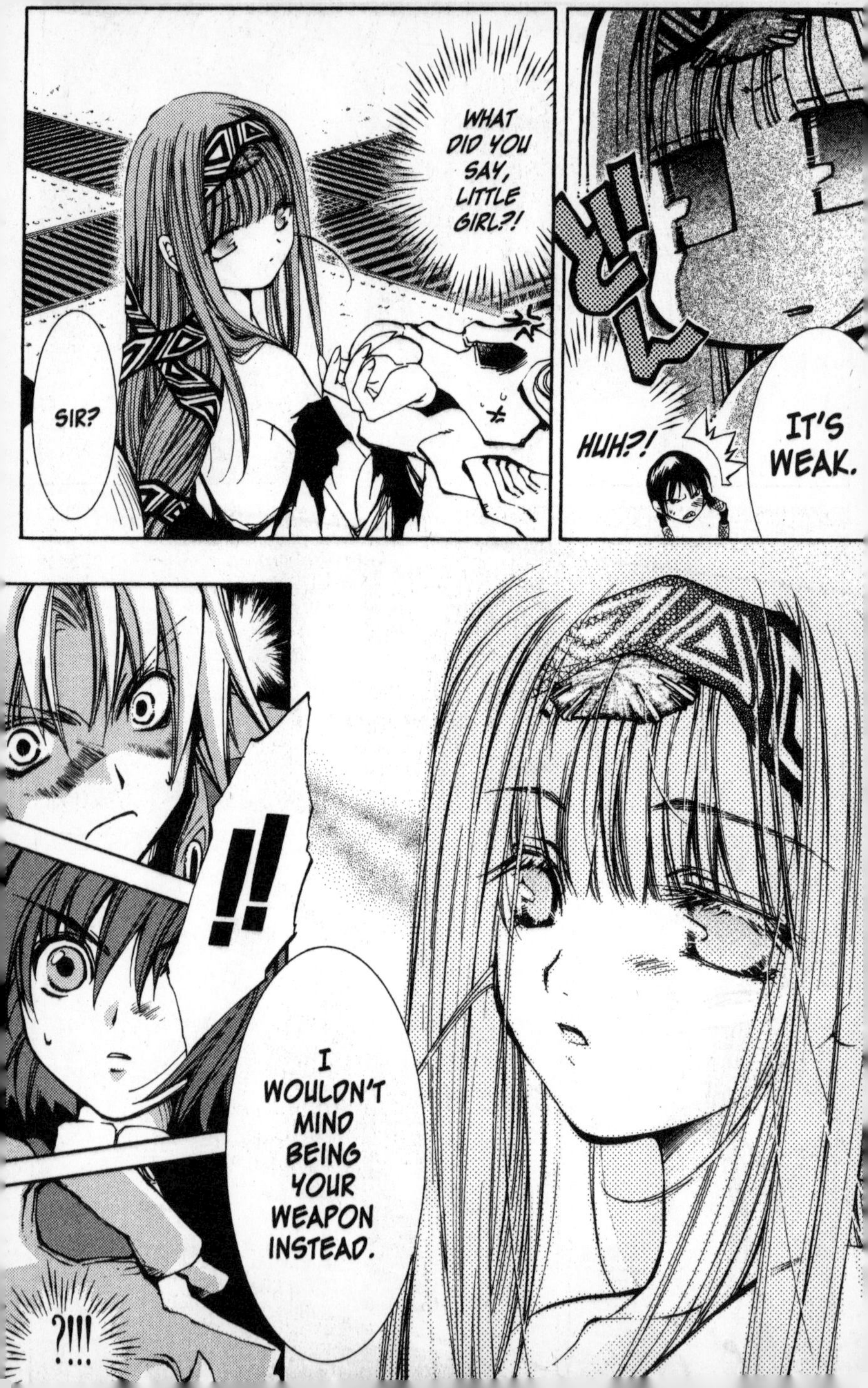
IT'S WEAK.
HUH?!
WHAT DID YOU SAY, LITTLE GIRL?!
SIR?
I WOULDN'T MIND BEING YOUR WEAPON INSTEAD.
!!
?!!!

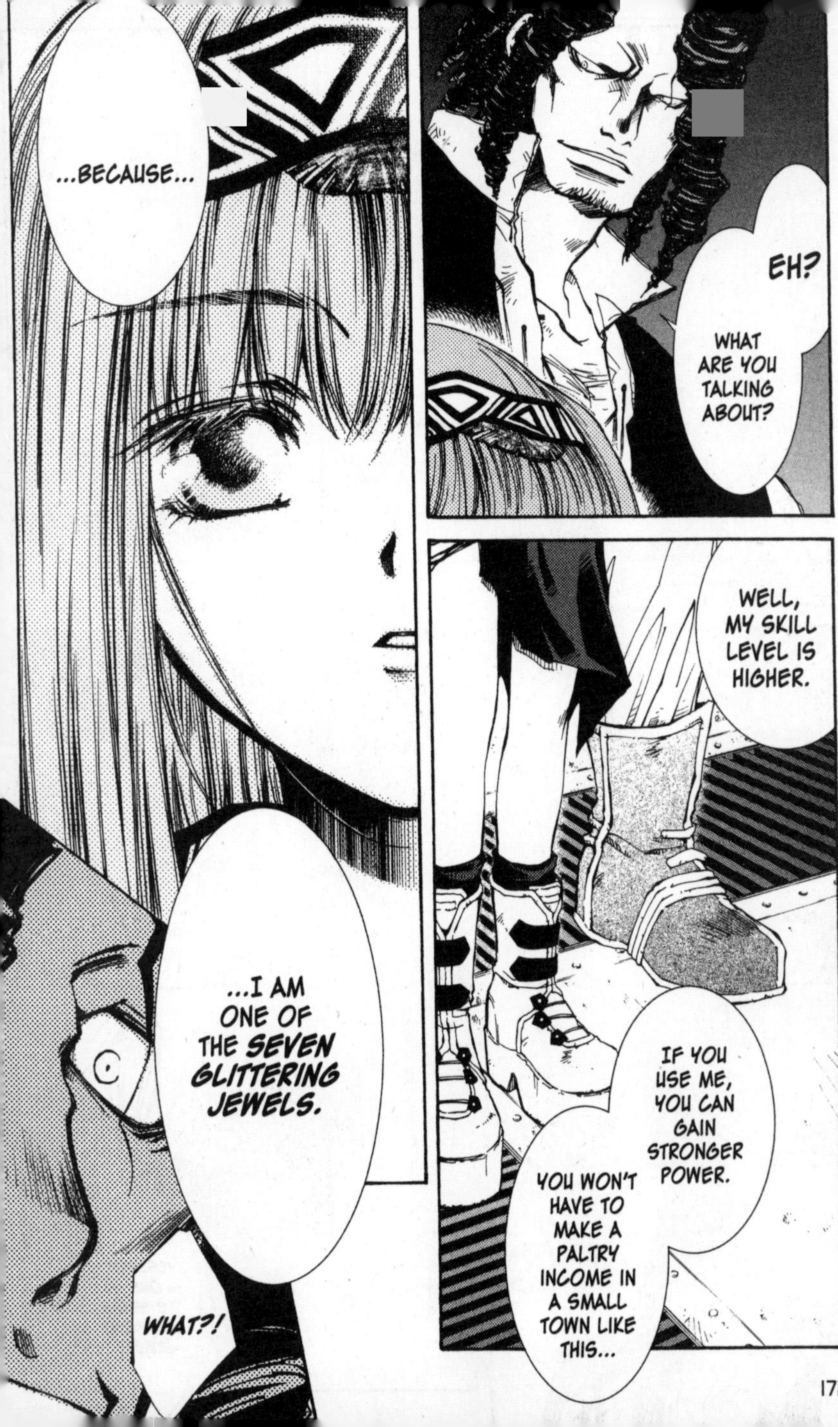
EH?
WHAT ARE YOU TALKING ABOUT?
WELL, MY SKILL LEVEL IS HIGHER.
IF YOU USE ME, YOU CAN GAIN STRONGER POWER.
YOU WON'T HAVE TO MAKE A PALTRY INCOME IN A SMALL TOWN LIKE THIS...
...BECAUSE...
...I AM ONE OF THE SEVEN GLITTERING JEWELS.
WHAT?!

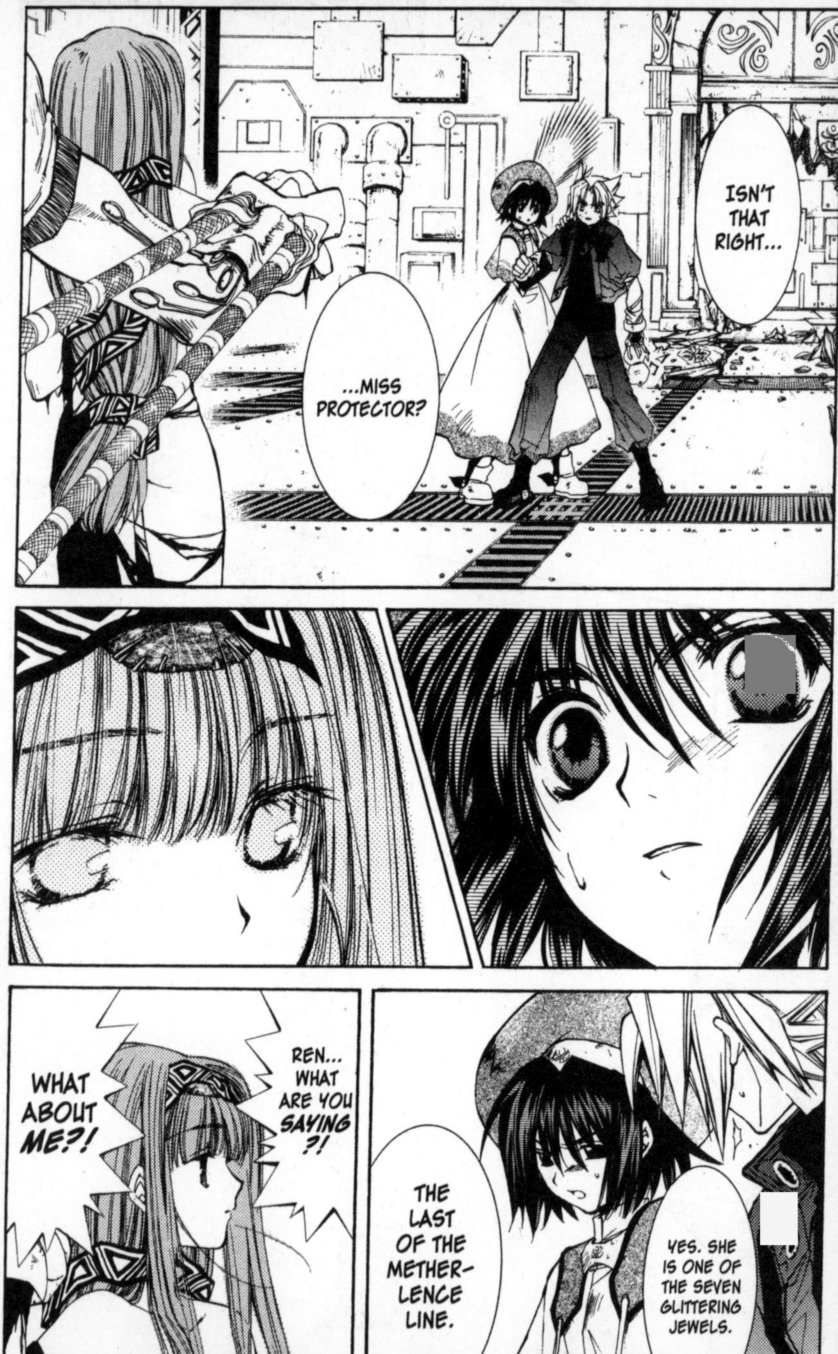
ISN'T THAT RIGHT...
...MISS PROTECTOR?
YES. SHE IS ONE OF THE SEVEN GLITTERING JEWELS.
THE LAST OF THE METHER-LENCE LINE.
REN... WHAT ARE YOU SAYING ?!
WHAT ABOUT ME?!

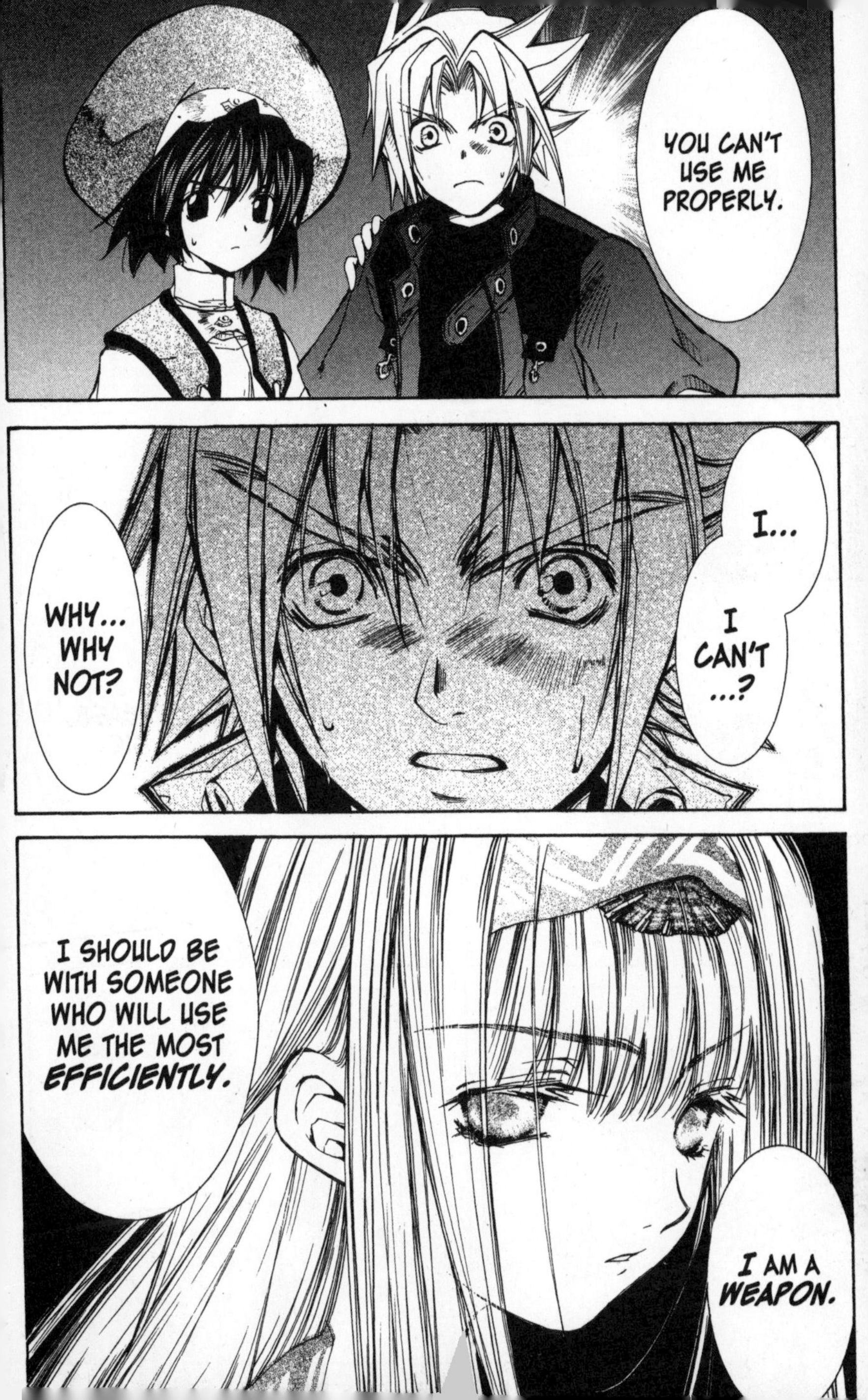
YOU CAN'T USE ME PROPERLY.
I...
I CAN'T ...?
WHY... WHY NOT?
I SHOULD BE WITH SOMEONE WHO WILL USE ME THE MOST EFFICIENTLY.
I AM A WEAPON.

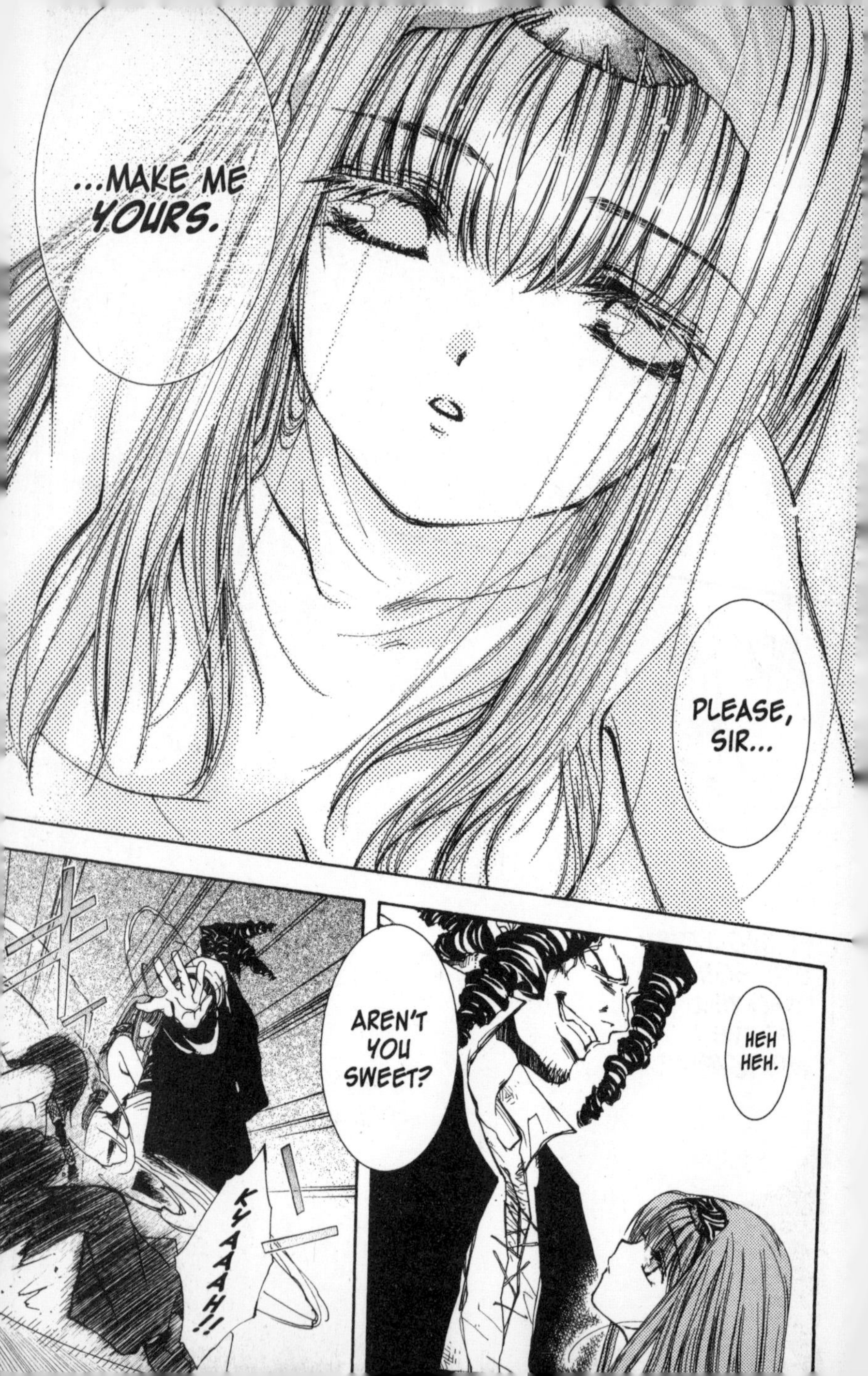
PLEASE, SIR...
...MAKE ME YOURS.
HEH HEH.
AREN'T YOU SWEET?
KYAAAAH!!

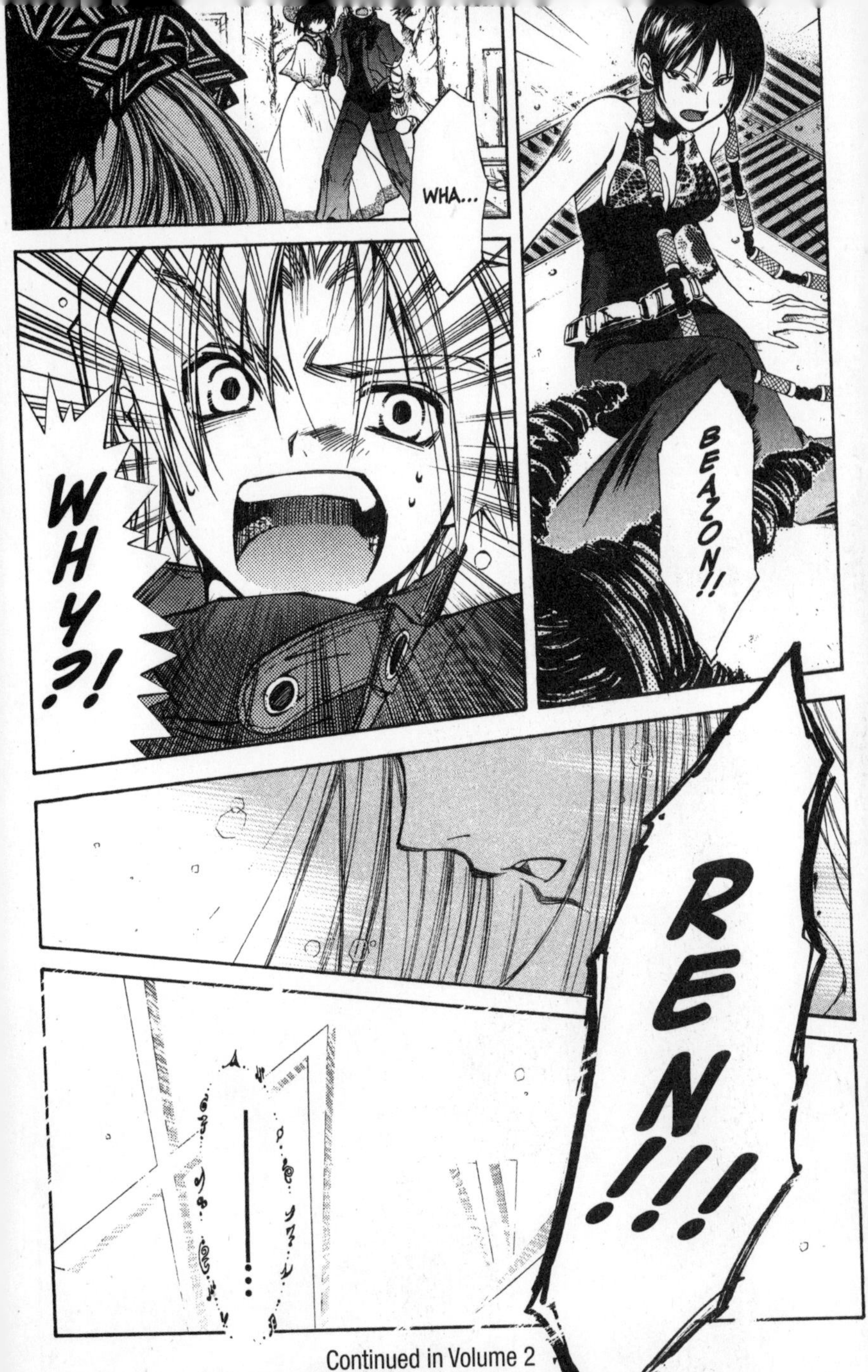
BEACON!!
WHA...
WHYY?!
REN!!!

Continued in Volume 2

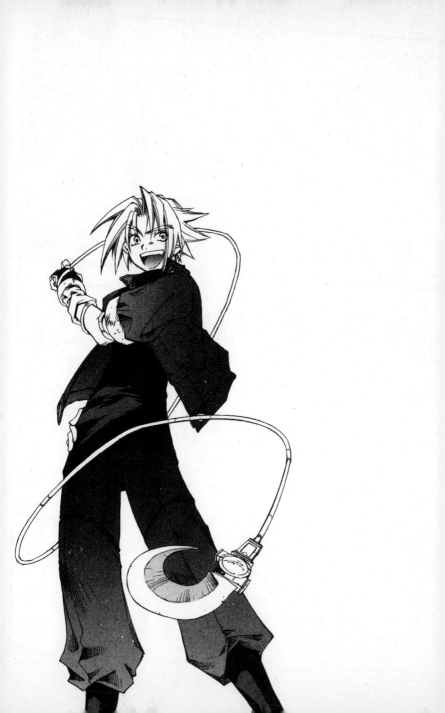

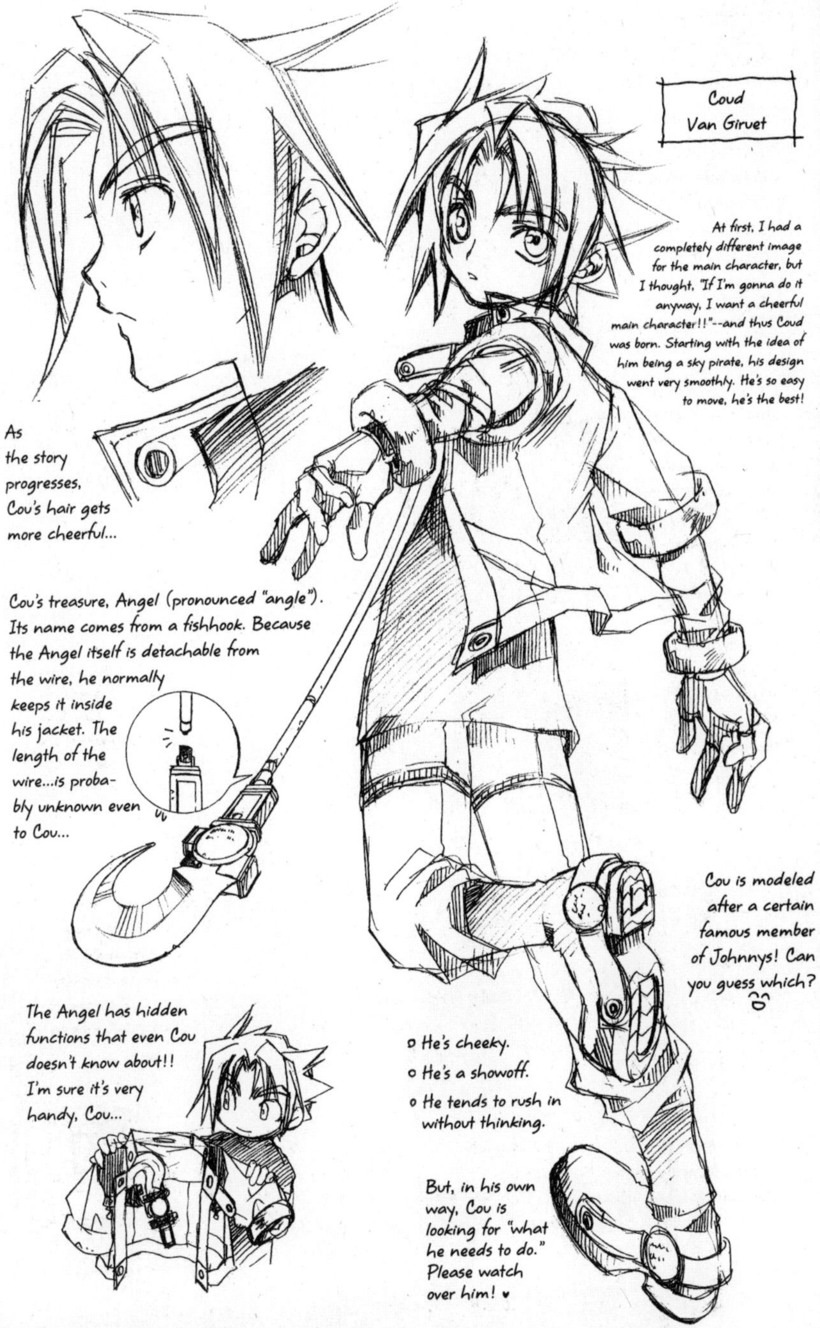
Coud
Van Giruet
At first, I had a completely different image for the main character, but I thought, "If I'm gonna do it anyway, I want a cheerful main character!!"--and thus Coud was born. Starting with the idea of him being a sky pirate, his design went very smoothly. He's so easy to move, he's the best!
As the story progresses, Cou's hair gets more cheerful...
Cou's treasure, Angel (pronounced "angle"). Its name comes from a fishhook. Because the Angel itself is detachable from the wire, he normally keeps it inside his jacket. The length of the wire...is probably unknown even to Cou...
Cou is modeled after a certain famous member of Johnnys! Can you guess which?
The Angel has hidden functions that even Cou doesn't know about!! I'm sure it's very handy, Cou...
o He's cheeky.
o He's a showoff.
o He tends to rush in without thinking.
But, in his own way, Cou is looking for "what he needs to do." Please watch over him! ♥

Reverie Metherlence

The last member of the Metherlence line, one of the Seven Glittering Jewels said to have power that far surpasses even other Edel Raids.

But, because she had been sealed for so long, she is still only half awake, and adding to that the sleepiness from recharging her Edel Raid power, she is usually very sleepy. She's always dozing off, yawning and bleary-eyed. In that way she's easygoing (laugh).

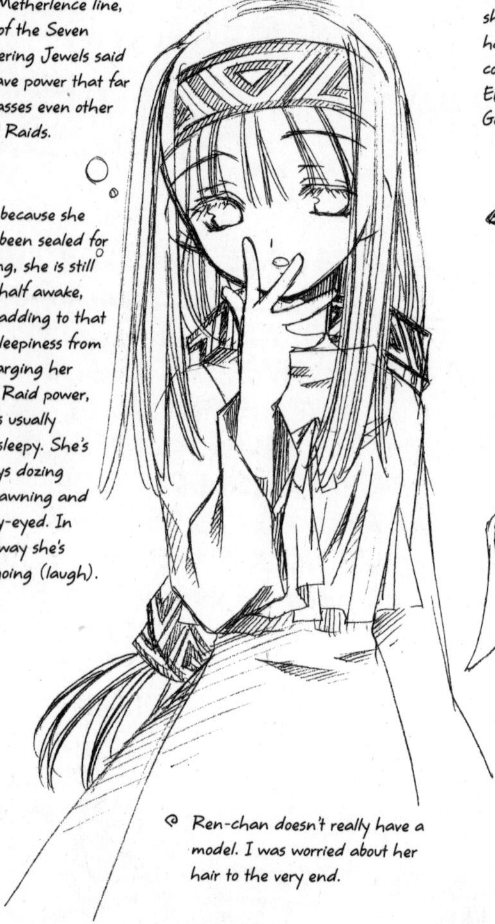

After reacting, Ren-chan takes the form of a giant sword wrapped in wind. Contrary to her appearance, she is as light as a feather and as sharp and as swift as the wind. It has a color like the malachite color of Ren-chan's Elemental Gelade.

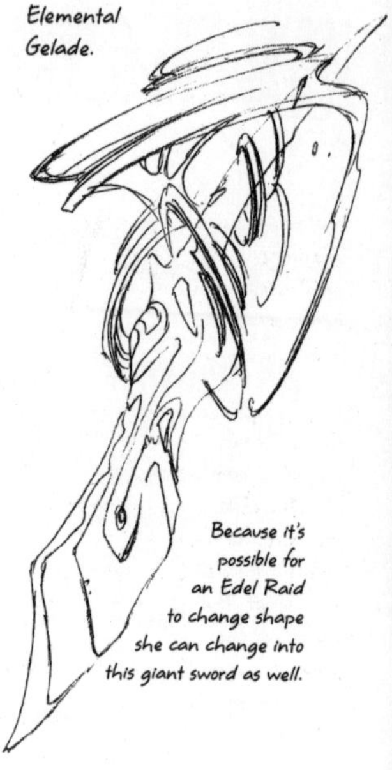

Because it's possible for an Edel Raid to change shape she can change into this giant sword as well.

Sleepy version Ren. Ren-chan often has vacant eyes and looks dazed. There is no doubt that Cou will continue to be brandished about by Ren-chan.

Ren-chan doesn't really have a model. I was worried about her hair to the very end.

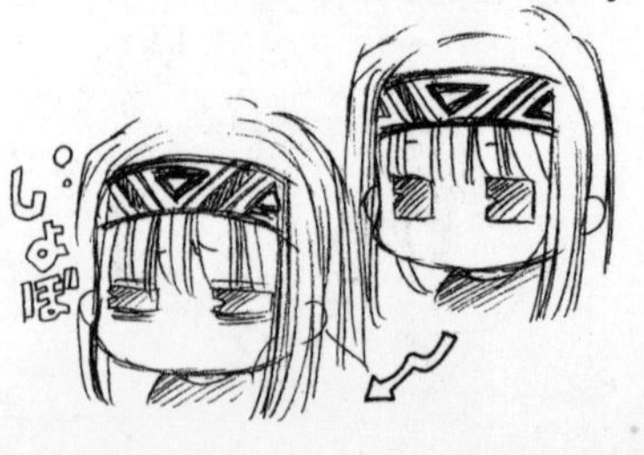
しょぼ

Sleepy Ren's goal is to go to "Edel Garden." I think that the reason she is aiming for Edel Garden will become clear as the story progresses. It would be nice if she could learn to get along (?) with everyone by then.

In The Next Volume of

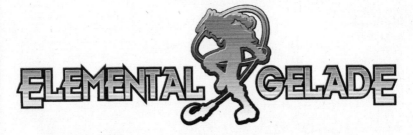

ELEMENTAL GELADE

THE SHOWDOWN CONTINUES AS REN OFFERS TO BE
BEAZON'S EDEL RAID. HAS SHE GONE TRAITOR? OR
DOES SHE HAVE A TRICK OR TWO UP HER SLEEVE?
EITHER WAY, COUD AND THE OTHERS WON'T GIVE HER
UP WITHOUT A FIGHT! BUT EVEN IF THEY DO DEFEAT
BEAZON, THE WORLD IS TEEMING WITH PEOPLE
ITCHING TO GET THEIR HANDS ON EDEL RAIDS...
A FACT MADE CLEAR WHEN KUEA IS STOLEN BY A
EDEL RAID HUNTER NAMED WOLX HOUND. WILL COUD
AND THE OTHERS BE ABLE TO RESCUE HER?
OR WILL THE HUNTER KEEP HIS PREY?

FIND OUT IN THE NEXT EXCITING VOLUME!

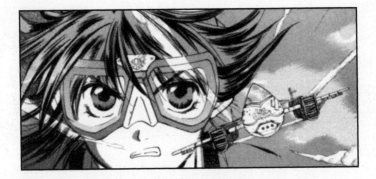

TOKYOPOP MANGA SUPPLEMENT

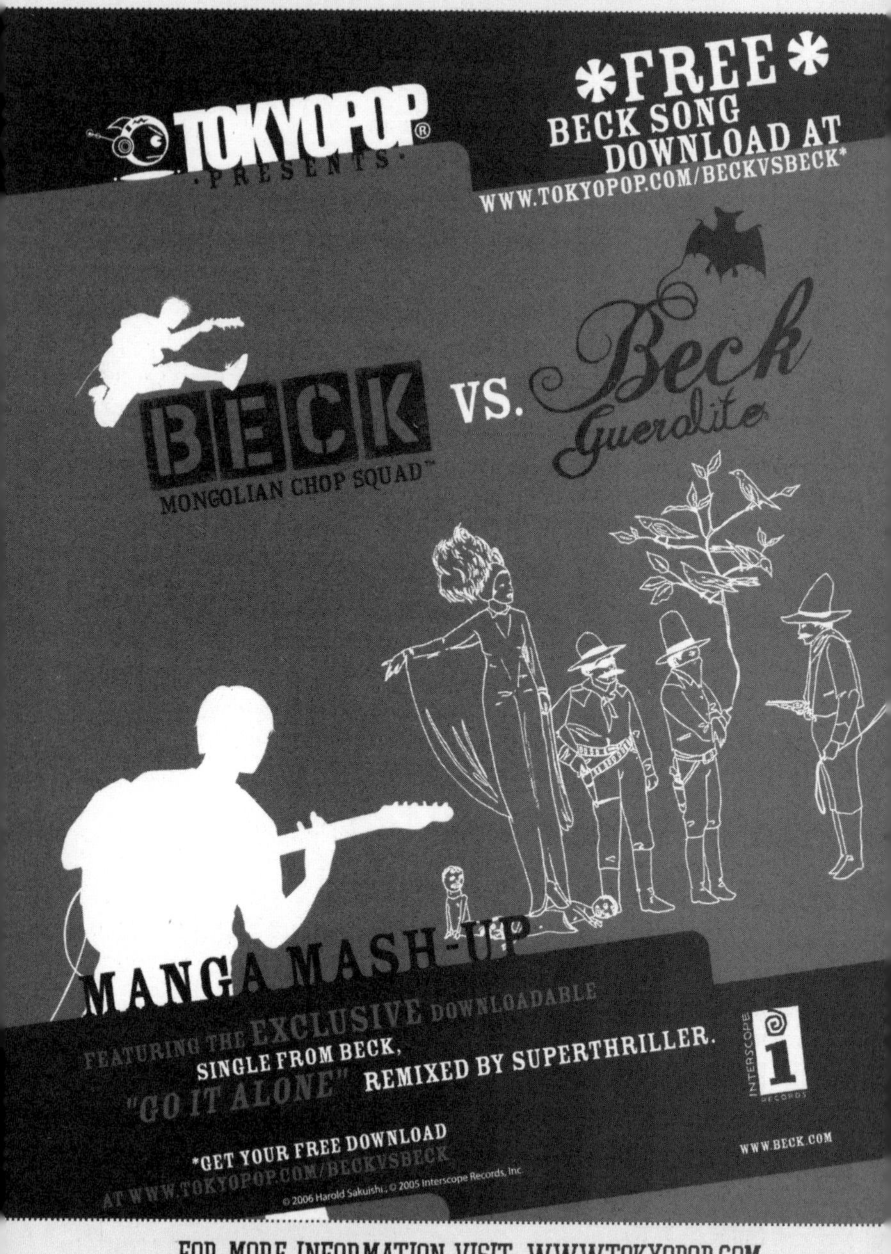

TOKYOPOP®
PRESENTS
FREE
BECK SONG
DOWNLOAD AT
TOKYOPOP.COM/BECKVSBECK*
WWW.TOKYOPOP.COM/BECKVSBECK
BECK
MONGOLIAN CHOP SQUAD™
VS.
Beck
Guerolito
MANGA MASH-UP
FEATURING THE EXCLUSIVE DOWNLOADABLE
SINGLE FROM BECK,
"GO IT ALONE" REMIXED BY SUPERTHRILLER.
INTERSCOPE RECORDS
*GET YOUR FREE DOWNLOAD
AT WWW.TOKYOPOP.COM/BECKVSBECK
© 2006 Harold Sakuishi, © 2005 Interscope Records, Inc
WWW.BECK.COM

FOR MORE INFORMATION VISIT: WWW.TOKYOPOP.COM

GRENADIER

CREATED BY: SOUSUKE KAISE

TWO BIG GUNS CAN BRING PEACE TO THE WORLD...

Rushuna is a golden-haired Senshi—
a gunslinger who travels the land
with one purpose: to make the world
a peaceful place with her high-
caliber revolver and enchanting
smile. However, her journey of
nonviolence won't be easy and she
may have to display her amazing
gun skills and talent for reloading
on the bounce.

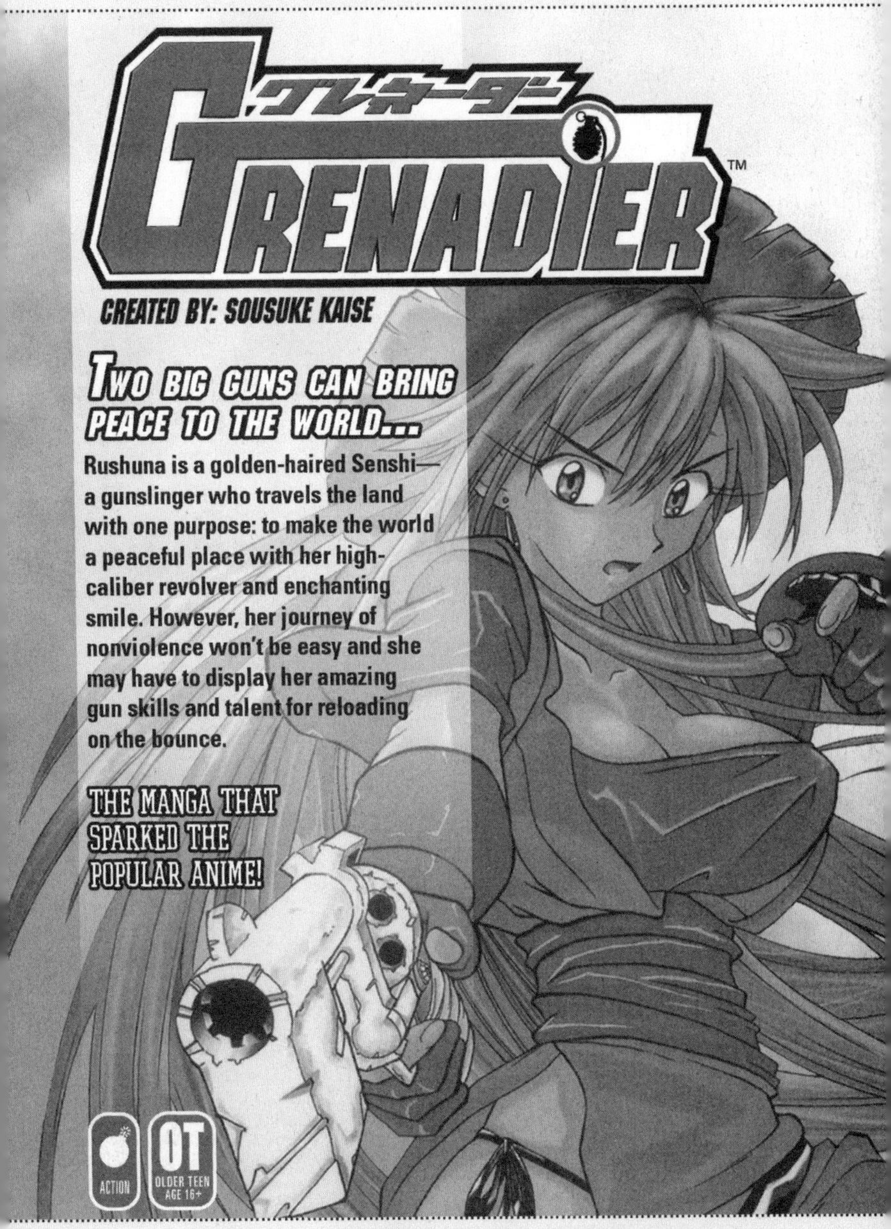

**THE MANGA THAT
SPARKED THE
POPULAR ANIME!**

ACTION

OT
OLDER TEEN
AGE 16+

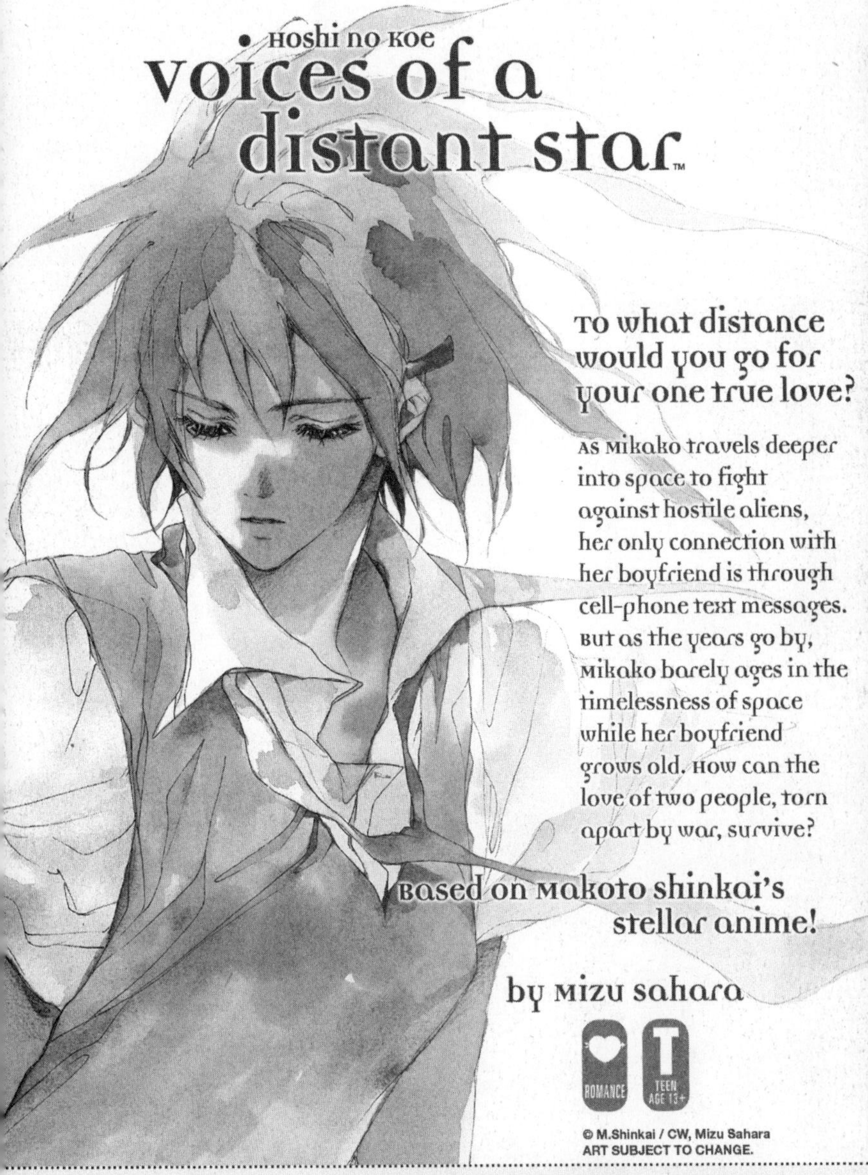

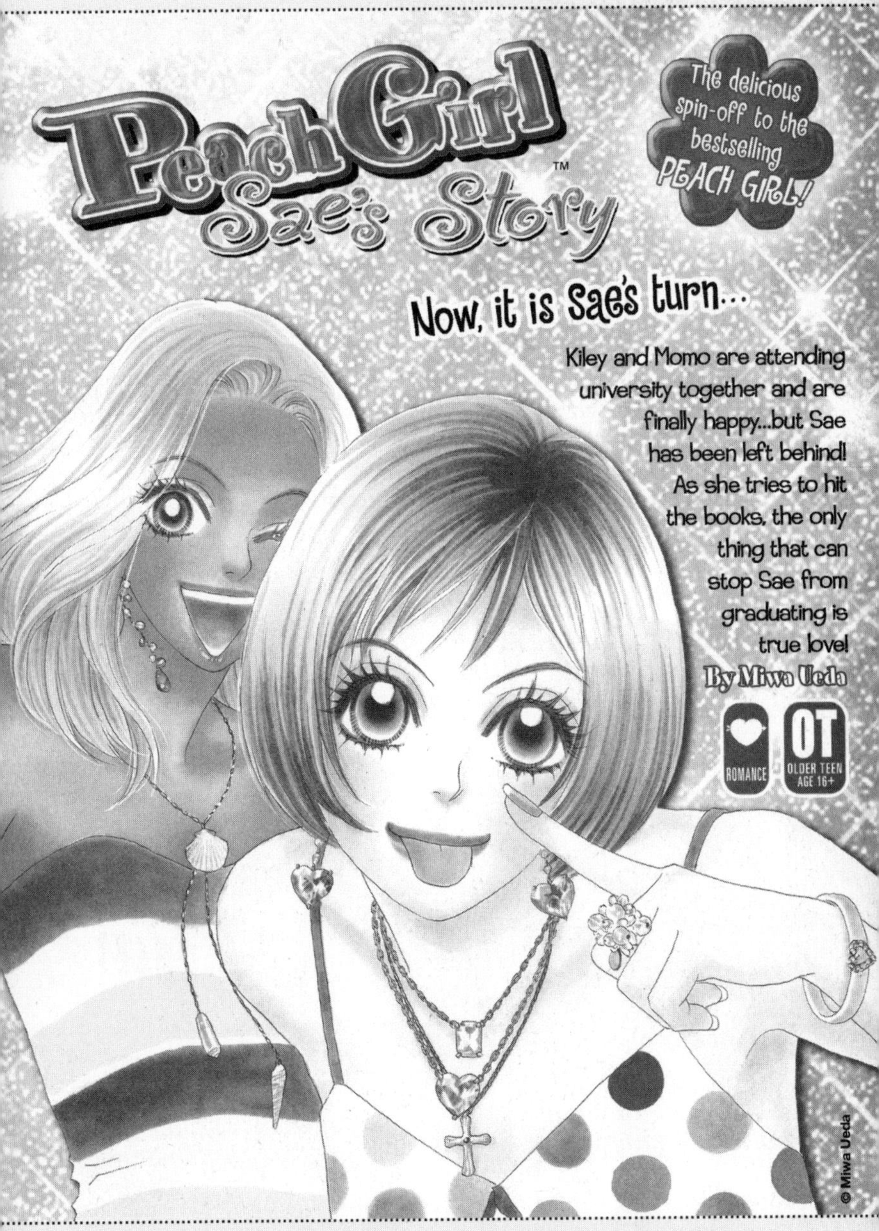

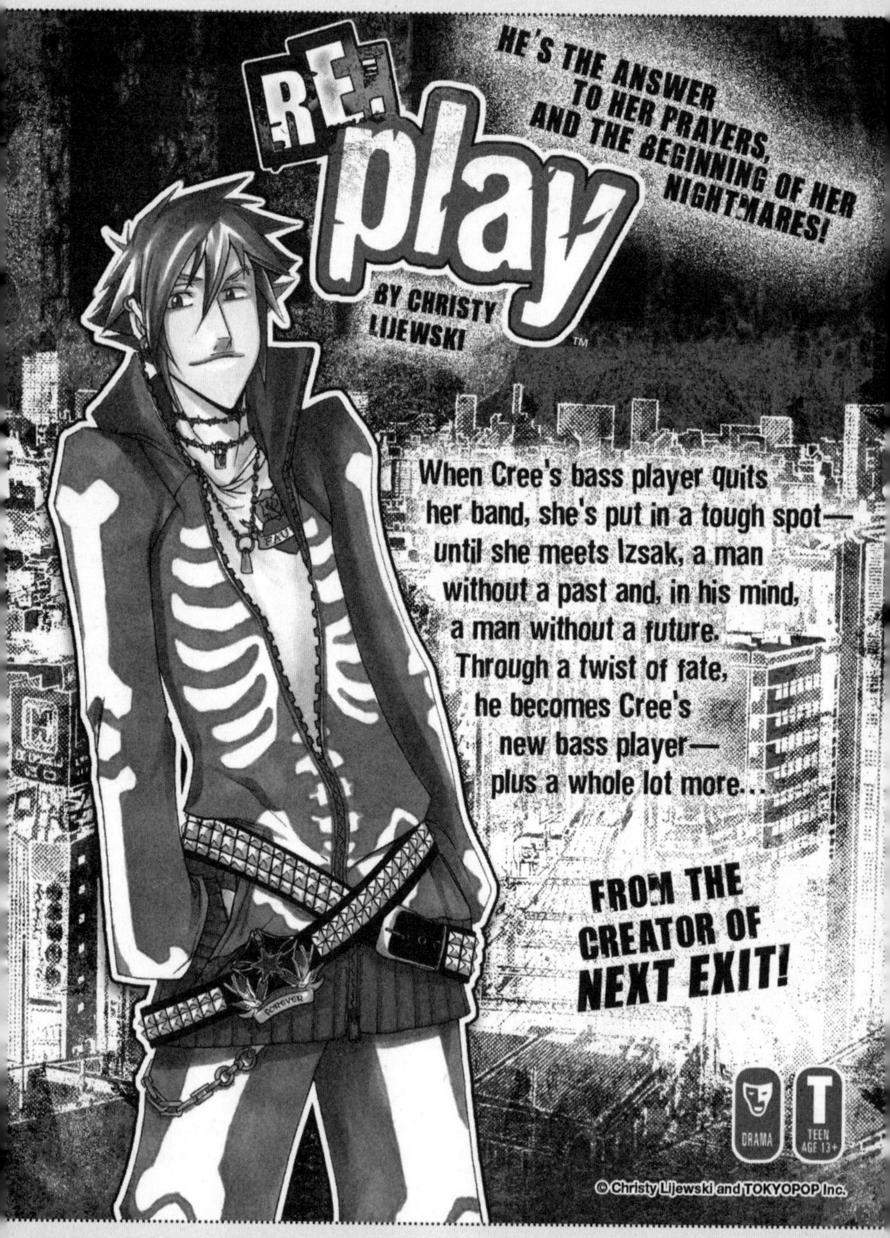
RE: play
BY CHRISTY LIJEWSKI
HE'S THE ANSWER TO HER PRAYERS, AND THE BEGINNING OF HER NIGHTMARES!
When Cree's bass player quits her band, she's put in a tough spot—until she meets Izsak, a man without a past and, in his mind, a man without a future. Through a twist of fate, he becomes Cree's new bass player—plus a whole lot more...
FROM THE CREATOR OF NEXT EXIT!
DRAMA
T
TEEN AGE 13+
© Christy Lijewski and TOKYOPOP Inc.

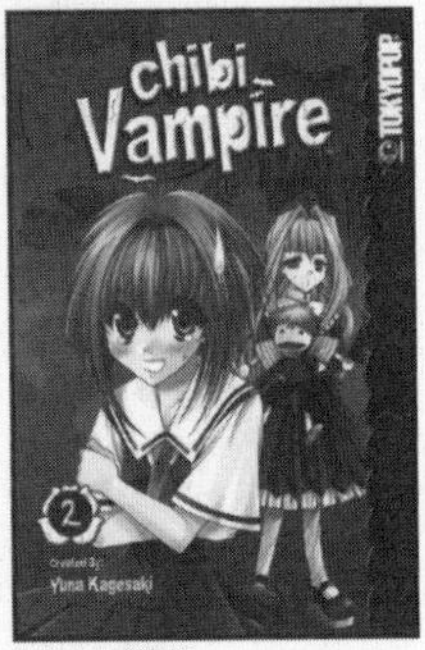
chibi Vampire
TOKYOPOP
Yuna Kagesaki

CHIBI VAMPIRE VOLUME 2

BY YUNA KAGESAKI

This bloody-good vampire has a big crush on her prey!

COMEDY OT OLDER TEEN AGE 16+

Inspired the hit anime!

DEVIL MAY CRY 3 VOLUME 2

BY SUGURO CHAYAMACHI

The secret of the seven seals will release the demon world unto the earth!

It's good against evil... and brother against brother!

ACTION OT OLDER TEEN AGE 16+

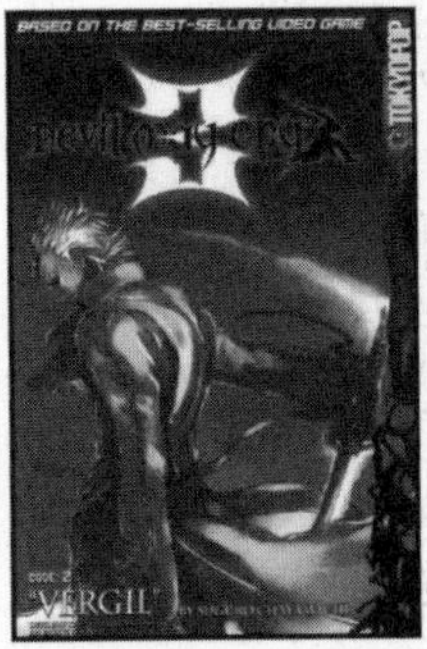
BASED ON THE BEST-SELLING VIDEO GAME
TOKYOPOP
"VERGIL"

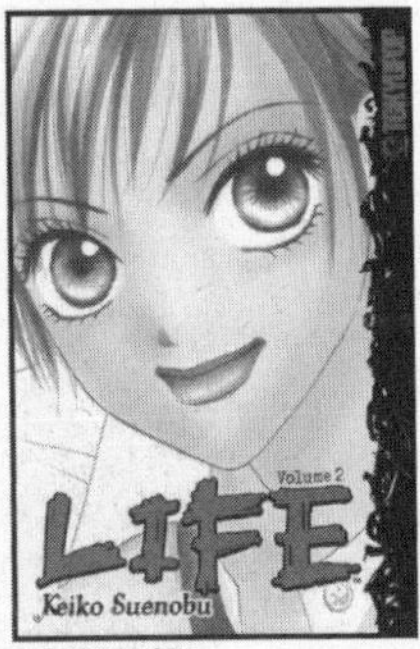
Volume 2
LIFE
Keiko Suenobu

LIFE VOLUME 2

BY KEIKO SUENOBU

It's about real teenagers...
real high school...
real life!

DRAMA OT OLDER TEEN AGE 16+

Every life has a story...
Every story has a life of its own.

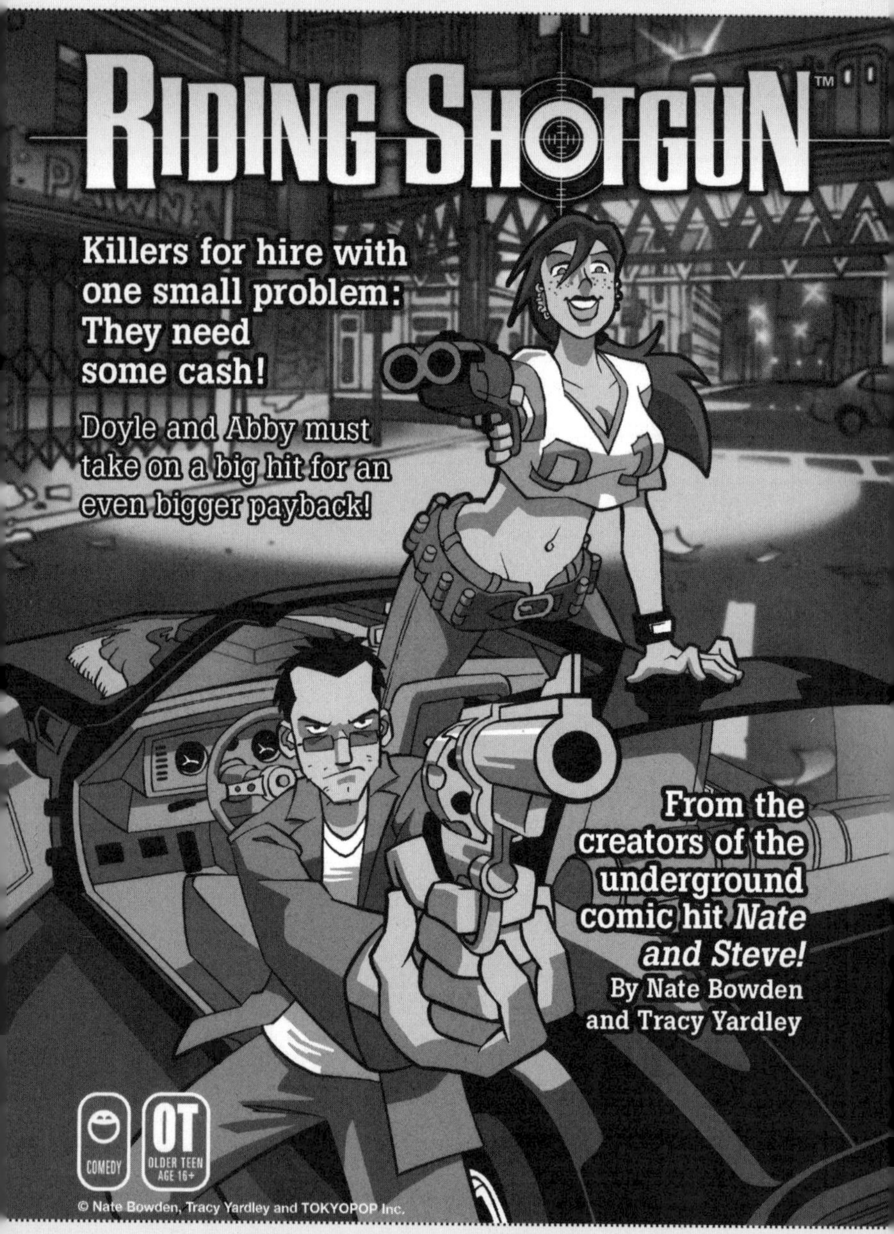
RIDING SHOTGUN™
Killers for hire with one small problem: They need some cash!
Doyle and Abby must take on a big hit for an even bigger payback!
From the creators of the underground comic hit *Nate and Steve!*
By Nate Bowden and Tracy Yardley
COMEDY
OT
OLDER TEEN AGE 16+
© Nate Bowden, Tracy Yardley and TOKYOPOP Inc.

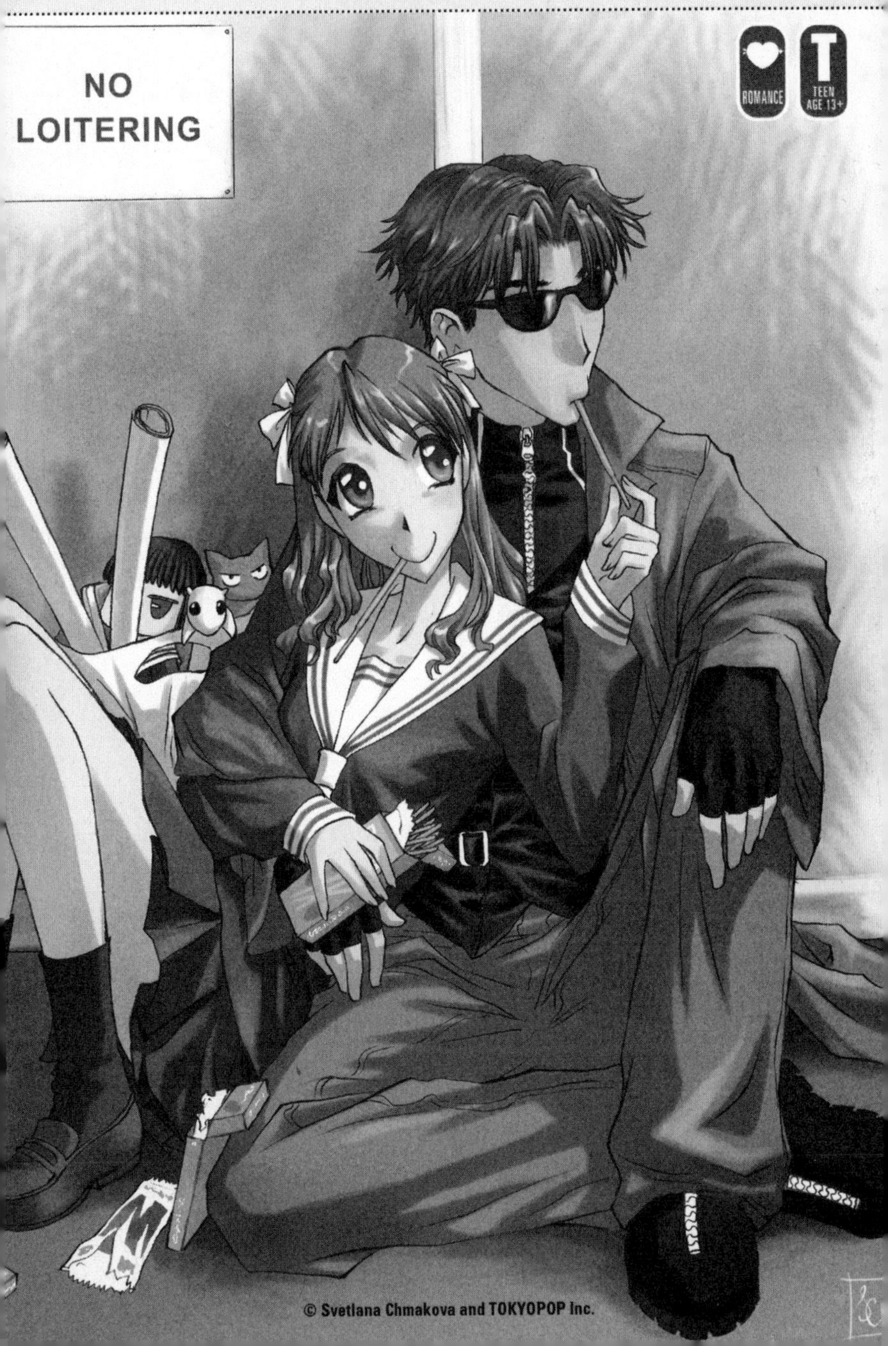
NO
LOITERING
ROMANCE
TEEN
AGE 13+

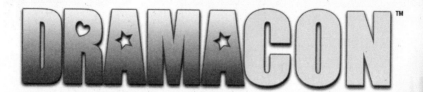
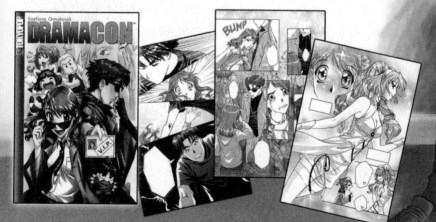

STOP!

This is the back of the book.
You wouldn't want to spoil a great ending!

This book is printed "manga-style," in the authentic Japanese right-to-left format. Since none of the artwork has been flipped or altered, readers get to experience the story just as the creator intended. You've been asking for it, so TOKYOPOP® delivered: authentic, hot-off-the-press, and far more fun!

DIRECTIONS

If this is your first time reading manga-style, here's a quick guide to help you understand how it works.

It's easy... just start in the top right panel and follow the numbers. Have fun, and look for more 100% authentic manga from TOKYOPOP®!

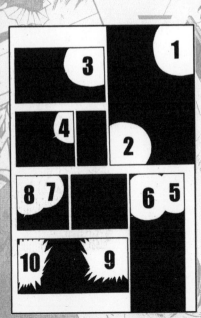

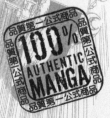